A BOOK ABOUT DOCTORS

LECTOR HOUSE PUBLIC DOMAIN WORKS

A BOOK ABOUT DOCTORS

JOHN CORDY JEAFFRESON

ISBN: 978-93-93794-57-4

Published: 1904

© 2022
LECTOR HOUSE LLP

LECTOR HOUSE LLP
E-MAIL: lectorpublishing@gmail.com

PROF. BILLROTH'S SURGICAL CLYNIC[1]

From the Original Painting by A. F. Seligmann, Pinx.

[1] Original by courtesy of William Wood & Co., New York.

A BOOK ABOUT DOCTORS

BY

JOHN CORDY JEAFFRESON

Author of "The Real Lord Byron," "The Real Shelley,"
`"A Book About Lawyers," etc., etc.

1904

PREFACE.

The writer of this volume has endeavoured to collect, in a readable and attractive form, the best of those medical Ana that have been preserved by tradition or literature. In doing so, he has not only done his best to combine and classify old stories, but also cautiously to select his materials, so that his work, while affording amusement to the leisure hours of Doctors learned in their craft, might contain no line that should render it unfit for the drawing-room table. To effect this, it has been found necessary to reject many valuable and characteristic anecdotes—some of them entering too minutely into the mysteries and technicalities of medicine and surgery, and some being spiced with a humour ill calculated to please the delicacy of the nineteenth century.

Much of the contents of this volume has never before been published, but, after being drawn from a variety of manuscript sources, is now for the first time submitted to the world. It would be difficult to enumerate all the persons to whom the writer is indebted for access to documents, suggestions, critical notes, or memoranda. He cannot, however, let the present occasion go by without expressing his gratitude to the College of Physicians, for the prompt urbanity with which they allowed him to inspect the treasures of their library. To Dr. Munk, the learned librarian of the College—who for many years, in the scant leisure allowed him by the urgent demands of an extensive practice, has found a dignified pastime in antiquarian and biographic research—the writer's best thanks are due. With a liberality by no means always found in a student possessed of "special information," the Doctor surrendered his precious stores to the use of a comparative stranger, apparently without even thinking of the value of his gift. But even more than to the librarian of the College of Physicians the writer is indebted for assistance to his very kind friend Dr. Diamond, of Twickenham House—a gentleman who, to all the best qualities of a complete physician, unites the graces of a scholarly mind, an enthusiasm for art, and the fascinations of a generous nature.

CONTENTS

LIST OF ILLUSTRATIONS

A BOOK ABOUT DOCTORS

CHAPTER I.

SOMETHING ABOUT STICKS,
AND RATHER LESS ABOUT WIGS.

Properly treated and fully expanded, this subject of "the stick" would cover all the races of man in all regions and all ages; indeed, it would hide every member of the human family. Attention could be called to the respect accorded in every chapter of the world's history, sacred and profane, to the *rabdos*—to the fasces of the Roman lictors, which every school-boy honours (often unconsciously) with an allusion when he says he will *lick*, or vows he won't be *licked*,—to the herald's staff of Hermes, the caduceus of Mercury, the wand of Æsculapius, and the rods of Moses and the contending sorcerers—to the mystic bundles of nine twigs, in honour of the nine muses, that Dr. Busby loved to wield, and which many a simple English parent believes Solomon, in all his glory, recommended as an element in domestic jurisdiction—to the sacred wands of savage tribes, the staffs of our constables and sheriffs, and the highly polished gold sticks and black rods that hover about the anterooms of St. James's or Portsoken. The rule of thumb has been said to be the government of this world. And what is this thumb but a short stick, a *sceptre*, emblematic of a sovereign authority which none dares to dispute? "The stick," says the Egyptian proverb, "came down from heaven."

The only sticks, however, that we here care to speak about are physicians' canes, barbers' poles, and the twigs of rue which are still strewn before the prisoner in the dock of a criminal court. Why should they be thus strung together?

The physician's cane is a very ancient part of his insignia. It is now disused, but up to very recent times no doctor of medicine presumed to pay a professional visit, or even to be seen in public, without this mystic wand. Long as a footman's stick, smooth and varnished, with a heavy gold knob or cross-bar at the top, it was an instrument with which, down to the present century, every prudent aspirant to medical practice was provided. The celebrated "gold-headed cane" which Radcliffe, Mead, Askew, Pitcairn and Baillie successively bore is preserved in the College of Physicians, bearing the arms which those gentlemen assumed, or were entitled to. In one respect it deviated from the physician's cane proper. It has a cross-bar almost like a crook; whereas a physician's wand ought to have a knob at the top. This knob in olden times was hollow, and contained a vinaigrette, which the man of science always held to his nose when he approached a sick person, so that its fumes might protect him from the noxious exhalations of his patient. We know timid people who, on the same plan, have their handkerchiefs washed in camphor-water, and bury their faces in them whenever they pass the corner of a dingy street, or cross an open drain, or come in contact with an ill-looking man. When Howard, the philanthropist, visited Exeter, he found that the medical officer of the county gaol had caused a clause to be inserted in his agreement with the magistrates, exonerating him from attendance and services during any outbreak of the gaol fever. Most likely this gentleman, by books or experience, had been enlightened as to the inefficacy of the vinaigrette.

But though the doctor, like a soldier skulking from the field of battle, might with impunity decline visiting the wretched captives, the judge was forced to do his part of the social duty to them—to sit in their presence during their trial in a close, fetid court; to brow-beat them when they presumed to make any declaration of their innocence beyond a brief "not guilty"; to read them an energetic homily on the consequences of giving way to corrupt passions and evil manners; and, finally, to order them their proper apportionments of whipping, or incarceration, or banishment, or death. Such was the abominable condition of our prisons, that the poor creatures dragged from them and placed in the dock often by the noxious effluvia of their bodies made seasoned criminal lawyers turn pale—partly, perhaps, through fear, but chiefly through physical discomfort. Then arose the custom of sprinkling aromatic herbs before the prisoners—so that if the health of his Lordship and the gentlemen of the long robe suffered from the tainted atmosphere, at least their senses of smell might be shocked as little as possible. Then, also, came the chaplain's bouquet, with which that reverend officer was always provided when accompanying a criminal to Tyburn. Coke used to go circuit carrying in his hand an enormous fan furnished with a handle, in the shape of a goodly stick—the whole forming a weapon of offence or defence. It is not improbable that the shrewd lawyer caused the end of this cumbrous instrument to be furnished with a vinaigrette.

So much for the head of the physician's cane. The stick itself was doubtless a relic of the conjuring paraphernalia with which the healer, in ignorant and superstitious times, worked upon the imagination of the credulous. Just as the **R** which the doctor affixes to his prescription is the old astrological sign (ill-drawn) of Jupiter, so his cane descended to him from Hermes and Mercurius. It was a relic of old jugglery, and of yet older religion—one of those baubles which we know well where to find, but which our conservative tendencies disincline us to sweep away without some grave necessity.

The charming-stick, the magic Æsculapian wand of the Medicine-man, differed in shape and significance from the pole of the barber-surgeon. In the "British Apollo," 1703, No. 3, we read:—

> "I'd know why he that selleth ale
> Hangs out a chequer'd part per pale:
> And why a barber at port-hole
> Puts forth a parti-coloured pole?"

ANSWER.

"In ancient Rome, when men loved fighting,
And wounds and scars took much delight in,
Man-menders then had noble pay—
Which we call surgeons to this day.
'Twas order'd that a huge long pole,
With basin deck'd, should grace the hole,
To guide the wounded, who unlopt
Could walk, on stumps the other hopt;
But when they ended all their wars,
And men grew out of love with scars.
Their trade decaying, to keep swimming,
They joined the other trade of trimming;
And to their poles, to publish either,
Thus twisted both their trades together."

The principal objection that can be made to this answer is that it leaves the question unanswered, after making only a very lame attempt to answer it. Lord Thurlow, in a speech delivered in the House of Peers on 17th of July, 1797, opposing the surgeons' incorporation bill, said that, "By a statute still in force, the barbers and surgeons were each to use a pole. The barbers were to have theirs blue and white, striped with no other appendage; but the surgeons', which was the same in other respects, was likewise to have a gallipot and a red rag, to denote the particular nature of their vocation."

But the reason why the surgeon's pole was adorned with both blue and red seems to have escaped the Chancellor. The chirurgical pole, properly tricked, ought to have a line of blue paint, another of red, and a third of white, winding round its length, in a regular serpentine progression—the blue representing the venous blood, the more brilliant colour the arterial, and the white thread being symbolic of the bandage used in tying up the arm after withdrawing the ligature. The stick itself is a sign that the operator possesses a stout staff for his patients to hold, continually tightening and relaxing their grasp during the operation—accelerating the flow of the blood by the muscular action of the arm. The phlebotomist's staff is of great antiquity. It is to be found amongst his properties, in an illuminated missal of the time of Edward the First, and in an engraving of the "Comenii Orbis Pictus."

Possibly in ancient times the physician's cane and the surgeon's club were used more actively. For many centuries fustigation was believed in as a sovereign remedy for bodily ailment as well as moral failings, and a beating was prescribed for an ague as frequently as for picking and stealing. This process Antonius Musa employed to cure Octavius Augustus of Sciatica. Thomas Campanella believed that it had the same effect as colocynth administered internally. Galen recommended it as a means of fattening people. Gordonius prescribed it in certain cases of nervous irritability—"Si sit juvenis, et non vult obedire, flagelletur frequenter et fortiter." In some rural districts ignorant mothers still flog the feet of their children to cure them of chilblains. And there remains on record a case in which club-tincture produced excellent results on a young patient to whom Desault gave a liberal dose of it.

In 1792, when Sir Astley Cooper was in Paris, he attended the lectures of Desault and Chopart in the Hotel Dieu. On one occasion, during this part of his student course, Cooper saw a young fellow, of some sixteen years of age, brought before Desault complaining of paralysis in his right arm. Suspecting that the boy was only shamming, "Abraham," Desault observed, unconcernedly, "Otez votre chapeau."

Forgetting his paralytic story, the boy instantly obeyed, and uncovered his head.

"Donnez moi un baton!" screamed Desault; and he beat the boy unmercifully.

"D'ou venez vous?" inquired the operator when the castigation was brought to a close.

"Faubourg de St. Antoine," was the answer.

"Oui, je le crois," replied Desault, with a shrug—speaking a truth experience had taught him—"tous les coquins viennent de ce quartier la."

But enough for the present of the barber-surgeon and his pole. "Tollite barberum,"—as Bonnel Thornton suggested, when in 1745 (a year barbarous in more ways than one), the surgeons, on being disjoined from the barbers, were asking what ought to be their motto.

Next to his cane, the physician's wig was the most important of his accoutrements. It gave profound learning and wise thought to lads just out of their teens. As the horse-hair skull-cap gives idle Mr. Briefless all the acuteness and gravity of aspect which one looks for in an attorney-general, so the doctor's artificial locks were to him a crown of honour. One of the Dukes of Holstein, in the eighteenth century, just missed destruction through being warned not to put on his head a poisoned wig which a traitorous peruke-maker offered him. To test the value of the advice given him, the Duke had the wig put upon the head of its fabricator. Within twelve minutes the man expired! We have never heard of a physician finding death in a wig; but a doctor who found the means of life in one is no rare bird in history.

> "Each son of Sol, to make him look more big,
> Had on a large, grave, decent, three-tailed wig;
> His clothes full-trimmed, with button-holes behind,
> Stiff were the skirts, with buckram stoutly lined;
> The cloth-cut velvet, or more reverend black,
> Full-made, and powder'd half-way down his back;
> Large decent cuffs, which near the ground did reach,
> With half a dozen buttons fix'd on each.
> Grave were their faces—fix'd in solemn state,
> These men struck awe; their children carried weight,
> In reverend wigs old heads young shoulders bore,
> And twenty-five or thirty seemed threescore."

The three-tailed wig was the one worn by Will Atkins, the gout doctor in Charles the Second's time (a good specialty then!). Will Atkins lived in the Old Bailey, and had a vast practice. His nostrums, some of which were composed of *thirty* different ingredients, were wonderful—but far less so than his wig, which was combed and frizzled over each cheek. When Will walked about the town, visiting his patients, he sometimes carried a cane, but never wore a hat. Such an article of costume would have disarranged the beautiful locks, or, at least, have obscured their glory.

> "Physic of old her entry made
> Beneath th' immense full-bottom's shade;
> While the gilt cane, with solemn pride,
> To each sagacious nose applied,
> Seem'd but a necessary prop
> To bear the weight of wig at top."

One of the most magnificent wigs on record was that of Colonel Dalmahoy, which was celebrated in a song beginning:—

> "If you would see a noble wig,
> And in that wig a man look big,
> To Ludgate Hill repair, my joy,
> And gaze on Col'nel Dalmahoy."

On Ludgate Hill, in close proximity to the Hall of the Apothecaries in Water Lane, the Colonel vended drugs and nostrums of all sorts—sweetmeats, washes for the complexion, scented oil for the hair, pomades, love-drops, and charms. Wadd, the humorous collector of anecdotes relating to his profession, records of him—

> "Dalmahoy sold infusions and lotions,
> Decoctions, and gargles, and pills;
> Electuaries, powders, and potions,
> Spermaceti, salts, scammony, squills.

> "Horse-aloes, burnt alum, agaric,
> Balm, benzoine, blood-stone, and dill;
> Castor, camphor, and acid tartaric,
> With specifics for every ill.

> "But with all his specifics in store,
> Death on Dalmahoy one day did pop;
> And although he had doctors a score,
> Made poor Dalmahoy shut up his shop."

The last silk-coated physician was Henry Revell Reynolds, M. D., one of the physicians who attended George III. during his long and melancholy affliction. Though this gentleman came quite down to living times, he persisted to the end in wearing the costume—of a well-powdered wig, silk coat, breeches, stockings, buckled shoes, gold-headed cane, and lace ruffles—with which he commenced his career. He was the Brummel of the Faculty, and retained his fondness for delicate apparel to the last. Even in his grave-clothes the coxcombical tastes of the man exhibited themselves. His very cerements were of "a good make."

> "Here well-dressed Reynolds lies.
> As great a beau as ever;
> We may perhaps see one as wise,
> But sure a smarter never."

Whilst Brocklesby's wig is still bobbing about in the distance, we may as well tell a good story of him. He was an eccentric man, with many good points, one of which was his friendship for Dr. Johnson. The Duchess of Richmond requested Brocklesby to visit her maid, who was so ill that she could not leave her bed. The physician proceeded forthwith to Richmond House, in obedience to the command. On arriving there he was shown up-stairs by the invalid's husband, who held the post of valet to the Duke. The man was a very intelligent fellow, a character with whom all visitors to Richmond House conversed freely, and a vehement politician. In this last characteristic the Doctor resembled him. Slowly the physician and the valet ascended the staircase, discussing the fate of parties, and the merits of ministers. They became excited, and declaiming at the top of their voices entered the sick room. The valet—forgetful of his marital duties in the delights of an intellectual contest—poured in a broadside of sarcasms, ironical inquiries, and red-hot declamation; the doctor—with true English pluck—returning fire, volley for volley. The battle lasted for upwards of an hour, when the two combatants walked down-stairs, and the man of medicine took his departure. When the doctor arrived at his door, and was stepping from his carriage, it flashed across his mind that he had not applied his finger to his patient's pulse, or even asked her how she felt herself!

Previous to Charles II.'s reign physicians were in the habit of visiting their patients on horse-back, sitting sideways on foot-cloths like women. Simeon Fox and Dr. Argent were the last Presidents of the College of Physicians to go their rounds in this undignified manner. With the "Restoration" came the carriage of the London physician. The *Lex Talionis* says, "For there must now be a little coach and two horses; and, being thus attended, half-a-piece, their usual fee, is but ill-taken, and popped into their left pocket, and possibly may cause the patient to send for his worship twice before he will come again to the hazard of another angel."

The fashion, once commenced, soon prevailed. In Queen Anne's reign, no physician with the slightest pretensions to practice could manage without his chariot and four, sometimes even six, horses. In our own day an equipage of some sort is considered so necessary an appendage to a medical practitioner, that a physician without a carriage (or a fly that can pass muster for one) is looked on with suspicion. He is marked down *mauvais sujet* in the same list with clergymen without duty, barristers without chambers, and gentlemen whose Irish tenantry obstinately refuse to keep them supplied with money. On the whole the carriage system is a good one. It protects stair carpets from being soiled with muddy boots (a great thing!), and bears cruelly on needy aspirants after professional employment (a yet greater thing! and one that manifestly ought to be the object of all professional etiquette!). If the early struggles of many fashionable physicians were fully and courageously written, we should have some heart-rending stories of the screwing and scraping and shifts by which their first equipages were maintained. Who hasn't heard of the darling doctor who taught singing under the moustachioed and bearded guise of an Italian Count, at a young ladies' school at Clapham, in order that he might make his daily West-end calls between 3 p. m. and 6 p. m. in a well-built brougham drawn by a fiery steed from a livery stable? There was one noted case of a young physician who provided himself with the means of figuring in a brougham during the May-fair morning, by condescending to the garb and duties of a flyman during the hours of darkness. He used the same carriage at both periods of the four-and-twenty hours, lolling in it by daylight, and sitting on it by gaslight. The poor fellow forgetting himself on one occasion, so far as to jump *in* when he ought to have jumped *on*, or jump *on* when he ought to have jumped *in*, he published his delicate secret to an unkind world.

It is a rash thing for a young man to start his carriage, unless he is sure of being able to sustain it for a dozen years. To drop it is sure destruction. We remember an ambitious Phaeton of Hospitals who astonished the world—not only of his profession, but of all London—with an equipage fit for an ambassador—the vehicle and the steeds being obtained, like the arms blazoned on his panels, upon credit. Six years afterwards he was met by a friend crushing the mud on the Marylebone pavements, and with a characteristic assurance, that even adversity was unable to deprive him of, said that his health was so much deranged that his dear friend, Sir James Clarke, had prescribed continual walking exercise for him as the only means of recovering his powers of digestion. His friends—good-natured people, as friends always are—observed that "it was a pity Sir James hadn't given him the advice a few years sooner—prevention being better than cure."

Though physicians began generally to take to carriages in Charles II.'s reign, it may not be supposed that no doctor of medicine before that time experienced the motion of a wheeled carriage. In "Stowe's Survey of London" one may read:—

> "In the year 1563, Dr. Langton, a physician, rid in a car, with a gown of damask, lined with velvet, and a coat of velvet, and a cap of the same (such, it seems, doctors then wore), but having a blue hood pinned over his cap; which was (as it seems) a customary mark of guilt. And so came through Cheapside on a market-day."

The doctor's offence was one against public morals. He had loved not wisely—but too well. The same generous weakness has brought learned doctors, since Langton's day, into extremely ridiculous positions.

The cane, wig, silk coat, stockings, side-saddle, and carriage, of the old physician have been mentioned. We may not pass over his muff in silence. That he might have his hands warm and delicate of touch, and so be able to discriminate to a nicety the qualities of his patient's arterial pulsations, he made his rounds, in cold weather, holding before him a large fur muff, in which his fingers and forearm were concealed.

CHAPTER II.

EARLY ENGLISH PHYSICIANS.

"Medicine is a science which hath been, as we have said, more professed than laboured, and yet more laboured than advanced; the labour having been, in my judgment, rather in circle than in progression. For I find much iteration, and small progression." —Lord Bacon's *Advancement of Learning*.

The British doctor, however, does not make his first appearance in sable dress and full-bottomed wig. Chaucer's physician, who was "groundit in Astronomy and Magyk Naturel," and whose "study was but lytyl in the Bible," had a far smarter and more attractive dress.

"In sanguyn and in perse he clad was al,
Lined with taffata and with sendal."

Taffeta and silk, of crimson and sky-blue colour, must have given an imposing appearance to this worthy gentleman, who, resembling many later doctors in his disuse of the Bible, resembled them also in his love of fees.

"And yit he was but esy of dispence,
He kepte that he won in pestelence;
For gold in physik is a cordial;
Therefore he lovede gold in special."

Amongst our more celebrated and learned English physicians was John Phreas, born about the commencement of the fifteenth century, and educated at Oxford, where he obtained a fellowship on the foundation of Balliol College. His M. D. degree he obtained in Padua, and the large fortune he made by the practice of physic was also acquired in Italy. He was a poet and an accomplished scholar. Some of his epistles in MS. are still preserved in the Balliol Library and at the Bodleian. His translation of Diodorus Siculus, dedicated to Paul II., procured for him from that pontiff the fatal gift of an English bishopric. A disappointed candidate for the same preferment is said to have poisoned him before the day appointed for his consecration.

Of Thomas Linacre, successively physician to Henry VII., Henry VIII., Edward VI., and Princess Mary, the memory is still green amongst men. At his request, in conjunction with the representations of John Chambre, Fernandus de Victoria, Nicholas Halswell, John Fraunces, Robert Yaxley (physicians), and Cardinal Wolsey, Henry VIII. granted letters patent, establishing the College of Physicians, and conferring on its members the sole privilege of practicing, and admitting persons to practice, within the city, and a circuit of seven miles. The college also was empowered to license practitioners throughout the kingdom, save such as were graduates of Oxford and Cambridge—who were to be exempt from the jurisdiction of the new college, save within London and its precincts. Linacre was the first President of the College of Physicians. The meetings of the learned corporation were held at Linacre's private house, No. 5, Knight-Rider Street, Doctors' Commons. This house (on which the Physician's arms, granted by Christopher Barker, Garter King-at-arms, Sept. 20, 1546, may still be seen,) was bequeathed to the college by Linacre, and long remained their property and abode. The original charter of the brotherhood states: "Before this period a great multitude of ignorant persons, of whom the greater part had no insight into physic, nor into any other kind of learning—some could not even read the letters and the book—so far forth, that common artificers, as smiths, weavers and women, boldly and accustomably took upon them great cures, to the high displeasure of God, great infamy of the Faculty, and the grievous hurt, damage, and destruction of many of the king's liege people."

Linacre died in the October of 1524. Caius, writing his epitaph, concludes, "Fraudes dolosque mire perosus, fidus amicis, omnibus juxta charus; aliquot annos antequam obierat Presbyter factus; plenus annes, ex hac vita migravit, multum desideratus." His motive for taking holy orders towards the latter part of his life is unknown. Possibly he imagined the sacerdotal garb would be a secure and comfortable clothing in the grave. Certainly he was not a profound theologian. A short while before his death he read the New Testament for the first time, when so great was his astonishment at finding the rules of Christians widely at variance with their practice, that he threw the sacred volume from him in a passion, and exclaimed, "Either this is not the gospel, or we are not Christians."

Of the generation next succeeding Linacre's was John Kaye, or Key (or Caius, as it has been long pedantically spelt). Like Linacre (the elegant writer and intimate friend of Erasmus), Caius is associated with letters not less than medicine. Born of a respectable Norfolk family, Caius raised, on the foundation of Gonvil Hall, the college in the University of Cambridge that bears his name—to which Eastern Counties' men do mostly resort. Those who know Cambridge remember the quaint humour with which, in obedience to the founder's will, the gates of Caius are named. As a president of the College of Physicians, Caius was a zealous defender of the rights of his order. It has been suggested that Shakespeare's Dr. Caius, in "The Merry Wives of Windsor," was produced in resentment towards the president, for his excessive fervor against the surgeons.

Caius terminated his laborious and honourable career on July the 29th, 1573, in the sixty-third year of his age.[2] He was buried in his college chapel, in a tomb constructed some time before his decease, and marked with the brief epitaph—"Fui Caius." In the same year in which this physician of Edward VI., Mary, and Elizabeth died, was born Theodore Turquet de Mayerne, Baron Aulbone of

---

[2] In Dr. Moussett's "Health's Improvement; or Rules concerning Food" is a curious passage relating to this eminent physician's decay.

France, and Sir Theodore Mayerne in England. Of Mayerne mention will be made in various places of these pages. There is some difficulty in ascertaining to how many crowned heads this lucky courtier was appointed physician. After leaving France and permanently fixing himself in England, he kept up his connection with the French, so that the list of his monarch-patients may be said to comprise two French and three English sovereigns—Henry IV. and Louis XIII. of France, and James I., Charles I., and Charles II. of England. Mayerne died at Chelsea, in the eighty-second year of his age, on the 15th of March, 1655. Like John Hunter, he was buried in the church of St. Martin's-in-the-Fields. His library went to the College of Physicians, and his wealth to his only daughter, who was married to the Marquis of Montpouvillon. Though Mayerne was the most eminent physician of his time, his prescriptions show that his enlightenment was not superior to the prevailing ignorance of the period. He recommended a monthly excess of wine and food as a fine stimulant to the system. His treatise on Gout, written in French, and translated into English (1676) by Charles II.'s physician in ordinary, Dr. Thomas Sherley, recommends a clumsy and inordinate administration of violent drugs. Calomel he habitually administered in scruple doses. Sugar of lead he mixed largely in his conserves; pulverized human bones he was very fond of prescribing; and the principal ingredient in his gout-powder was "raspings of a human skull unburied." But his sweetest compound was his "Balsam of Bats," strongly recommended as an unguent for hypochondriacal persons, into which entered adders, bats, suckling whelps, earth-worms, hog's grease, the marrow of a stag, and the thigh-bone of an ox. After such a specimen of the doctor's skill, possibly the reader will not care to study his receipts for canine madness, communicated to the Royal Society in 1687, or his "Excellent and well-approved Receipts and Experiments in Cookery, with the best way of Preserving." Nor will the reader be surprised to learn that the great physician had a firm belief in the efficacy of amulets and charms.

But the ignorance and superstition of which Mayerne was the representative were approaching the close of their career; and Sir Theodore's court celebrity and splendour were to become contemptible by the side of the scientific achievements of a contemporary. The grave closed over Mayerne in 1655; but in the December of 1652, the College of Physicians had erected in their hall a statue of Harvey, who died on the third of June, 1657, aged seventy-nine years.

> "The circling streams, once thought but pools of blood
> (Whether life's fuel, or the body's food),
> From dark oblivion Harvey's name shall save."

Aubrey says of Harvey—"He was not tall, but of the lowest stature; round-faced, olivaster (waintscott) complexion; little eie—round, very black, full of spirit; his haire was black as a raven, but quite white twenty years before he dyed. I remember he was wont to drink coffee, which he and his brother Eliab did, before coffee-houses were in fashion in London. He was, as all the rest of his brothers, very cholerique; and in his younger days wore a dagger (as the fashion then was); but this doctor would be apt to draw out his dagger upon every slight occasion. He rode on *horse-back with a foot-cloth to visit his patients, his man following on foot, as the fashion then was, was very decent, now quite discontinued.*"

Harvey's discovery dates a new era in medical and surgical science. Its influence on scientific men, not only as a stepping-stone to further discoveries, but as a power rousing in all quarters a spirit of philosophic investigation, was immediately perceptible. A new class of students arose, before whom the foolish dreams of medical superstition and the darkness of empiricism slowly disappeared.

Of the physicians[3] of what may be termed the Elizabethan era, beyond all others the most sagacious and interesting, is William Bulleyn. He belongs to a bevy of distinguished Eastern Counties' physicians. Dr. Butts, Henry VIII.'s physician, mentioned in Strype's "Life of Cranmer," and made celebrated amongst doctors by Shakespeare's "Henry the Eighth," belonged to an honourable and gentle family sprinkled over Norfolk, Suffolk, and Cambridgeshire. The butcher king knighted him by the style of William Butts of Norfolk. Caius was born at Norwich; and the eccentric William Butler, of whom Mayerne, Aubrey, and Fuller tell fantastic stories, was born at Ipswich, about the year 1535.

William Bulleyn was born in the isle of Ely; but it is with the eastern division of the county of Suffolk that his name is especially associated. Sir William Bulleyn, the Sheriff of Norfolk and Suffolk in the fifteenth year of Henry VII., and grandfather of the unfortunate Anne Boleyn, was one of the magnates of the doctor's family—members of which are still to be found in Ipswich and other parts of East Anglia, occupying positions of high respectability. In the reigns of Edward VI., Mary, and Elizabeth, no one ranked higher than William Bulleyn as botanist and physician. The record of his acuteness and learning is found in his numerous works, which are amongst the most interesting prose writings of the Elizabethan era. If Mr. Bohn, who has already done so much to render old and neglected authors popular, would present the public with a well-edited reprint of Bulleyn's works, he would make a valuable addition to the services he has already conferred on literature.

After receiving a preliminary education in the University of Cambridge, Bulleyn enlarged his mind by extended travel, spending much time in Germany and Scotland. During the reign of Queen Mary he practiced in Norwich; but he moved to Blaxhall, in Suffolk (of which parish it is believed his brother was for some years rector). Alluding to his wealthy friend, Sir Thomas Rushe, of Oxford, he says, with a pun, "I myself did know a Rushe, growing in the fenne side, by Orford, in Suffolke, that might have spent three hundred marks by year. Was not this a *rush* of estimation? A fewe sutche rushes be better than many great trees or bushes. But thou doste not know that countrey, where sometyme I did dwell, at a place called Blaxall, neere to that *Rushe Bushe*. I would all rushes within this realme were as riche in value." (The ancient family still maintain their connection with the county.) Speaking of the rushes near Orford, in Suffolk, and about the isle of Ely, Bulleyn says, "The playne people make mattes and horse-collars of the greater rushes, and of the smaller they make lightes or candles for the winter. Rushes that growe

---

[3] To the acquirements of the Elizabethan physicians in every department of learning, *save* the sciences immediately concerning their own profession, Lord Bacon bears emphatic testimony—"For you shall have of them antiquaries, poets, humanists, statesmen, merchants, divines."

upon dry groundes be good to strewe in halles, chambers, and galleries, to walk upon—defending apparell, as traynes of gownes and kirtles, from the dust."

He tells of the virtues of Suffolk sage (a herb that the nurses of that county still believe in as having miraculous effects, when administered in the form of "sage-tea"). Of Suffolk hops (now but little grown in the county) he mentions in terms of high praise—especially of those grown round Framlingham Castle, and "the late house of nunnes at Briziarde." "I know in many places of the country of Suffolke, where they brew theyr beere with hoppes that growe upon theyr owne groundes, as in a place called Briziarde, near an old famous castle called Framingham, and in many other places of the country." Of the peas of Orford the following mention is made:—"In a place called Orforde, in Suffolke, betwene the haven and the mayne sea, wheras never plow came, nor natural earth was, but stones onely, infinite thousand ships loden in that place, there did pease grow, whose roots were more than iii fadome long, and the coddes did grow uppon clusters like the keys of ashe trees, bigger than fitches, and less than the fyeld peason, very sweete to eat upon, and served many pore people dwelling there at hand, which els should have perished for honger, the scarcity of bread was so great. In so much that the playne pore people did make very much of akornes; and a sickness of a strong fever did sore molest the commons that yere, the like whereof was never heard of there. Now, whether th' occasion of these peason, in providence of God, came through some shipwracke with much misery, or els by miracle, I am not able to determine thereof; but sowen by man's hand they were not, nor like other pease."[4]

In the same way one has in the Doctor's "Book of Simples" pleasant gossip about the more choice productions of the garden and of commerce, showing that horticulture must have been far more advanced at that time than is generally supposed, and that the luxuries imported from foreign countries were largely consumed throughout the country. Pears, apples, peaches, quinces, cherries, grapes, raisins, prunes, barberries, oranges, medlars, raspberries and strawberries, spinage, ginger, and lettuces are the good things thrown upon the board.

Of pears, the author says: "There is a kynd of peares growing in the city of Norwich, called the black freere's peare, very delicious and pleasaunt, and no lesse profitable unto a hoate stomacke, as I heard it reported by a ryght worshipful phisicion of the same city, called Doctour Manfield." Other pears, too, are mentioned, "sutch as have names as peare Robert, peare John, bishop's blessyngs, with other prety names. The red warden is of great vertue, conserved, roasted or baken to quench choller." The varieties of the apple especially mentioned are "the costardes, the greene cotes, the pippen, the queene aple."

Grapes are spoken of as cultivated and brought to a high state of perfection in Suffolk and other parts of the country. Hemp is humorously called "gallow grasse or neckweede." The heartesease, or paunsie, is mentioned by its quaint old name, "three faces in one hodde." Parsnips, radishes, and carrots are offered for sale. In the neighborhood of London, large quantities of these vegetables were grown for the London market; but Bulleyn thinks little of them, describing them as "more

---

[4] The tradition of this timely and unaccountable growth of peas still exists amongst the peasants in the neighbourhood of Orford. J. C. J.

plentiful than profytable." Of figs—"Figges be good agaynst melancholy, and the falling evil, to be eaten. Figges, nuts, and herb grace do make a sufficient medicine against poison or the pestilence. Figges make a good gargarism to cleanse the throates."

The double daisy is mentioned as growing in gardens. Daisy tea was employed in gout and rheumatism—as herb tea of various sorts still is by the poor of our provinces. With daisy tea (or *bellis-tea*) "I, Bulleyn, did recover one Belliser, not onely from a spice of the palsie, but also from the quartan. And afterwards, the same Belliser, more unnatural than a viper, sought divers ways to have murthered me, taking part against me with my mortal enemies, accompanied with bloudy ruffins for that bloudy purpose." Parsley, also, was much used in medicine. And as it was the custom for the doctor to grow his own herbs in his garden, we may here see the origin of the old nursery tradition of little babies being brought by the doctor from the parsley bed.[5]

Scarcely less interesting than "The Book of Simples" is Bulleyn's "Dialogue betweene Soarenes and Chirurgi." It opens with an honourable mention of many distinguished physicians and chirurgians. Dr. John Kaius is praised as a worthy follower of Linacre. Dr. Turner's "booke of herbes will always grow greene." Sir Thomas Eliot's "'castel of health' cannot decay." Thomas Faire "is not deade, but is transformed and chaunged into a new nature immortal." Androwe Borde, the father of "Merry Andrews," "wrote also wel of physicke to profit the common wealth withal." Thomas Pannel, the translator of the Schola Saternitana, "hath play'd ye good servant to the commonwealth in translating good bookes of physicke." Dr. William Kunyngham "hath wel travailed like a good souldiour agaynst the ignorant enemy." Numerous other less eminent practitioners are mentioned— such as Buns, Edwards, Hatcher, Frere, Langton, Lorkin, Wendy—educated at Cambridge; Gee and Simon Ludford, of Oxford; Huyck (the Queen's physician), Bartley, Carr; Masters, John Porter, of Norwich; Edmunds of York, Robert Baltrop, and Thomas Calfe, apothecary.

"Soft chirurgians," says Bulleyn, "make foul sores." He was a bold and courageous one. "Where the wound is," runs the Philippine proverb, "the plaster must be." Bulleyn was of the same opinion; but, in dressing a tender part, the surgeon is directed to have "a gladsome countenance," because "the paciente should not be greatly troubled." For bad surgeons he has not less hostility than he has for

> "Petty Foggers, in cases of the law,
> Who make mountaynes of molhils, and trees of a straw."

The state of medicine in Elizabeth's reign may be discovered by a survey of the best recipes of this physician, who, in sagacity and learning, was far superior to Sir Theodore Mayerne, his successor by a long interval.

"*An Embrocation.*—An embrocation is made after this manner:—R. Of a decoction of mallowes, vyolets, barly, quince seed, lettice leaves, one pint; of barly meale, two ounces; of oyle of vyolets and roses, of each, an ounce and half; of but-

---

[5] The classical reader who is acquainted with the significations of the Greek [Greek: Selinon], will not be at a loss to account for this medicinal use of the crisp green leaves.

ter, one ounce; and then seeth them all together till they be like a broathe, puttyng thereto, at the ende, four yolkes of eggs; and the maner of applying them is with peeces of cloth, dipped in the aforesaid decoction, being actually hoate."

"*A Good Emplaster.*—You shall mak a plaster with these medicines following, which the great learned men themselves have used unto their pacientes:—R. Of hulled beanes, or beane flower that is without the brane, one pound; of mallow-leaves, two handfuls; seethe them in lye, til they be well sodden, and afterwarde let them be stamped and incorporate with four ounces of meale of lint or flaxe, two ounces of meale of lupina; and forme thereof a plaster with goat's grease, for this openeth the pores, avoideth the matter, and comforteth also the member; but if the place, after a daye or two of the application, fall more and more to blackness, it shall be necessary to go further, even to sacrifying and incision of the place."

Pearl electuaries and pearl mixtures were very fashionable medicines with the wealthy down to the commencement of the eighteenth century. Here we have Bulleyn's recipe for

> "*Electuarium de Gemmis.*—Take two drachms of white perles; two little peeces of saphyre; jacinth, corneline, emerauldes, granettes, of each an ounce; setwal, the sweate roote doronike, the rind of pomecitron, mace, basel seede, of each two drachms; of redde corall, amber, shaving of ivory, of each two drachms; rootes both of white and red behen, ginger, long peper, spicknard, folium indicum, saffron, cardamon, of each one drachm; of troch, diarodon, lignum aloes, of each half a small handful; cinnamon, galinga, zurubeth, which is a kind of setwal, of each one drachm and a half; thin pieces of gold and sylver, of each half a scruple; of musk, half a drachm. Make your electuary with honey emblici, which is the fourth kind of mirobalans with roses, strained in equall partes, as much as will suffice. This healeth cold diseases of ye braine, harte, stomack. It is a medicine proved against the tremblynge of the harte, faynting and souning, the weaknes of the stomacke, pensivenes, solitarines. Kings and noble men have used this for their comfort. It causeth them to be bold-spirited, the body to smell wel, and ingendreth to the face good coloure."

Truly a medicine for kings and noblemen! During the railway panic in '46 an unfortunate physician prescribed for a nervous lady:—

> R. Great Western, 350 shares.
>
> Eastern Counties   }
> North Middlesex   } a—a 1050
>
> Mft. Haust. 1. Om. noc. cap.

This direction to a delicate gentlewoman, to swallow nightly two thousand four hundred and fifty railway shares, was regarded as evidence of the physician's insanity, and the management of his private affairs was forthwith taken out of his hands. But assuredly it was as rational a prescription as Bulleyn's "Electuarium de Gemmis."

"*A Precious Water.*—Take nutmegges, the roote called doronike, which the apothecaries have, setwall, gatangall, mastike, long peper, the bark of pomecitron, of mellon, sage, bazel, marjorum, dill, spiknard, wood of aloes, cubebe, cardamon, called graynes of paradise, lavender, peniroyall, mintes, sweet catamus, germander, enulacampana, rosemary, stichados, and quinance, of eche lyke quantity; saffron, an ounce and half; the bone of a harte's heart grated, cut, and stamped; and beate your spyces grossly in a morter. Put in ambergrice and musk, of each half a drachm. Distil this in a simple aqua vitæ, made with strong ale, or sackeleyes and aniseedes, not in a common styll, but in a serpentine; to tell the vertue of this water against colde, phlegme, dropsy, heavines of minde, comming of melancholy, I cannot well at thys present, the excellent virtues thereof are sutch, and also the tyme were to long."

The cure of cancers has been pretended and attempted by a numerous train of knaves and simpletons, as well as men of science. In the Elizabethan time this most terrible of maladies was thought to be influenced by certain precious waters—*i. e.* precious messes.

"Many good men and women," says Bulleyn, "wythin thys realme have dyvers and sundry medicines for the canker, and do help their neighboures that bee in perill and daunger whyche be not onely poore and needy, having no money to spende in chirurgie. But some do well where no chirurgians be neere at hand; in such cases, as I have said, many good gentlemen and ladyes have done no small pleasure to poore people; as that excellent knyght, and worthy learned man, Syr Thomas Eliot, whose works be immortall. Syr William Parris, of Cambridgeshire, whose cures deserve prayse; Syr William Gascoigne, of Yorkshire, that helped many soare eyen; and the Lady Tailor, of Huntingdonshire, and the Lady Darrell of Kent, had many precious medicines to comfort the sight, and to heale woundes withal, and were well seene in herbes.

"The commonwealth hath great want of them, and of theyr medicines, whych if they had come into my handes, they should have bin written in my booke. Among al other there was a knight, a man of great worshyp, a Godly hurtlesse gentleman, which is departed thys lyfe, hys name is Syr Anthony Heveningham. This gentleman learned a water to kyll a canker of hys owne mother, whych he used all hys lyfe, to the greate helpe of many men, women, and chyldren."

This water "learned by Syr Anthony Heveningham" was, Bulleyn states on report, composed thus:—

"*Precious Water to Cure a Canker*:—Take dove's foote, a herbe so named, Arkangell ivy wyth the berries, young red bryer toppes, and leaves, whyte roses, theyr leaves and buds, red sage, selandyne, and woodbynde, of eche lyke quantity, cut or chopped and put into pure cleane whyte wyne, and clarified hony. Then breake into it alum glasse and put in a little of the pouder of aloes hepatica. Destill these together softly in a limbecke of glasse or pure tin; if not, then in limbecke wherein aqua vitæ is made. Keep this water close. It will not onely kyll the canker, if it be duly washed therewyth; but also two droppes dayly put into the eye wyll sharp the syght, and breake the pearle and spottes, specially if it be dropped in with a little fenell water, and close the eys after."

There is reason to wish that all empirical applications, for the cure of cancer, were as harmless as this.

The following prescription for pomatum differs but little from the common domestic receipts for lip-salve in use at the present day:—

"*Sickness.*—How make you pomatum?

"*Health.*—Take the fat of a young kyd one pound, temper it with the water of musk roses by the space of foure dayes; then take five apples, and dresse them, and cut them in pieces, and lard them with cloves, then boyle them altogeather in the same water of roses, in one vessel of glasse; set within another vessel; let it boyle on the fyre so long until all be white; then wash them with ye same water of muske roses; this done, kepe it in a glass; and if you wil have it to smel better, then you must put in a little civet or musk, or of them both, and ambergrice. Gentilwomen doe use this to make theyr faces smoth and fayre, for it healeth cliftes in the lyppes, or in any other place of the hands and face."

The most laughable of all Bulleyn's receipts is one in which, for the cure of a child suffering under a certain nervous malady, he prescribes "a smal yong mouse rosted." To some a "rosted mouse" may seem more palatable than the compound in which snails are the principal ingredient. "Snayles," says Bulleyn, "broken from the shelles and sodden in whyte wyne with oyle and sugar are very holsome, because they be hoat and moist for the straightnes of the lungs and cold cough. Snails stamped with camphory, and leven wil draw forth prycks in the flesh." So long did this belief in the virtue of snails retain its hold on Suffolk, that the writer of these pages remembers a venerable lady (whose memory is cherished for her unostentatious benevolence and rare worth) who for years daily took a cup of snail broth, for the benefit of a weak chest.

One minor feature of Bulleyn's works is the number of receipts given in them for curing the bites of mad dogs. The good man's horror of Suffolk witches is equal to his admiration of Suffolk dairies. Of the former he says, "I dyd know wythin these few yeres a false witch, called M. Line, in a towne of Suffolke called Derham, which with a payre of ebene beades, and certain charmes, had no small resort of foolysh women, when theyr chyldren were syck. To thys lame wytch they resorted, to have the fairie charmed and the spyrite conjured away; through the prayers of the ebene beades, whych she said came from the Holy Land, and were sanctifyed at Rome. Through whom many goodly cures were don, but my chaunce was to burn ye said beades. Oh that damnable witches be suffred to live unpunished and so many blessed men burned; witches be more hurtful in this realm than either quarten or pestilence. I know in a towne called Kelshall in Suffolke, a witch, whose name was M. Didge, who with certain *Ave Marias* upon her ebene beades, and a waxe candle, used this charme for S. Anthonies fyre, having the sycke body before her, holding up her hande, saying—

'There came two angels out of the North-east,

One brought fyre, the other brought frost,—
Out fyre, and in frost!'

"I could reherse an hundred of sutch knackes, of these holy gossips. The fyre take them all, for they be God's enemyes."

On leaving Blaxhall in Suffolk, Bulleyn migrated to the north. For many years he practised with success at Durham. At Shields he owned a considerable property. Sir Thomas, Baron of Hilton, Commander of Tinmouth Castle under Philip and Mary, was his patron and intimate friend. His first book, entitled "Government of Health," he dedicated to Sir Thomas Hilton; but the MS., unfortunately, was lost in a shipwreck before it was printed. Disheartened by this loss, and the death of his patron, Bulleyn bravely set to work in London, to "revive his dead book." Whilst engaged on the laborious work of recomposition, he was arraigned on a grave charge of murder. "One William Hilton," he says, telling his own story, "brother to the sayd Syr Thomas Hilton, accused me of no less cryme then of most cruel murder of his owne brother, who dyed of a fever (sent onely of God) among his owne frends, fynishing his lyfe in the Christian fayth. But this William Hilton caused me to be arraigned before that noble Prince, the Duke's Grace of Norfolke, for the same; to this end to have had me dyed shamefully; that with the covetous Ahab he might have, through false witnes and perjury, obtayned by the counsel of Jezabell, a wineyard, by the pryce of blood. But it is wrytten, *Testis mendax peribit*, a fals witnes shal com to naught; his wicked practise was wisely espyed, his folly deryded, his bloudy purpose letted, and fynallye I was with justice delivered."

This occurred in 1560. His foiled enemy afterwards endeavoured to get him assassinated; but he again triumphed over the machinations of his adversary. Settling in London, he obtained a large practice, though he was never enrolled amongst the physicians of the college. His leisure time he devoted to the composition of his excellent works. To the last he seems to have kept up a close connection with the leading Eastern Counties families. His "Comfortable Regiment and Very Wholsome order against the moste perilous Pleurisie," was dedicated to the Right Worshipful Sir Robart Wingfelde of Lethryngham, Knight.

William Bulleyn died in London, on the 7th of January, 1576, and was buried in the church of St. Giles's, Cripplegate, in the same tomb wherein his brother Richard had been laid thirteen years before; and wherein John Fox, the martyrologist, was interred eleven years later.

CHAPTER III.

SIR THOMAS BROWNE AND SIR KENELM DIGBY.

Amongst the physicians of the seventeenth century were three Brownes—father, son, and grandson. The father wrote the "Religio Medici," and the "Pseudoxia Epidemica"—a treatise on vulgar errors. The son was the traveller, and author of "Travels in Hungaria, Servia, Bulgaria, Macedonia, Thessaly, Austria, Styria, Carinthia, Carniola, Friuli &c.," and the translator of the Life of Themistocles in the English version of "Plutarch's Lives" undertaken by Dryden. He was also a physician of Bartholomew's, and a favourite physician of Charles II., who on one occasion said of him, "Doctor Browne is as learned as any of the college, and as well bred as any of the court." The grandson was a Fellow of the Royal Society, and, like his father and grandfather, a Fellow of the Royal College of Physicians; but he was by no means worthy of his distinguished progenitors. Alike unknown in literature, science, and art, he was a miserable sot, and was killed by a fall from his horse, between Southfleet and Gravesend, when in a state of intoxication. He was thus cut off in the July of 1710, having survived his father not quite two years.

The author of the "Religio Medici" enjoys as good a chance of an immortality of fame as any of his contemporaries. The child of a London merchant, who left him a comfortable fortune, Thomas Browne was from the beginning of his life (Oct. 19, 1605) to its close (Oct. 19, 1682), well placed amongst the wealthier of those who occupied the middle way of life. From Winchester College, where his schoolboy days were spent, he proceeded to the University of Oxford, becoming a member of Broadgates Hall, i.e., Pembroke College—the college of Blackstone, Shenstone, and Samuel Johnson. After taking his B.A. and M.A. degrees, he turned his attention to medicine, and for some time practised as a physician in Oxfordshire. Subsequently to this he travelled over different parts of Europe, visiting France, Italy, and Holland, and taking a degree of Doctor in Physic at Leyden. Returning to England, he settled at Norwich, married a rich and beautiful Norfolk lady, named Mileham; and for the rest of his days resided in that ancient city, industriously occupied with an extensive practice, the pursuits of literature, and the education of his children. When Charles II. visited Norwich in 1671, Thomas Browne, M.D., was knighted by the royal hand. This honour, little as a man of letters would now esteem it, was highly prized by the philosopher. He thus alludes to it in his "Antiquities of Norwich"—"And it is not for some wonder, that Norwich having been for so long a time so considerable a place, so few kings have visited it; of which number among so many monarchs since the Conquest we find but four; viz., King Henry III., Edward I., Queen Elizabeth, and our gracious sovereign now reigning,

King Charles II., of which I had a particular reason to take notice."

Amongst the Norfolk people Sir Thomas was very popular, his suave and un-obtrusive manners securing him many friends, and his philosophic moderation of temper saving him from ever making an enemy. The honour conferred on him was a subject of congratulation—even amongst his personal friends, when his back was turned. The Rev. John Whitefoot, M.A., Rector of Heigham, in Norfolk, in his "Minutes for the Life of Sir Thomas Browne," says, that had it been his province to preach his funeral sermon, he should have taken his text from an uncanonical book—"I mean that of Syracides, or Jesus, the son of Syrach, commonly called Ec-clesiasticus, which, in the 38th chapter, and the first verse, hath these words, 'Hon-our a physician with the honour due unto him; for the uses which you may have of him, for the Lord hath created him; for of the Most High cometh healing, and he shall receive Honour of the King' (as ours did that of knighthood from the present King, when he was in this city). 'The skill of the physician shall lift up his head, and in the sight of great men shall he be in admiration'; so was this worthy person by the greatest man of this nation that ever came into this country, by whom also he was frequently and personally visited."

Widely and accurately read in ancient and modern literature, and possessed of numerous accomplishments, Sir Thomas Browne was in society diffident al-most to shyness. "His modesty," says Whitefoot, "was visible in a natural habitual blush, which was increased upon the least occasion, and oft discovered without any observable cause. Those who knew him only by the briskness of his writings were astonished at his gravity of aspect and countenance, and freedom from lo-quacity." As was his manner, so was his dress. "In his habit of cloathing he had an aversion to all finery, and affected plainness both in fashion and ornaments."

The monuments of Sir Thomas and his lady are in the church of St. Peter's, Mancroft, Norwich, where they were buried. Some years since Sir Thomas Browne's tomb was opened for the purpose of submitting it to repair, when there was discovered on his coffin a plate, of which Dr. Diamond, who happened at the time to be in Norwich, took two rubbings, one of which is at present in the writer's custody. It bears the following interesting inscription:—"Amplissimus vir Dr. Thomas Browne Miles Medicinæ Dr. Annos Natus et Denatus 19 Die Mensis Anno Dmi., 1682—hoc loculo indormiens corporis spagyrici pulvere plumbum in aurum convertit."

The "Religio Medici" not only created an unprecedented sensation by its er-udition and polished style, but it shocked the nervous guardians of orthodoxy by its boldness of inquiry. It was assailed for its infidelity and scientific heresies. According to Coleridge's view of the "Religio Medici," Sir Thomas Browne, "a fine mixture of humourist, genius, and pedant," was a Spinosist without knowing it. "Had he," says the poet, "lived nowadays, he would probably have been a very ingenious and bold infidel in his real opinions, though the kindness of his nature would have kept him aloof from vulgar, prating, obtrusive infidelity."

Amongst the adverse critics of the "Religio Medici" was the eccentric, gallant, brave, credulous, persevering, frivolous, Sir Kenelm Digby. A Mæcenas, a Sir Philip Sydney, a Dr. Dee, a Beau Fielding, and a Dr. Kitchener, all in one, this man is chief of those extravagant characters that astonish the world at rare intervals, and are found nowhere except in actual life. No novelist of the most advanced section of the idealistic school would dare to create such a personage as Sir Kenelm. The eldest son of the ill-fated Sir Everard Digby, he was scarcely three years old when his father atoned on the scaffold for his share in the gunpowder treason. Fortunately a portion of the family estate was entailed, so Sir Kenelm, although the offspring of attainted blood, succeeded to an ample revenue of about £3000 a-year. In 1618 (when only in his fifteenth year) he entered Gloucester Hall, now Worcester College, Oxford. In 1621 he commenced foreign travel. He attended Charles I. (then Prince of Wales) at the Court of Madrid; and returning to England in 1623, was knighted by James I. at Hinchinbroke, the house of Lord Montague, on the 23rd of October in that year. From that period he was before the world as courtier, cook, lover, warrior, alchemist, political intriguer, and man of letters. He became a gentleman of the bedchamber, and commissioner of the navy. In 1628 he obtained a naval command, and made his brilliant expedition against the Venetians and Algerians, whose galleys he routed off Scanderon. This achievement is celebrated by his client and friend, Ben Jonson:—

> "Though, happy Muse, thou know my Digby well,
> Yet read in him these lines: he doth excel
> In honour, courtesy, and all the parts
> Court can call hero, or man could call his arts.
> He's prudent, valiant, just, and temperate;
> In him all virtue is beheld in state;
> And he is built like some imperial room
> For that to dwell in, and be still at home.
> His breast is a brave palace, a broad street,
> Where all heroic, ample thoughts do meet;
> Where nature such a large survey hath ta'en,
> As other souls, to his, dwelt in a lane:
> Witness his action done at Scanderoon
> Upon his birthday, the eleventh of June."

Returning from war, he became once more the student, presenting in 1632 the library he had purchased of his friend Allen, to the Bodleian Library, and devoting his powers to the mastery of controversial divinity. Having in 1636 entered the Church of Rome, he resided for some time abroad. Amongst his works at this period were his "Conference with a Lady about the Choice of Religion," published in 1638, and his "Letters between Lord George Digby and Sir Kenelm Digby, Knt., concerning Religion," not published till 1651. It is difficult to say to which he was most devoted—his King, his Church, literature, or his beautiful and frail wife, Venetia Stanley, whose charms fascinated the many admirers on whom she distributed her favours, and gained her Sir Kenelm for a husband when she was the discarded mistress of Richard, Earl of Dorset. She had borne the Earl children, so his Lordship on parting settled on her an annuity of £500 per annum. After her marriage, this annuity not being punctually paid, Sir Kenelm sued the Earl for it.

Well might Mr. Lodge say, "By the frailties of that lady much of the noblest blood of England was dishonoured, for she was the daughter of Sir Edward Stanley, Knight of the Bath, grandson of the great Edward, Earl of Derby, by Lucy, daughter and co-heir of Thomas Percy, Earl of Northumberland." Such was her unfair fame. "The *fair fame* left to Posterity of that Truly Noble Lady, the Lady Venetia Digby, late wife of Sir Kenelm Digby, Knight, a Gentleman Absolute in all Numbers," is embalmed in the clear verses of Jonson. Like Helen, she is preserved to us by the sacred poet.

> "Draw first a cloud, all save her neck,
> And out of that make day to break;
> Till like her face it do appear,
> And men may think all light rose there."

In other and more passionate terms Sir Kenelm painted the same charms in his "Private Memoirs."

But if Sir Kenelm was a chivalric husband, he was not a less loyal subject. How he avenged in France the honour of his King, on the body of a French nobleman, may be learnt in a curious tract, "Sir Kenelme Digby's Honour Maintained. By a most courageous combat which he fought with Lord Mount le Ros, who by base and slanderous words reviled our King. Also the true relation how he went to the King of France, who kindly intreated him, and sent two hundred men to guard him so far as Flanders. And now he is returned from Banishment, and to his eternall honour lives in England."

Sir Kenelm's "Observations upon Religio Medici," are properly characterized by Coleridge as those of a pedant. They were written whilst he was kept a prisoner, by order of the Parliament, in Winchester House; and the author had the ludicrous folly to assert that he both read the "Religio Medici" through for the first time, and wrote his bulky criticism upon it, in less than twenty-four hours. Of all the claims that have been advanced by authors for the reputation of being rapid workmen, this is perhaps the most audacious. For not only was the task one that at least would require a month, but the impudent assertion that it was accomplished in less than a day and night was contradicted by the title-page, in which "the observations" are described as "occasionally written." Beckford's vanity induced him to boast that "Vathek" was composed at one sitting of two days and three nights; but this statement—outrageous falsehood though it be—was sober truth compared with Sir Kenelm's brag.

But of all Sir Kenelm's vagaries, his Sympathetic Powder was the drollest. The composition, revealed after the Knight's death by his chemist and steward, George Hartman, was effected in the following manner:—English vitriol was dissolved in warm water; this solution was filtered, and then evaporated till a thin scum appeared on the surface. It was then left undisturbed and closely covered in a cool place for two or three days, when fair, green, and large crystals were evolved. "Spread these crystals," continues the chemist, "abroad in a large flat earthen dish, and expose them to the heat of the sun in the dog-days, turning them often, and the sun will calcine them white; when you see them all white without, beat them grossly, and expose them again to the sun, securing them from the rain; when they are well calcined, powder them finely, and expose this powder again to the sun, turning and stirring it often. Continue this until it be reduced to a white powder, which put up in a glass, and tye it up close, and keep it in a dry place."

The virtues of this powder were unfolded by Sir Kenelm, in a French oration delivered to "a solemn assembly of Nobles and Learned Men at Montpellier, in France." It cured wounds in the following manner:—If any piece of a wounded person's apparel, having on it the stain of blood that had proceeded from the wound, was dipped in water holding in solution some of this sympathetic powder, the wound of the injured person would forthwith commence a healing process. It mattered not how far distant the sufferer was from the scene of operation. Sir Kenelm gravely related the case of his friend Mr. James Howel, the author of the "Dendrologia," translated into French by Mons. Baudoin. Coming accidentally on two of his friends whilst they were fighting a duel with swords, Howel endeavoured to separate them by grasping hold of their weapons. The result of this interference was to show the perils that

> "Environ
> The man who meddles with cold iron."

His hands were severely cut, insomuch that some four or five days afterwards, when he called on Sir Kenelm, with his wounds plastered and bandaged up, he said his surgeons feared the supervention of gangrene. At Sir Kenelm's request, he gave the knight a garter which was stained with his blood. Sir Kenelm took it, and without saying what he was about to do, dipped it in a solution of his powder of vitriol. Instantly the sufferer started.

"What ails you?" cried Sir Kenelm.

"I know not what ails me," was the answer; "but I find that I feel no more pain. Methinks that a pleasing kind of freshnesse, as it were a cold napkin, did spread over my hand, which hath taken away the inflammation that tormented me before."

"Since that you feel," rejoined Sir Kenelm, "already so good an effect of my medicament, I advise you to cast away all your plaisters. Only keep the wound clean, and in moderate temper 'twixt heat and cold."

Mr. Howel went away, sounding the praises of his physician; and the Duke of Buckingham, hearing what had taken place, hastened to Sir Kenelm's house to talk about it. The Duke and Knight dined together; when, after dinner, the latter, to show his guest the wondrous power of his powder, took the garter out of the solution, and dried it before the fire. Scarcely was it dry, when Mr. Howel's servant ran in to say that his master's hand was worse than ever—burning hot, as if "it were betwixt coales of fire." The messenger was dismissed with the assurance that ere he reached home his master would be comfortable again. On the man retiring, Sir Kenelm put the garter back into the solution—the result of which was instant relief to Mr. Howel. In six days the wounds were entirely healed. This remarkable case occurred in London, during the reign of James the First. "King James," says Sir Kenelm, "required a punctuall information of what had passed touching this cure;

and, after it was done and perfected, his Majesty would needs know of me how it was done—having drolled with me first (which he could do with a very good grace) about a magician and sorcerer." On the promise of inviolable secrecy, Sir Kenelm communicated the secret to his Majesty; "whereupon his Majesty made sundry proofs, whence he received singular satisfaction."

The secret was also communicated by Sir Kenelm to Mayerne, through whom it was imparted to the Duke of Mayerne—"a long time his friend and protector." After the Duke's death, his surgeon communicated it to divers people of quality; so that, ere long, every country-barber was familiar with the discovery. The mention made of Mayerne in the lecture is interesting, as it settles a point on which Dr. Aikin had no information; viz.,—Whether Sir Theodore's Barony of Aubonne was hereditary or acquired? Sir Kenelm says, "A little while after the Doctor went to France, to see some fair territories that he had purchased near Geneva, which was the Barony of Aubonne."

For a time the Sympathetic Powder was very generally believed in; and it doubtless did as much good as harm, by inducing people to throw from their wounds the abominable messes of grease and irritants which were then honoured with the name of plaisters. "What is this?" asked Abernethy, when about to examine a patient with a pulsating tumour, that was pretty clearly an aneurism.

"Oh! that is a plaister," said the family doctor.

"Pooh!" said Abernethy, taking it off, and pitching it aside.

"That was all very well," said the physician, on describing the occurrence; "but that 'pooh' took several guineas out of my pocket."

Fashionable as the Sympathetic Powder was for several years, it fell into complete disrepute in this country before the death of Sir Kenelm. Hartman, the Knight's attached servant, could, of his own experience, say nothing more for it than, when dissolved in water, it was a useful astringent lotion in cases of bleeding from the nose; but he mentions a certain "Mr. Smith, in the city of Augusta, in Germany, who told me that he had a great respect for Sir D. K.'s books, and that he made his sympatheticall powder every year, and did all his chiefest cures with it in green wounds, with much greater ease to the patient than if he had used ointments or plaisters."

In 1643 Sir Kenelm Digby was released from the confinement to which he had been subjected by the Parliament. The condition of his liberty was that he forthwith retired to the Continent—having previously pledged his word as a Christian and a gentleman, in no way to act or plot against the Parliament. In France he became a celebrity of the highest order. Returning to England with the Restoration, he resided in "the last fair house westward in the north portico of Covent Garden," and became the centre of literary and scientific society. He was appointed a member of the council of the Royal Society, on the incorporation of that learned body in the year 1663. His death occurred in his sixty-second year, on the 11th of June, 1665; and his funeral took place in Christ's Church, within Newgate, where, several years before, he had raised a splendid tomb to the memory of the lovely and abandoned Venetia. His epitaph, by the pen of R. Ferrar, is concise, and not too eulogistic for a monumental inscription:—

> "Under this tomb the matchless Digby lies—
> Digby the great, the valiant, and the wise;
> This age's wonder for his noble parts,
> Skill'd in six tongues, and learned in all the arts.
> Born on the day he died—the Eleventh of June—
> And that day bravely fought at Scanderoon.
> It's rare that one and the same day should be
> His day of birth, and death, and victory."

After his death, with the approval of his son, was published (1669), "The Closet of the Eminently Learned Sir Kenelme Digbie, Kt., Opened: Whereby is discovered Several ways for making of Metheglin, Sider, Cherry-Wine, &c.; together with excellent Directions for Cookery: as also for Preserving, Conserving, Candying, &c." The frontispiece of this work is a portrait of Sir Kenelm, with a shelf over his head, adorned with his five principal works, entitled, "Plants," "Sym. Powder," "His Cookery," "Rects. in Physick, &c.," "Sr. K. Digby of Bodyes."

In Sir Kenelm's receipts for cookery the gastronome would find something to amuse him, and more to arouse his horror. Minced pies are made (as they still are amongst the homely of some counties) of *meat*, raisins, and spices, mixed. Some of the sweet dishes very closely resemble what are still served on English tables. The potages are well enough. But the barley-puddings, pear-puddings, and oat-meal puddings give ill promise to the ear. It is recommended to batter up a couple of eggs and a lot of brown sugar in a cup of tea;—a not less impious profanation of the sacred leaves than that committed by the Highlanders, mentioned by Sir Walter Scott, who, ignorant of the proper mode of treating a pound of fragrant Bohea, served it up in—melted butter!

CHAPTER IV.

SIR HANS SLOANE.

The lives of three physicians—Sydenham, Sir Hans Sloane, and Heberden—completely bridge over the uncertain period between old empiricism and modern science. The son of a wealthy Dorsetshire squire, Sydenham was born in 1624, and received the most important part of his education in the University of Oxford, where he was created Bachelor of Medicine 14th April, 1648. Settling in London about 1661, he was admitted a Licentiate of the Royal College of Physicians 25th June, 1665. Subsequently he acquired an M.D. degree at Cambridge, but this step he did not take till 17th May, 1676. He also studied physic at Montpellier; but it may be questioned if his professional success was a consequence of his labours in any seat of learning, so much as a result of that knowledge of the world which he gained in the Civil war as a captain in the Parliamentary army. It was he who replied to Sir Richard Blackmore's inquiry after the best course of study for a medical student to pursue—"Read Don Quixote; it is a very good book—I read it still." Medical critics have felt it incumbent on themselves to explain away this memorable answer—attributing it to the doctor's cynical temper rather than his scepticism with regard to medicine. When, however, the state of medical science in the seventeenth century is considered, one has not much difficulty in believing that the shrewd physician meant exactly what he said. There is no question but that as a practitioner he was a man of many doubts. The author of the capital sketch of Sydenham in the "Lives of British Physicians" says—"At the commencement of his professional life it is handed down to us by tradition, that it was his ordinary custom, when consulted by his patients for the first time, to hear attentively the story of their complaints, and then say, 'Well, I will consider of your case, and in a few days will order something for you.' But he soon discovered that this deliberate method of proceeding was not satisfactory, and that many of the persons so received forgot to come again; and he was consequently obliged to adopt the usual practice of prescribing immediately for the diseases of those who sought his advice." A doctor who feels the need for such deliberation must labour under considerable perplexity as to the proper treatment of his patient. But the low opinion he expressed to Blackmore of books as instructors in medicine, he gave publicly with greater decorum, but almost as forcibly, in a dedication addressed to Dr. Mapletoft, where he says, "The medical art could not be learned so well and so surely as by use and experience; and that he who would pay the nicest and most accurate attention to the symptoms of distempers would succeed best in finding out the true means of cure."

Sydenham died in his house, in Pall Mall, on the 29th of December, 1689. In his last years he was a martyr to gout, a malady fast becoming one of the good things of the past. Dr. Forbes Winslow, in his "Physic and Physicians"—gives a picture, at the same time painful and laughable, of the doctor's sufferings. "Sydenham died of the gout; and in the latter part of his life is described as visited with that dreadful disorder, and sitting near an open window, on the ground floor of his house, in St. James's Square, respiring the cool breeze on a summer's evening, and reflecting, with a serene countenance and great complacency, on the alleviation to human misery that his skill in his art enabled him to give. Whilst this divine man was enjoying one of these delicious reveries, a thief took away from the table, near to which he was sitting, a silver tankard filled with his favourite beverage, small beer, in which a sprig of rosemary had been immersed, and ran off with it. Sydenham was too lame to ring his bell, and too feeble in his voice to give the alarm."

Heberden, the medical friend of Samuel Johnson, was born in London in 1710, and died on the 17th of May, 1801. Between Sydenham and Heberden came Sir Hans Sloane, a man ever to be mentioned honourably amongst those physicians who have contributed to the advancement of science, and the amelioration of society.

Pope says:—

"'Tis strange the miser should his cares employ,
To gain those riches he can ne'er enjoy;
Is it less strange the prodigal should waste
His wealth to purchase what he ne'er can taste?
Not for himself he sees, or hears, or eats,
Artists must chuse his pictures, music, meats;
He buys for Topham drawings and designs,
For Pembroke statues, dirty gods, and coins;
Rare monkish manuscripts, for Hearne alone,
And books for Mead, and butterflies for Sloane."

Pope's *Moral Essays*, Epistle IV.

Hans Sloane (the seventh and youngest child of Alexander Sloane, receiver-general of taxes for the county of Down, before and after the Civil war, and a commissioner of array, after the restoration of Charles II.) was born at Killileagh in 1660. An Irishman by birth, and a Scotchman by descent, he exhibited in no ordinary degree the energy and politeness of either of the sister countries. After a childhood of extreme delicacy he came to England, and devoted himself to medical study and scientific investigation. Having passed through a course of careful labour in London, he visited Paris and Montpellier, and, returning from the Continent, became the intimate friend of Sydenham. On the 21st of January, 1685, he was elected a Fellow of the Royal Society; and on the 12th of April, 1687, he became a Fellow of the College of Physicians. In the September of the latter year he sailed to the West Indies, in the character of physician to the Duke of Albemarle, who had been appointed Governor of Jamaica. His residence in that quarter of the globe was not of long duration. On the death of his Grace the doctor attended the Duchess back to England, arriving once more in London in the July of 1689. From that time he remained in the capital—his professional career, his social position, and his scientific reputation being alike brilliant. From 1694 to 1730, he was a physician of Christ's Hospital. On the 30th of November, 1693, he was elected Secretary of the Royal Society. In 1701 he was made an M.D. of Oxford; and in 1705 he was elected into the fellowship of the College of Physicians of Edinburgh. In 1708 he was chosen a Fellow of the Royal Academy of Sciences of Paris. Four years later he was elected a member of the Royal Society of Berlin. In 1719 he became president of the College of Physicians; and in 1727 he was created President of the Royal Society (on the death of Sir Isaac Newton), and was appointed physician to King George II. In addition to these honours, he won the distinction of being the first[6] medical practitioner advanced to the dignity of a baronetcy.

In 1742, Sir Hans Sloane quitted his professional residence at Bloomsbury; and in the society of his library, museum, and a select number of scientific friends, spent the last years of his life at Chelsea, the manor of which parish he had purchased in 1722.

In the *Gentleman's Magazine* for 1748, there is a long but interesting account of a visit paid by the Prince and Princess of Wales to the Baronet's museum. Sir Hans received his royal guests and entertained them with a banquet of curiosities, the tables being cleverly shifted, so that a succession of "courses," under glass cases, gave the charm of variety to the labours of observation.

In his old age Sir Hans became sadly penurious, grudging even the ordinary expenses of hospitality. His intimate friend, George Edwards, F.R.S., gives, in his "Gleanings of Natural History," some particulars of the old Baronet, which present a stronger picture of his parsimony than can be found in the pages of his avowed detractors.

"Sir Hans, in the decline of his life, left London and retired to his manor-house, at Chelsea, where he resided about fourteen years before he died. After his retirement at Chelsea, he requested it as a favour to him (though I embraced it as an honour due to myself), that I would visit him every week, in order to divert him for an hour or two with the common news of the town, and with everything particular that should happen amongst his acquaintance of the Royal Society, and other ingenious gentlemen, many of whom I was weekly conversant with; and I seldom missed drinking coffee with him on a Saturday, during the whole time of his re-

[6] The learned Librarian of the College of Physicians in a letter to me, elicited by the first edition of "The Book About Doctors," observes on this point: "Sir Hans Sloane is commonly stated to have been the first medical baronet, but I think incorrectly. Sir Edmund Greaves, M. D., a Fellow of the College, who died 11th Nov., 1680, is said, and I am disposed to think with truth, to have been created a Baronet at Oxford in 1645. Anthony A. Wood it is true calls him a 'pretended baronet,' but he was acknowledged to be a true and veritable one by his colleagues of our college, and considering the jealousy of physicians, which is not quite so great by the way as you seem to think, this is no small testimony in favour of my belief. In the 5th edition of Guillim's Heraldry he is made to be the 450th baronet from the first institution of the order, and is placed between William de Borcel of Amsterdam and George Carteret of Jersey. If you think the matter worthy of investigation you may turn to Nash's Worcestershire, vol. i., p. 198."

tirement at Chelsea. He was so infirm as to be wholly confined to his house, except sometimes, though rarely, taking a little air in his garden in a wheeled chair; and this confinement made him very desirous to see any of his old acquaintance, to amuse him. He was strictly careful that I should be at no expense in my journeys from London to Chelsea to wait on him, knowing that I did not superabound in the gifts of fortune. He would calculate what the expense of coach-hire, waterage, or any other little charge that might attend on my journeys backward and forward would amount to, and would oblige me annually to accept of it, though I would willingly have declined it."

Such generosity speaks of a parsimonious temper and habit more forcibly than positive acts of stinginess would.

On the death of Sir Hans Sloane, on the 11th of January, 1753, his museum and library passed into the hands of the nation for a comparatively small sum of money, and became the nucleus of our British Museum.

The Royal Society of Sir Hans Sloane's time differed widely from the Royal Society of the present day. The reader of Mr. Charles Weld's history of that distinguished fraternity smiles a painful smile at the feeble steps of its first members in the direction of natural science. The efficacy of the divining rod, and the merits of Sir Kenelm Digby's sympathetic powder, were the subjects that occupied the attention of the philosophers of Charles II.'s reign. Entries such as the following are the records of their proceedings:—

"*June 5.*—Col. Tuke related the manner of the rain like corn at Norwich, and Mr Boyle and Mr Evelyn were entreated to sow some of those rained seeds to try their product.

"Magneticall cures were then discoursed of. Sir Gilbert Talbot promised to bring what he knew of sympathetical cures. Those that had any powder of sympathy were desired to bring some of it at the next meeting.

"Mr Boyle related of a gentleman, who, having made some experiments of the ayre, essayed the quicksilver experiment at the top and bottom of a hill, when there was found three inches difference.

"Dr Charleton promised to bring in that white powder, which, put into water, heates that.

"The Duke of Buckingham promised to cause charcoal to be distilled by his chymist.

"His Grace promised to bring into the society a piece of a unicorne's horn.

"Sir Kenelme Digby related that the calcined powder of toades reverberated, applyed in bagges upon the stomach of a pestiferate body, cures it by several applications."

"*June 13.*—Colonel Tuke brought in the history of rained seedes, which were reported to have fallen downe from heaven in Warwickshire and Shropshire, &c.

"That the dyving engine be going forward with all speed, and the treasurer to procure the lead and moneys.

"Ordered, that Friday next the engine be tried at Deptford."

"June 26. — Dr Ent, Dr Clarke, Dr Goddard, and Dr Whistler, were appointed curators of the proposition made by Sir G. Talbot, to torment a man presently with the sympatheticall powder.

"Sir G. Talbot brought in his experiments of the sympathetick cures."

It is true that these passages relate to transactions of the Royal Society that occurred long before Sir Hans was one of the body. But even in his time the advances made towards greater enlightenment were few and feeble, when compared with the strides of science during the last century. So simple and childish were the operations and speculations of the Society in the first half of the eighteenth century, that even Sir John Hill was able to cover them with ridicule.

Sir Hans had two medical successors in the presidentship of the Royal Society — Sir John Pringle, Bart., elected Nov. 30, 1772, and William Hyde Wollaston, M.D., elected June 29, 1820. The last-mentioned physician had but a brief tenure of the dignity, for he retired from the exalted post on Nov. 30, 1820, in favor of Sir Humphrey Davy, Bart.

Humphrey Davy (the son of the Penzance woodcarver, who was known to his acquaintances as "Little Carver Davy") was the most acute natural philosopher of his generation, and at the same time about the vainest and most eccentric of his countrymen. With all his mental energy, he was disfigured by a moral pettiness, which, to a certain extent, justified Wordsworth's unaccustomed bitterness in "A Poet's Epitaph": —

> "Physician art thou? one all eyes;
> Philosopher? a fingering slave,
> One that would peep and botanize
> Upon his mother's grave!
>
> "Wrapt closely in thy sensual fleece,
> O turn aside — and take, I pray,
> That he below may rest in peace,
> Thy ever-dwindling soul away!"

At the summit of his success, Davy was morbidly sensitive of the humility of his extraction. That his father had been a respectable mechanic — that his mother, on her husband's death, had established herself as milliner in Penzance, in order to apprentice her son to an apothecary in that town — that by his own intellects, in the hard battle of life, he had raised himself from obscure poverty to a brilliant eminence — were to him facts of shame, instead of pride. In contradiction to this moral cowardice, there was in him, on some points, an extravagant eccentricity, which, in most men, would have pointed to imperviousness to ridicule. The demands of society, and the labours of his laboratory, of course left him with but little leisure. He, however, affected not to have time enough for the ordinary decencies of the toilet. Cold ablutions neither his constitution nor his philosophic temperament required, so he rarely washed himself. And, on the plea of saving time, he used to put on his clean linen over his dirty — so that he has been known to wear at the same time five shirts and five pairs of stockings. On the rare occasions when he divested himself of his superfluous integuments, he caused infinite perplexity to his less intimate friends, who could not account for his rapid transition from corpulence to tenuity.

The ludicrousness of his costume did not end there. Like many other men of powerful and excitable minds, he was very fond of angling; and on the banks of the Thames he might be found, at all unsuitable seasons, in a costume that must have been a source of no common merriment to the river nymphs. His coat and breeches were of green cloth. On his head he wore a hat that Dr. Paris describes as "having been originally intended for a coal-heaver, but as having, when in its raw state, been dyed green by some sort of pigment." In this attire Davy flattered himself that he resembled vegetable life as closely as it was possible for mortal to do.

But if his angling dress was droll, his shooting costume was more so. His great fear as an angler was that the fish should escape him; his greatest anxiety as a bearer of a gun was to escape being shot. In the one character, concealment was his chief object—in the other, revelation. So that he might be seen from a distance, and run fewer chances of being fired into by accident, he was accustomed on shooting excursions, to crown himself with a broad-brimmed hat, covered with scarlet. It never struck him that, in our Protestant England, he incurred imminent peril of being mistaken for a cardinal, and knocked over accordingly.

Naturally, Davy was of a poetical temperament; and some of his boyish poetry possesses merit that unquestionably justifies the anticipation formed by his po-et-friends of the flights his more mature muse would take. But when his intellect became absorbed in the pursuits by which he rendered inestimable service to his species, he never renewed the bright imaginings of his day-spring.

On passing (in 1809) through the galleries of the Louvre, he could find nothing more worthy of admiration than the fine frames of the pictures. "What an extraor-dinary collection of fine frames!" he observed to the gentleman who acted as his guide, amidst the treasures of art gathered from every part of the Continent. His attention was directed to the "Transfiguration"; when, on its being suggested to him that he was looking at a rather well-executed picture, he said, coldly, "Indeed! I am glad I have seen it." In the same way, the statues were to him simply blocks of material. In the Apollo Belvidere, the Laocoon, and the Venus dei Medici, he saw no beauty; but when his eyes rested on the Antinous, treated in the Egyptian style, and sculptured in alabaster, he made an exclamation of delight, and cried, "Gracious powers, what a beautiful stalactite!"

More amusing than even these criticisms, is a story told of Lady Davy, who accompanied her husband to Paris. She was walking in the Tuileries garden, wear-ing the fashionable London bonnet of the day—shaped like a cockle-shell. The Parisians, who just then were patronizing bonnets of enormous dimensions, were astounded at the apparition of a head-dress so opposed to their notions of the ev-erlasting fitness of things; and with the good breeding for which they are and have long been proverbial, they surrounded the daring stranger, and stared at her. This was sufficiently unpleasant to a timid English lady. But her discomfort had only commenced. Ere another minute or two had elapsed, one of the inspectors of the garden approached, and telling her Ladyship that no cause of *rassemblement* could be permitted in that locality, requested her to retire. Alarmed and indignant, she appealed to some officers of the Imperial Guard, but they could afford her no assistance. One of them politely offered her his arm, and proposed to conduct her to a carriage. But by the time she had decided to profit by the courtesy, such a crowd had gathered together, that it was found necessary to send for a guard of infantry, and remove *la belle Anglaise*, surrounded with bayonets.

CHAPTER V.

THE APOTHECARIES AND SIR SAMUEL GARTH.

Baldwin Hamey, whose manuscript memoirs of eminent physicians are among the treasures of the College, praises Winston because he treated his apothecary as a master might a slave. "Heriliter imperavit," says the Doctor. The learned Thomas Winston, anatomy lecturer at Gresham College, lived to the age of eighty years, and died on the 24th of October, 1655. He knew, therefore, apothecaries in the day of their humility—before prosperity had encouraged them to compete with their professional superiors.

The apothecaries of the Elizabethan era compounded their medicines much as medicines are compounded at the present—as far as manipulation and measuring are concerned. Prescriptions have altered, but shop-customs have undergone only a very slight change. The apothecaries' table of weights and measures, still in use, was the rule in the sixteenth century, and the symbols (for a pound, an ounce, a drachm, a scruple, a grain, &c.) remain at this day just what they were three hundred years ago.

Our good friend, William Bulleyn, gave the following excellent rules for an apothecary's life and conduct:—

"THE APOTICARYE.

"1.—Must fyrst serve God, forsee the end, be clenly, pity the poore.

"2.—Must not be suborned for money to hurt mankynde.

"3.—His place of dwelling and shop to be clenly to please the sences withal.

"4.—His garden must be at hand with plenty of herbes, seedes, and rootes.

"5.—To sow, set, plant, gather, preserve and kepe them in due tyme.

"6.—To read Dioscorides, to know ye natures of plants and herbes.

"7.—To invent medicines to chose by coloure, tast, odour, figure, &c.

"8.—To have his morters, stilles, pottes, filters, glasses, boxes, cleane and sweete.

"9.—To have charcoals at hand, to make decoctions, syrupes, &c.

"10.—To kepe his cleane ware closse, and cast away the baggage.

"11.—To have two places in his shop—one most cleane for the phisik, and a baser place for the chirurgie stuff.

"12.—That he neither increase nor diminish the physician's bill (*i. e.* prescription), and kepe it for his own discharge.

"13.—That he neither buy nor sel rotten drugges.

"14.—That he peruse often his wares, that they corrupt not.

"15.—That he put not in *quid pro quo* (*i. e.*, use one ingredient in the place of another, when dispensing a physician's prescription) without advysement.

"16.—That he may open wel a vein for to helpe pleuresy.

"17.—That he meddle only in his vocation.

"18.—That he delyte to reede Nicolaus Myrepsus, Valerius Cordus, Johannes Placaton, the Lubik, &c.

"19.—That he do remember his office is only to be ye physician's cooke.

"20.—That he use true measure and waight.

"21.—To remember his end, and the judgment of God: and thus I do commend him to God, if he be not covetous, or crafty, seeking his own lucre before other men's help, succour, and comfort."

The apothecaries to whom these excellent directions were given were only tradesmen—grocers who paid attention to the commands of physicians. They were not required to have any knowledge of the medical science, beyond what might be obtained by the perusal of two or three writers; they were not to presume to administer drugs on their own judgment and responsibility—or to perform any surgical operation, except phlebotomy, and that only for one malady. The custom was for the doctors to sell their most valuable remedies as nostrums, keeping their composition a secret to themselves, and themselves taking the price paid for them by the sick. The commoner drugs were vended to patients by the drug-merchants (who invariably dealt in groceries for culinary use, as well as in medicinal simples), acting under the directions of the learned graduates of the Faculty.

In the fourth year of James I., a charter was obtained, that "Willed, ordained, and granted, that all and singular the Freemen of the Mystery of Grocers and Apothecaries of the City of London ... should and might be ... one body corporate and politique, in deed, fact, and name, by the name of Warden and Commonalty of the Mystery of Grocers of the City of London." But in the thirteenth year of the same king, the apothecaries and grocers were disunited. At the advice of Theodore de Mayerne and Henry Atkins, doctors in physick, another charter was granted, constituting drug-venders a distinct company. Amongst the apothecaries mentioned in this charter are the names of the most respectable families of the country. Gideon de Laune, one of this first batch of apothecaries, amassed a very large fortune in his vocation, and founded a family at Sharsted, in Kent, from which several persons of distinction draw part of their origin; and not a few of De Laune's brethren were equally lucky.

At their first foundation as a company the apothecaries were put completely under control of the College of Physicians, who were endowed with dangerous powers of inspecting their wares and punishing their malpractices. But before a generation had passed away, the apothecaries had gained such a firm footing in society that the more prosperous of them could afford to laugh at the censures of the College; and before the close of a century they were fawned upon by young physicians, and were in a position to quarrel with the old.

The doctors of that day knew so little that the apothecaries found it easy to know as much. A knowledge of the herbals, an acquaintance with the ingredients and doses of a hundred empirical compounds and systems of maltreating eruptive fevers, gout, and consumption, constituted all the medical learning of such men as Mayerne or Gibbons. To pick up that amount of information was no hard task for an ambitious apothecary.

Soon the leading apothecaries began to prescribe on their own responsibility, without the countenance of a member of the College. If they were threatened with censure or other punishment by a regular physician, they retorted by discontinuing to call him in to consultations. Jealousies soon sprang up. Starving graduates, with the diplomas of Oxford and Cambridge and the certificates of the College in their pockets, were embittered by having to trudge the pavements of London, and see the mean medicine-mixers (who had scarce scholarship enough to construe a Latin bill) dashing by in their carriages. Ere long the heartburnings broke out in a paper warfare, as rancorous and disreputable as any squabble embalmed in literature. The scholars called the rich tradesmen thieves, swindlers, and unlettered blockheads. The rich tradesmen taunted the scholars with discontent, falsehood, and ignorance of everything except Latin and Greek.

Pope took the side of the physicians. Like Johnson, Parr, and all men of enlightenment and sound scholarship, he had a high opinion of the Faculty. It is indeed told of him, on questionable authority, that on his death-bed, when he heard the bickerings of Dr. Burton and Dr. Thompson, each accusing the other of maltreating his patient, he levelled with his last breath an epigram at the two rivals—

> "Dunces, rejoice, forgive all censures past—
> The greatest dunce has killed your foe at last."

To Dr. Arbuthnot he wrote—

> "Friend to my life, which did not you prolong,
> The world had wanted many an idle song."

His feeble health, making his life a long disease, never allowed him vigour and confidence enough to display ingratitude to the Faculty, and illustrate the truth of the lines—

> "God and the doctor we alike adore,
> But only when in danger, not before;
> The danger o'er, both are alike requited,
> God is forgotten, and the doctor slighted."

His habitual tone, when speaking of the medical profession, was that of warm admiration and affection. In the "Imitations of Horace" he says—

> "Weak though I am of limb, and short of sight,
> Far from a lynx, and not a giant quite,

> I'll do what Mead and Cheselden advise,
> To keep these limbs, and to preserve these eyes."

It is true that he elsewhere ridicules Mead's fondness for rare books and Sloane's passion for butterflies; but at the close of his days he wrote in a confidential letter to a friend of the Faculty, "They are in general the most amiable companions and the best friends, as well as the most learned men I know."

In the protracted dissensions between the physicians and the apothecaries Pope was a cordial supporter of the former. When he accused, in the "Essay on Criticism," the penny-a-lining critics of acquiring their slender knowledge of the poetic art from the poets they assailed, he compared them to apothecaries whose scientific information was pilfered from the prescriptions they were required to dispense.

> "Then Criticism the Muse's handmaid proved,
> To dress her charms and make her more beloved:
> But following wits from that intention stray'd.
> Who could not win the mistress, woo'd the maid;
> Against the poets their own arms they turn'd,
> Sure to hate most the men from whom they learn'd.
> So modern 'Pothecaries, taught the art
> By Doctors' bills to play the Doctor's part,
> Bold in the practice of mistaken rules,
> Prescribe, apply, and call their masters fools."

The origin of the memorable Dispensarian Campaign between the College of Physicians and the Company of Apothecaries is a story that can be briefly told. The younger physicians, impatient at beholding the prosperity and influence of the apothecaries, and the older ones indignant at seeing a class of men they despised creeping into their quarters and craftily laying hold of a portion of their monopoly, concocted a scheme to reinstate themselves in public favour. Without a doubt many of the physicians who countenanced this scheme gave it their support from purely charitable motives; but it cannot be questioned that as a body the dispensarians were actuated in their humanitarian exertions by a desire to lower the apothecaries, and raise themselves in the eyes of the world. With all its genuine and sterling benevolence, the medical profession, by the unworthy and silly conduct of its obscure members, has repeatedly laid itself open to the charge of trading on its reputation for humanity. In Smollett's time, as his novels show, the recognized mode employed by unknown doctors to puff themselves into notoriety and practice, was to get up little hospitals and infirmaries, and advertise to the charitable for aid in the good task of ameliorating the condition of the poor. And half the peddling little charitable institutions, infirmaries, dispensaries, or hospitals, that at the present time rob the rich and do harm to the poor in every quarter of London, originated in "the friends" of young physicians and surgeons conspiring together to get them "the position of being attached to an hospital staff." In 1687, the physicians at a college-meeting, voted "that all members of the College, whether Fellows, Candidates, or Licentiates, should give their advice gratis to all their sick neighbouring poor, when desired, within the city of London, or seven miles round."

To give prescriptions to the very poor, unaccompanied with the means of getting them dispensed, is of little use. Sir Astley Cooper used to see in the vicinity of his residence the slips of paper, marked with his pen, which it was his wont to distribute gratuitously to indigent applicants. The fact was, the poor people, finding it beyond their means to pay the druggist for dispensing them, threw them away in disgust. It was just the same in 1687. The poor folk carried their prescriptions to the apothecaries, to learn that the trade charge for dispensing them was beyond their means. The physicians asserted that the demands of the drug-venders were extortionate, and were not reduced to meet the finances of the applicants, to the end that the undertakings of benevolence might prove abortive. This was of course absurd. The apothecaries knew their own interests better than so to oppose a system which at least rendered drug-consuming fashionable with the lower orders. Perhaps they regarded the poor as their peculiar field of practice, and felt insulted at having the same humble people—for whom they had pompously prescribed and put up boluses at two-pence apiece—now entering their shops with papers dictating what the two-penny bolus was to be composed of. But the charge preferred against them was groundless. Indeed, a numerous body of the apothecaries expressly offered to sell medicines "to the poor within their respective parishes, at such rates as the committee of physicians should think reasonable."

But this would not suit the game of the physicians. "A proposal was started by a committee of the College, that the College should furnish the medicines of the poor, and perfect alone that charity which the apothecaries refused to concur in; and after divers methods ineffectually tried, and much time wasted in endeavouring to bring the Apothecaries to terms of reason in relation to the poor, an instrument was subscribed by divers charitably disposed members of the College, now in number about fifty, wherein they obliged themselves to pay ten pounds apiece towards the preparing and delivering medicines at their intrinsic value." Such was the version of the affair given by the College apologists. The plan was acted upon; and a dispensary was eventually established (some nine years after the vote of 1687) in the College of Physicians, Warwick Lane, where medicines were vended to the poor at cost price.

This measure of the College was impolitic and unjustifiable. It was unjust to that important division of the trade who were ready to vend the medicines at rates to be fixed by the College authorities—for it took altogether out of their hands the small amount of profit which they, as *dealers*, could have realized on those terms. It was also an eminently unwise course. The College sank to the level of the Apothecaries' Hall, becoming an emporium for the sale of medicines. It was all very well to say that no profit was made on such sale—the censorious world would not believe it. The apothecaries and their friends denied that such was the fact, and avowed that the benevolent dispensarians were bent only on underselling and ruining them.

Again, the movement introduced dissension within the walls of the College. Many of the first physicians, with the conservatism of success, did not care to offend the apothecaries, who were continually calling them in, and paying them fees. They therefore joined in the cry against the dispensary. The profession was split up into dispensarians and anti-dispensarians. The apothecaries combined and agreed not to recommend the dispensarians. The anti-dispensarians repaid this ill service by refusing to meet dispensarians in consultation. Sir Thomas Millington, the president of the College, Edward Hulse, Hans Sloane, John Woodward, Sir Edmund King, and Samuel Garth were amongst the latter. Of them the last-named was the man who rendered the most efficient service to his party.

Garth is perhaps the most cherished by the present generation of all the physicians of Pope's time. He was a Whig without rancour, and a bon-vivant without selfishness. Full of jest and amiability, he did more to create merriment at the Kit-Kat club than either Swift or Arbuthnot. He loved wine to excess; but then wine loved him too, ripening and warming his wit, and leaving no sluggish humour behind. His practice was a good one, but his numerous patients prized his *bon-mots* more than his prescriptions. His enemies averred that he was not only an epicure, but a profligate voluptuary and an infidel. Pope, however, wrote of him after his death, "If ever there was a good Christian, without knowing himself to be so, it was Dr. Garth." Pope had honoured him when alive by dedicating his second pastoral to him.

> "Accept, O Garth, the muse's early lays,
> That adds this wreath of ivy to thy bays;
> Hear what from love unpractised hearts endure,
> From love, the sole disease thou canst not cure."

A good picture of Garth the politician is found in the "Journal to Stella." "London, Nov. 17, 1711," writes Swift—"This is Queen Elizabeth's birthday, usually kept in this town by apprentices, &c.; but the Whigs designed a mighty procession by midnight, and had laid out a thousand pounds to dress up the pope, devil, cardinals, Sacheverel, &c., and carry them with torches about and burn them. They did it by contribution. Garth gave five guineas; Dr. Garth I mean, if ever you heard of him. But they were seized last night by order from the Secretary.... The figures are now at the Secretary's Office at Whitehall. I design to see them if I can."

A Whig, but the friend of Tories, Garth cordially disliked Sir Richard Blackmore, a member of his own profession and political party. Blackmore was an anti-dispensarian, a bad poet, and a pure and rigid moralist. Naturally Garth abominated him, and sneered at him for his pomposity and bad scholarship. It is to be regretted that Garth, with the vulgarity of the age, twitted him with his early poverty, and with having been—a schoolmaster. To ridicule his enemy Garth composed the following verses:—

"TO THE MERRY POETASTER, AT SADLER'S HALL, IN CHEAPSIDE.

> "Unwieldy pedant, let thy awkward muse
> With censures praise, with flatteries abuse;
> To lash, and not be felt, in thee's an art,
> That ne'er mad'st any but thy school-boys smart.
> Then be advised and scribble not again—
> Thou'rt fashion'd for a flail and not a pen.

> If B— —l's immortal wit thou would'st decry,
> Pretend 'tis he that wrote thy poetry.
> Thy feeble satire ne'er can do him wrong—
> Thy poems and thy patients live not long."

Garth's death, as described by William Ayre, was characteristic. He was soon tired of an invalid's suffering and helplessness, the *ennui* and boredom of the sick-room afflicting him more than the bodily pain. "Gentlemen," said he to the crowd of weeping friends who stood round his bed, "I wish the ceremony of death was over." And so, sinking lower in the bed, he died without a struggle. He had previously, on being informed that his end was approaching, expressed pleasure at the intelligence, because he was tired of having his shoes pulled off and on. The manner of Garth's exit reminds one of the death of Rabelais, also a physician. The presence of officious friends troubled him; and when he saw his doctors consulting together, he raised his head from his pillow and said with a smile, "Dear gentlemen, let me die a natural death." After he had received extreme unction, a friend approached him, and asked him how he did. "I am going on my journey," was the answer—"they have greased my boots already."

Garth has, apart from his literary productions, one great claim on posterity. To him Dryden owed honourable interment. When the great poet died, Garth caused his body to be conveyed to the College of Physicians, and started a public subscription to defray the expenses of the funeral. He pronounced an oration over the deceased at the College in Warwick Lane, and then accompanied it to Westminster Abbey.

Of the stories preserved of Garth's social humour some are exquisitely droll. Writing a letter at a coffee-house, he found himself overlooked by a curious Irishman, who was impudently reading every word of the epistle. Garth took no notice of the impertinence, until he had finished and signed the body of the letter, when he added a postscript, of unquestionable legibility: "I would write you more by this post, but there's a d— — tall impudent Irishman looking over my shoulder all the time."

"What do you mean, sir?" roared the Irishman in a fury. "Do you think I looked over your letter?"

"Sir," replied the physician, "I never once opened my lips to you."

"Ay, but you have put it down, for all that."

"'Tis impossible, sir, that you should know that, for you have never once looked over my letter."

Stumbling into a Presbyterian church one Sunday, for pastime, he found a pathetic preacher shedding tears over the iniquity of the earth.

"What makes the man greet?" asked Garth of a bystander.

"By my faith," was the answer, "and you too would greet if you were in his place and had as little to say."

"Come along, my dear fellow," responded Garth to his new acquaintance, "and dine with me. You are too good a fellow to be here."

At the Kit-Kat he once stayed to drink long after he had said that he must be off to see his patients. Sir Richard, more humane than the physician, or possibly, like the rest of the world, not disinclined to be virtuous at another's expense, observed, "Really, Garth, you ought to have no more wine, but be off to see those poor devils."

"It's no great matter," Garth replied, "whether I see them to-night or not, for nine of them have such bad constitutions, that all the physicians in the world can't save them; and the other six have such good constitutions, that all the physicians in the world can't kill them."

Born of a respectable north-country family, Garth was educated first at a provincial school, and then at Cambridge. He was admitted a Fellow of the College of Physicians on June 26, 1692, just when the quarrel of the Physicians and Apothecaries was waxing to its hottest, *i. e.* between the College edict of 1687, ordaining gratuitous advice, and the creation of the dispensary in 1696. As a young man he saw that his right place was with the dispensarians—and he took it. For a time his great poem, "The Dispensary," covered the apothecaries and anti-dispensarians with ridicule. It rapidly passed through numerous editions—in each of which, as was elegantly observed, the world lost and gained much. To say that of all the books, pamphlets, and broad-sheets thrown out by the combatants on both sides, it is by far the one of the greatest merit, would be scant justice, when it might almost be said that it is the only one of them that can now be read by a gentleman without a sense of annoyance and disgust. There is no point of view from which the medical profession appears in a more humiliating and contemptible light than that which the literature of this memorable squabble presents to the student. Charges of ignorance, dishonesty, and extortion were preferred on both sides; and the dispensarian physicians did not hesitate to taunt their brethren of the opposite camp with playing corruptly into the hands of the apothecaries—prescribing enormous and unnecessary quantities of medicine, so that the drug-venders might make heavy bills, and, as a consequence, recommend in all directions such complacent *superiors* to be called in. Garth's poem, unfair and violent though it is, seldom offends against decency. As a work of art it cannot be ranked high, and is now deservedly forgotten, although it has many good lines, and some felicitous satire. Johnson rightly pointed to the secret of its success, though he took a one-sided and unjust view of the dissensions which called it forth. "The poem," observes the biographer, "as its subject was present and popular, co-operated with passions and prejudices then prevalent; and, with such auxiliaries to its intrinsic merit, was universally and liberally applauded. It was on the side of charity against the intrigues of interest, and of regular learning against licentious usurpation of medical authority."

Sir Samuel Garth (knighted by the sword of Marlborough) died January 18, 1718-19, and was buried at Harrow-on-the-Hill.

But he lived to see the apothecaries gradually emancipate themselves from the ignominious regulations to which they consented, when their vocation was first separated from the grocery trade. Four years after his death they obtained legal acknowledgment of their right to dispense and sell medicines without the prescription of a physician; and six years later the law again decided in their favour, with regard to the physicians' right of examining and condemning their drugs. In 1721, Mr. Rose, an apothecary, on being prosecuted by the College for prescribing as well as compounding medicines, carried the matter into the House of Lords, and obtained a favourable decision. And from 1727, in which year Mr. Goodwin, an apothecary, obtained in a court of law a considerable sum for an illegal seizure of his wares (by Drs. Arbuthnot, Bale, and Levit), the physicians may be said to have discontinued to exercise their privileges of inspection.

Arbuthnot did not exceed Garth in love to the apothecaries. His contempt for, and dislike of, the fraternity, inspired him to write his "Essay on an Apothecary." He thinks it a pity that, to prevent the country from being overrun with apothecaries, it should not be allowed to anatomize them, for the improvement of natural knowledge. He ridicules them for pedantically "dressing all their discourse in the language of the Faculty."

"At meals," he says, "they distributed their wine with a little lymph, dissected a widgeon, cohobated their pease-porridge, and amalgamated a custard. A morsel of beef was a bolus; a grillard was sacrificed; eating was mastication and deglutition; a dish of steaks was a compound of many powerful ingredients; and a plate of soup was a very exalted preparation. In dress, a suit of cloaths was a system, a loophole a valve, and a surtout an integument. Cloth was a texture of fibres spread into a drab or kersey; a small rent in it was cutaneous; a thread was a filament; and the waistband of the breeches the peritoneum."

The superior branch of the Faculty invited in many ways the same satire. Indeed, pedantry was the prevalent fault of the manners of the eighteenth century. The physician, the divine, the lawyer, the parliament-man, the country gentleman, the author by profession—all had peculiarities of style, costume, speech, or intonation, by which they were well pleased they should be recognised. In one respect, this was well; men were proud of being what they were, and desired to be known as belonging to their respective vocations. They had no anxiety to be free from trade-marks. The barrister's smirk, the physician's unctuous smiles, the pedagogue's frown, did not originate in a mean desire to be taken for something of higher mark and esteem than they really were.

From the time when Bulleyn called him the physician's cook, down to the present, generation, the pure apothecary is found holding a very subordinate position. His business is to do unpleasant drudgery that a gentleman finds it unpleasant to perform, but which cannot be left to the hands of a nurse. The questions to be considered previous to becoming an apprentice to an apothecary, put in Chemberlaine's "Tyrocinium Medicum," well describe the state of the apothecary's pupil. "Can you bear the thoughts of being obliged to get up out of your warm bed, on a cold winter's night, or rather morning, to make up medicines which your employer, just arrived through frost and snow, prescribes for a patient taken suddenly or dangerously ill?—or, supposing that your master is not in sufficient business to keep a boy to take out medicines, can you make up your mind to think it no hardship to take them to the patient after you have made them up?" &c., &c. When such services were expected from pupils studying for admittance to the craft, of course boys with ample means, or prospects elsewhere, did not as a rule desire to become apothecaries.

Within the last fifty years changes have been affected in various departments of the medical profession, that have rendered the apothecary a feature of the past, and transferred his old functions to a new labourer. Prior to 1788, it is stated on authority there were not in all London more than half-a-dozen druggists who dispensed medicines from physicians' prescriptions. Before that time, the apothecaries—the members of the Apothecaries' Company—were almost the sole compounders and preparers of drugs. At the present time it is exceptional for an apothecary to put up prescriptions, unless he is acting as the family or ordinary medical attendant to the patient prescribed for. As a young man, indeed, he sometimes condescends to keep an open shop; but as soon as he can get on without "counter" business, he leaves the commercial part of his occupation to the druggist, as beneath his dignity. The dispensing chemists and druggists, whose shops, flashing with blue bottles (last remnant of empiric charlatanry), brighten our street corners and scare our horses at night, are the apothecaries of the last century. The apothecary himself—that is, the member of the Company—is hardly ever found as an apothecary *pur et simple*. He enrolls himself at "the hall" for the sake of being able to sue ungrateful patients for money due to him. But in the great majority of cases he is also a Fellow or Member of the College of Surgeons, and acts as a general practitioner; that is, he does anything and everything—prescribes and dispenses his prescriptions; is at the same time physician, surgeon, accoucheur, and dentist. Physic and surgery were divided at a very early date in theory, but in practice they were combined by eminent physicians till a comparatively recent period. And yet later the physician performed the functions of the apothecary, just as the apothecary presumed to discharge the offices of physician. It was not derogatory to the dignity of a leading physician, in the reign of Charles the Second, to keep a shop, and advertise the wares vended in it, announcing in the same manner their prices. Dr. Mead realized large sums by the sale of worthless nostrums. And only a few years since, a distinguished Cambridge physician, retaining as an octogenarian the popularity he had achieved as a young man, in one of our eastern counties, used to sell his "gout tincture"—a secret specific against gout—at so many shillings per bottle. In many respects the general practitioner of this century would consider his professional character compromised if he adopted the customs generally in vogue amongst the physicians of the last.

CHAPTER VI.

QUACKS.

"So then the subject being so variable, hath made the art by consequence more conjectural; an art being conjectural hath made so much the more place to be left for imposture. For almost all other arts and sciences are judged by acts or masterpieces, as I may term them, and not by the successes and events. The lawyer is judged by the virtue of his pleading, and not by the issue of the cause. The master of the ship is judged by the directing his course aright, and not by the fortune of the voyage. But the physician, and perhaps the politician, hath no particular acts demonstrative of his ability, but is judged most by the event; which is ever but as it is taken: for who can tell, if a patient die or recover, or if a state be preserved or ruined, whether it be art or accident? and therefore many times the impostor is prized, and the man of virtue taxed. *Nay, we see the weakness and credulity of men is such, as they will often prefer a mountebank or witch before a learned physician.*" —Lord Bacon's "*Advancement of Learning.*"

The history of quackery, if it were written on a scale that should include the entire number of those frauds which may be generally classed under the head of humbug, would be the history of the human race in all ages and climes. Neither the benefactors nor the enemies of mankind would escape mention; and a searching scrutiny would show that dishonesty has played as important, though not as manifest, a part in the operations of benevolence, as in the achievements of the devil. But a more confined use of the word must satisfy us on the present occasion. We are not about to enter on a philosophic inquiry into the causes that contributed to the success of Mahomet and Cromwell, but only to chronicle a few of the most humorous facts connected with the predecessors of Dr. Townsend and Mr. Morrison.

In the success that has in every century attended the rascally enterprises of pretenders to the art of medicine, is found a touching evidence of the sorrow, credulity, and ignorance of the generations that have passed, or are passing, to the silent home where the pain and joy, the simplicity and cunning, of this world are alike of insignificance. The hope that to the last lurks in the breast of the veriest wretch under heaven's canopy, whether his trials come from broken health, or an empty pocket, or wronged affection, speaks aloud in saddest tones, as one thinks of the multitudes who, worn with bodily malady and spiritual dejection, ignorant of the source of their sufferings, but thirsting for relief from them, have gone from charlatan to charlatan, giving hoarded money in exchange for charms, cramp-rings, warming-stones, elixirs, and trochees, warranted to cure every ill that flesh is heir to. The scene, from another point of view, is more droll, but scarcely less mournful. Look away for a few seconds from the throng of miserable objects who press round the empiric's stage; wipe out for a brief while the memory of their woes, and regard the style and arts of the practitioner who, with a trunk full of nostrums, bids disease to vanish, and death to retire from the scenes of his triumph. There he stands—a lean, fantastic man, voluble of tongue, empty-headed, full of loud words and menaces, prating about kings and princes who have taken him by the hand and kissed him in gratitude for his benefits showered upon them—dauntless, greedy, and so steeped in falsehood that his crazy-tainted brain half believes the lies that flow from his glib tongue. Are there no such men amongst us now—not standing on carts at the street-corners, and selling their wares to a dingy rabble, but having their seats of exchange in honoured places, and vending their prescriptions to crowds of wealthy clients?

In the feudal ages medicine and quackery were the same, as far as any principles of science are concerned. The only difference between the physician and the charlatan was, that the former was a fool and the latter a rogue. Men did not meddle much with the healing art. A few clerks devoted themselves to it, and in the exercise of their spiritual and medical functions discovered how to get two fleeces from a sheep at one shearing; but the care of the sick was for the most part left to the women, who then, as in every other period of the world's history, prided themselves on their medical cunning, and, with the exception of intrigue, preferred attending on the sick to any other occupation. From the time of the Reformation, however, the number of lady doctors rapidly diminished. The fair sex gradually relinquished the ground they had so long occupied, to men, who, had the monastic institutions continued to exist, would have assumed the priestly garb and passed their days in sloth. Quackery was at length fairly taken out of the hands of women and the shelter of domestic life, and was practised, not for love, and in a superstitious belief in its efficacy, but for money, and frequently with a perfect knowledge of its worthlessness as a remedial system.

As soon as the printing-press had become an institution of the country, and there existed a considerable proportion of the community capable of reading, the empirics seized hold of Caxton's invention, and made it subservient to their honourable ends. The advertising system was had recourse to in London, during the Stuart era, scarcely less than it is now. Handbills were distributed in all directions by half-starved wretches, whose withered forms and pallid cheeks were of themselves a sufficient disproof of the assertions of their employers.

The costume, language, style, and artifices of the pretenders to physic in the seventeenth century were doubtless copied from models of long standing, and differed little in essentials from those of their predecessors. Professions retain their characteristics with singular obstinacy. The doctor of Charles the Second's London transmitted all his most salient features to the quack of the Regency.

Cotgrave, in his "Treasury of "Wit and Language," published 1655, thus paints the poor physician of his time:—

> "My name is Pulsefeel, a poor Doctor of Physick,
> That does wear three pile velvet in his hat,
> Has paid a quarter's rent of his house before-hand,
> And (simple as he stands here) was made doctor beyond sea.
> I vow, as I am right worshipful, the taking
> Of my degree cost me twelve French crowns, and
> Thirty-five pounds of butter in Upper Germany.
> I can make your beauty, and preserve it,
> Rectifie your body and maintain it,
> Clarifie your blood, surfle your cheeks, perfume
> Your skin, tinct your hair, enliven your eye,
> Heighten your appetite; and as for Jellies,
> Dentifrizes, Dyets, Minerals, Fricasses,
> Pomatums, Fumes, Italia masks to sleep in,
> Either to moisten or dry the superficies, Faugh! Galen
> Was a goose, and Paracelsus a Patch,
> To Doctor Pulsefeel."

This picture would serve for the portrait of Dr. Pulsefeel in the eighteenth and nineteenth, as well as the seventeenth century. How it calls to mind the image of Oliver Goldsmith, when, with a smattering of medical knowledge, a cane, and a dubious diploma, he tried to pick out of the miseries and ignorance of his fellow-creatures the means of keeping body and soul together! He too, poet and scholar though he was, would have sold a pot of rouge to a faded beauty, or a bottle of hair-dye, or a nostrum warranted to cure the bite of a mad dog.

A more accurate picture, however, of the charlatan, is to be found in "The Quack's Academy; or, The Dunce's Directory," published in 1678, of which the following is a portion:—

"However, in the second place, to support this title, there are several things very convenient: of which some are external accoutrements, others internal qualifications.

"Your outward requisites are a decent black suit, and (if your credit will stretch so far in Long Lane) a plush jacket; not a pin the worse though threadbare as a tailor's cloak—it shows the more reverend antiquity.

"Secondly, like Mercury, you must always carry a caduceus or conjuring japan in your hand, capt with a civet-box; with which you must walk with Spanish gravity, as in deep contemplation upon an arbitrament between life and death.

"Thirdly, a convenient lodging, not forgetting a hatch at the door; a chamber hung with Dutch pictures, or looking-glasses, belittered with empty bottles, gallipots, and vials filled with tapdroppings, or fair water, coloured with saunders. Any sexton will furnish your window with a skull, in hope of your custom; over which hang up the skeleton of a monkey, to proclaim your skill in anatomy.

"Fourthly, let your table be never without some old musty Greek or Arabick author, and the 4th book of Cornelius Agrippa's 'Occult Philosophy,' wide open to amuse spectators; with half-a-dozen of gilt shillings, as so many guineas received that morning for fees.

"Fifthly, fail not to oblige neighbouring ale-houses, to recommend you to inquirers; and hold correspondence with all the nurses and midwives near you, to applaud your skill at gossippings."

The directions go on to advise loquacity and impudence, qualities which quacks of all times and kinds have found most useful. But in cases where the practitioner has an impediment in his speech, or cannot by training render himself glib of utterance, he is advised to persevere in a habit of mysterious silence, rendered impressive by grave nods of the head.

When Dr. Pulsefeel was tired of London, or felt a want of country air, he concentrated his powers on the pleasant occupation of fleecing rustic simplicity. For his journeys into the provinces he provided himself with a stout and fast-trotting hack—stout, that it might bear without fatigue weighty parcels of medicinal composition; and fleet of foot, so that if an ungrateful rabble should commit the indecorum of stoning their benefactor as an impostor (a mishap that would occasionally occur), escape might be effected from the infatuated and excited populace. In his circuit the doctor took in all the fairs, markets, wakes, and public festivals; not, however, disdaining to stop an entire week, or even month, at an assize town, where he found the sick anxious to benefit by his wisdom.

His plan of making acquaintance with a new place was to ride boldly into the thickest crowd of a fair or market, with as much speed as he could make without imperilling the lives of by-standers; and then, when he had checked his steed, inform all who listened that he had come straight from the Duke of Bohemia, or the most Serene Emperor of Wallachia, out of a desire to do good to his fellow-creatures. He was born in that very town,—yes, that very town in which he then was speaking, and had left it when an orphan child of eight years of age, to seek his fortune in the world. He had found his way to London, and been crimped on board a vessel bound for Morocco, and so had been carried off to foreign parts. His adventures had been wonderful. He had visited the Sultan and the Great Mogul. There was not a part of the Indies with which he was not familiar. If any one doubted him, let his face be regarded, and his bronze complexion bear witness of the scorching suns he had endured. He had cured hundreds—ay, thousands—of emperors, kings, queens, princes, margravines, grand duchesses, and generalissimos, of their diseases. He had a powder which would stay the palsy, jaundice, hot fever, and cramps. It was expensive; but that he couldn't help, for it was made of pearls, and the dried leaves of violets brought from the very middle of Tartary; still he could sell a packet of the medicine for a crown—a sum which would just pay him back his outlaid money, and leave him no profit. But he didn't want to make money of them. He was their fellow-townsman; and in order to find them out and cure them he had refused offers of wealth from the king of Mesopotamia, who wanted him to accept a fortune of a thousand gold pieces a month, tarry with the Mesopotamians, and keep them out of Death's clutches. Sometimes this harangue was made from the back of a horse; sometimes from a rude hustings, from which he was called *mountebank*. He sold all kinds of medicaments: dyes for the hair, washes for the complexion, lotions to keep young men youthful; rings which, when worn on the fore-finger of the right hand, should make a chosen favourite desperately in love with the wearer, and when worn on the same finger of the left hand, should drive the said favourite to commit suicide. Nothing could surpass the impudence of the fellow's lies, save the admiration with which his credulous auditors swallowed his assertions. There they stood,—stout yeomen, drunken squires, merry peasant girls, gawky hinds, gabbling dames, deeming themselves in luck's way to have lived to see such a miracle of learning. Possibly a young student home from Oxford, with the rashness of inexperience, would smile scornfully, and in a loud voice designate the pretender a quack—a quacksalvar (kwabzalver), from the liniment he vended for the cure of wens. But such an interruption, in ninety and nine cases out of every hundred, was condemned by the orthodox friends of the young student, and he was warned that he would come to no good if he went on as he had begun—a contemptuous unbeliever, and a mocker of wise men.

The author of the "Discourse de l'Origine des Mœurs, Fraudes, et Impostures des Ciarlatans, avec leur Découverte, Paris, 1662," says, "Premièrement, par ce mot de Ciarlatans, j'entens ceux que les Italiens appellent Saltambaci, basteleurs, bouffons, vendeurs de bagatelles, et generalement toute autre personne, laquelle en place publique montée en banc, à terre, ou à cheval, vend medecines, baumes, huilles ou poudres, composées pour guerir quelque infirmité, louant et exaltant sa drogue, avec artifice, et mille faux sermens, en racontant mille et mille merveilles.

*   *   *   *   *

"Mais c'est chose plaisante de voir l'artifice dont se servent ces medecins de banc pour vendre leur drogue, quand avec mille faux sermens ils affirment d'avoir appris leur secret du roi de Dannemarc, au d'un prince de Transilvanie."

The great quack of Charles the Second's London was Dr. Thomas Saffold. This man (who was originally a weaver) professed to cure every disease of the human body, and also to foretell the destinies of his patients. Along Cheapside, Fleet-street, and the Strand, even down to the sacred precincts of Whitehall and St. James's, he stationed bill-distributors, who showered prose and poetry on the passers-by—just as the agents (possibly the poets) of the Messrs. Moses cast their literature on the town of Queen Victoria. When this great benefactor of his species departed this life, on May the 12th, 1691, a satirical broadsheet called on the world to mourn for the loss of one—

> "So skilled in drugs and verse, 'twas hard to show it,
> Whether was best, the doctor or the poet."

The ode continues:—

> "Lament, ye damsels of our London city,
> (Poor unprovided girls) tho' fair and witty,
> Who, maskt, would to his house in couples come,
> To understand your matrimonial doom;
> To know what kind of men you were to marry,

And how long time, poor things, you were to tarry;
Your oracle is silent, none can tell
On whom his astrologick mantle fell:
For he when sick refused all doctors' aid,
And only to his pills devotion paid!
Yet it was surely a most sad disaster,
The saucy pills at last should kill their master."

EPITAPH.

"Here lies the corpse of Thomas Saffold,
By death, in spite of physick, baffled;
Who, leaving off his working loom,
Did learned doctor soon become.
To poetry he made pretence,
Too plain to any man's own sense;
But he when living thought it sin
To hide his talent in napkin;
Now death does doctor (poet) crowd
Within the limits of a shroud."

The vocation of fortune-teller was exercised not only by the quacks, but also by the apothecaries, of that period. Garth had ample foundation, in fact, for his satirical sketch of Horoscope's shop in the second canto of "The Dispensary."

"Long has he been of that amphibious fry,
Bold to prescribe and busie to apply;
His shop the gazing vulgars' eyes employs,
With foreign trinkets and domestick toys.
Here mummies lay most reverendly stale,
And there the tortoise hung her coat of mail.
Not far from some huge shark's devouring head
The flying fish their finny pinions spread;
Aloft in rows large poppy-heads were strung,
And near a scaly alligator hung;
In this place, drugs in musty heaps decay'd,
In that, dry'd bladders and drawn teeth were laid.

"An inner room receives the num'rous shoals
Of such as pay to be reputed fools;
Globes stand by globes, volumes by volumes lye,
And planetary schemes amuse the eye.
The sage, in velvet chair, here lolls at ease,
To promise future health for present fees.
Then, as from Tripod, solemn shams reveals,
And what the stars know nothing of reveals.

"One asks how soon Panthea may be won,
And longs to feel the marriage fetters on;
Others, convinced by melancholy proof,

Enquire when courteous fates will strike them off;
Some by what means they may redress the wrong,
When fathers the possession keep too long;
And some would know the issue of their cause,
And whether gold can solder up its flaws.

*   *   *   *   *

"Whilst Iris his cosmetick wash would try,
To make her bloom revive, and lovers die;
Some ask for charms, and others philters choose,
To gain Corinna, and their quartans lose."

Queen Anne's weak eyes caused her to pass from one empiric to another, for the relief they all promised to give, and in some cases even persuaded that they gave her. She had a passion for quack oculists; and happy was the advertising scoundrel who gained her Majesty's favour with a new collyrium. For, of course, if the greatest personage in the land said that Professor Bungalo was a wonderful man, a master of his art, and inspired by God to heal the sick, there was no appeal from so eminent an authority. How should an elderly lady with a crown on her head be mistaken? Do we not hear the same arguments every day in our own enlightened generation, when the new Chiropodist, or Rubber, or inventor of a specific for consumption, points to the social distinctions of his dupes as conclusive evidence that he is neither supported by vulgar ignorance, nor afraid to meet the most searching scrutiny of the educated? Good Queen Anne was so charmed with two of the many knaves who by turns enjoyed her countenance, that she had them sworn in as her own oculists in ordinary; and one of them she was even so silly as to knight. This lucky gentleman was William Reade, originally a botching tailor, and to the last a very ignorant man, as his "Short and Exact Account of all Diseases Incident to the Eyes" attests; yet he rose to the honour of knighthood, and the most lucrative and fashionable physician's practice of his period. Surely every dog has his day. Lazarus never should despair; a turn of fortune may one fine day pick him from the rags which cover his nakedness in the kennel, and put him to feast amongst princes, arrayed in purple and fine linen, and regarded as an oracle of wisdom. It was true that Sir William Reade was unable to read the book which he had written (by the hand of an amanuensis), but I have no doubt that many worthy people who listened to his sonorous voice, beheld his lace ruffles and gold-headed cane, and saw his coach drawn along to St. James's by superb horses, thought him in every respect equal, or even superior, to Pope and Swift.

When Sir William was knighted he hired a poet, who lived in Grub Street, to announce the fact to posterity and "the town," in decasyllabic verse. The production of this bard, "The Oculist, a Poem," was published in the year 1705, and has already (thanks to the British Museum, which like the nets of fishermen receiveth of "all sorts") endowed with a century and a half of posthumous renown; and no one can deny that so much fame is due, both to the man who bought, and the scribbler who sold the following strain:—

"Whilst Britain's Sovereign scales such worth has weighed,
And Anne herself her smiling favours paid,

> That sacred hand does your fair chaplet twist,
> Great Reade her own entitled Oculist,
> With this fair mark of honour, sir, assume
> No common trophies from this shining plume;
> Her favours by desert are only shared—
> Her smiles are not her gift, but her reward.
> Thus in your new fair plumes of Honour drest,
> To hail the Royal Foundress of the feast;
> When the great Anne's warm smiles this favourite raise,
> 'Tis not a royal grace she gives, but pays."

Queen Anne's other "sworn oculist," as he and Reade termed themselves, was Roger Grant, a cobbler and Anabaptist preacher. He was a prodigiously vain man, even for a quack, and had his likeness engraved in copper. Impressions of the plate were distributed amongst his friends, but were not in all cases treated with much respect; for one of those who had been complimented with a present of the eminent oculist's portrait, fixed it on a wall of his house, having first adorned it with the following lines:—

> "See here a picture of a brazen face,
> The fittest lumber of this wretched place.
> A tinker first his scene of life began;
> That failing, he set up for cunning man;
> But wanting luck, puts on a new disguise,
> And now pretends that he can mend your eyes;
> But this expect, that, like a tinker true,
> Where he repairs one eye he puts out two."

The charge of his being a tinker was preferred against him also by another lampoon writer. "In his stead up popped Roger Grant, the tinker, of whom a friend of mine once sung.—

> "'Her Majesty sure was in a surprise,
> Or else was very short-sighted;
> When a tinker was sworn to look after her eyes,
> And the mountebank Reade was knighted.'"

This man, according to the custom of his class, was in the habit of publishing circumstantial and minute accounts of his cures. Of course his statements were a tissue of untruths, with just the faintest possible admixture of what was not altogether false. His plan was to get hold of some poor person of imperfect vision, and, after treating him with medicines and half-crowns for six weeks, induce him to sign a testimonial to the effect that he had been born stone-blind, and had never enjoyed any visual power whatever, till Providence led him to good Dr. Grant, who had cured him in little more than a month. This certificate the clergyman and churchwardens of the parish, in which the patient had been known to wander about the streets in mendicancy, were asked to attest; and if they proved impregnable to the cunning representations of the importunate suitors, and declined to give the evidence of their handwriting, either on the ground that they had reason to question the fact of the original blindness, or because they were not thoroughly acquainted with the particulars of the case, Dr. Grant did not scruple to sign their names himself, or by the hands of his agents. The *modus operandi* with which he carried out these frauds may be learned by the curious in a pamphlet, published in the year 1709, and entitled "A Full and True Account of a Miraculous Cure of a Young Man in Newington that was Born Blind."

But the last century was rife with medical quacks. The Rev. John Hancocke, D.D., Rector of St. Margaret's, Lothbury, London, Prebendary of Canterbury, and chaplain to the Duke of Bedford, preached up the water-cure, which Pliny the naturalist described as being in his day the fashionable remedy in Rome. He published a work in 1723 that immediately became popular, called "Febrifugum Magnum; or, Common Water the best Cure for Fevers, and probably for the Plague."

The good man deemed himself a genius of the highest order, because he had discovered that a draught of cold water, under certain circumstances, is a powerful diaphoretic. His pharmacopeia, however, contained another remedy—namely, stewed prunes, which the Doctor regarded as a specific in obstinate cases of blood-spitting. Then there was Ward, with his famous pill, whose praises that learned man, Lord Chief Baron Reynolds, sounded in every direction. There was also a tar-water mania, which mastered the clear intellect of Henry Fielding, and had as its principal advocate the supreme intellect of the age, Bishop Berkeley. In volume eighteen of the *Gentleman's Magazine* is a list of the quack-doctors then practising; and the number of those named in it is almost as numerous as the nostrums, which mount up to 202. These accommodating fellows were ready to fleece every rank of society. The fashionable impostor sold his specific sometimes at the rate of 2*s*. 6*d*. a pill, while the humbler knave vended his boluses at 6*d*. a box. To account for society tolerating, and yet more, warmly encouraging such a state of things, we must remember the force of the example set by eminent physicians in vending medicines the composition of which they kept secret. Sir Hans Sloane sold an eye-salve; and Dr. Mead had a favourite nostrum—a powder for the bite of a mad dog.

The close of the seventeenth century was not in respect of its quacks behind the few preceding generations. In 1789 Mr. and Mrs. Loutherbourg became notorious for curing people without medicine. God, they proclaimed, had endowed them with a miraculous power of healing the impoverished sick, by looking upon them and touching them. Of course every one who presumed to doubt the statement was regarded as calling in question the miracles of holy writ, and was exclaimed against as an infidel. The doctor's house was besieged with enormous crowds. The good man and his lady refused to take any fee whatever, and issued gratuitous tickets amongst the mob, which would admit the bearers into the Loutherbourgian presence. Strange to say, however, these tickets found their way into the hands of venal people, who sold them to others in the crowd (who were tired of waiting) for sums varying from two to five guineas each; and ere long it was discovered that these barterers of the healing power were accomplices in the pay of the poor man's friend. A certain Miss Mary Pratt, in all probability a puppet acting in obedience to Loutherbourg's instructions, wrote an account of the cures performed by the physician and his wife. In a dedicatory letter to the Archbishop of Canterbury, Miss Pratt says:—"I therefore presume when these testimonies are searched into (which will corroborate with mine) your Lordship will compose a form of prayer, to be used in all churches and chapels, that nothing may impede or prevent this inestimable gift from having its free course; and publick thanks may be offered up in all churches and chapels, for such an astonishing proof of God's love to this favoured land." The publication frankly states that "Mr. De Loutherbourg, who lives on Hammersmith Green, has received a most glorious power from the Lord Jehovah—viz. the gift of healing all manner of diseases incident to the human body, such as blindness, deafness, lameness, cancers, loss of speech, palsies." But the statements of "cases" are yet more droll. The reader will enjoy the perusal of a few of them.

"*Case of Thomas Robinson.*—Thomas Robinson was sent home to his parents at the sign of the Ram, a public-house in Cow Cross, so ill with what is called the king's evil, that they applied for leave to bring him into St Bartholomew's Hospital." (Of course he was discharged as "incurable," and was eventually restored to health by Mr. Loutherbourg.) "But how," continues Miss Pratt, "shall my pen paint ingratitude? The mother had procured a ticket for him from the Finsbury Dispensary, and with a shameful reluctance denied having seen Mr De Loutherbourg, waited on the kind gentleman belonging to the dispensary, and, *amazing*! thanked them for relief which they had no hand in; for she told me and fifty more, she took the drugs and medicines and threw them away, reserving the phials, &c. Such an imposition on the public ought to be detected, as she deprived other poor people of those medicines which might have been useful; not only so—robbed the Lord of Life of the glory due to him only, by returning thanks at the dispensary for a cure which they had never performed. The lad is now under Mr De Loutherbourg's care, who administered to him before me yesterday in the public healing-room, amongst a large concourse of people, amongst whom was some of the first families in the kingdom."

"*Case.—Mary Ann Hughes.*—Her father is chairman to her Grace the Duchess of Rutland, who lives at No. 37, in Ogle Street. She had a most violent fever, *fell into her knee*, went to Middlesex Hospital, where they made every experiment in order to cure her—but in vain; she came home worse than she went in, her leg contracted and useless. In this deplorable state she waited on Mrs De Loutherbourg, who, with infinite condescension, saw her, administered to her, and the second time of waiting on Mrs De Loutherbourg she was perfectly cured."

"*Case.—Mrs Hook.*—Mrs Hook, Stableyard, St James's, has two daughters born deaf and dumb. She waited on the lady above-mentioned, *who looked on them with an eye of benignity, and healed them.* (I heard them both speak.)"

Mary Pratt, after enumerating several cases like the foregoing, concludes thus:

"Let me repeat, with horror and detestation, the wickedness of those who have procured tickets of admission, and sold them for five and two guineas apiece!— whereas this gift was chiefly intended for the poor. Therefore Mr De Loutherbourg has retired from the practice into the country (for the present), having suffered all the indignities and contumely that man could suffer, joined to ungrateful behaviour, and tumultuous proceedings. I have heard people curse him and threaten his life, instead of returning him thanks; and it is my humble wish that prayers may be put up in all churches for his great gifts to multiply."

"FINIS.

"Report says three thousand persons have waited for tickets at a time."

Forming a portion of this interesting work by Miss Pratt is a description of a case which throws the Loutherbourgian miracles into the shade, and is apparently cited only for the insight it affords into the state of public feeling in Queen Anne's time, as contrasted with the sceptical enlightenment of George III.'s reign:—

"I hope the public will allow me to adduce a case which history will evince the truth of. A girl, whose father and mother were French refugees, had her hip dislocated from her birth. She was apprentice to a milliner, and obliged to go out about the mistress's business; the boys used to insult her for her lameness continually, as she limped very much.... Providence directed her to read one of the miracles performed by our blessed Saviour concerning the withered arm. The girl exclaimed, 'Oh, madam, was Jesus here on earth he would cure me.' Her mistress answered, 'If you have faith, his power is the same now.' She immediately cried, 'I have faith!' and the bone flew into its place with a report like the noise of a pistol. The girl's joy was ecstatic. She jumped about the room in raptures. The servant was called, sent for her parents, and the minister under whom she sat. They spent the night praising God. Hundreds came to see her, amongst whom was the Bishop of London, by the command of her Majesty Queen Anne (for in those days people were astonished at this great miracle.)"

Dr. Loutherbourg was not the first quack to fleece the good people of Hammersmith. In the 572nd paper of the *Spectator*, dated July 26, 1714, there is a good story of a consummate artist, who surrounded himself with an enormous crowd, and assured them that Hammersmith was the place of his nativity; and that, out of strong natural affection for his birth-place, he was willing to give each of its inhabitants a present of five shillings. After this exordium, the benevolent fellow produced from his cases an immense number of packets of a powder warranted to cure everything and kill nothing. The price of each packet was properly five shillings and sixpence; but out of love for the people of Hammersmith the good doctor offered to let any of his audience buy them at the rate of sixpence apiece. The multitude availed themselves of this proposition to such an extent that it is to be feared the friend of Hammersmith's humanity suffered greatly from his liberality.

Steele has transmitted to us some capital anecdotes of the empirics of his day. One doctor of Sir Richard's acquaintance resided in Moore Alley, near Wapping, and proclaimed his ability to cure cataracts, *because he had lost an eye in the emperor's service*. To his patients he was in the habit of displaying, as a conclusive proof of his surgical prowess, a muster-roll showing that either he, or a man of his name, had been in one of his imperial Majesty's regiments. At the sight of this document of course mistrust fled. Another man professed to treat ruptured children, because his father and grandfather were born bursten. But more humorous even than either of these gentlemen was another friend of Sir Richard's, who announced to the public that "from eight to twelve and from two till six, he attended for the good of the public to bleed for threepence."

The fortunes which pretenders to the healing art have amassed would justify a belief that empiricism, under favourable circumstances, is the best trade to be found in the entire list of industrial occupations. Quacks have in all ages found staunch supporters amongst the powerful and affluent. Dr. Myersbach, whom Lettsom endeavoured to drive back into obscurity, continued, long after the publication of the "Observations," to make a large income out of the credulity of the fashionable classes of English society. Without learning of any kind, this man raised himself to opulence. His degree was bought at Erfurth for a few shillings, just before that university raised the prices of its academical distinctions, in consequence of the pleasant raillery of a young Englishman, who paid the fees for a Doctor's diploma, and had it duly recorded in the Collegiate archives as having been presented to Anglicus Ponto; Ponto being no other than his mastiff dog. With such a degree Myersbach set up for a philosopher. Patients crowded to his consulting-room, and those who were unable to come sent their servants with descriptions of their cases. But his success was less than that of the inventor of Ailhaud's powders, which ran their devastating course through every country in Europe, sending to the silence of the grave almost as many thousands as were destroyed in all Napoleon's campaigns. Tissot, in his "Avis au Peuple," published in 1803, attacked Ailhaud with characteristic vehemence, and put an end to his destructive power; but ere this took place the charlatan had mounted on his slaughtered myriads to the possession of three baronies, and was figuring in European courts as the Baron de Castelet.

The tricks which these practitioners have had recourse to for the attainment of their ends are various. Dr. Katterfelto, who rose into eminence upon the evil wind that brought the influenza to England in the year 1782, always travelled about the country in a large caravan, containing a number of black cats. This gentleman's triumphant campaign was brought to a disastrous termination by the mayor of Shrewsbury, who gave him a taste of the sharp discipline provided at that time by the law for rogues and vagabonds.—"The Wise Man of Liverpool," whose destiny it was to gull the canny inhabitants of the North of England, used to traverse the country in a chariot drawn by six horses, attended by a perfect army of outriders in brilliant liveries, and affecting all the pomp of a prince of the royal blood.

The quacks who merit severe punishment the least of all their order are those who, while they profess to exercise a powerful influence over the bodies of their patients, leave nature to pursue her operations pretty much in her own way. Of this comparatively harmless class was Atwell, the parson of St. Tue, who, according to the account given of him by Fuller, in his English Worthies, "although he now and then used blood-letting, mostly for all diseases prescribed milk, and often milk and apples, which (although contrary to the judgments of the best-esteemed practitioners) either by virtue of the medicine, or fortune of the physician, or fancy of the patient, recovered many out of desperate extremities." Atwell won his reputation by acting on the same principle that has brought a certain degree of popularity to the homœopathists—that, namely, of letting things run their own course. The higher order of empirics have always availed themselves of the wonderful faculty possessed by nature of taking good care of herself. Simple people who enlarge on the series of miraculous cures performed by their pet charlatan, and find in them proofs of his honesty and professional worth, do not reflect that in ninety-and-nine cases out of every hundred where a sick person is restored to health, the result is achieved by nature rather than art, and would have been arrived at as speedily without as with medicine. Again, the fame of an ordinary medical practitioner is never backed up by simple and compound addition. His cures and half cures are never summed up to magnificent total by his employers, and then flaunted about on a bright banner before the eyes of the electors. 'Tis a mere matter of course that *he* (although he *is* quite wrong, and knows not half as much about his art as any great lady who has tested the efficacy of the new system on her sick poodle) should cure people. 'Tis only the cause of globules which is to be supported by documentary evidence, containing the case of every young lady who has lost a severe headache under the benign influence of an infinitesimal dose of flour and water.

Dumoulin, the physician, observed at his death that "he left behind him two great physicians, Regimen and River Water." A due appreciation of the truth embodied in this remark, coupled with that masterly assurance, without which the human family is not to be fleeced, enabled the French quack, Villars, to do good to others and to himself at the same time. This man, in 1723, confided to his friends that his uncle, who had recently been killed by an accident at the advanced age of one hundred years, had bequeathed to him the recipe for a nostrum which would prolong the life of any one who used it to a hundred and fifty, provided only that the rules of sobriety were never transgressed. Whenever a funeral passed him in the street he said aloud, "Ah! if that unfortunate creature had taken my nostrum, he might be carrying that coffin, instead of being carried in it." This nostrum was composed of nitre and Seine water, and was sold at the ridiculously cheap rate of five francs a bottle. Those who bought it were directed to drink it at certain stated periods, and also to lead regular lives, to eat moderately, drink temperately, take plenty of bodily exercise, go to and rise from bed early, and to avoid mental anxiety. In an enormous majority of cases the patient was either cured or benefitted. Some possibly died, who, by the ministrations of science, might have been preserved from the grave. But in these cases, and doubtless they were few, the blunder was set down to Nature, who, somewhat unjustly, was never credited with any of the recoveries. The world was charitable, and the doctor could say—

> "The grave my faults does hide,
> The world my cures does see;
> What youth and time provide,
> Are oft ascribed to me."

Anyhow Villars succeeded, and won the approbation not only of his dupes, but of those also who were sagacious enough to see the nature of his trick. The Abbe Pons declared him to be the superior of the marshal of the same name. "The latter," said he, "kills men—the former prolongs their existence." At length Villars' secret leaked out; and his patients, unwise in coming to him, unwisely deserted him. His occupation was gone.

The displeasure of Villars' dupes, on the discovery of the benevolent hoax played upon them, reminds us of a good story. Some years since, at a fashionable watering-place, on the south-east coast of England, resided a young surgeon—handsome, well-bred, and of most pleasant address. He was fast rising into public favour and a good practice, when an eccentric and wealthy maiden lady, far advanced in years, sent for him. The summons of course was promptly obeyed, and the young practitioner was soon listening to a most terrible story of suffering. The afflicted lady, according to her own account, had a year before, during the performance of her toilet, accidentally taken into her throat one of the bristles of her tooth-brush. This bristle had stuck in the top of the gullet, and set up an irritation which, she was convinced, was killing her. She had been from one surgeon of eminence to another, and everywhere in London and in the country the Faculty had assured her that she was only the victim of a nervous delusion—that her throat was in a perfectly healthy condition—that the disturbance existed only in her own imagination. "And so they go on, the stupid, obstinate, perverse, unfeeling creatures," concluded the poor lady, "saying there is nothing the matter with me, while I am—dying—dying—dying!" "Allow me, my dear lady," said the adroit surgeon in reply, "to inspect for myself—carefully—the state of your throat." The inspection was made gravely, and at much length. "My dear Miss — —," resumed the surgeon, when he had concluded his examination, "you are quite right, and Sir Benjamin Brodie and Sir James Clark are wrong. I can see the head of the bristle low down, almost out of sight; and if you'll let me run home for my instruments, I'll forthwith extract it for you." The adroit man retired, and in a few minutes re-entered the room, armed with a very delicate pair of forceps, into the teeth of which he had inserted a bristle taken from an ordinary tooth-brush. The rest can be imagined. The lady threw back her head; the forceps were introduced into her mouth; a prick—a scream! and 'twas all over; and the surgeon, with a smiling face, was holding up to the light, and inspecting with lively curiosity, the extracted bristle. The patient was in raptures at a result that proved that she was right, and Sir Benjamin Brodie wrong. She immediately recovered her health and spirits, and went about everywhere sounding the praises of "her saviour," as she persisted in calling the dexterous operator. So enthusiastic was her gratitude, she offered him her hand in marriage and her noble fortune. The fact that the young surgeon was already married was an insuperable obstacle to this arrangement. But other proofs of gratitude the lady lavishly showered on him. She compelled him to accept a carriage and horses, a service of plate, and a new house. Unfortunately the lucky fellow could not keep his own counsel. Like foolish Samson with Delilah, he imparted the secret of his cunning to the wife of his bosom; she confided it to Louise Clarissa, her especial friend, who had been her bridesmaid; Louise Clarissa told it under vows of inviolable secrecy to six other particular friends; and the six other particular friends—base and unworthy girls!—told it to all the world. Ere long the story came round to the lady herself. Then what a storm arose! She was in a transport of fury! It was of no avail for the surgeon to remind her that he had unquestionably raised her from a pitiable condition to health and happiness. That mattered not. He had tricked, fooled, bamboozled her! She would not forgive him, she would pursue him with undying vengeance, she would ruin him! The writer of these pages is happy to know that the surgeon here spoken of, whose prosperous career has been adorned by much genuine benevolence, though unforgiven, was not ruined.

The ignorant are remarkable alike for suspicion and credulity; and the quack makes them his prey by lulling to sleep the former quality, and artfully arousing and playing upon the latter. Whatever the field of quackery may be, the dupe must ever be the same. Some years since a canny drover, from the north of the Tweed, gained a high reputation throughout the Eastern Counties for selling at high prices the beasts intrusted to him as a salesman. At Norwich and Earl Soham, at Bury and Ipswich, the story was the same—Peter M'Dougal invariably got more per head for "a lot" than even his warmest admirers had calculated he would obtain. He managed his business so well, that his brethren, unable to compete with him, came to a conclusion not altogether supported by the facts of the case, but flattering to their own self-love. Clearly Peter could only surpass them by such a long distance, through the agency of some charm or witch's secret. They hinted as much; and Peter wisely accepted the suggestion, with a half-assenting nod of cunning, and encouraged his mates to believe in it. A year or so passed on, and it was generally allowed that Peter M'Dougal was in league on honourable terms with the unseen world. To contend with him was useless. The only line open to his would-be imitators was to buy from him participations in his mysterious powers. "Peter," at length said a simple southern, at the close of Halesworth cattle-fair, acting as spokesman for himself and four other conspirators, "lets us into yer secret, man. Yer ha' made here twelve pun a yead by a lot that aren't woth sex. How ded yer doo it? We are all owld friens. Lets us goo to 'Th' Alter'd Case,' an I an my mets ull stan yar supper an a dead drunk o' whiskey or rom poonch, so be yar jine hans to giv us the wink." Peter's eyes twinkled. He liked a good supper and plenty of hot grog at a friend's expense. Indeed, of such fare, like Sheridan with wine, he was ready to take any given quantity. The bargain was made, and an immediate adjournment effected to the public-house rejoicing in the title of "The Case is Altered." The supper was of hot steak-pudding, made savoury with pepper and onions. Peter M'Dougal ate plentifully and deliberately. Slowly also he drank two stiff tumblers of whiskey punch, smoking his pipe meanwhile without uttering a word. The second tumbler was followed by a third, and as he sipped the latter half of it, his entertainers closed round him, and intimated that their part of the contract being accomplished, he, as a man of honour, ought to fulfill his. Peter was a man of few words, and without any unnecessary prelude or comment, he stated in one laconic speech the secret of his professional success. Laying down his pipe by his empty glass, and emitting from his gray eyes a light of strange humour, he said drily, "Ye'd knoo hoo it was I cam to mak sae guid a sale o' my beasties? Weel, I ken it was joost this—*I fund a fule!*"

The drover who rises to be a capitalist, and the lawyer who mounts to the woolsack, ascend by the same process. They know how to find out fools, and how to turn their discoveries to advantage.

It is told of a Barbadoes physician and slaveholder, that having been robbed to a serious extent in his sugar-works, he discovered the thief by the following ingenious artifice. Having called his slaves together, he addressed them thus:—"My friends, the great serpent appeared to me during the night, and told me that the person who stole my money should, at this instant—*this very instant*—have a parrot's feather at the point of his nose." On this announcement, the dishonest thief, anxious to find out if his guilt had declared itself, put his finger to his nose. "Man," cried the master instantly, "'tis thou who hast robbed me. The great serpent has just told me so."

Clearly this piece of quackery succeeded, because the quack had "fund a fule."

CHAPTER VII.

JOHN RADCLIFFE.

Radcliffe, the Jacobite partisan, the physician without learning, and the luxurious *bon-vivant*, who grudged the odd sixpences of his tavern scores, was born at Wakefield in Yorkshire, in the year 1650. His extraction was humble, his father being only a well-to-do yeoman. In after life, when he lived on intimate terms with the leading nobility of the country, he put in a claim for aristocratic descent; and the Earl of Derwentwater recognized him as a kinsman deriving his blood from the Radcliffes of Dilston, in the county of Northumberland, the chiefs of which honourable family had been knights, barons, and earls, from the time of Henry IV. It may be remembered that a similar countenance was given to Burke's patrician pretensions, which have been related by more than one biographer, with much humorous pomp. In Radcliffe's case the Heralds interfered with the Earl's decision; for after the physician's decease they admonished the University of Oxford not to erect any escutcheon over or upon his monument. But though Radcliffe was a plebeian, he contrived, by his shrewd humour, arrogant simplicity, and immeasurable insolence, to hold both Whigs and Tories in his grasp. The two factions of the aristocracy bowed before him—the Tories from affection to a zealous adherent of regal absolutism; and the Whigs, from a superstitious belief in his remedial skill, and a fear that in their hours of need he would leave them to the advances of Death.

At the age of fifteen he became a member of the University College, Oxford; and having kept his terms there, he took his B. A. degree in 1669, and was made senior-scholar of the college. But no fellowship falling vacant there, he accepted one on the foundation of Lincoln College. His M. B. degree he took in 1675, and forthwith obtained considerable practice in Oxford. Owing to a misunderstanding with Dr. Marshall, the rector of Lincoln College, Radcliffe relinquished a fellowship, which he could no longer hold, without taking orders, in 1677. He did not take his M. D. degree till 1682, two years after which time he went up to London, and took a house in Bow Street, next that in which Sir Godfrey Kneller long resided; and with a facility which can hardly be credited in these days, when success is achieved only by slow advances, he stept forthwith into a magnificent income.

The days of mealy-mouthed suavity had not yet come to the Faculty. Instead of standing by each other with lip-service, as they now do in spite of all their jealousies, physicians and surgeons vented their mutual enmities in frank, honest abuse. Radcliffe's tongue was well suited for this part of his business; and if that unruly member created for him enemies, it could also contend with a legion of adversaries at the same time. Foulks and Adams, then the first apothecaries in Oxford, tried to discredit the young doctor, but were ere long compelled to sue for a cessation of hostilities. Luff, who afterwards became Professor of Physic in the University, declared that all "Radcliffe's cures were performed only by guesswork"; and Gibbons, with a sneer, said, "that it was a pity that his friends had not made a scholar of the young man." In return Radcliffe always persisted in speaking of his opponent as *Nurse* Gibbons—because of his slops and diet drinks, whereas he (Radcliffe the innovator) preached up the good effects of fresh air, a liberal table, and cordials. This was the Dr. Gibbons around whom the apothecaries rallied, to defend their interests in the great Dispensarian contest, and whom Garth in his poem ridicules, under the name of "Mirmillo," for entertaining drug-venders:—

> "Not far from that frequented theatre,
> Where wandering punks each night at five repair,
> Where purple emperors in buskins tread,
> And rule imaginary worlds for bread;
> Where Bentley, by old writers, wealthy grew,
> And Briscoe lately was undone by new;
> There triumphs a physician of renown,
> To none, but such as rust in health, unknown.
> *　　　*　　　*　　　*　　　*
> The trading tribe oft thither throng to dine,
> And want of elbow-room supply in wine."

Gibbons was not the only dangerous antagonist that Radcliffe did battle with in London. Dr. Whistler, Sir Edmund King, Sir Edward Hannes, and Sir Richard Blackmore were all strong enough to hurt him and rouse his jealousy. Hannes, also an Oxford man, was to the last a dangerous and hated rival. He opened his campaign in London with a carriage and four horses. The equipage was so costly and imposing that it attracted the general attention of the town. "By Jove! Radcliffe," said a kind friend, "Hannes's horses are the finest I have ever seen." "Umph!" growled Radcliffe savagely, "then he'll be able to sell them for all the more."

To make his name known Hannes used to send his liveried footmen running about the streets with directions to put their heads into every coach they met and inquire, with accents of alarm, if Dr. Hannes was in it. Acting on these orders, one of his fellows, after looking into every carriage between Whitehall and the Royal Exchange, without finding his employer, ran up Exchange Alley into Garraway's Coffee-house, which was one of the great places of meeting for the members of the medical profession. (Apothecaries used regularly to come and consult the physicians, while the latter were over their wine, paying only half fees for the advice so given, without the patients being personally examined. Batson's coffee-house in Corn-hill was another favourite spot for these Galenic re-unions, Sir William Blizard being amongst the last of the medical authorities who frequented that hostelry for the purpose of receiving apothecaries.) "Gentlemen, can your honours tell me if Dr. Hannes is here?" asked the man, running into the very centre of the exchange of medicine-men. "Who wants Dr. Hannes, fellow?" demanded Radcliffe, who happened to be present. "Lord A—— and Lord B——, your honour!" answered the man. "No, no, friend," responded the doctor slowly, and with pleasant irony, "you are mistaken. Those lords don't want your master—'tis he who wants them."

But Hannes made friends and a fine income, to the deep chagrin of his contemptuous opponent. An incessant feud existed between the two men. The virulence of their mutual animosity may be estimated by the following story. When the poor little Duke of Gloucester was taken ill, Sir Edward Hannes and Blackmore (famous as Sir Richard Blackmore, the poet) were called in to attend him. On the case taking a fatal turn, Radcliffe was sent for; and after roundly charging the two doctors with the grossest mismanagement of a simple attack of rash, went on, "It would have been happy for this nation had you, sir, been bred up a basket-maker—and you, sir, had remained a country schoolmaster, rather than have ventured out of your reach, in the practice of an art which you are an utter stranger to, and for your blunders in which you ought to be whipped with one of your own rods." The reader will not see the force of this delicate speech if he is not aware that Hannes was generally believed to be the son of a basket-maker, and Sir Richard Blackmore had, in the period of his early poverty, like Johnson and Oliver Goldsmith, been a teacher of boys. Whenever the "Amenities of the Faculty" come to be published, this consultation, on the last illness of Jenkin Lewis's little friend, ought to have its niche in the collection.

Towards the conclusion of his life, Radcliffe said that, "when a young practitioner, he possessed twenty remedies for every disease; and at the close of his career he found twenty diseases for which he had not one remedy." His mode of practice, however, as far as anything is known about it, at the outset was the same as that which he used at the conclusion of his career. Pure air, cleanliness, and a wholesome diet were amongst his most important prescriptions; though he was so far from running counter to the interests of the druggists, that his apothecary, Dandridge, whose business was almost entirely confined to preparing the doctor's medicines, died worth 50,000*l*. For the imaginary maladies of his hypochondriacal male and fanciful female patients he had the greatest contempt, and neither respect for age or rank, nor considerations of interest, could always restrain him from insulting such patients. In 1686 he was appointed physician to Princess Anne of Denmark, and was for some years a trusted adviser of that royal lady; but he lacked the compliant temper and imperturbable suavity requisite for a court physician. Shortly after the death of Queen Mary, the Princess Anne, having incurred a fit of what is by the vulgar termed "blue devils," from not paying proper attention to her diet, sent in all haste to her physician. Radcliffe, when he received the imperative summons to hurry to St. James's was sitting over his bottle in a tavern. The allurements of Bacchus were too strong for him, and he delayed his visit to the distinguished sufferer. A second messenger arrived, but by that time the physician was so gloriously ennobled with claret, that he discarded all petty considerations of personal advantage, and flatly refused to stir an inch from the room where he was experiencing all the happiness humanity is capable of. "Tell her Royal Highness," he exclaimed, banging his fist on the table, "that her distemper is nothing but the vapours. She's in as good state of health as any woman breathing—only she can't make up her mind to believe it."

The next morning prudence returned with sobriety; and the doctor did not fail to present himself at an early hour in the Princess's apartment in St. James's Palace. To his consternation he was stopped in the ante-room by an officer, and informed that he was dismissed from his post, which had already been given to Dr. Gibbons. Anne never forgave the sarcasm about "the vapours." It so rankled in her breast, that, though she consented to ask for the Doctor's advice both for herself and those dear to her, she never again held any cordial communication with him. Radcliffe tried to hide the annoyance caused him by his fall, in a hurricane of insolence towards his triumphant rival: Nurse Gibbons had gotten a new nursery—Nurse Gibbons was not to be envied his new acquisition—Nurse Gibbons was fit only to look after a woman who merely fancied herself ill.

Notwithstanding this rupture with the Court, Radcliffe continued to have the most lucrative practice in town, and in all that regarded money he was from first to last a most lucky man. On coming to town he found Lower, the Whig physician, sinking in public favour—and Thomas Short, the Roman Catholic doctor, about to drop into the grave. Whistler, Sir Edmund King, and Blackmore had plenty of patients. But there was a "splendid opening," and so cleverly did Radcliffe slip into it, that at the end of his first year in town he got twenty guineas per diem. The difference in the value of money being taken into consideration, it may be safely affirmed that no living physician makes more. Occasionally the fees presented to him were very large. He cured Bentinck, afterwards Earl of Portland, of a diarrhœa, and Zulestein, afterwards Earl of Rochford, of an attack of congestion of the brain. For these services William III. presented him with 500 guineas out of the privy-purse, and offered to appoint him one of his physicians, with £200 per annum more than he gave any other of his medical officers. Radcliffe pocketed the fee, but his Jacobite principles precluded him from accepting the post. William, however, notwithstanding the opposition of Bidloe and the rest of his medical servants, held Radcliffe in such estimation that he continually consulted him; and during the first eleven years of his reign paid him, one year with another, 600 guineas per annum. And when he restored to health William, Duke of Gloucester (the Princess of Denmark's son), who in his third year was attacked with severe convulsions, Queen Mary sent him, through the hand of her Lord Chamberlain, 1000 guineas. And for attending the Earl of Albemarle at Namur he had 400 guineas and a diamond ring, 1200 guineas from the treasury, and an offer of a baronetcy from the King.

For many years he was the neighbour of Sir Godfrey Kneller, in Bow Street. A dispute that occurred between the two neighbours and friends is worth recording. Sir Godfrey took pleasure in his garden, and expended large sums of money in stocking it with exotic plants and rare flowers. Radcliffe also enjoyed a garden, but loved his fees too well to expend them on one of his own. He suggested to Sir Godfrey that it would be a good plan to insert a door into the boundary wall between their gardens, so that on idle afternoons, when he had no patients to visit, he might slip into his dear friend's pleasure-grounds. Kneller readily assented to this proposition, and ere a week had elapsed the door was ready for use. The plan, however, had not been long acted on when the painter was annoyed by Radcliffe's servants wantonly injuring his parterres. After fruitlessly expostulating against these depredations, the sufferer sent a message to his friend, threatening, if the annoyance recurred, to brick up the wall. "Tell Sir Godfrey," answered Radcliffe to the messenger, "that he may do what he likes to the door, so long as he does not paint it." When this vulgar jeer was reported to Kneller, he replied, with equal good humour and more wit, "Go back and give my service to Dr. Radcliffe, and tell him, I'll take anything from him—but physic."

Radcliffe was never married, and professed a degree of misogyny that was scarcely in keeping with his conduct on certain occasions. His person was handsome and imposing, but his manners were little calculated to please women. Overbearing, truculent, and abusive, he could not rest without wounding the feelings of his companions with harsh jokes. Men could bear with him, but ladies were like Queen Anne in vehemently disliking him. King William was not pleased with his brutal candour in exclaiming, at the sight of the dropsical ancles uncovered for inspection, "I would not have your Majesty's legs for your three kingdoms"; but William's sister-in-law repaid a much slighter offence with life-long animosity. In 1693, however, the doctor made an offer to a citizen's daughter, who had beauty and a fortune of £15,000. As she was only twenty-four years of age, the doctor was warmly congratulated by his friends when he informed them that he, though well advanced in middle age, had succeeded in his suit. Before the wedding-day, however, it was discovered that the health of the lady rendered it incumbent on her honour that she should marry her father's book-keeper. This mishap soured the doctor's temper to the fair sex, and his sarcasms at feminine folly and frailty were innumerable.

He was fond of declaring that he wished for an Act of Parliament entitling nurses to the sole and entire medical care of women. A lady who consulted him about a nervous singing in the head was advised to "curl her hair with a ballad." His scorn of women was not lessened by the advances of certain disorderly ladies of condition, who displayed for him that morbid passion which medical practitioners have often to resist in the treatment of hysterical patients. Yet he tried his luck once again at the table of love. "There's no fool so great as an old fool." In the summer of 1709, Radcliffe, then in his sixtieth year, started a new equipage; and having arrayed himself in the newest mode of foppery, threw all the town into fits of laughter by paying his addresses, with the greatest possible publicity, to a lady who possessed every requisite charm—(youth, beauty, wealth)—except a tenderness for her aged suitor. Again was there an unlucky termination to the doctor's love, which Steele, in No. 44 of *The Tatler*, ridiculed in the following manner:—

"This day, passing through Covent Garden, I was stopped in the Piazza by Pacolet, to observe what he called *The Triumph of Love and Youth*. I turned to the object he pointed at, and there I saw a gay gilt chariot, drawn by fresh prancing horses, the coachman with a new cockade, and the lacqueys with insolence and plenty in their countenances. I asked immediately, 'What young heir, or lover, owned that glittering equipage!' But my companion interrupted, 'Do not you see there the mourning Æsculapius?' 'The mourning!' said I. 'Yes, Isaac,' said Pacolet, 'he is in deep mourning, and is the languishing, hopeless lover of the divine Hebe, the emblem of Youth and Beauty. That excellent and learned sage you behold in that furniture is the strongest instance imaginable that love is the most powerful of all things.

"'You are not so ignorant as to be a stranger to the character of Æsculapius, as the patron and most successful of all who profess the Art of Medicine. But as most of his operations are owing to a natural sagacity or impulse, he has very little troubled himself with the Doctrine of Drugs, but has always given Nature more room to help herself than any of her learned assistants; and consequently has done greater wonders than in the power of Art to perform; for which reason he is half deified by the people, and has ever been courted by all the world, just as if he were a seventh son.

"'It happened that the charming Hebe was reduc'd, by a long and violent fever, to the most extreme danger of Death; and when all skill failed, they sent for Æsculapius. The renowned artist was touched with the deepest compassion, to see the faded charms and faint bloom of Hebe; and had a generous concern, too, in beholding a struggle, not between Life, but rather between Youth, and Death. All his skill and his passion tended to the recovery of Hebe, beautiful even in sickness; but, alas! the unhappy physician knew not that in all his care he was only sharpening darts for his own destruction. In a word, his fortune was the same with that of the statuary who fell in love with an image of his own making; and the unfortunate Æsculapius is become the patient of her whom he lately recovered. Long before this, Æsculapius was far gone in the unnecessary and superfluous amusements of old age, in the increase of unwieldy stores, and the provision in the midst of an incapacity of enjoyment, of what he had for a supply of more wants than he had calls for in Youth itself. But these low considerations are now no more; and Love has taken place of Avarice, or rather is become an Avarice of another kind, which still urges him to pursue what he does not want. But behold the metamorphosis: the anxious mean cares of an usurer are turned into the languishments and complaints of a lover. "Behold," says the aged Æsculapius, "I submit; I own, great Love, thy empire. Pity, Hebe, the fop you have made. What have I to do with gilding but on Pills? Yet, O Fate! for thee I sit amidst a crowd of painted deities on my chariot, buttoned in gold, clasp'd in gold, without having any value for that beloved metal, but as it adorns the person and laces the hat of the dying lover. I ask not to live, O Hebe! Give me but gentle death. Euthanasia, Euthanasia! that is all I implore."' When Æsculapius had finished his complaint, Pacolet went on in deep morals on the uncertainty of riches, with this remarkable explanation—'O wealth! how impatient art thou! And how little dost thou supply us with real happiness, when the usurer himself cannot forget thee, for the love of what is foreign to his felicity, as thou art!'"

Seven days after the *Tatler* resumed the attack, but with less happy effect. In this picture, the justice of which was not questioned, even by the Doctor's admirers, the avarice of the veteran is not less insisted on as the basis of his character, than his amorousness is displayed as a ludicrous freak of vanity. Indeed, love of money was the master-defect of Radcliffe's disposition. Without a child, or a prospect of offspring, he screwed and scraped in every direction. Even his debaucheries had an alloy of discomfort that does not customarily mingle in the dissipations of the rich. The flavour of the money each bottle cost gave ungrateful smack to his wine. He had numerous poor relations, of whom he took, during his life, little or no notice. Even his sisters he kept at arm's distance, lest they should show their affection for him by dipping their hands in his pockets. It is true, he provided liberally for them at his death—leaving to the one (a married lady—Mrs. Hannah Redshaw) a thousand a year for life, and to the other (a spinster lady) an income of half that amount as long as she lived. But that he treated them with unbrotherly neglect there is no doubt.

After his decease, a letter was found in his closet, directed to his unmarried sister, Millicent Radcliffe, in which, with contrition, and much pathos, he bids her farewell. "You will find," says he, in that epistle, "by my will that I have taken better care of you than perhaps you might expect from my former treatment of you; for which, with my dying breath, I most heartily ask pardon. I had indeed acted the brother's part much better, in making a handsome settlement on you while living, than after my decease; and can plead nothing in excuse, but that the love of money, which I have emphatically known to be the root of all evil, was too predominant over me. Though, I hope, I have made some amends for that odious sin of covetousness, in my last dispositions of those worldly goods which it pleased the great Dispenser of Providence to bless me with."

What made this meanness of disposition in money matters the more remarkable was, that he was capable of occasional munificence, on a scale almost beyond his wealth, and also of a stoical fortitude under any reverse of fortune that chanced to deprive him of some of his beloved guineas.

In the year 1704, at a general collection for propagating the Gospel in foreign parts, he settled on the Society established for that purpose £50 per annum for ever. And this noble gift he unostentatiously made under an assumed name. In the same year he presented £520 to the Bishop of Norwich, to be distributed among the poor non-juring clergy; and this donation he also desired should be kept a secret from the world.

His liberality to Oxford was far from being all of the *post-mortem* sort. In 1687 he presented the chapel of University College with an east window, representing, in stained glass, the Nativity, and having the following inscription:—"D.D. Johan Radcliffe, M.D., hujus Collegii quondam Socius, Anno Domini MDCLXXXVII." In 1707 he gave Sprat, Bishop of Rochester, bills for £300, drawn under the assumed name of Francis Andrews, on Waldegrave the goldsmith, of Russell Street, Covent Garden, for the relief of distressed Scotch Episcopal clergy.

As another instance of how his niggard nature could allow him to do good by stealth, and blush to find it fame, his liberality to James Drake, the Tory writer, may be mentioned. Drake was a physician, as well as a political author. As the latter, he was well liked, as the former he was honestly hated by Radcliffe. Two of a trade—where one of the two is a John Radcliffe—can never agree. Each of the two doctors had done his utmost to injure the reputation of the other. But when Drake, broken in circumstances by a political persecution, was in sore distress from want of money, Radcliffe put fifty guineas into a lady's hands, and begged her to convey it to Drake. "Let him," said Radcliffe, with the delicacy of a fine heart, "by no means be told whence it comes. He is a gentleman, and has often done his best to hurt me. He could, therefore, by no means brook the receipt of a benefit from a person whom he had used all possible means to make an enemy."

After such instances of Ratcliffe's generosity, it may seem unnecessary to give more proofs of the existence of that quality, disguised though it was by miserly habits. His friend Nutley, a loose rollicking gentleman about town, a barrister without practice, a man of good family, and no fortune, a jovial dog, with a jest always on his lips, wine in his head, and a death's-head grinning over each shoulder [such bachelors may still be found in London], was in this case the object of the doctor's benevolence. Driven by duns and tippling to the borders of distraction, Nutley crept out of his chambers under the cover of night to the "Mitre Tavern," and called for "a bottle." "A bottle" with Nutley meant "many bottles." The end of it was that the high-spirited gentleman fell down in a condition of — — well! in a condition that Templars, in this age of earnest purpose and decent morals, would blush to be caught in. Mr. Nutley was taken hold of by the waiters, and carried up-stairs to bed.

The next morning the merry fellow is in the saddest of all possible humours. The memory of a few little bills, the holders of which are holding a parliament on his stair-case in Pump-court; the recollection that he has not a guinea left—either to pacify those creditors with, or to use in paying for the wine consumed over night; a depressing sense that the prominent features of civilized existence are tax-gatherers and sheriff's officers; a head that seems to be falling over one side of the pillow, whilst the eyes roll out on the other;—all these afflict poor Mr. Nutley! A knock at the door, and the landlady enters. The landlady is the Widow Watts, daughter of the widow Bowles, also in the same line. As now, so a hundred and fifty years ago, ladies in licensed victualling circles played tricks with their husbands' night-caps—killed them with kindness, and reigned in their stead. The widow Watts has a sneaking fondness for poor Mr. Nutley, and is much affected when, in answer to her inquiry how "his honour feels his-self," he begins to sob like a child, narrate the troubles of his infancy, the errors of his youth, and the sorrows of his riper age. Mistress Watts is alarmed. Only to think of Mr. Nutley going on like that, talking of his blessed mother who had been dead these twenty years, and vowing he'd kill himself, because he is an outcast, and no better than a disgrace to his family. "To think of it! and only yesterday he were the top of company, and would have me drink his own honourable health in a glass of his own wine." Mistress Watts sends straightway for Squire Nutley's friend, the Doctor. When Radcliffe makes his appearance, he sees the whole case at a glance, rallies Billy Nutley about his rascally morals, estimates his assertion that "it's only his liver a little out of order" exactly at its worth, and takes his leave shortly, saying to himself, "If poor Billy could only be freed from the depression caused by his present pecuniary difficulties, he would escape for this once a return of the deliri...." At the end of another half hour, a goldsmith's man enters the bed-room, and puts into Nutley's hand a letter and a bag of gold containing 200 guineas. The epistle is from

Radcliffe, begging his friend to accept the money, and to allow the donor to send him in a few days 300 more of the same coins. Such was the physician's prescription, in dispensing which he condescended to act as his own apothecary. Bravo, doctor!—who of us shall say which of the good deeds—thy gift to Billy Nutley or thy princely bequest to Oxford—has the better right to be regarded as the offspring of sincere benevolence? Some—and let no "fie!" be cried upon them—will find in this story more to make them love thy memory than they have ever found in that noble library whose dome stands up amidst the towers, and steeples, and sacred walls of beloved Oxford.

It would not be hard to say which of the two gifts has done the greater good. Poor Will Nutley took his 500 guineas, and had "more bottles," went a few more times to the theatres in lace and velvet and brocade, roared out at a few more drinking bouts, and was carried off by [his biographer calls it "a violent fever"] in the twenty-ninth year of his age. And possibly since Willy Nutley was Willy Nutley, and no one else, this was the best possible termination for him. That Radcliffe, the head of a grave profession, and a man of fifty-seven years of age, should have conceived an enthusiastic friendship for a youngster of half his age, is a fact that shows us one of the consequences of the tavern life of our great-grandfathers. It puts us in mind of how Fielding, ere he had a beard, burst into popularity with the haunters of coffee-houses. When roistering was in fashion, a young man had many chances which he no longer possesses. After the theatres were closed, he reeled into the hostels of the town, singing snatches with the blithe, clear voice of youth, laughing and jesting with all around, and frequently amongst that "all" he came in contact with the highest and most powerful men of the time. A boy-adventurer could display his wit and quality to statesmen and leaders of all sorts; whereas now he must wait years before he is even introduced to them, and years more ere he gets an invitation to their formal dinners, at which Barnes Newcome cuts as brilliant a figure as the best and the strongest.

Throughout his life Radcliffe was a staunch and manly Jacobite. He was for "the king"; but neither loyalty nor interest could bind him to higher considerations than those of attachment to the individual he regarded as the rightful head of the realm. In 1688, when Obadiah Walker tried to wheedle him into the folly of becoming a Romanist, the attempt at perversion proved a signal failure. Nothing can be more truly manly than his manner of rejecting the wily advances of the proselytizing pervert. "The advantages you propose to me," he writes, "may be very great, for all that I know; God Almighty can do very much and so can the king; but you'll pardon me if I cease to speak like a physician for once, and, with an air of gravity, am very apprehensive that I may anger the one in being too complaisant to the other. You cannot call this pinning my faith to any man's sleeve; those that know me are too well apprized of my quite contrary tendency. As I never flattered a man myself, so 'tis my firm resolution never to be wheedled out of my real sentiments—which are, that since it has been my good fortune to be educated according to the usage of the Church of England, established by law, I shall never make myself so unhappy as to shame my teachers and instructors by departing from what I have imbibed from them."

Thus was Walker treated when he abused his position as head of University College. But when the foolish man was deprived of his office, he found a good friend in him whom he had tried to seduce from the Church in which he had been reared. From the time of his first coming to London from Oxford, on the abdication of James the Second, up to the time of his death, Walker subsisted on a handsome allowance made to him out of Radcliffe's purse. When, also, the discarded principal died, it was the doctor who gave him an honourable interment in Pancras churchyard, and years afterwards erected a monument to his memory.

As years passed on, without the restitution of the proscribed males of the Stuart House, Radcliffe's political feelings became more bitter. He was too cautious a man to commit himself in any plot having for its object a change of dynasty; but his ill-humour at the existing state of things vented itself in continual sarcasms against the chiefs of the Whig party with whom he came in contact. He professed that he did not wish for practice amongst the faction to which he was opposed. He had rather only preserve the lives of those citizens who were loyal to their king. One of the immediate results of this affectation was increased popularity with his political antagonists. Whenever a Whig leader was dangerously ill, his friends were sure to feel that his only chance of safety rested on the ministrations of the Jacobite doctor. Radcliffe would be sent for, and after swearing a score of times that nothing should induce him to comply with the summons, would make his appearance at the sick-bed, where he would sometimes tell the sufferer that the devil would have no mercy on those who put constitutional governments above the divine right of kings. If the patient recovered, of course his cure was attributed to the Tory physician; and if death was the result, the same cause was pointed to.

It might be fancied that, rather than incur a charge of positively killing his political antagonists, Radcliffe would have left them to their fates. But this plan would have served him the reverse of well. If he failed to attend a Whig's death-bed to which he had been summoned, the death was all the same attributed to him. "He might," exclaimed the indignant survivors, "have saved poor Tom if he had liked; only poor Tom was a Whig, and so he left him to die." He was charged alike with killing Queen Mary, whom he did attend in her dying illness—and Queen Anne, whom he didn't.

The reader of the Harleian MS. of Burnet's "History" is amused with the following passage, which does not appear in the printed editions:—"I will not enter into another province, nor go out of my own profession, and so will say no more of the physician's part, but that it was universally condemned; so that the Queen's death was imputed to the unskilfulness and wilfulness of Dr. Radcliffe, an impious and vicious man, who hated the Queen much, but virtue and religion more. He was a professed Jacobite, and was, by many, thought a very bad physician; but others cried him up to the highest degree imaginable. He was called for, and it appeared but too evident that his opinion was depended on. Other physicians were called when it was too late; all symptoms were bad, yet still the Queen felt herself well."

Radcliffe's negative murder of Queen Anne was yet more amusing than his positive destruction of Mary. When Queen Anne was almost *in extremis*, Radcliffe was sent for. The Queen, though she never forgave him for his drunken ridicule of her vapours, had an exalted opinion of his professional talents, and had, more than once, winked at her ladies, consulting him about the health of their royal mistress. Now that death was at hand, Lady Masham sent a summons for the doctor; but he was at Carshalton, sick of his dying illness, and returned answer that it would be impossible for him to leave his country-seat and wait on her Majesty. Such was the absurd and superstitious belief in his mere presence, that the Queen was popularly pictured as having died because he was not present to see her draw her last breath. Whom he liked he could kill, and whom he liked could keep alive and well. Even Arbuthnot, a brother physician, was so tinctured with the popular prejudice, that he could gravely tell Swift of the pleasure Radcliffe had "in preserving my Lord Chief Justice Holt's wife, whom he attended out of spite to her husband, who wished her dead."

It makes one smile to read Charles Ford's letter to the sarcastic Dean on the subject of the Queen's last illness. "She continued ill the whole day. In the evening I spoke to Dr Arbuthnot, and he told me that he did not think her distemper was desperate. Radcliffe was sent for to Carshalton about noon, by order of council; but said he had taken physic and could not come. *In all probability he had saved her life; for I am told the late Lord Gower had been often in the condition with the gout in the head, and Radcliffe kept him alive many years after.*" The author of Gulliver must have grinned as he read this sentence. It was strange stuff to write about "that puppy Radcliffe" (as the Dean calls the physician in his journal to Stella) to the man who coolly sent out word to a Dublin mob that he had put off an eclipse to a more suitable time. The absurdity of Ford's letter is heightened by the fact that it was written before the Queen's death. It is dated July 31, 1714, and concludes with the following postscript:—"The Queen is something better, and the council again adjourned till eight in the morning." Surely the accusation, then, of negative womanslaughter was preferred somewhat prematurely. The next day, however, the Queen died; and then arose a magnificent hubbub of indignation against the impious doctor. The poor man himself sinking into the grave, was at that country-seat where he had entertained his medical friends with so many noisy orgies. But the cries for vengeance reached him in his retreat. "Give us back our ten days!" screamed the rabble of London round Lord Chesterfield's carriage. "Give us back our Queen!" was the howl directed against Radcliffe. The accused was a member of the House of Commons, having been elected M.P. for the town of Buckingham in the previous year; and positively a member (one of Radcliffe's intimate personal acquaintances) moved that the physician should be summoned to attend in his place and be censured for not attending her late Majesty. To a friend the doctor wrote from Carshalton on August 7, 1714:—"Dear Sir,—I could not have thought so old an acquaintance, and so good a friend as Sir John always professed himself, would have made such a motion against me. God knows my will to do her Majesty any service has ever got the start of my ability, and I have nothing that gives me greater anxiety and trouble than the death of that great and glorious Princess. I must do that justice to the physicians that attended her in her illness, from a sight of the method that was taken for her preservation, transmitted to me by Dr Mead, as to declare nothing was omitted for her preservation; but the people about her (the plagues of Egypt fall upon them!) put it out of the power of physick to be of any benefit to her. I know the nature of attending crowned heads to their last moments too well to be fond of waiting upon them, without being sent for by a proper authority. You have heard of pardons signed for physicians before a sovereign's demise. However, as ill as I was, I would have went to the Queen in a horse-litter, had either her Majesty, or those in commission next to her, commanded me so to do. You may tell Sir John as much, and assure him, from me, that his zeal for her Majesty will not excuse his ill usage of *a friend who has drunk many a hundred bottles with him*, and cannot, even after this breach of good understanding, that was ever preserved between us, but have a very good esteem for him."

So strong was the feeling against the doctor, that a set of maniacs at large formed a plan for his assassination. Fortunately, however, the plot was made known to him in the following letter:—

"Doctor,—Tho' I am no friend of yours, but, on the contrary, one that could wish your destruction in a legal way, for not preventing the death of our most excellent Queen, whom you had it in your power to save, yet I have such an aversion to the taking away men's lives unfairly, as to acquaint you that if you go to meet the gentlemen you have appointed to dine with at the 'Greyhound,' in Croydon, on Thursday next, you will be most certainly murthered. I am one of the persons engaged in the conspiracy, with twelve more, who are resolved to sacrifice you to the *Ghost of her late Majesty, that cries aloud for blood*; therefore, neither stir out of doors that day, nor any other, nor think of exchanging your present abode for your house at Hammersmith, since there and everywhere else we shall be in quest of you. I am touched with remorse, and give you this notice; but take care of yourself, lest I repent of it, and give proofs of so doing, by having it in my power to destroy you, who am your sworn enemy.—N. G."

That thirteen men could have been found to meditate such a ridiculous atrocity is so incredible, that one is inclined to suspect a hoax in this epistle. Radcliffe, however, did not see the letter in that light. Panic-struck, he kept himself a close prisoner to his house and its precincts, though he was very desirous of paying another visit to London—the monotony of his rural seclusion being broken only by the customary visits of his professional associates who came down to comfort and drink with him. The end, however, was fast approaching. The maladies under which he suffered were exacerbated by mental disquiet; and his powers suddenly failing him, he expired on the 1st of November, 1714, just three months after the death of the murdered Queen, of whose vapours he had spoken so disrespectfully.

His original biographer (from whose work all his many memoirs have been taken) tells the world that the great physician *"fell a victim to the ingratitude of a thankless world, and the fury of the gout."*

Radcliffe was an ignorant man, but shrewd enough to see that in the then existing state of medical science the book-learning of the Faculty could be but of little service to him. He was so notoriously deficient in the literature of his profession, that his warmest admirers made merry about it. Garth happily observed that for Radcliffe to leave a library was as if a eunuch should found a seraglio. Nor was Radcliffe ashamed to admit his lack of lore. Indeed, he was proud of it; and on the inquiry being made by Bathurst, the head of Trinity College, Oxford, where his study was, he pointed to a few vials, a skeleton, and an herbal, and answered, "This is Radcliffe's library." Mead, who rose into the first favour of the town as the doctor retired from it, was an excellent scholar; but far from assuming on that ground a superiority to his senior, made it the means of paying him a graceful compliment. The first time that Radcliffe called on Mead when in town he found his young friend reading Hippocrates.

"Do you read Hippocrates in Greek?" demanded the visitor.

"Yes," replied Mead, timidly fearing his scholarship would offend the great man.

"I never read him in my life," responded Radcliffe, sullenly.

"You, sir," was the rejoinder, "have no occasion—you are Hippocrates himself."

A man who could manufacture flattery so promptly and courageously deserved to get on. Radcliffe swallowed the fly, and was glad to be the prey of the expert angler. Only the day before, Mead had thrown in his ground-bait. As a promising young man, Radcliffe had asked him to a dinner-party at Carshalton, with the hospitable resolve of reducing such a promising young man to a state of intoxication, in the presence of the assembled elders of his profession. Mead, however, was not to be so managed. He had strong nerves, and was careful to drink as little as he could without attracting attention by his abstinence. The consequence was that Mead saw magnate after magnate disappear under the table, just as he had before seen magnum after magnum disappear above it; and still he retained his self-possession. At last he and his host were the only occupants of the banqueting-room left in a non-recumbent position. Radcliffe was delighted with his youthful acquaintance—loved him almost as well as he had loved Billy Nutley.

"Mead," cried the enthusiastic veteran to the young man, who anyhow had not *fallen* from his chair, "you are a *rising* man. You will succeed me."

"That, sir, is impossible," Mead adroitly answered; "You are Alexander the Great, and no one can succeed Radcliffe; to succeed to one of his kingdoms is the utmost of my ambition."

Charmed with the reply, Radcliffe exclaimed,

"By — —, I'll recommend you to my patients."

The promise was kept; and Mead endeavoured to repay the worldly advancement with spiritual council. "I remember," says Kennett (*vide* Lansdowne MSS., Brit. Mus.), "what Dr Mede has told to several of his friends, that he fell much into the favour of Dr Radcliffe a few years before his death, and visited him often at Carshalton, where he observed upon occasion that there was no Bible to be found in the house. Dr Mede had a mind to supply that defect, without taking any notice of it; and therefore one day carried down with him a very beautiful Bible that he had lately bought, which had lain in a closet of King William for his Majesty's own use, and left it as a curiosity that he had picked up by the way. When Dr Mede made the last visit to him he found that Dr R. had read in it as far as the middle of the Book of Exodus, from whence it might be inferred that he had never before read the Scriptures; as I doubt must be inferred of Dr Linacre, from the account given by Sir John Cheke."

The allusion to "the kingdom of Alexander the Great" reminds one of Arbuthnot's letter to Swift, in which the writer concludes his sketch of the proposed map of diseases for Martinus Scriblerus with—"Then the great diseases are like capital cities, with their symptoms all like streets and suburbs, with the roads that lead to other diseases. It is thicker set with towns than any Flanders map you ever saw. Radcliffe is painted at the corner of the map, contending for the universal empire of this world, and the rest of the physicians opposing his ambitious designs, with a project of a treaty of partition to settle peace."

As a practitioner, Radcliffe served the public as well as he did his own interests. The violent measures of bleeding, and the exhibition of reducing medicines, which constituted the popular practice even to the present generation, he regarded with distrust in some cases and horror in others. There is a good story told of him, that well illustrates his disapproval of a kill-or-cure system, and his hatred of Nurse Gibbons. John Bancroft, the eminent surgeon, who resided in Russell Street, Covent Garden, had a son attacked with inflammation of the lungs. Gibbons was called in, and prescribed the most violent remedies, or rather the most virulent irritants. The child became rapidly worse, and Radcliffe was sent for. "I can do nothing, sir," observed the doctor, after visiting his patient, "for the poor little boy's preservation. He is killed to all intents and purposes. But if you have any thoughts of putting a stone over him, I'll help you to an inscription." The offer was accepted, and over the child's grave, in Covent Garden churchyard, was placed a stone sculptured with a figure of a child laying one hand on his side, and saying, "Hic dolor," and pointing with the other to a death's head on which was engraved, "Ibi medicus." This is about the prettiest professional libel which we can point to in all the quarrels of the Faculty.

The uses to which the doctor applied his wealth every one knows. Notwithstanding his occasional acts of munificence, and a loss of £5000 in an East Indian venture, into which Betterton, the tragedian, seduced him, his accumulations were very great. In his will, after liberally providing for the members of his family and his dependents, he devoted his acquisitions to the benefit of the University of Oxford. From them have proceeded the Radcliffe Library, the Radcliffe Infirmary, the Radcliffe Observatory, and the Radcliffe Travelling Fellowships. It is true that nothing has transpired in the history of these last-mentioned endowments to justify us in reversing the sentiment of Johnson, who remarked to Boswell: "It is wonderful how little good Radcliffe's Travelling Fellowships have done. I know nothing that has been imported by them."

After lying in state at his own residence, and again in the University, Radcliffe's body was interred, with great pomp, in St. Mary's Church, Oxford. The royal gift of so large an estate (which during life he had been unable thoroughly to enjoy) to purchase a library, the contents of which he at no time could have read, of course provoked much comment. It need not be said that the testator's memory was, for the most part, extolled to the skies. He had died rich—a great virtue in itself. He was dead; and as men like to deal out censure as long as it can cause pain, and scatter praise when it can no longer create happiness, Radcliffe, the physician, the friend of suffering humanity, the benefactor of ancient and Tory Oxford, was spoken of in "most handsome terms." One could hardly believe that this great good man, this fervent Christian and sublime patriot, was the same man as he whom Steele had ridiculed for servile vanity, and to bring whom into contempt a play was written, and publicly acted, only ten years before, to the intense delight of the Duchess of Marlborough, and the applauding maids of honour.

The philosophic Mandeville, far from approving the behaviour of the fickle multitude, retained his old opinion of the doctor, and gave it to the world in his "Essay on Charity and Charity Schools." "That a man," writes Mandeville, "with small skill in physic, and hardly any learning, should by vile arts get into practice, and lay up great wealth, is no mighty wonder; but that he should so deeply work himself into the good opinion of the world as to gain the general esteem of a nation, and establish a reputation beyond all his contemporaries, with no other qualities but a perfect knowledge of mankind, and a capacity of making the most of it, is something extraordinary.

"If a man arrived to such a height of glory should be almost distracted with pride—sometime give his attendance on a servant, or any mean person, for nothing and at the same time neglect a nobleman that gives exhorbitant fees—at other times refuse to leave his bottle for his business, without any regard to the quality of the persons that sent for him, or the danger they are in; if he should be surly and morose, affect to be an humourist, treat his patients like dogs, though people of distinction, and value no man but what would deify him, and never call in question the certainty of his oracles; if he should insult all the world, affront the first nobility, and extend his insolence even to the royal family; if to maintain, as well as to increase, the fame of his sufficiency, he should scorn to consult his betters, on what emergency soever, look down with contempt on the most deserving of his profession, and never confer with any other physician but what will pay homage to his genius, creep to his humour, and ever approach him with all the slavish obsequiousness a court flatterer can treat a prince with; if a man in his life-time should discover, on the one hand, such manifest symptoms of superlative pride, and an insatiable greediness after wealth at the same time; and, on the other, no regard to religion or affection to his kindred, no compassion to the poor, and hardly any humanity to his fellow-creatures; if he gave no proofs that he loved his country, had a public spirit, or was a lover of the arts, of books, or of literature—what must we judge of his motive, the principle he acted from, when, after his death, we find that he has left a trifle among his relations who stood in need of it, and an immense treasure to a University that did not want it.

"Let a man be as charitable as it is possible for him to be, without forfeiting his reason or good sense, can he think otherwise, but that this famous physician did, in the making of his will, as in everything else, indulge his darling passion, entertaining his vanity with the happiness of the contrivance?"

This severe portrait is just about as true as the likeness of a man, painted by a conscientious enemy, usually is. Radcliffe was not endowed with a kindly nature. "Mead, I love you," said he to his fascinating adulator; "and I'll tell you a sure secret to make your fortune—use all mankind ill." Radcliffe carried out his rule by wringing as much as possible from, and returning as little as possible to, his fellowmen. He could not pay a tradesman's bill without a sense of keen suffering. Even a poor pavior, who had been employed to do a job to the stones before the doctor's house in Bloomsbury Square (whither the physician removed from Bow Street), could not get his money without a contest. "Why, you rascal!" cried the debtor, as he alighted from his chariot, "do you pretend to be paid for such a piece of work! Why, you have spoiled my pavement, and then covered it over with earth to hide the bad work."

"Doctor," responded the man, dryly, "mine is not the only bad work the earth hides."

Of course, the only course to pursue with a creditor who could dun in this sarcastic style was to pay, and be rid of him. But the doctor made up for his own avarice by being ever ready to condemn it in others.

Tyson, the miser, being near his last hour, magnanimously resolved to pay two of his 3,000,000 guineas to Radcliffe, to learn if anything could be done for his malady. The miserable old man came up with his wife from Hackney, and tottered into the consulting-room in Bloomsbury Square, with two guineas in his hand—

"You may go, sir," exclaimed Radcliffe, to the astonished wretch, who trusted he was unknown—"you may go home, and die, and be — —, without a speedy repentance; for both the grave and the devil are ready for Tyson of Hackney, who has grown rich out of the spoils of the public and the tears of orphans and widows. You'll be a dead man, sir, in ten days."

There are numerous stories extant relative to Radcliffe's practice; but nearly all those which bear the stamp of genuineness are unfit for publication in the present polite age. Such stories as the hasty-pudding one, re-edited by the pleasant author of "The Gold-headed Cane," can be found by the dozen, but the cumbrous workmanship of Mr. Joseph Miller is manifest in them all.

CHAPTER VIII.

THE DOCTOR AS A BON-VIVANT.

"What must I do, sir!" inquired an indolent bon-vivant of Abernethy.

"Live on sixpence a day, and earn it, sir," was the stern answer.

Gabriel Fallopius, who has given his name to a structure with which anatomists are familiar, gave the same reproof in a more delicate manner. With a smile he replied in the words of Terence,

"Otio abundas Antipho," — "Sir, you're as lazy as Hall's dog."

But, though medical practitioners have dealt in sayings like these, to do them bare justice, it must be admitted that their preaching has generally been contradicted by the practice. When medicine remained very much in the hands of the ladies, the composition of remedies, and the making of dinners, went on in the same apartment. Indeed hunger and thirst were but two out of a list of diseases that were ministered to by the attendants round a kitchen table. The same book held the receipts for dishes and the recipes for electuaries. In many an old hall of England the manual still remains from which three centuries ago the lady of the house learned to dress a boar's head or cure a cold. Most physicians would now disdain to give dietetic instruction to a patient beyond the most general directions; but there are cases where, even in these days, they stoop to do so, with advantage to themselves and their patients.

"I have ordered twelve dinners this morning," a cheery little doctor said to the writer of these pages, on the white cliffs of a well-known sea-side town.

"Indeed — I did not know that was your business."

"But it is. A host of rich old invalids come down here to be medicinally treated. They can't be happy without good living, and yet are so ignorant of the science and art of eating, that they don't know how to distinguish between a luxurious and pernicious diet, and a luxurious and wholesome one. They flock to the 'Duke's Hotel,' and I always tell the landlord what they are to have. Each dinner costs three or four guineas. They'd grudge them, and their consciences would be uneasy at spending so much money, if they ordered their dinners themselves. But when they regard the fare as medicine recommended by the doctor, there is no drawback to their enjoyment of it. Their confidence in me is unbounded."

The bottle and the board were once the doctor's two favourite companions. More than one eminent physician died in testifying his affection for them. In the days of tippling they were the most persevering of tavern-haunters. No wonder that some of them were as fat as Daniel Lambert, and that even more died sudden deaths from apoplexy. The obesity of Dr. Stafford was celebrated in an epitaph:—

"Take heed, O good traveller, and do not tread hard,
For here lies Dr. Stafford in all this churchyard."

Dr. Beddoes was so stout that the Clifton ladies used to call him their "walking feather-bed."

Dr. Flemyng weighed twenty stone and eleven pounds, till he reduced his weight by abstinence from the delicacies of the table, and by taking a quarter of an ounce of common Castile soap every night.

Dr. Cheyne's weight was thirty-two stone, till he cured himself by persevering in a temperate diet. Laughing at two unwieldly noblemen whose corpulence was the favourite jest of all the wits in the court, Louis XV. said to one of them, "I suppose you take little or no exercise."

"Your Majesty will pardon me," replied the bulky duke, "for I generally walk two or three times round my cousin every morning."

Sir Theodore Mayerne, who, though he was the most eminent physician of his time, did not disdain to write "Excellent and Well-Approved Receipts in Cookery, with the best way of Preserving," was killed by tavern wine. He died, after returning from supper in a Strand hotel; his immediate friends attributing his unexpected death to the quality of the beverage, but others, less charitable, setting it down to the quantity.

Not many years ago, about a score surgeons were dining together at a tavern, when, about five minutes after some very "particular port" had been sent round for the first time, they all fell back in their chairs, afflicted in various degrees with sickness, vertigo, and spasm. A more pleasant sight for the waiters can hardly be conceived. One after one the gentlemen were conveyed to beds or sofas. Unfortunately for the startling effect which the story would otherwise have produced, they none of them expired. The next day they remembered that, instead of relishing the "particular port," they had detected a very unpleasant smack in it. The black bottles were demanded from the trembling landlord, when chemical analysis soon discovered that they had been previously used for fly-poison, and had not been properly cleansed. A fine old crust of such a kind is little to be desired.

It would perhaps have been well had old Butler (mentioned elsewhere in these volumes) met with a similar mishap, if it had only made him a less obstinate frequenter of beer-shops. He loved tobacco, deeming it

"A physician
Good both for sound and sickly;
'Tis a hot perfume
That expels cold Rheume,
And makes it flow down quickly."

It is on record that he made one of his patients smoke twenty-five pipes at a sitting. But fond though he was of tobacco, he was yet fonder of beer. He invented a drink called "Butler's Ale," afterwards sold at the Butler's Head, in Mason's Alley, Basinghall Street. Indeed, he was a sad old scamp. Nightly he would go to the tavern, and drink deeply for hours, till his maid-servant, old Nell, came between nine and ten o'clock and *fetched* him home, scolding him all the way for being such a sot. But though Butler liked ale and wine for himself, he thought highly of water for other people. When he occupied rooms in the Savoy, looking over the Thames, a gentleman afflicted with an ague came to consult him. Butler tipped the wink to his servants, who flung the sick man, in the twinkling of an eye, slap out of the window into the river. We are asked to believe that "the surprise absolutely cured" the patient of his malady.

The physicians of Charles the Second's day were jolly fellows. They made deep drinking and intrigue part of their profession as well as of their practice. Their books contain arguments in favour of indulgence, which their passions suggested and the taste of the times approved. Tobias Whitaker and John Archer, both physicians in ordinary to the merry monarch, were representative men of their class. Whitaker, a Norfolk man, practised with success at Norwich before coming up to London. He published a discourse upon waters, that proved him very ignorant on the subject; and a treatise on the properties of wine, that is a much better testimony to the soundness of his understanding. Prefixed to his "Elenchus of opinions on Small-Pox," is a portrait that represents him as a well-looking fellow. That he was a sincere and discerning worshipper of Bacchus, is shown by his "Tree of Humane Life, or the Bloud of the Grape. Proving the possibilitie of maintaining humane life from infancy to extreame old age without any sicknesse by the use of Wine." In this work (sold, by the way, in the author's shop, Pope's Head Alley) we read of wine, —"This is the phisick that doth not dull, but sets a true edge upon nature, after operation leaveth no venomous contact. Sure I am this was ancient phisick, else what meant Avicenna, Rhasis, and Averroes, to move the body twice every month with the same; as it is familiar to Nature, so they used it familiarly. As for my own experience, though I have not lived yet so long as to love excesse, yet have I seene such powerful effects, both on my selfe and others, as if I could render no other reason, they were enough to persuade me of its excellencie, seeing extenuate withered bodies by it caused to be faire, fresh, plumpe, and fat, old and infirme to be young and sound, when as water or small-beer drinkers looke like apes rather than men."

John Archer, the author of "Every Man his own Doctor," and "Secrets Disclosed," was an advocate of generous diet and enlightened sensuality. His place of business was "a chamber in a Sadler's howse over against the Black Horse nigh Charing-cross," where his hours of attendance for some years were from 11 A. M. to 5 P. M. each day. On setting up a house at Knightsbridge, where he resided in great style, he shortened the number of hours daily passed in London. In 1684 he announced in one of his works—"For these and other Directions you may send to the Author, at his chamber against the *Mews* by Charing-cross, who is certainly there from twelve to four, at other times at his house at Knightsbridge, being a mile from Charing-cross, where is good air for cure of consumptions, melancholy, and other infirmities." He had also a business established in Winchester Street, near Gresham College, next door to the *Fleece Tavern.* Indeed, physician-in-ordinary to the King though he was, he did not think it beneath him to keep a number of apothecaries' shops, and, like Whitaker, to live by the sale of drugs as well as fees. His cordial dyet drink was advertised as costing 2*s*. 6*d*. per quart; for a box containing 30 morbus pills, the charge was 5*s*.; 40 corroborating pills were to be had for the same sum. Like Dr. Everard, he recommended his patients to smoke, saying that "tobacco smoke purified the air from infectious malignancy by its fragrancy, sweetened the breath, strengthened the brain and memory, and revived the sight to admiration." He sold tobacco, of a superior quality to the ordinary article of commerce, at 2*s*. and 1*s*. an ounce. "The order of taking it is like other tobacco at any time; its virtues may be perceived by taking one pipe, after which you will spit more, and your mouth will be dryer than after common tobacco, which you may moisten by drinking any warm drink, as coffee, &c., or with sugar candy, liquorish, or a raisin, and you will find yourself much refreshed."

Whilst Whitaker and Archer were advising men to smoke and drink, another physician of the Court was inventing a stomach-brush, in some respects much like the bottle-brush with which fly-poison ought to be taken from the interior of black bottles before wine is committed to them. This instrument was pushed down the gullet, and then poked about and turned round, much in the same way as a chimney-sweeper's brush is handled by a dexterous operator on soot. It was recommended that gentlemen should thus sweep out their insides not oftener than once a week, but not less frequently than once a month. The curious may find not only a detailed description but engraved likeness of this remarkable stomach-brush in the *Gentleman's Magazine*, vol. xx., for the year 1750.

It would be unfair to take leave of Dr. Archer without mentioning his three inventions, on which he justly prided himself not a little. He constructed a hot steam-bath, an oven "which doth with a small faggot bake a good quantity of anything," and "a compleat charriot that shall with any ordinary horse run swift with four or five people within, and there is place for more without, all which one horse can as easily draw as two horses." In these days of vapour baths, bachelors' kettles, and broughams, surely Dr. Archer ought to have a statue by the side of Jenner in Trafalgar Square.

The doctors of Anne's time were of even looser morals than their immediate predecessors. In taverns, over wine, they received patients and apothecaries. It became fashionable (a fashion that has lasted down to the present day) for a physician to scratch down his prescriptions illegibly; the mode, in all probability, arising from the fact that a doctor's hand was usually too unsteady to write distinctly.

Freind continually visited his patients in a state of intoxication. To one lady of high rank he came in such a state of confusion that when in her room he could only grumble to himself, "Drunk—drunk—drunk, by God!" Fortunately the fair patient was suffering from the same malady as her doctor, who (as she learnt from her maid on returning to consciousness) had made the above bluff comment on *her* case, and then had gone away. The next day, Freind was sitting in a penitent state over his tea, debating what apology he should offer to his aristocratic patient, when he was relieved from his perplexity by the arrival of a note from the lady herself enclosing a handsome fee, imploring her dear Dr. Freind to keep her secret, and begging him to visit her during the course of the day.

On another occasion Freind wrote a prescription for a member of an important family, when his faculties were so evidently beyond his control that Mead was sent for. On arriving, Mead, with a characteristic delicacy towards his professional friend, took up the tipsy man's prescription, and having looked at it, said, "'Pon my honour, Dr. Freind can write a better prescription when drunk than I can when sober."

Gibbons—the "Nurse Gibbons" of our old friend Radcliffe—was a deep drinker, disgusting, by the grossness of his debaucheries, the polite and epicurean Garth. But Gibbons did something for English dinner-tables worth remembering. He brought into domestic use the mahogany with which we have so many pleasant associations. His brother, a West Indian Captain, brought over some of the wood as ballast, thinking it might possibly turn to use. At first the carpenters, in a truly conservative spirit, refused to have anything to do with the "new wood," saying it was too hard for their tools. Dr. Gibbons, however, had first a candle-box and then a bureau made for Mrs. Gibbons out of the condemned material. The bureau so pleased his friends, amongst whom was the Duchess of Buckingham, that her Grace ordered a similar piece of furniture, and introduced the wood into high life, where it quickly became the fashion.

Of Radcliffe's drunkenness mention is made elsewhere. As an eater, he was a *gourmand*, not a *gourmet*. When Prince Eugene of Savoy came over to England on a diplomatic mission, his nephew, the Chevalier de Soissons, fell into the fashion of the town, roaming it at night in search of frays—a roaring, swaggering mohock. The sprightly Chevalier took it into his head that it would be a pleasant thing to thrash a watchman; so he squared up to one, and threatened to kill him. Instead of succumbing, the watchman returned his assailant's blows, and gave him an awful thrashing. The next day, what with the mauling he had undergone, and what with *delirium tremens*, the merry roisterer was declared by his physician, Sieur Swartenburgh, to be in a dying state. Radcliffe was called in, and acting on his almost invariable rule, told Prince Eugene that the young man must die, *because* Swartenburgh had maltreated him. The prophecy was true, if the criticism was not. The Chevalier died, and was buried amongst the Ormond family in Westminster Abbey—it being given out to the public that he had died of small-pox.

Prince Eugene conceived a strong liking for Radcliffe, and dined with him at the Doctor's residence. The dinner Radcliffe put before his guest is expressive of the coarseness both of the times and the man. On the table the only viands were barons of beef, jiggets of mutton, legs of pork, and such other ponderous masses of butcher's stuff, which no one can look at without discomfort, when the first edge has been taken off the appetite. Prince Eugene expressed himself delighted with "the food and liquors!"

George Fordyce, like Radcliffe, was fond of substantial fare. For more than twenty years he dined daily at Dolly's Chop-house. The dinner he there consumed was his only meal during the four-and-twenty hours, but its bulk would have kept a boa-constrictor happy for a twelvemonth. Four o'clock was the hour at which the repast commenced, when, punctual to a minute, the Doctor seated himself at a table specially reserved for him, and adorned with a silver tankard of strong ale, a bottle of port-wine, and a measure containing a quarter of a pint of brandy. Before the dinner was first put on, he had one light dish of a broiled fowl, or a few whitings. Having leisurely devoured this plate, the doctor took one glass of brandy, and asked for his steak. The steak was always a prime one, weighing one pound and a half. When the man of science had eaten the whole of it, he took the rest of his brandy, then drank his tankard of heady ale, and, lastly, sipped down his bottle of port. Having brought his intellects, up or down, to the standard of his pupils, he rose and walked down to his house in Essex Street to give his six o'clock lecture on Chemistry.

Dr. Beauford was another of the eighteenth-century physicians who thought temperance a vice that hadn't even the recommendation of transient pleasure. A Jacobite of the most enthusiastic sort, he was not less than Freind a favourite with the aristocracy who countenanced the Stuart faction. As he was known to be very intimate with Lord Barrymore, the Doctor was summoned, in 1745, to appear before the Privy-Council, and answer the questions of the custodians of his Majesty's safety and honour.

"You know Lord Barrymore?" said one of the Lords of Council.

"Intimately—most intimately,"—was the answer.

"You are continually with him?"

"We dine together almost daily when his Lordship is in town."

"What do you talk about?"

"Eating and drinking."

"And what else?"

"Oh, my lord, we never talk of anything except eating and drinking—drinking and eating."

A good deal of treasonable sentiment might have been exchanged in these discussions of eating and drinking. "God send this *crum-well down!*" was the ordinary toast of the Cavalier during the glorious Protectorate of Oliver. And long afterwards, English gentlemen of Jacobite sympathies, drinking "to the King," before they raised the glass to their lips, put it over the water-bottle, to indicate where the King was whose prosperity they pledged.

At the tavern in Finch Lane, where Beauford received the apothecaries who followed him, he drank freely, but never was known to give a glass from his bottle to one of his clients. In this respect he resembled Dr. Gaskin of Plymouth, a physician in fine practice in Devonshire at the close of the last century, who once said to a young beginner in his profession, "Young man, when you get a fee, don't give fifteen shillings of it back to your patient in beef and port-wine."

Contemporary with Beauford was Dr. Barrowby—wit, scholar, political partisan, and toper. Barrowby was the hero of an oft-told tale, recently attributed in the newspapers to Abernethy. When canvassing for a place on the staff of St.

Bartholomew's Hospital, Barrowby entered the shop of one of the governors, a grocer on Snow-hill, to solicit his influence and vote. The tradesman, bursting with importance, and anticipating the pleasure of getting a very low bow from a gentleman, strutted up the shop, and, with a mixture of insolent patronage and insulting familiarity, cried, "Well, friend, and what is your business?"

Barrowby paused for a minute, cut him right through with the glance of his eye, and then said, quietly and slowly, "I want a pound of plums."

Confused and blushing, the grocer did up the plums. Barrowby put them in his pocket, and went away without asking the fellow for his vote.

A good political story is told of Barrowby, the incident of which occurred in 1749, eleven years after his translation of Astruc's "Treatise" appeared. Lord Trentham (afterwards Lord Gower) and Sir George Vandeput were contesting the election for Westminster. Barrowby, a vehement supporter of the latter, was then in attendance on the notorious Joe Weatherby, master of the "Ben Jonson's Head," in Russell Street, who lay in a perilous state, emaciated by nervous fever. Mrs. Weatherby was deeply afflicted at her husband's condition, because it rendered him unable to vote for Lord Trentham. Towards the close of the polling days the Doctor, calling one day on his patient, to his great astonishment found him up, and almost dressed by the nurse and her assistants.

"Hey-day! what's the cause of this?" exclaims Barrowby. "Why are you up without my leave?"

"Dear Doctor," says Joe, in a broken voice, "I am going to poll."

"To poll!" roars Barrowby, supposing the man to hold his wife's political opinions, "you mean going to the devil! Get to bed, man, the cold air will kill you. If you don't get into bed instantly you'll be dead before the day is out."

"I'll do as you bid me, doctor," was the reluctant answer. "But as my wife was away for the morning, I thought I could get as far as Covent Garden Church, and vote for Sir George Vandeput."

"How, Joe, for Sir George?"

"Oh, yes, sir, I don't go with my wife. I am a Sir George's man."

Barrowby was struck by a sudden change for the better in the man's appearance, and said, "Wait a minute, nurse. Don't pull off his stockings. Let me feel his pulse. Humph—a good firm stroke! You took the pills I ordered you?"

"Yes, sir, but they made me feel very ill."

"Ay, so much the better; that's what I wished. Nurse, how did he sleep?"

"Charmingly, sir."

"Well, Joe," said Barrowby, after a few seconds' consideration, "if you are bent on going to this election, your mind ought to be set at rest. It's a fine sunny day, and a ride will very likely do you good. So, bedad, I'll take you with me in my chariot."

Delighted with his doctor's urbanity, Weatherby was taken off in the carriage to Covent Garden, recorded his vote for Sir George Vandeput, was brought back in the same vehicle, and died *two* hours afterwards, amidst the reproaches of his wife and her friends of the Court party.

Charles the Second was so impressed with the power of the Medical Faculty in influencing the various intrigues of political parties, that he averred that Dr. Lower, Nell Gwynn's physician, did more mischief than a troop of horse. But Barrowby was prevented, by the intrusion of death, from rendering effectual service to his party. Called away from a dinner-table, where he was drinking deeply and laughing much, to see a patient, he got into his carriage, and was driven off. When the footman opened the door, on arriving at the house of sickness, he found his master dead. A fit of apoplexy had struck him down, whilst he was still a young man, and just as he was ascending to the highest rank of his profession.

John Sheldon was somewhat addicted to the pleasures of the table. On one occasion, however, he had to make a journey fasting. The son of a John Sheldon, an apothecary who carried on business in the Tottenham Court Road, a few doors from the Black Horse Yard, Sheldon conceived in early life a strong love for mechanics. At Harrow he was birched for making a boat and floating it. In after life he had a notable scheme for taking whales with poisoned harpoons; and, to test its merit, actually made a voyage to Greenland. He was moreover the first Englishman to make an ascent in a balloon. He went with Blanchard, and had taken his place in the car, when the aeronaut, seeing that his machine was too heavily weighted, begged him to get out.

"If you are my friend, you will alight. My fame, my all, depends on success," exclaimed Blanchard.

"I won't," bluntly answered Sheldon, as the balloon manifested symptoms of rising.

In a furious passion, the little air-traveller exclaimed, "Then I starve you! Point du chicken, by Gar, you shall have no chicken." So saying, he flung the hamper of provisions out of the car, and, thus lightened, the balloon went up.

Abernethy is said to have reproved an over-fed alderman for his excesses at table in the following manner. The civic footman was ordered to put a large bowl under the sideboard, and of whatever he served his master with to throw the same quantity into the bowl as he put on the gourmand's plate. After the repast was at an end, the sated feaster was requested to look into the bowl at a nauseous mess of mock turtle, turbot, roast-beef, turkey, sausages, cakes, wines, ale, fruits, cheese.

Sir Richard Jebb showed little favour to the digestion thinking it was made to be used — not nursed. Habitually more rough and harsh than Abernethy in his most surly moods, Jebb offended many of his patients. "That's *my* way," said he to a noble invalid, astonished at his rudeness. "Then," answered the sick man, pointing to the door, "I beg you'll make that your way."

To all questions about diet Jebb would respond tetchily or carelessly.

"Pray, Sir Richard, may I eat a muffin?" asked a lady.

"Yes, madam, 'tis the *best* thing you can take."

"Oh, dear! Sir Richard, I am glad of that. The other day you said it was the worst thing in the world for me."

"Good, madam, I said so last Tuesday. This isn't a Tuesday—is it?"

To another lady who asked what she might eat he said contemptuously, "Boiled turnips."

"Boiled turnips!" was the answer; "you forget, Sir Richard—I told you I could not bear boiled turnips."

"Then, madam," answered Sir Richard, sternly, as if his sense of the moral fitness of things was offended, "you must have a d— —d vitiated appetite."

Sir Richard's best set of dietetic directions consisted of the following negative advice, given to an old gentleman who put the everlasting question, "What may I eat?" "My directions, sir, are simple. You must not eat the poker, shovel, or tongs, for they are hard of digestion; nor the bellows; but anything else you please."

Even to the King, Sir Richard was plain-spoken. George the Third lamented to him the restless spirit of his cousin, Dr. John Jebb, the dissenting minister. "And please your Majesty," was the answer, "if my cousin were in heaven he would be a reformer."

Dr. Babington used to tell a story of an Irish gentleman, for whom he prescribed an emetic, saying, "My dear doctor, it is of no use your giving me an emetic. I tried it twice in Dublin, and it would not stay on my stomach either time." Jebb's stomach would have gone on tranquilly, even when entertaining an emetic.

Jebb, with all his bluntness, was a mean lover of the atmosphere of the Court. His income was subject to great fluctuations, as the whims of his fashionable employers ran for or against him. Sir Edward Wilmont's receipts sank from £3000 to £300, in consequence of his having lost two ladies of quality at the Court. Jebb's revenue never varied so much as this, but the £15,000 (the greatest sum he ever made in one year) often fell off by thousands. This fact didn't tend to lessen his mortification at the loss of a great patient. When George the Third dismissed him, and took Sir George Baker in his place, he nearly died of chagrin. And when he was recalled to attend the royal family in the measles, he nearly died of delight. This ruling passion exhibited itself strongly in death. When he was on his deathbed, the Queen, by the hand of a German lady, wrote to inquire after his condition. So elated was the poor man with this act of royal benignity, that he grasped the letter, and never let go his hold of it till the breath of life quitted his attenuated body.

This chapter has been for the most part on the feasting of physicians. We'll conclude it with a few words on their fasts. In the house of a Strand grocer there used to be a scientific club, of which the principal members were—W. Heberden, M.D., J. Turton, M.D., G. Baker, M.D., Sir John Pringle, Sir William Watson, and Lord C. Cavendish who officiated as president. Each member paid sixpence per evening for the use of the grocer's dining-room. The club took in one newspaper, and the only refreshment allowed to be taken at the place of meeting was—water.

The most abstemious of eminent physicians was Sir Hans Sloane, the president of the Royal Society and of the College of Physicians, and (in a certain sense) the founder of the British Museum. A love of money made him a hater of all good things, except money and his museum. He gave up his winter soirées in Blooms-bury Square, in order to save his tea and bread and butter. At one of these scientific entertainments Handel offended the scientific knight deeply by laying a muffin on one of his books. "To be sure it was a gareless trick," said the composer, when telling the story, "bud it tid no monsdrous mischief; pode it but the old poog-vorm treadfully oud of sorts. I offered my best apologies, but the old miser would not have done with it. If it had been a biscuit, it would not have mattered; but muffin and pudder. And I said, *Ah, mine Gotd, that is the rub!—it is the pudder!* Now, mine worthy friend, Sir Hans Sloane, you have a nodable excuse, you may save your doast and pudder, and lay it to that unfeeling gormandizing German; and den I knows it will add something to your life by sparing your *burse*."

The eccentric Dr. Glyn of Cambridge, rarely dined, but used to satisfy his hunger at chance times by cutting slices off a cold joint (a constant ornament of the side-table in his study), and eating them while standing. To eat such a dinner in such an attitude would be to fare little better than the ascetic physician who used twice a week to dine off two Abernethy biscuits, consumed as he walked at the pace of four miles an hour. However wholesome they may be, the hard biscuits, known as Abernethies (but in the construction of which, by-the-by, Abernethy was no more concerned than were Wellington and Blucher in making the boots that bear their names), are not convivial cates, though one would rather have to consume them than the calomel sandwiches which Dr. Curry (popularly called Dr. Calomel Curry) used to give his patients.

CHAPTER IX.

FEES.

From the earliest times the Leech (Leighis), or healer, has found, in the exercise of his art, not only a pleasant sense of being a public benefactor, but also the means of private advancement. The use the churchmen made of their medical position throughout Christendom (both before and after that decree of the council of Tours, A.D. 1163, which forbade priests and deacons to perform surgical operations in which cauteries and incisions were employed), is attested by the broad acres they extracted, for their religious corporations, as much from the gratitude as from the superstition of their patients. And since the Reformation, from which period the vocations of the spiritual and the bodily physician have been almost entirely kept apart, the practitioners of medicine have had cause to bless the powers of sickness. A good story is told of Arbuthnot. When he was a young man (ere he had won the patronage of Queen Anne, and the friendship of Swift and Pope), he settled at Dorchester, and endeavoured to get practice in that salubrious town. Nature obviated his good intentions: he wished to minister to the afflicted, if they were rich enough to pay for his ministrations, but the place was so healthy that it contained scarce half-a-dozen sick inhabitants. Arbuthnot determined to quit a field so ill-adapted for a display of his philanthropy. "Where are you off to?" cried a friend, who met him riding post towards London. "To leave your confounded place," was the answer, "for a man can neither live nor die there." But to arrive at wealth was not amongst Arbuthnot's faculties; he was unable to use his profession as a trade; and only a few weeks before his death he wrote, "I am as well as a man can be who is gasping for breath, and has a house full of men and women unprovided for."

Arbuthnot's ill-luck, however, was quite out of the ordinary rule. Fuller says (1662), "Physic hath promoted many more, and that since the reign of King Henry VIII. Indeed, before his time, I find a doctor of physic, father to Reginald, first and last Lord Bray. But this faculty hath flourished much the three last fifty years; it being true of physic, what is said of Sylla, 'suos divitiis explevit.' Sir William Butts, physician to King Henry VIII., Doctor Thomas Wendy, and Doctor Hatcher, Queen Elizabeth's physician, raised worshipful families in Norfolk, Cambridge, and Lincolnshire, having borne the office of Sheriff in this county." Sir William Butts was rewarded for his professional services by Henry VIII. with the honour of Knighthood, and he attended that sovereign when the royal confirmation was given, in 1512, to the charter of the barber-surgeons of London. Another eminent physician of the same period, who also arrived at the dignity of knighthood, was

John Ayliffe, a sheriff of London, and merchant of Blackwell-Hall. His epitaph records:—

> "In surgery brought up in youth,
> A knight here lieth dead;
> A knight and eke a surgeon, such
> As England seld' hath bred.
>
> "For which so sovereign gift of God,
> Wherein he did excell,
> King Henry VIII. called him to court,
> Who loved him dearly well.
>
> "King Edward, for his service sake,
> Bade him rise up a knight;
> A name of praise, and ever since
> He Sir John Ayliffe hight."

This mode of rewarding medical services was not unfrequent in those days, and long before. Ignorance as to the true position of the barber in the middle ages has induced the popular and erroneous belief that the barber-surgeon had in olden times a contemptible social status. Unquestionably his art has been elevated during late generations to a dignity it did not possess in feudal life; but it might be argued with much force, that the reverse has been the case with regard to his rank. Surgery and medicine were arts that nobles were proud to practise for honour, and not unfrequently for emolument. The reigns of Elizabeth and her three predecessors in sovereign power abounded in medical and surgical amateurs. Amongst the fashionable empirics Bulleyn mentions Sir Thomas Elliot, Sir Philip Paris, Sir William Gasgoyne, Lady Taylor and Lady Darrel, and especially that "goodly hurtlesse Gentleman, Sir Andrew Haveningham, who learned water to kill a canker of his own mother." Even an Earl of Derby, about this time, was celebrated for his skill in *chirurgerie* and *bone-setting*, as also was the Earl of Herfurth. The Scots nobility were enthusiastic dabblers in such matters; and we have the evidence of Buchanan and Lindsay as to James IV. of Scotland, "quod vulnera scientissime tractaret," to use the former authority's words, and in the language of the latter, that he was "such a *cunning chirurgeon*, that none in his realm who used that craft but would take his counsel in all their proceedings." The only art which fashionable people now-a-days care much to meddle with is literature. In estimating the difference between the position of an eminent surgeon now, and that which he would have occupied in earlier times, we must remember that life and hereditary knighthood are the highest dignities to which he is now permitted to aspire; although since this honour was first accorded to him it has so fallen in public estimation, that it has almost ceased to be an honour at all. It can scarcely be questioned that if Sir Benjamin Brodie were to be elevated to the rank of a Baron of the realm, he would still not occupy a better position, in regard to the rest of society, than that which Sir William Butts and Sir John Ayliffe did after they were knighted. A fact that definitely fixes the high esteem in which Edward III. held his medical officers, is one of his grants—"Quod Willielmus Holme Sirurgicus Regis pro vitâ suâ possit, fugare, capere, et asportare omnimodas feras in quibuscunque forestis, chaccis parcis et warrennis regis." Indeed, at a time when the highest dignitaries of the Church, the proudest bishops and the wealthiest abbots, practised as physicians, it followed, as a matter of course, that everything pertaining to their profession was respected.

From remote antiquity the fee of the healer has been regarded as a voluntary offering for services gratuitously rendered. The pretender to the art always stuck out for a price, and in some form or other made the demand which was imprinted on the pillboxes of Lilly's successor, John Case,

> "Here's fourteen pills for thirteen pence,
> Enough in any man's own con-sci-ence."

But the true physician always left his reward to be measured by the gratitude and justice of the benefited. He extorted nothing, but freely received that which was freely given. Dr. Doran, with his characteristic erudition, says, "Now there is a religious reason why fees are supposed not to be taken by physicians. Amongst the Christian martyrs are reckoned the two eastern brothers, Damian and Cosmas. They practised as physicians in Cilicia, and they were the first mortal practitioners who refused to take recompense for their work. Hence they were called Anargyri, or 'without money.' All physicians are pleasantly supposed to follow this example. They never take fees, like Damian and Cosmas; but they meekly receive what they know will be given out of Christian humility, and with a certain or uncertain reluctance, which is the nearest approach that can be made in these times to the two brothers who were in partnership at Egea in Cilicia."

But, with all due respect to our learned writer, there is a much better reason for the phenomenon. Self-interest, and not a Christian ambition to resemble the charitable Cilician brothers, was the cause of physicians preferring a system of gratuities to a system of legal rights. They could scarcely have put in *a claim* without defining the *amount claimed*; and they soon discovered that a rich patient, left to his generosity, folly, and impotent anxiety to propitiate the mysterious functionary who presided over his life, would, in a great majority of cases, give ten, or even a hundred times as much as they in the wildest audacity of avarice would ever dare to ask for.

Seleucus, for having his son Antiochus restored to health, was fool enough to give sixty thousand crowns to Erasistratus: and for their attendance on the Emperor Augustus, and his two next successors, no less than four physicians received annual pensions of two hundred and fifty thousand sesterces apiece. Indeed, there is no saying what a sick man will not give his doctor. The "cacoethes donandi" is a manifestation of enfeebled powers which a high-minded physician is often called upon to resist, and an unprincipled one often basely turns to his advantage. Alluding to this feature of the sick, a deservedly successful and honourable practitioner, using the language of one of our Oriental pro-consuls, said with a laugh to the writer of these pages, "I wonder at my moderation."

But directly health approaches, this desirable frame of mind disappears. When the devil was sick he was a very different character from what he was on getting well. 'Tis so with ordinary patients, not less than satanic ones. The man who, when he is in his agonies, gives his medical attendant double fees three times a day (and vows, please God he recover, to make his fortune by trumpeting his praises to the world), on becoming convalescent, grows irritable, suspicious, and distant,—and by the time he can resume his customary occupations, looks on his dear benefactor and saviour as a designing rascal, bent on plundering him of his worldly possessions. Euricus Cordus, who died in 1535, seems to have taken the worst possible time for getting his payment; but it cannot be regretted that he did so, as his experiences inspired him to write the following excellent epigram:—

> "Tres medicus facies habet; unam quando rogatur,
> Angelicam; mox est, cum juvat, ipse Deus.
> Post ubi curato, poscit sua proemia, morbo,
> Horridus apparet, terribilisque Sathan."

> "Three faces wears the doctor: when first sought,
> An angel's—and a God's the cure half wrought:
> But when, that cure complete, he seeks his fee,
> The Devil looks then less terrible than he."

Illustrative of the same truth is a story told of Bouvart. On entering one morning the chamber of a French Marquis, whom he had attended through a very dangerous illness, he was accosted by his noble patient in the following terms:—

"Good day to you, Mr. Bouvart; I feel quite in spirits, and think my fever has left me."

"I am sure it has," replied Bouvart, dryly. "The very first expression you used convinced me of it."

"Pray, explain yourself."

"Nothing is easier. In the first days of your illness, when your life was in danger, I was your *dearest friend*; as you began to get better, I was your *good Bouvart*; and now I am Mr. Bouvart: depend upon it you are quite recovered."

In fact, the affection of a patient for his physician is very like the love a candidate for a borough has for an individual elector—he is very grateful to him, till he has got all he wants out of him. The medical practitioner is unwise not to recognize this fact. Common prudence enjoins him to act as much as possible on the maxim of "accipe dum dolet"—"take your fee while your patient is in pain."

But though physicians have always held themselves open to take as much as they can get, their ordinary remuneration has been fixed in divers times by custom, according to the locality of their practice, the rank of their patients, the nature of the particular services rendered, and such other circumstances. In China the rule is "no cure, no pay," save at the Imperial court, where the physicians have salaries that are cut off during the continuance of royal indisposition. For their sakes it is to be hoped that the Emperor is a temperate man, and does not follow the example of George the Fourth, who used to drink Maraschino between midnight and four o'clock in the morning; and then, when he awoke with a furred tongue, from disturbed sleep, used to put himself under the hands of his doctors. Formerly the medical officers of the English monarch were paid by salary, though doubtless they were offered, and were not too proud to accept, fees as well. Coursus de Gungeland, Edward the Third's apothecary, had a pension of sixpence a-day—a considerable sum at that time; and Ricardus Wye, the surgeon of the same king, had twelve-pence a day, and eight marks per annum. "Duodecim denarios per diem, et octo marcas per annum, pro vadiis suis pro vitâ." In the royal courts of Wales, also, the fees of surgeons and physicians were fixed by law—a surgeon receiving, as payment for curing a slight wound, only the blood-stained garments of the injured person; but for healing a dangerous wound he had the bloody apparel, his board and lodging during the time his services were required, and one hundred and eighty pence.

At a very early period in England a doctor looked for his palm to be crossed with gold, if his patient happened to be a man of condition. In Henry VIII.'s reign a Cambridge physician was presented by the Earl of Cumberland with a fee of £1—but this was at least double what a commoner would then have paid. Stow complains that while in Holland half-a-crown was looked upon as a proper remuneration for a single visit paid by a skilled physician, the medical practitioners of London scorned "to touch any metal but gold."

It is no matter of uncertainty what the physician's ordinary fee was at the close of the sixteenth and the commencement of the seventeenth century. It was ten shillings, as is certified by the following extract from "Physick lies a-bleeding: the Apothecary turned Doctor"—published in 1697:—

"*Gallipot*—Good sir, be not so unreasonably passionate and I'll tell you. Sir, the Pearl Julep will be 6*s.* 8*d.*, Pearls being dear since our clipt money was bought. The Specific Bolus, 4*s.* 6*d.*, I never reckon less; my master in Leadenhall Street never set down less, be it what it would. The Antihysterick Application 3*s.* 6*d.* (a common one is but 2*s.* 6*d.*), and the Anodyne Draught 3*s.* 4*d.*—that's all, sir; a small matter and please you, sir, for your lady. My fee is what you please, sir. All the bill is *but* 18*s.*

"*Trueman*—Faith, then, d'ye make a *but* at it? I do suppose, to be very genteel, I must give you a crown.

"*Gallipot*—If your worship please; I take it to be a fair and an honest bill.

"*Trueman*—Do you indeed? But I wish you had called a doctor, perhaps he would have advised her to have forebore taking anything, as yet at least, so I had saved 13*s.* in my pocket."

"Physick lies a-bleeding" was written during the great Dispensarian War, which is touched upon in another part of these pages; and its object was to hold up physicians as models of learning and probity, and to expose the extortionate practices of the apothecaries. It must therefore be read with caution, and with due allowance for the license of satire, and the violence of a party statement. But the statement that 10*s.* was the *customary* fee is clearly one that may be accepted as truthful. Indeed, the unknown and needy doctors were glad to accept less. The author of "The Dispensarians are the Patriots of Britain," published in 1708, represents the humbler physicians being nothing better than the slaves of the opulent apothecaries, accepting half their right fee, and taking instead 25 or 50 per cent. of the amount paid for drugs to the apothecary. "They (the powerful traders)," says the writer, "offered the Physicians 5*s.* and 10*s.* in the pound, to excite their industry to prescribe the larger abundance to all the disorders."

But physicians daily received more than their ten shillings at a time. In confirmation of this, a good anecdote may be related of Sir Theodore Mayerne. Sir Theodore Mayerne, a native of Geneva, was physician to Henry IV. and Louis XIII. of France, and subsequently to James I., Charles I., and Charles II. of England. As a physician, who had the honour of attending many crowned heads, he ranks above Caius, who was physician to Edward VI., Mary, and Elizabeth—Ambrose Paré, the inventor of ligatures for severed arteries, who was physician and surgeon to Henry II., Francis II., Charles IX., and Henry III. of France—and Sir Henry Halford, who attended successively George III., George IV., William IV., and Victoria. It is told of Sir Theodore, that when a friend, after consulting him, foolishly put two broad gold pieces (six-and-thirty shillings each) on the table, he quietly pocketed them. The patient, who, as a friend, expected to have his fee refused, and therefore (deeming it well to indulge in the magnificence of generosity when it would cost him nothing) had absurdly exhibited so large a sum, did not at all relish the sight of its being netted. His countenance, if not his tongue, made his mortification manifest. "Sir," said Sir Theodore, "I made my will this morning; and if it should appear that I refused a fee, I might be deemed *non compos.*"

The "Levamen Infirmi," published in 1700, shows that a century had not, at that date, made much difference in the scale of remuneration accorded to surgeons and physicians. "To a graduate in physick," this authority states, "his due is about ten shillings, though he commonly expects or demands twenty. Those that are only licensed physicians, their due is no more than six shillings and eight-pence, though they commonly demand ten shillings. A surgeon's fee is twelve-pence a mile, be his journey far or near; ten groats to set a bone broke, or out of joint; and for letting blood one shilling; the cutting off or amputation of any limb is five pounds, but there is no settled price for the cure." These charges are much the same as those made at the present day by country surgeons to their less wealthy patients, with the exception of a fee for setting a bone, or reducing a dislocation, which is absurdly out of proportion to the rest of the sums mentioned.

Mr William Wadd, in his very interesting "Memorabilia," states, that the physicians who attended Queen Caroline had five hundred guineas, and the surgeons three hundred guineas each; and that Dr. Willis was rewarded for his successful attendance on his Majesty King George III., by £1500 per annum for twenty years, and £650 per annum to his son for life. The other physicians, however, had only thirty guineas each visit to Windsor, and ten guineas each visit to Kew.

These large fees put us in mind of one that ought to have been paid to Dr. King for his attendance on Charles the Second. Evelyn relates—"1685, Feb. 4, I went to London, hearing his Majesty had ben, the Monday before (2 Feb.), surprised in his bed-chamber with an apoplectic fit; so that if, by God's providence, Dr King (that excellent chirurgeon as well as physitian) had not been actually present, to let his bloud (having his lancet in his pocket), his Majesty had certainly died that moment, which might have ben of direful consequence, there being nobody else present with the king save this doctor and one more, as I am assured. It was a mark of the extraordinary dexterity, resolution, and presence of mind in the Dr to let him bloud in the very paroxysm, without staying the coming of other physicians, which regularly should have ben done, and for want of which he must have a regular pardon, as they tell me." For this promptitude and courage the Privy-Council ordered £1000 to be given to Dr. King—but he never obtained the money.

In a more humourous, but not less agreeable manner, Dr. Hunter (John Hunter's brother), was disappointed of payment for his professional services. On a certain occasion he was suffering under such severe indisposition that he was compelled to keep his bed, when a lady called and implored to be admitted to his chamber for the benefit of his advice. After considerable resistance on the part of the servants, she obtained her request; and the sick physician, sitting up in his bed, attended to her case, and prescribed for it. "What is your fee, sir?" the lady asked when the work was done. The doctor, with the prudent delicacy of his order, informed his patient that it was a rule with him never to fix his fee; and, on repeated entreaty that he would depart from his custom, refused to do so. On this the lady rose from her seat, and courteously thanking the doctor, left him—not a little annoyed at the result of his squeamishness or artifice.

This puts us in mind of the manner in which an eminent surgeon not long since was defrauded of a fee, under circumstances that must rouse the indignation of every honourable man against the delinquent. Mr. — — received, in his consulting room, a gentleman of military and prepossessing exterior, who, after detailing the history of his sufferings, implored the professional man he addressed to perform for him a certain difficult and important operation. The surgeon consented, and on being asked what remuneration he would require, said that his fee was a hundred guineas.

"Sir," replied the visitor with some embarrassment, "I am very sorry to hear you say so. I feel sure my case without you will terminate fatally; but I am a poor half-pay officer, in pecuniary difficulties, and I could not, even if it were to save my soul, raise half the sum you mention."

"My dear sir," responded the surgeon frankly, and with the generosity which is more frequently found amongst medical practitioners than any other class of men, "don't then disturb yourself. I cannot take a less fee than I have stated, for my character demands that I should not have two charges, but I am at liberty to remit my fee altogether. Allow me, then, the very great pleasure of attending a retired officer of the British army gratuitously."

This kindly offer was accepted. Mr. — — not only performed the operation, but visited his patient daily for more than three weeks without ever accepting a guinea—and three months after he had restored the sick man to health, discovered that, instead of being in necessitous circumstances, he was a magistrate and deputy-lieutenant for his county, and owner of a fine landed estate.

"And, by — —!" exclaimed the fine-hearted surgeon—when he narrated this disgraceful affair, "I'll act exactly in the same way to the next poor man who gives me his *word of honour* that he is not rich enough to pay me."

The success of Sir Astley Cooper was beyond that of any medical practitioner of modern times; but it came very gradually. His earnings for the first nine years of his professional career progressed thus:—In the first year he netted five guineas; in the second, twenty-six pounds; in the third, sixty-four pounds; in the fourth, ninety-six pounds; in the fifth, a hundred pounds; in the sixth, two hundred pounds; in the seventh, four hundred pounds; in the eighth, six hundred and ten pounds; and in the ninth, the year in which he secured his hospital appointment, eleven hundred pounds. But the time came when the patients stood for hours in his ante-rooms waiting to have an interview with the great surgeon, and after all, their patients were dismissed without being admitted to the consulting-room. Sir Astley's man, Charles, with all the dignity that became so eminent a man's servant, used to say to these disappointed applicants, in a tone of magnificent patronage, when they reappeared the next morning after their effectless visit, "I am not at all sure that *we* shall be able to attend to-day to you, gentlemen, for *we* are excessively busy, and our list is perfectly full for the day; but if you'll wait I will see what can be done for you!"

The highest amount that Sir Astley received in any one year was £21,000. This splendid income was an exceptional one. For many years, however, he achieved more than £15,000 per annum. As long as he lived in the City after becoming celebrated he made an enormous, but fluctuating, revenue, the state of the money-market having an almost laughable effect on the size of the fees paid him. The capitalists who visited the surgeon in Broad Street, in three cases out of four, paid in cheques, and felt it beneath their dignity to put pen to paper for a smaller sum than five guineas. After Sir Astley moved to the West End he had a more numerous and at the same time more aristocratic practice; but his receipts were never so much as they were when he dwelt within the Lord Mayor's jurisdiction. His more distinguished patients invariably paid their guineas in cash, and many of them did not consider it inconsistent with patrician position to give single fees. The citizens were the fellows to pay. Mr. William Coles, of Mincing Lane, for a long period paid Sir Astley £600 a year, the visits of the latter being principally made to Mr. Cole's seat near Croydon. Another "City man," who consulted the surgeon in Broad Street, and departed without putting down any honorarium whatever, sent a cheque for £63 10*s.*, with the following characteristic note:—

"DEAR SIR—When I had first the pleasure of seeing you, you requested, as a favour, that I would consider your visit on the occasion as a friend. I now, sir, must request you will return the compliment by accepting the enclosed draft as an act of friendship. It is the profit on £2000 of the ensuing loan, out of a small sum Sir F. Baring had given, of appropriating for your chance."

The largest fee Sir Astley Cooper ever received was paid him by a West Indian millionaire named Hyatt. This gentleman having occasion to undergo a painful and perilous operation, was attended by Drs. Lettsom and Nelson as physicians, and Sir Astley as chirurgeon. The wealthy patient, his treatment having resulted most successfully, was so delighted that he fee'd his physicians with 300 guineas each. "But you, sir," cried the grateful old man, sitting up in his bed, and speaking to his surgeon, "shall have something better. There, sir—take *that*." The *that* was the convalescent's night-cap, which he flung at the dexterous operator. "Sir," replied Sir Astley, picking up the cap, "I'll pocket the affront." It was well he did so, for on reaching home he found in the cap a draft for 1000 guineas. This story has been told in various ways, but all its tellers agree as to the amount of the prize.

Catherine, the Empress of Russia, was even more munificent than the West Indian planter. When Dr. Dimsdale, for many years a Hertford physician, and subsequently the parliamentary representative of that borough, went over to Russia and inoculated the Empress and her son, in the year 1768, he was rewarded with a fee of £12,000, a pension for life of £500 per annum, and the rank of Baron of the Empire. But if Catherine paid thus handsomely for increased security of life, a modern emperor of Austria put down a yet more royal fee for his death-warrant. When on his death-bed the Emperor Joseph asked Quarin his opinion of his case, the physician told the monarch that he could not possibly live forty-eight hours. In acknowledgment of this frank declaration of the truth, the Emperor created Quarin a Baron, and gave him a pension of more than £2000 per annum to support the rank with.

A goodly collection might be made of eccentric fees given to the practitioners of the healing art. William Butler, who, in his moroseness of manner, was the prototype of Abernethy, found (*vide* Fuller's "English Worthies") more pleasure in "presents than money; loved what was pretty rather than what was costly; and preferred rarities to riches." The number of physicians is large who have won the hands of heiresses in the discharge of their professional avocations. But of them we purpose to speak at length hereafter. Joshua Ward, the Thames Street drysalter, who made a fortune by his "Drop and Pill,"

> "Of late, without the least pretence to skill,
> Ward's grown a famed physician by a pill,"

was so successfully puffed by Lord Chief Baron Reynolds and General Churchill, that he was called in to prescribe for the king. The royal malady disappeared in consequence, or in spite, of the treatment; and Ward was rewarded with a solemn vote of the House of Commons, protecting him from the interdictions of the College of Physicians; and, as an additional fee, he asked for, and obtained, the privilege of driving his carriage through St. James's Park.

The pertinacity with which the members of the medical profession cling to the shilling of "the guinea" is amusing. When Erskine used to order "The Devil's Own" to *charge*, he would cry out "Six-and-eightpence!" instead of the ordinary word of command. Had his Lordship been colonel of a volunteer corps of physicians, he would have roused them to an onward march by "A guinea!" Sometimes patients object to pay the extra shilling over the sovereign, not less than their medical advisers insist on having it. "We surgeons do things by guineas," we recollect a veteran hospital surgeon saying to a visitor who had put down the largest current gold piece of our present coinage. The patient (an irritable old gentleman) made it a question of principle; he hated humbug—he regarded "that shilling" as sheer humbug, and he would not pay it. A contest ensued, which terminated in the eccentric patient paying, not the shilling, but an additional sovereign. And to this day he is a frequent visitor of our surgical ally, and is well content to pay his two sovereigns, though he would die rather than countenance "a sham" by putting down "a guinea."

But of all the stories told of surgeons who have grown fat at the expense of the public, the best is the following one, for which Mr. Alexander Kellet, who died at his lodgings in Bath, in the year 1788 is our authority. A certain French surgeon residing in Georgia was taken prisoner by some Indians, who having acquired from the French the art of larding their provisions, determined to lard this particular Frenchman, and then roast him alive. During the culinary process, when the man was half larded, the operators were surprised by the enemy, and their victim, making his escape, lived many days in the woods on the bacon he had in his skin.

If full reliance may be placed on the following humorous verses, it is not unknown for a physician to be paid in commodities, without the intervention of the circulating medium, or the receipt of such creature comforts as Johnson's friendly apothecary was wont to accept in lieu of cash: —

> "An adept in the sister arts,
> Painter, poet, and musician,
> Employ'd a doctor of all parts,
> Druggist, surgeon, and physician.
>
> "The artist with M.D. agrees,
> If he'd attend him when he grew sick,
> Fully to liquidate his fees
> With painting, poetry, and music.
>
> "The druggist, surgeon, and physician,
> So often physick'd, bled, prescribed,
> That painter, poet, and musician
> (Alas! poor artist!) sunk—and died.
>
> "But ere death's stroke, 'Doctor,' cried he,
> 'In honour of your skill and charge,
> Accept from my professions three—
> A *hatchment*, *epitaph*, and *dirge*.'

A double fee for good news has long been a rule in the profession. A father just presented with an heir, or a lucky fellow just made one, is expected to bleed freely for the benefit of the Faculty.

> "Madam scolded one day so long,
> She sudden lost all use of tongue!
> The doctor came—with hum and haw,
> Pronounc'd th' affection a lock'd jaw!
>
> 'What hopes, good sir?' —'Small, small, I see!'
> The husband slips a *double fee*;
> 'What, no hopes, doctor?' —'None, I fear;'
> Another fee for issue clear.

"Madam deceased—'Pray, sir, don't grieve!'
'My friends, one comfort I receive—
A *lock'd jaw* was the only case
From which my wife could die—in peace.'"

CHAPTER X.

PEDAGOGUES TURNED DOCTORS.

In the church of St. Mary Magdalen, Taunton, is a monumental stone engraved with the following inscription:—

"Qui medicus doctus, prudentis nomine clarus,
Eloquii splendor, Pieridumque decus,
Virtutis cultor, pietatis vixit amicus;
Hoc jacet in tumulo, spiritus alta tenet."

It is in memory of John Bond, M.A., the learned commentator on Horace and Persius. Educated at Winchester school, and then at New College, Oxford, he was elected master of the Taunton Grammar-school in the year 1579. For many years he presided over that seminary with great efficiency, and sent out into the world several eminent scholars. On arriving, however, at the middle age of life, he relinquished the mastership of the school, and turned his attention to the practice of medicine. His reputation and success as a physician were great—the worthy people of Taunton honouring him as "a wise man." He died August 3, 1612.

More than a century later than John Bond, schoolmaster and physician, appeared a greater celebrity in the person of James Jurin, who, from the position of a provincial pedagogue, raised himself to be regarded as first of the London physicians, and conspicuous amongst the philosophers of Europe. Jurin was born in 1684, and received his early education at Christ's Hospital—better known to the public as the Bluecoat school. After graduating in arts at Cambridge, he obtained the mastership of the grammar-school of Newcastle-upon-Tyne, January, 1710. In the following year he acquired the high academic distinction of a fellowship on the foundation of Trinity College; and the year after (1712) he published through the University press, his edition of Varenius's Geography, dedicated to Bentley. In 1718 and 1719 he contributed to the Philosophical Transactions the essays which involved him in controversies with Keill and Senac, and were, in the year 1732, reprinted in a collected form, under the title of "Physico-Mathematical Dissertations." Another of his important contributions to science was "An Essay on Distinct and Indistinct Vision," added to Smith's "System of Optics." Voltaire was not without good reason for styling him, in the *Journal de Savans*, "the famous Jurin."

Besides working zealously in his school, Jurin delivered lectures at Newcastle, on Experimental Philosophy. He worked very hard, his immediate object being to get and save money. As soon as he had laid by a clear thousand pounds, he left Newcastle, and returning to his University devoted himself to the study of medicine. From that time his course was a prosperous one. Having taken his M.D. degree, he settled in London, became a Fellow of the College of Physicians, a Fellow of the Royal Society (to which distinguished body he became secretary on the resignation of Dr. Halley in 1721), and a Physician of Guy's Hospital, as well as Governor of St. Thomas's. The friend of Sir Isaac Newton and Bentley did not lack patients. The consulting-rooms and ante-chambers of his house in Lincoln's Inn Fields received many visitors; so that he acquired considerable wealth, and had an estate and an imposing establishment at Clapton. Nichols speaks of him in one of his volumes as "James Jurin, M.D., sometime of Clapton in Hackney." It was, however, at his town residence that he died, March 22, 1750, of what the *Gentleman's Magazine* calls "a dead palsy," leaving by his will a considerable legacy to Christ's Hospital.

One might make a long list of Doctors Pedagogic, including poor Oliver Goldsmith, who used to wince and redden with shame and anger when the cant phrase, "It's all a holiday at Peckham," saluted his ears. Between Bond and Jurin, however, there were two tutors turned physicians, who may not be passed over without especial attention. Only a little prior to Jurin they knew many of his friends, and doubtless met him often in consultation. They were both authors—one of rare wit, and the other (as he himself boasted) of no wit; and they hated each other, as literary men know how to hate. In every respect, even down to the quarters of town which they inhabited, they were opposed to each other. One was a brilliant talker and frequented St. James's; the other was a pompous drone, and haunted the Mansion-house: a Jacobite the one, a Whig the other. The reader sees that these two worthies can be none other than Arbuthnot and Blackmore.

A wily, courtly, mirth-loving Scotchman, Arbuthnot had all the best qualities that are to be ordinarily found in a child of North Britain. Everybody knew him—nearly every one liked him. His satire, that was only rarely tinctured with bitterness—his tongue, powerful to mimic, flatter, or persuade—his polished manners and cordial bearing, would alone have made him a favourite with the ladies, had he not been what he was—one of the handsomest men about town. (Of course, in appearance he did not approach that magnificent gentleman, Beau Fielding). In conversation he was frank without being noisy; and there hung about him—tavern-haunting wit though he was—an air of simplicity, tempering his reckless fun, that was very pleasant and very winning. Pope, Parnell, Garth, Gay, were society much more to his taste than the stately big-wigs of Warwick Hall. And next to drinking wine with such men, the good-humoured doctor enjoyed flirting with the maids of honour, and taking part in a political intrigue. No wonder that Swift valued him as a priceless treasure—"loved him," as he wrote to Stella, "ten times as much" as jolly, tippling Dr. Freind.

It was arm in arm with him that the Dean used to peer about St. James's, jesting, snarling, laughing, causing dowagers to smile at "that dear Mr. Dean," and young girls, up for their first year at Court—green and unsophisticated—to blush with annoyance at his coarse, shameless badinage; bowing to this great man (from whom he hoped for countenance), staring insolently at that one (from whom he was sure of nothing but enmity), quoting Martial to a mitred courtier (because the prelate couldn't understand Latin), whispering French to a youthful diploma-tist (because the boy knew no tongue but English), preparing impromptu compli-ments for "royal Anna" (as our dear worthy ancestors used to call Mrs. Masham's intimate friend), or with his glorious blue eyes sending a glance, eloquent of admi-ration and homage, at a fair and influential supporter; cringing, fawning, flatter-ing—in fact, angling for the bishopric he was never to get. With Arbuthnot it was that Swift tried the dinners and wine of every hotel round Covent Garden, or in the city. From Arbuthnot it was that the Dean, during his periods of official exile, received his best and surest information of the battles of the cliques, the scandals of the Court, the contentions of parties, the prospects of ministers, and (most im-portant subject by far) the health of the Queen.

Some of the most pleasant pictures in the "Journal to Stella" are those in which the kindly presence of the Doctor softens the asperity of the Dean. Most readers of these pages have accompanied the two "brothers" in their excursion to the course the day before the horse-races, when they overtook Miss Forrester, the pretty maid of honour, and made her accompany them. The lady was taking the air on her pal-frey, habited in the piquant riding-dress of the period—the natty three-cornered cocked hat, ornamented with gold lace, and perched on the top of a long flowing periwig, powdered to the whiteness of snow, the long coat cut like a coachman's, the waistcoat flapped and faced, and lastly the habit-skirt. One sees the belle at this time smiling archly, with all the power of beauty, and shaking the handle of her whip at the divine and the physician. So they took her with them (and they weren't wrong in doing so). Then the old Queen came by, gouty and hypochon-driac. Off went the hats of the two courtiers in the presence of her Majesty. The beauty, too, raised her little three-cornered cock-boat (rising on her stirrup as she did so), and returned it to the summit of the flowing wig, with a knowing side-glance, as much as to say, "See, sirs, we women can do that sort of thing quite as gracefully as the lords of the creation." (Oh, Mr. Spectator, how could you find it in you to quarrel with that costume?) Swift was charmed, and described enough of the scene to make that foolish Stella frantically jealous; and then, prudent, canny love-tyrant that he was, added with a sneer—"I did not like her, though she be a toast, and was dressed like a man." And you may be sure that poor little Stella was both fool enough and wise enough both to believe and disbelieve this assurance at the same time.

Arbuthnot owed his success in no degree whatever to the influence of his family, and only in a very slight degree to his professional knowledge. His father was only a poor episcopalian clergyman, and his M.D. degree was only an Aber-deen one. He rose by his wit, rare conversational powers, and fascinating address, achieving eminence at Court because he was the greatest master of fence with the weapon that is most used in courts—the tongue. He failed to get a living amongst rustic boors, who appreciated no effort of the human voice but a fox-hunter's whoop. Dorchester, where as a young man he endeavoured to establish himself in practice, refused to give him an income, but it doubtless maintained more than one dull empiric in opulence. In London he met with a different reception. For a time he was very poor, and resorted to the most hateful of all occupations—the personal instruction of the ignorant. How long he was so engaged is uncertain. Something of Goldsmith's "Peckham" sensibility made him not care in after-life to talk of the days when he was a teacher of mathematics—starving on pupils until he should be permitted to grow fat on patients.

The patients were not long in coming. The literary reputation he obtained by his "Examination of Dr Woodward's Account of the Deluge," elicited by Woodward's "Essay towards a Natural History of the Earth," instead of frightening the sick from him, brought them to him. Accidentally called in to Prince George of Denmark, when his Royal Highness was suddenly taken ill at Epsom, he made himself so agreeable that the casual introduction became a permanent connection. In 1709, on the illness of Hannes (a physician who also understood the art of rising in spite of obstacles) he was appointed physician-in-ordinary to Queen Anne.

To secure the good graces of his royal patient, and rise yet higher in them, he adopted a tone of affection for her as a person, as well as loyal devotion to her as a queen. The fall of Radcliffe warned him that he had need of caution in dealing with the weak-minded, querulous, crotchety, self-indulgent invalid.

"What's the time?" asked the Queen of him one day.

"Whatever it may please your Majesty," answered the court-physician, with a graceful bow.

After all, the best testimony of a man's merit is the opinion held of him by those of his acquaintance who know him intimately—at home as well as abroad. By all who came within the circle of Arbuthnot's privacy he was respected as much as loved. And his associates were no common men. Pope, addressing him as "the friend of his life," says:—

> "Why did I write? what sin, to me unknown,
> Dipp'd me in ink?—my parents' or my own?
> As yet a child, nor yet a fool to fame,
> I lisp'd in numbers, for the numbers came.
> I left no calling for this idle trade,
> No duty broke, no father disobey'd.
> The muse but served to ease some friend, not wife,
> To help me through this long disease, my life,
> To second, Arbuthnot! thy art and care,
> And teach the being you preserved to bear."

Pope's concluding wish—

> "Oh, friend! may each domestic bliss be thine."

was ineffectual. Arbuthnot's health failed under his habits of intemperance, and during his latter years he was a terrible sufferer from asthma and melancholy. After the Queen's death he went for the benefit of his health on the continent, and visited his brother, a Paris banker. Returning to London he took a house in Dover Street, from which he moved to the residence in Cork Street, Burlington Gardens, where he died Feb. 27, 1734-5. He died in straitened circumstances; for unlike his fellow-countryman, Colonel Chartres, he had not the faculty of saving. But with failing energies, an excruciated frame, and the heart-burden of a family unprovided for, he maintained a philosophic equanimity, and displayed his old unvarying consideration for all who surrounded him.

Arbuthnot's epitaph on Colonel Chartres (almost as well known as Martinus Scriblerus) is a good specimen of his humour: —

"Here continueth to rot,
The Body of Francis Chartres.
Who, with an indefatigable constancy,
And inimitable Uniformity of life,
Persisted,
In spite of Age and Infirmities,
In the practice of every Human Vice,
Excepting Prodigality and Hypocrisy:
His insatiable Avarice exempting him from the First,
His matchless impudence from the Second.
Nor was he more singular in the Undeviating Pravity
Of his manners, than successful
In accumulating Wealth:
For, without Trade or Profession,
Without trust of public money,
And without bribe-worthy service,
He acquired, or more properly created,
A ministerial estate.
He was the only person of this time
Who could cheat without the Mask of Honesty,
Retain his primæval meanness when possessed of
Ten thousand a-year:
And having duly deserved the Gibbet for what he did,
Was at last condemned to it for what he could not do.
Oh, indignant reader!
Think not his life useless to mankind:
Providence connived at his execrable designs,
To give to After-age a conspicuous
Proof and Example
Of how small estimation is exorbitant Wealth
In the sight of God, by His bestowing it on
The most unworthy of Mortals."

The history of the worthy person whose reputation is here embalmed is interesting. Beginning life as an ensign in the army, he was drummed out of his regiment, banished Brussels, and ignominiously expelled from Ghent, for cheating. As a miser he saved, and as a usurer he increased, the money which he won as a blackleg and card-sharper. Twice was he condemned to death for heinous offences, but contrived to purchase pardon; and, after all, he was fortunate enough to die in his own bed, in his native country, Scotland, A. D. 1731, aged sixty-two. At his funeral the indignant mob, feeling that justice had not been done to the dear departed, raised a riot, insulted the mourners, and, when the coffin was lowered into the grave, threw upon it a magnificent collection of dead dogs!

In a similar and scarcely less magnificent vein of humour, Arbuthnot wrote another epitaph—on a greyhound:—

"To the memory of
Signor Fido,
An Italian of Good Extraction:
Who came into England,
Not to bite us, like most of his countrymen,
But to gain an honest livelihood:
He hunted not after fame,
Yet acquired it:
Regardless of the Praise of his Friends,
But most sensible of their love:
Tho' he liv'd amongst the great,
He neither learn'd nor flatter'd any vice:
He was no Bigot,
Tho' he doubted of none of the thirty-nine articles;
And if to follow Nature,
And to respect the laws of Society,
Be Philosophy,
He was a perfect Phi losopher,
A faithful Friend,
An agreeable Companion,
A loving Husband,
Distinguished by a numerous Offspring,
All of which he lived to see take good courses;
In his old age he retired
To the House of a Clergyman in the Country,
Where he finished his earthly Race,
And died an Honour and an Example to the whole Species.
Reader,
This stone is guiltless of Flattery,
For he to whom it is inscribed
Was not a man,
But a
Greyhound."

In the concluding lines there is a touch of Sterne. They also call to mind Byron's epitaph on his dog.

These epitaphs put the writer in mind of the literary ambition of the eminent Dr. James Gregory of Edinburgh. His great aim was to be *the* Inscriptor (as he styled it) of his age. No distinguished person died without the doctor promptly striking off his characteristics in a mural legend. For every statue erected to heroes, real or sham, he composed an inscription, and interested himself warmly to have it adopted. Amongst the public monuments on which his compositions may be found are the Nelson Monument at Edinburgh, and the Duke of Wellington's shield at Gibraltar. On King Robert Bruce, Charles Edward Stuart, his mother, Sir James Foulis de Collington, and Robertson the historian, he also produced commemorative inscriptions of great excellence. As a very fair specimen of his style the inscription on the Scott Flagon is transcribed:—

"Gualterum Scott,
De Abbotsford,
Virum summi Ingenii
Scriptorem Elegantem
Poetarum sui seculi facile Principem
Patriæ Decus
Ob varia ergo ipsam merita
In civium suorum numerum
Grata adscripsit Civitas Edinburgensis
Et hoc Cantharo donavit
A. D. MDCCCXIII."

Sir Richard Blackmore, the other pedagogue physician, was one of those good, injudicious mortals who always either praise or blame too much—usually the latter. The son of a Wiltshire attorney, he was educated at Westminster School and Oxford, taking his degree of M.A. June, 1676, and residing, in all, thirteen years in the university, during a portion of which protracted period of residence he was (though Dr. Johnson erroneously supposed the reverse) a laborious student. On leaving Oxford he passed through a course of searching poverty, and became a schoolmaster. In this earlier part of his life he travelled in France, Germany, the Low Countries, and Italy, and took his doctor's degree in the University of Padua. On turning his attention to medicine, he consulted Sydenham as to what authors he ought to read. "Don Quixote," replied the veteran. A similar answer has been attributed to Lord Erskine on being asked by a law student the best literary sources for acquiring legal knowledge and success. The scepticism of the reply reminds one of Garth, who, to an anxious patient inquiring what physician he had best call in in case of his (Garth's) death, responded, "One is e'en as good as t'other, and surgeons are not less knowing."

As a poet, Blackmore failed, but as a physician he was for many years one of the most successful men in his profession. Living at Sadler's Hall, Cheapside, he was the oracle of all the wealthiest citizens, and was blessed with an affluence that allowed him to drive about town in a handsome equipage, and make an imposing figure to the world. Industrious, honourable, and cordially liked by his personal friends, he was by no means the paltry fellow that Dryden and Pope represented him. Johnson, in his brilliant memoir, treated him very unfairly, and clearly was annoyed that his conscience would not allow him to treat him worse. On altogether insufficient grounds the doctor argued that his knowledge of ancient authors was superficial, and for the most part derived from secondary sources. Passages indeed are introduced to show that the ridicule and contempt showered on the poet by his adversaries, and re-echoed by the laughing world, were unjust; but the effect of these admissions, complete in themselves, is more than counterbalanced by the sarcasms (and some of them vulgar sarcasms too) which the biographer, in imitation of Colonel Codrington, Sir Charles Sedley, and Colonel Blount, directs against the city knight.

A sincerely religious man, Blackmore was offended with the gross licentiousness of the drama, and all those productions of the poets which constituted the light literature of the eighteenth century. To his eternal honour, Blackmore was the first man who had the courage to raise his voice against the evil, and give utterance to a manly indignation at the insults offered nightly in every theatre to public decency. Unskilled in the use of the pen, of an age when he could not hope to perfect himself in an art to which he had not in youth systematically trained himself, and immersed in the cares of an extensive practice, he set himself to work on the production of a poem, which should elevate and instruct, not vitiate and deprave youthful readers. In this spirit "Prince Arthur" was composed and published in 1695, when the author was between forty and fifty years of age. It was written, as he frankly acknowledged, "by such catches and starts, and in such occasional uncertain hours as his profession afforded, and for the greatest part in coffee-houses, or in passing up and down streets." The wits laughed at him for writing "to the rumbling of his chariot-wheels," but at this date, ridicule thrown on a man for doing good at odd scraps of a busy day, has a close similarity to the laughter of fools. Let any reader compare the healthy gentlemanlike tone of the preface to "Prince Arthur," with the mean animosity of all the virulent criticisms and sarcasms that were directed against the author and his works, and then decide on which side truth and good taste lie.

Blackmore made the fatal error of writing too much. His long poems wearied the patience of those who sympathized with his goodness of intention. What a list there is of them, in Swift's inscription, "to be put under Sir Richard's picture!"

> "See, who ne'er was, or will be half read,
> Who first sung Arthur, then sung Alfred,[7]
> Praised great Eliza[8] in God's anger,
> Till all true Englishmen cried, hang her!
> *   *   *   *   *
>
> Then hiss'd from earth, grown heavenly quite,
> Made every reader curse the light.[9]
> Mauled human wit in one thick satire;[10]
> Next, in three books, spoil'd human nature;[11]
> Ended Creation[12] at a jerk,
> And of Redemption[13] made damn'd work:
> Then took his muse at once, and dipp'd her
> Full in the middle of the Scripture.

[7] Two heroic Poems, folio, twenty books.
[8] An heroic Poem, in twelve books.
[9] Hymn to Light.
[10] Satire against Wit.
[11] Of the Nature of Man.
[12] Creation, in seven books.
[13] Redemption, in six books.

What wonders there the man grown old did!
Sternhold himself he out-sternholded;
Made David[14] seem so mad and freakish,
All thought him just what thought king Achish.
No mortal read his Solomon,[15]
But judged R'oboam his own son.
Moses[16] he served, as Moses Pharaoh,
And Deborah as she Sisera:
Made Jeremy[17] full sore to cry,
And Job[18] himself curse God and die."

Nor is this by any means a complete list of Sir Richard's works; for he was also a voluminous medical writer, and author of a "History of the Conspiracy against the Person and Government of King William the Third, of glorious memory, in the year 1695."

Dryden, unable to clear himself of the charge of pandering for gain to the licentious tastes of the age, responded to his accuser by calling him an "ass," a "pedant," a "quack," and a "canting preacher."

"Quack Maurus, though he never took degrees
In either of our universities,
Yet to be shown by some kind wit he looks,
Because he play'd the fool, and writ three books.
But if he would be worth a poet's pen,
He must be more a fool, and write again;
For all the former fustian stuff he wrote
Was dead-born doggerel, or is quite forgot:
His man of Uz, stript of his Hebrew robe,
Is just the proverb, and 'as poor as Job.'
One would have thought he could no longer jog;
But Arthur was a level, Job's a bog.
There though he crept, yet still he kept in sight;
But here he founders in, and sinks downright.
*   *   *   *   *

At leisure hours in epic song he deals,
Writes to the rumbling of his coach's wheels.
*   *   *   *   *

Well, let him go—'tis yet too early day
To get himself a place in farce or play;
We know not by what name we should arraign him,
For no one category can contain him.
A pedant, canting preacher, and a quack,
Are load enough to break an ass's back.

[14] Translation of all the Psalms.
[15] Canticles and Ecclesiastes.
[16] Canticles of Moses, Deborah, &c.
[17] The Lamentations.
[18] The Whole Book of Job, in folio.

> At last, grown wanton, he presumed to write,
> Traduced two kings, their kindness to requite;
> One made the doctor, and one dubbed the knight."

The former of the kings alluded to is James the Second, Blackmore having obtained his fellowship of the College of Physicians, April 12, 1687, under the new charter granted to the college by that monarch; the latter being William the Third, who, in recognition of the doctor's zeal and influence as a Whig, not less than of his eminence in his profession, made him a physician of the household, and knighted him.

Pope says:—

> "The hero William, and the martyr Charles,
> One knighted Blackmore, and one pension'd Quarles."

The bard of Twickenham had of course a few ill words for Blackmore. In the Dunciad he says:—

> "Ye critics, in whose heads, as equal scales,
> I weigh what author's heaviness prevails;
> Which most conduce to soothe the soul in slumbers,
> My H— —ley's periods, or my Blackmore's numbers."

Elsewhere, in the same poem, the little wasp of poetry continues his hissing song:—

> "But far o'er all, sonorous Blackmore's strain,
> Walls, steeples, skies, bray back to him again.
> In Tot'nham fields, the brethren, with amaze,
> Prick all their ears up, and forget to graze;
> 'Long Chancery Lane retentive rolls the sound,
> And courts to courts return it round and round;
> Thames wafts it thence to Rufus' roaring hall,
> And Hungerford re-echoes bawl for bawl;
> All hail him victor in both gifts and song,
> Who sings so loudly, and who sings so long."

Such being the tone of the generals, the reader can imagine that of the petty scribblers, the professional libellers, the coffee-house rakes, and literary amateurs of the Temple, who formed the rabble of the vast army against which the doctor had pitted himself, in defence of public decency and domestic morality. Under the title of "Commendatory Verses, on the author of the two Arthurs, and the Satyr against Wit, by some of his particular friends," were collected, in the year 1700, upwards of forty sets of ribald verses, taunting Sir Richard with his early poverty, with his having been a school-master, with the unspeakable baseness of—living in the city. The writers of these wretched dirty lampoons, that no kitchen-maid could in our day read without blushing, little thought what they were doing. Their obscene stupidity has secured for them the lasting ignominy to which they imagined they were consigning their antagonist. What a crew they are!—with chivalric Steel and kindly Garth, forgetting their better natures, and joining in the miserable riot!

To "The City Quack"; "The Cheapside Knight"; "The Illustrious Quack, Pedant, Bard"; "The Merry Poetaster of Sadler's Hall"—such are the titles by which they address the doctor, who had presumed to say that authors and men of wit ought to find a worthier exercise for their intellects than the manufacture of impure jests.

Colonel Codrington makes his shot thus—

> "By Nature meant, by Want a Pedant made,
> Blackmore at first profess'd the whipping trade;
> *   *   *   *   *
> In vain his drugs as well as Birch he try'd—
> His boys grew blockheads, and his patients dy'd.
> Next he turn'd Bard, and, mounted on a cart,
> Whose hideous rumbling made Apollo start,
> Burlesqued the Bravest, Wisest son of Mars,
> In ballad rhymes, and all the pomp of Farce.
> *   *   *   *   *

The same dull sarcasms about killing patients and whipping boys into block-heads are repeated over and over again. As if to show, with the greatest possible force, the pitch to which the evil of the times had risen, the coarsest and most disgusting of all these lampoon-writers was a lady of rank—the Countess of Sand-wich. By the side of her Ladyship, Afra Behn and Mistress Manley become timid blushing maidens. A better defence of Sir Richard than the Countess's attack on him it would be impossible to imagine.

And after all—the slander and the maledictions—Sir Richard Blackmore gained the victory, and the wits who never wearied of calling him "a fool" were defeated. The preface to "Prince Arthur" provoked discussion; the good sense and better taste of the country were roused, and took the reformer's side of the con-troversy. Pope and his myrmidons, it was true, were still able to make the *beau monde* merry about the city knight's presumption—but they could not refute the city knight's arguments; and they themselves were compelled to shape their con-duct, as writers, in deference to a new public feeling which he was an important instrument in calling into existence. "Prince Arthur" appeared in 1695, and to the commotion caused by its preface may be attributed much of the success of Jeremy Collier's "Short View of the Immorality and Profaneness of the Stage," which was published some three years afterwards.

As a poet Sir Richard Blackmore can command only that praise which the charitable bestow on goodness of intention. His muse was a pleasant, well-look-ing, right-minded young lady, but nothing more. But it must be remembered, be-fore we measure out our criticisms on his productions, that he never arrogated to himself the highest honours of poesy. "I am a gentleman of taste and culture, and though I cannot ever hope to build up the nervous lines of Dryden, or attain the polish and brilliance of Congreve, I believe I can write what the generation sorely needs—works that intelligent men may study with improvement, devout Christians may read without being offended, and pure-minded girls may peruse without blushing from shame. 'Tis true I am a hard-worked doctor, spending my days in coffee-houses, receiving apothecaries, or driving over the stones in my carriage, visiting my patients. Of course a man so circumstanced must fail to achieve artistic excellence, but still I'll do my best." Such was the language with which he introduced himself to the public.

His best poem, *The Creation*, had such merit that his carping biographer, Johnson, says, "This poem, if he had written nothing else, would have transmitted him to posterity one of the first favourites of the English muse"; and Addison designated the same poem "one of the most useful and noble productions in our English verse."

Of Sir Richard's private character Johnson remarks—"In some part of his life, it is not known when, his indigence compelled him to teach a school—a humiliation with which, though it certainly lasted but a little while, his enemies did not forget to reproach him when he became conspicuous enough to excite malevolence; and let it be remembered, for his honour, that to have been a schoolmaster is the only reproach which all the perspicacity of malice, animated by wit, has ever fixed upon his private life."

CHAPTER XI.

THE GENEROSITY AND THE PARSIMONY OF PHYSICIANS.

Of the generosity of physicians one *need* say nothing, for there are few who have not experienced or witnessed it; and one *had better* say nothing, as no words could do justice to such a subject. This writer can speak for at least one poor scholar, to whose sick-bed physicians have come from distant quarters of the town, day after day, never taking a coin for their precious services, and always in their graceful benevolence seeming to find positive enjoyment in their unpaid labour. In gratitude for kindness shown to himself, and yet more for beneficence exhibited to those whom he loves, that man of the goose-quill and thumbed books would like to put on record the names of certain members of "the Faculty" to whom he is so deeply indebted. Ah, dear Dr. — — and Dr. — — and Dr. — —, do not start!— your names shall not be put down on this cheap common page. Where they are engraved, you know!

Cynics have been found in plenty to rail at physicians for loving their fees; and one might justly retort on the Cynics, that they love *nothing but* their fees. Who doesn't love the sweet money earned by his labour—be it labour of hand or brain, or both? One thing is sure—that doctors are underpaid. The most successful of them in our own time get far less than their predecessors of any reign, from Harry the Eighth downwards. And for honours, though the present age has seen an author raised to the peerage, no precedent has as yet been established for ennobling eminent physicians and surgeons.

Queen Elizabeth gave her physician-in-ordinary £100 per annum, besides diet, wine, wax, and other perquisites. Her apothecary, Hugo Morgan, must too have made a good thing out of her. For a quarter's bill that gentleman was paid £83 7s. 8d., a large sum in those days; but then it was for such good things. What Queen of England could grudge eleven shillings for "a confection made like a manus Christi, with bezoar stone and unicorn's horn"?—sixteen pence for "a royal sweetmeat with incised rhubarb"?—twelve pence for "Rosewater for the King of Navarre's ambassador"?—six shillings for "a conserve of barberries, with preserved damascene plums, and other things for Mr. Raleigh"?—two shillings and sixpence for "sweet scent to be used at the christening of Sir Richard Knightley's son"?

Coytier, the physician of Charles the XI. of France, was better paid by far. The extent to which he fleeced that monarch is incredible. Favour after favour he wrung from him. When the royal patient resisted the modest demands of his physician, the latter threatened him with speedy dissolution. On this menace the king, succumbing to that fear of death which characterized more than one other of his family, was sure to make the required concession. Theodore Hook's valet, who was a good servant in the first year of his service, a sympathizing friend in the second, and a hard tyrant in the third, was a timid slave compared with Coytier. Charles, in order to be freed from his despotism, ordered him to be dispatched. The officer, intrusted with the task of carrying out the royal wishes, waited on Coytier, and said, in a most gentlemanlike and considerate manner, "I am very sorry, my dear fellow, but I must kill you. The king can't stand you any longer." "All right," said Coytier, with perfect unconcern, "whenever you like. What time would it be most convenient for you to kill me? But still, I am deuced sorry for his Majesty, for I know by occult science that he can't outlive me more than four days." The officer was so struck with the announcement, that he went away and forthwith imparted it to the king. "Liberate him instantly—don't hurt a hair of his head!" cried the terrified monarch. And Coytier was once again restored to his place in the king's confidence and pocket.

Henry Atkins managed James the First with some dexterity. Atkins was sent for to Scotland, to attend Charles the First (then an infant), who was dangerously ill of a fever. The king gave him the handsome fee of £6000. Atkins invested the money in the purchase of the manor of Clapham.

Radcliffe, with a rare effort of generosity, attended a friend for a twelvemonth gratuitously. On making his last visit his friend said, "Doctor, here is a purse in which I have put every day's fee; and your goodness must not get the better of my gratitude. Take your money." Radcliffe looked, made a resolve to persevere in benevolence, just touched the purse to reject it, heard the chink of the gold pieces in it, and put the bag into his pocket. "Singly, sir, I could have refused them for a twelvemonth; but, all together, *they are irresistible*," said the doctor, walking off with a heavy prize and a light heart.

Louis XIV. gave his physician and his surgeon 75,000 crowns each, after successfully undergoing a painful and at that time novel operation. By the side of such munificence, the fees paid by Napoleon I. to the Faculty who attended Marie Louise in March, 1811, when the Emperor's son was born, seem insufficient. Dubois, Corvisart, Bourdier, and Ivan were the professional authorities employed, and they had among them a remuneration of £4000, £2000 being the portion assigned to Dubois.

Even more than fee gratefully paid does a humorous physician enjoy an extra fee adroitly drawn from the hand of a reluctant payer. Sir Richard Jebb was once paid three guineas by a nobleman from whom he had a right to expect five. Sir Richard dropped the coins on the carpet, when a servant picked them up and restored them—three, and only three. Instead of walking off Sir Richard continued his search on the carpet. "Are all the guineas found?" asked his Lordship looking round. "There must be two still on the floor," was the answer, "for I have only three." The hint of course was taken and the right sum put down. An eminent Bristol doctor accomplished a greater feat than this, and took a fee from—a dead commoner, not a live lord. Coming into his patient's bed-room immediately after death had taken place, he found the right hand of the deceased tightly clenched. Opening the fingers he discovered within them a guinea. "Ah, that was for me—clearly," said the doctor putting the piece into his pocket.

Reminding the reader, in its commencement, of Sir Richard Jebb's disappointment at the three-guinea fee, the following story may here be appropriately inserted. A physician on receiving two guineas, when he expected three, from an old lady patient, who was accustomed to give him the latter fee, had recourse to one part of Sir Richard's artifice, and assuming that the third guinea had been dropt through his carelessness on the floor, looked about for it. "Nay, nay," said the lady with a smile, "you are not in fault. It is I who dropt it."

There is an abundance of good stories of physicians fleecing their lambs. To those that are true the comment may be made—"Doubtless the lambs were all the better for being shorn." For the following anecdote we are indebted to Dr. Moore, the author of "Zeluco." A wealthy tradesman, after drinking the Bath waters, took a fancy to try the effect of the Bristol hot wells. Armed with an introduction from a Bath physician to a professional brother at Bristol, the invalid set out on his journey. On the road he gave way to his curiosity to read the doctor's letter of introduction, and cautiously prying into it read these instructive words: "Dear sir, the bearer is a fat Wiltshire clothier—make the most of him."

Benevolence was not a virtue in old Monsey's line; but he could be generous at another's expense, when the enjoyment his malignity experienced in paining one person counterbalanced his discomfort at giving pleasure to another. Strolling through Oxford market he heard a poor woman ask the price of a piece of meat that lay on a butcher's stall.

"A penny a pound!" growled the man to whom the question was put, disdaining to give a serious answer to such a poverty-stricken customer.

"Just weigh that piece of beef, my friend," said Monsey, stepping up.

"Ten pounds and a half, sir," observed the butcher, after adjusting the scales and weights.

"Here, my good woman," said Monsey, "out with your apron, and put the beef into it, and make haste home to your family."

Blessing the benevolent heart of the eccentric old gentleman, the woman did as she was bid, took possession of her meat, and was speedily out of sight.

"And there, my man," said Monsey, turning to the butcher, "is tenpence halfpenny, the price of your beef."

"What do you mean?" demanded the man.

"Simply that that's all I'll pay you. You said the meat was a penny a pound. At that price I bought it of you—to give to the poor woman. Good morning!"

A fee that Dr. Fothergill took of Mr. Grenville was earned without much trouble. Fothergill, like Lettsom, was a Quaker, and was warmly supported by his brother sectarians. In the same way Mead was brought into practice by the Nonconformists, to whom his father ministered spiritually. Indeed, Mead's satirists affirmed that when his servant (acting on instructions) had called him out from divine service, the parson took his part in the "dodge" by asking the congregation to pray for the bodily and ghostly welfare of the patient to whom his son had just been summoned. Dissenters are remarkable for giving staunch support, and thorough confidence, to a doctor of their own persuasion. At the outbreak of the American war, therefore Grenville knew that he could not consult a better authority than the Quaker doctor, Fothergill, on the state of feeling amongst the Quaker colonists. Fothergill was consequently summoned to prescribe for the politician. The visit took the form of an animated discussion on American affairs, which was brought to a conclusion by Grenville's putting five guineas into the physician's hand, saying—"Really, doctor, I am so much better, that I don't want you to prescribe for me." With a canny significant smile Fothergill, keeping, like a true Quaker, firm hold of the money, answered, "At this rate, friend, I will spare thee an hour now and then."

Dr. Glynn, of Cambridge, was as benevolent as he was eccentric. His reputation in the fen districts as an ague doctor was great, and for some years he made a large professional income. On one occasion a poor peasant woman, the widowed mother of an only son, trudged from the heart of the fens into Cambridge, to consult the doctor about her boy, who was ill of an ague. Her manner so interested the physician, that though it was during an inclement winter, and the roads were almost impassable to carriages, he ordered horses, and went out to see the sick lad. After a tedious attendance, and the exhibition of much port wine and bark (bought at the doctor's expense), the patient recovered, and Glynn took his leave. A few days after the farewell visit, the poor woman again presented herself in the consulting room.

"I hope, my good woman," said Glynn, "your son is not ill again?"

"No, sir, he was never better," answered the woman, gratefully; "but we can't get no rest for thinking of all the trouble that you have had, and so my boy resolved this morning on sending you his favourite magpie."

In the woman's hand was a large wicker basket, which she opened at the conclusion of the speech, affording means of egress to an enormous magpie, that hopped out into the room, demure as a saint and bold as a lord. It was a fee to be proud of!

The free-will offerings of the poor to their doctors are sometimes very droll, and yet more touching. They are presented with such fervour and simplicity, and such a sincere anxiety that they should be taken as an expression of gratitude for favours past, not for favours to come. The writer of these pages has known the humble toilers of agricultural districts retain for a score of years the memory of kind services done to them in sickness. He could tell of several who, at the anniversary of a particular day (when a wife died, or child was saved from fever, or an accident crushed a finger or lacerated a limb), trudge for miles over the country to the doctor's house, and leave there a little present—a pot of honey, a basket of apples, a dish of the currants from the bush which "the doctor" once praised, and said was fit for a gentleman's garden.

Of eminent physicians Dr. Gregory of Edinburgh was as remarkable for his amiability as for his learning. It was his custom to receive from new pupils at his own house the fees for the privilege of attending his lectures. Whilst thus engaged one day, he left a student in his consulting-room, and went into an adjoining apartment for a fresh supply of admission tickets. In a mirror the doctor saw the student rise from his seat, and sweep into his pocket some guineas from a heap of gold (the fees of other students) that lay on the consulting-room table. Without saying a word at the moment, Dr. Gregory returned, dated the admission ticket, and gave it to the thief. He then politely attended him to the door, and on the threshold said to the young man, with deep emotion, "I saw what you did just now. Keep the money. I know what distress you must be in. But for God's sake never do it again—it can never succeed." The pupil implored Gregory to take back the money, but the doctor said, "Your punishment is this, you must keep it—now you have taken it." The reproof had a salutary effect. The youth turned out a good and honest man.

An even better anecdote can be told of this good physician's benevolence. A poor medical student, ill of typhus fever, sent for him. The summons was attended to, and the visit paid, when the invalid proffered the customary guinea fee. Dr. Gregory turned away, insulted and angry. "I beg your pardon, Dr. Gregory," exclaimed the student, apologetically, "I didn't know your rule. Dr. — — has always taken one." "Oh," answered Gregory, "he has—has he? Look you, then, my young friend; ask him to meet me in consultation, and then offer him a fee; or stay—offer me the fee first." The directions were duly acted upon. The consultation took place, and the fee was offered. "Sir," exclaimed the benevolent doctor, "do you mean to insult me? Is there a professor who would in this University degrade himself so far as to take payment from one of his brotherhood—and a junior?" The confusion of the man on whom this reproof was really conferred can be imagined. He had the decency, ere the day closed, to send back to the student all the fees he had taken of him.

Amongst charitable physicians a high place must be assigned to Brocklesby, of whom mention is made in another part of these pages. An ardent Whig, he was the friend of enthusiastic Tories as well as of the members of his own body. Burke on the one hand, and Johnson on the other, were amongst his intimate associates, and experienced his beneficence. To the latter he offered a hundred-a-year for life. And when the Tory writer was struggling with the heavy burden of increasing disease, he attended him with affectionate solicitude, taking no fee for his services—Dr. Heberden, Dr. Warren, Dr. Butler, and Mr. Cruikshank the surgeon, displaying a similar liberality. It was Brocklesby who endeavored to soothe the mental agitation of the aged scholar's death-bed, by repeating the passage from the Roman satirist, in which occurs the line:—

"Fortem posce animum et mortis terrore carentem."

Burke's pun on Brocklesby's name is a good instance of the elaborate ingenuity with which the great Whig orator adorned his conversation and his speeches. Pre-eminent amongst the advertising quacks of the day was Dr. Rock. It was therefore natural that Brocklesby should express some surprise at being accosted by Burke as Dr. Rock, a title at once infamous and ridiculous. "Don't be offended.

Your name is Rock," said Burke, with a laugh; "I'll prove it algebraically: *Brock—b = Rock*; or, Brock less *b* makes Rock." Dr. Brocklesby, on the occasion of giving evidence in a trial, had the ill fortune to offend the presiding judge, who, amongst other prejudices not uncommon in the legal profession, cherished a lively contempt for medical evidence. "Well, gentlemen of the jury," said the noble lawyer in his summing up, "what's the medical testimony? First we have a Dr. Rocklesby or—Brocklesby. What does he say? *First of all he* swears—*he's a physician.*"

Abernethy is a by-word for rudeness and even brutality of manner; but he was as tender and generous as a man ought to be, as a man of great intelligence usually is. The stories current about him are nearly all fictions of the imagination; or, where they have any foundation in fact, relate to events that occurred long before the hero to whom they are tacked by anecdote-mongers had appeared on the stage. He was eccentric—but his eccentricities always took the direction of common sense; whereas the extravagances attributed to him by popular gossip are frequently those of a heartless buffoon. His time was precious, and he rightly considered that his business was to set his patients in the way of recovering their lost health—not to listen to their fatuous prosings about their maladies. He was therefore prompt and decided in checking the egotistic garrulity of valetudinarians. This candid expression of his dislike to unnecessary talk had one good result. People who came to consult him took care not to offend him by bootless prating. A lady on one occasion entered his consulting-room, and put before him an injured finger, without saying a word. In silence Abernethy dressed the wound, when instantly and silently the lady put the usual fee on the table, and retired. In a few days she called again, and offered the finger for inspection. "Better?" asked the surgeon. "Better," answered the lady, speaking to him for the first time. Not another word followed during the rest of the interview. Three or four similar visits were made, at the last of which the patient held out her finger free from bandages and perfectly healed. "Well?" was Abernethy's monosyllabic inquiry. "Well," was the lady's equally brief answer. "Upon my soul, madam," exclaimed the delighted surgeon, "*you are the most rational woman I ever met with.*"

To curb his tongue, however, out of respect to Abernethy's humour, was an impossibility to John Philpot Curran. Eight times Curran (personally unknown to Abernethy) had called on the great surgeon; and eight times Abernethy had looked at the orator's tongue (telling him, by-the-by, that it was the most unclean and utterly abominable tongue in the world), had curtly advised him to drink less, and not abuse his stomach with gormandizing, had taken a guinea, and had bowed him out of the room. On the ninth visit, just as he was about to be dismissed in the same summary fashion, Curran, with a flash of his dark eye, fixed the surgeon, and said—"Mr. Abernethy, I have been here on eight different days, and I have paid you eight different guineas; but you have never yet listened to the symptoms of my complaint. I am resolved, sir, not to leave the room till you satisfy me by doing so." With a good-natured laugh, Abernethy, half suspecting that he had to deal with a madman, fell back in his chair and said—"Oh! very well, sir; I am ready to hear you out. Go on, give me the whole—your birth, parentage, and education. I wait your pleasure. Pray be as minute and tedious as you can." With perfect gravity Curran began—"Sir, my name is John Philpot Curran. My parents were poor, but I believe honest people, of the province of Munster, where also I was born, at Newmarket, in the county of Cork, in the year one thousand seven hundred and fifty. My father being employed to collect the rents of a Protestant gentleman of small fortune, in that neighbourhood, procured my admission into one of the Protestant free-schools, where I obtained the first rudiments of my education. I was next enabled to enter Trinity College, Dublin, in the humble sphere of a sizar—" And so he went steadily on, till he had thrown his auditor into convulsions of laughter.

Abernethy was very careful not to take fees from patients if he suspected them to be in indigent circumstances. Mr. George Macilwain, in his instructive and agreeable "Memoirs of John Abernethy," mentions a case where an old officer of parsimonious habits, but not of impoverished condition, could not induce Abernethy to accept his fee, and consequently forbore from again consulting him. On another occasion, when a half-pay lieutenant wished to pay him for a long and laborious attendance, Abernethy replied, "Wait till you're a general; then come and see me, and we'll talk about fees." To a gentleman of small means who consulted him, after having in vain had recourse to other surgeons, he said—"Your recovery will be slow. If you don't feel much pain, depend upon it you are gradually getting round; if you do feel much pain, then come again, *but not else*. I don't want your money." To a hospital student (of great promise and industry, but in narrow circumstances), who became his dresser, he returned the customary fee of sixty guineas, and requested him to expend them in the purchase of books and securing other means of improvement. To a poor widow lady (who consulted him about her child), he, on saying good-bye in a friendly letter, returned all the fees he had taken from her under the impression that she was in good circumstances, and added £50 to the sum, begging her to expend it in giving her child a daily ride in the fresh air. He was often brusque and harsh, and more than once was properly reproved for his hastiness and want of consideration.

"I have heard of your rudeness before I came, sir," one lady said, taking his prescription, "but I was not prepared for such treatment. What am I to do with this?"

"Anything you like," the surgeon roughly answered. "Put it on the fire if you please."

Taking him at his word, the lady put her fee on the table, and the prescription on the fire; and making a bow, left the room. Abernethy followed her into the hall, apologizing, and begging her to take back the fee or let him write another prescription; but the lady would not yield her vantage-ground.

Of operations Abernethy had a most un-surgeon-like horror—"like Cheselden and Hunter, regarding them as the reproach of the profession." "I hope, sir, it will not be long," said a poor woman, suffering under the knife. "No, indeed," earnestly answered Abernethy, "that would be too horrible." This humanity, on a point on which surgeons are popularly regarded as being devoid of feeling, is very general in the profession. William Cooper (Sir Astley's uncle) was, like Abernethy, a most tender-hearted man. He was about to amputate a man's leg, in the hospital theatre, when the poor fellow, terrified at the display of instruments and apparatus, suddenly jumped off the table, and hobbled away. The students burst out laughing; and the surgeon, much pleased at being excused from the performance of a painful duty, exclaimed, "By God, I am glad he's gone!"

The treatment which one poor fellow received from Abernethy may at first sight seem to militate against our high estimate of the surgeon's humanity, and dislike of inflicting physical pain. Dr. — —, an eminent physician still living and conferring lustre on his profession, sent a favourite man-servant with a brief note, running—"Dear Abernethy, Will you do me the kindness to put a seton in this poor fellow's neck? Yours sincerely, — —." The man, who was accustomed and encouraged to indulge in considerable freedom of speech with his master's friends, not only delivered the note to Abernethy, but added, in an explanatory and confiding tone, "You see, sir, I don't get better, and as master thinks I ought to have a seton in my neck, I should be thankful if you'd put it in for me." It is not at all improbable that Abernethy resented the directions of master and man. Anyhow he inquired into the invalid's case, and then taking out his needles did as he was requested. The operation was attended with a little pain, and the man howled, as only a coward can howl, under the temporary inconvenience. "Oh! Lor' bless you! Oh, have mercy on me! Yarra—yarra—yarr! Oh, doctor—doctor—you'll kill me!" In another minute the surgeon's work was accomplished, and the acute pain having passed away, the man recovered his self-possession and impudence.

"Oh, well, sir, I do hope, now that it's done, it'll do me good. I do hope that."

"But it won't do you a bit of good."

"What, sir, no good?" cried the fellow.

"No more good," replied Abernethy, "than if I had spat upon it."

"Then, sir—why—oh, yarr! here's the pain again—why did you do it?"

"Confound you, man!" answered the surgeon testily. "Why did I do it?—why, *didn't you ask me to put a seton in your neck?*"

Of course the surgical treatment employed by Abernethy in this case was the right one; but he was so nettled with the fellow's impudence and unmanly lamentations, that he could not forbear playing off upon him a barbarous jest.

If for this outbreak of vindictive humour the reader is inclined to call Abernethy a savage, let his gift of £50 to the widow lady, to pay for her sick child's carriage exercise, be remembered. *Apropos* of £50, Dr. Wilson of Bath sent a present of that sum to an indigent clergyman, against whom he had come in the course of practice. The gentleman who had engaged to convey the gift to the unfortunate priest said, "Well, then, I'll take the money to him to-morrow." "Oh, my dear sir," said the doctor, "take it to him to-night. Only think of the importance to a sick man of one good night's rest!"

Side by side with stories of the benevolence of "the Faculty," piquant anecdotes of their stinginess might be told. This writer knew formerly a grab-all-you-can-get surgeon, who was entertaining a few professional brethren at a Sunday morning's breakfast, when a patient was ushered into the ante-room of the surgeon's bachelor chambers, and the surgeon himself was called away to the visitor. Unfortunately he left the folding-doors between the breakfast-room and the ante-room ajar, and his friends sitting in the former apartment overheard the following conversation:

"Well, my friend, what's the matter?"—the surgeon's voice.

The visitor's voice—"Plaze, yer honner, I'm a pore Hirish labourer, but I can spill a bit, and I read o' yer honner's moighty foine cure in the midical jarnal—the *Lancet*. And I've walked up twilve miles to have yer honner cure me. My complaint is — —"

Surgeon's voice, contemptuously—"Oh, my good man, you've made a mistake. You'd better go to the druggist's shop nearest your home, and he'll do for you all you want. You couldn't pay me as I require to be paid."

Visitor's voice, proudly and triumphantly—"Och, an' little ye know an Irish gintleman, dochter, if ye think he'd be beholden to the best of you for a feavor. Here's a bit o' gould—nocht liss nor a tin shillin' piece, but I've saved it up for ye, and ye'll heve the whole, tho' its every blissed farthing I hev."

The surgeon's voice altered. The case was gone into. The prescription was written. The poor Irish drudge rose to go, when the surgeon, with that delicate quantity of conscience that rogues always have to make themselves comfortable upon, said, "Now, you say you have no more money, my friend. Well, the druggist will charge you eighteenpence for the medicine I have ordered there. So there's eighteenpence for you out of your half-sovereign."

We may add that this surgeon was then, at a moderate computation, making three thousand a year. We have heard of an Old Bailey barrister boasting how he wrung the shillings (to convert the sovereigns already paid with his brief into guineas) from the grimed hands of a prisoner actually standing in the dock for trial, ere he would engage to defend him. But compared with this surgeon the man of the long robe was a disinterested friend of the oppressed.

A better story yet of a surgeon who seized on his fee like a hawk. A clergyman of — —shire, fell from a branch of a high pear-tree to the grass-plot of the little garden that surrounded his vicarage-house, and sustained, besides being stunned, a compound fracture of the right arm. His wife, a young and lovely creature, of a noble but poor family, to whom he had been married only three or four years, was terribly alarmed, and without regulating her conduct by considerations of her pecuniary means, dispatched a telegraphic message to an eminent London surgeon. In the course of three or four hours the surgeon made his appearance, and set the broken limb.

"And what, sir," the young wife timidly asked of the surgeon, when he had come down-stairs into her little drawing-room, "is your fee?"

"Oh, let's see—distance from town, hundred miles. Yes. Then my fee is a hundred guineas!"

Turning deadly pale with fright (for the sum was ten times the highest amount the poor girl had thought of as a likely fee) she rose, and left the room, saying, "Will you be kind enough to wait for a few minutes?"

Luckily her brother (like her husband, a clergyman, with very moderate preferment) was in the house, and he soon made his appearance in the drawing-room. "Sir," said he, addressing the operator, "my sister has just now been telling me the embarrassment she is in, and I think it best to repeat her story frankly. She is quite inexperienced in money matters, and sent for you without ever asking what the ordinary fee to so distinguished a surgeon as yourself, for coming so far from London, might be. Well, sir, it is right you should know her circumstances. My brother-in-law has no property but his small living, which does not yield him more than £400 per annum, and he has already two children. My sister has no private fortune whatever, at present, and all she has in prospect is the reversion of a trifling sum—at a distant period. Poverty is the only stigma that time has fixed upon my family. Now, sir, under the circumstances, if professional etiquette would allow of your reducing your fee to the straitened finances of my sister, it really would—would be—"

"Oh, my dear sir," returned the surgeon, in a rich, unctuous voice of benevolence, "pray don't think I'm a shark. I am really deeply concerned for your poor sister. As for my demand of *a hundred guineas*, since it would be beyond her means to satisfy it, why, my dear sir, I shall be only too delighted to be allowed—*to take a hundred pounds!*"

The fee-loving propensities of doctors are well illustrated by the admirable touches of Froissart's notice of Guyllyam of Harseley, who was appointed physician to Charles the Sixth, King of France, during his derangement. The writer's attention was first called to Friossart's sketch of the renowned mad-doctor by his friend Mr. Edgar—a gentleman whose valuable contributions to historical literature have endeared his name to both young and old. Of the measures adopted by Guyllyam for the king's cure the readers of Froissart are not particularly informed; but it would appear, from the physician's parting address to the "dukes of Orlyance, Berrey, Burgoyne, and Burbone," that his system was, in its enlightened humanity, not far behind that adopted at the present day by Dr. Conolly and Dr. Forbes Winslow. But, however this may be, Guyllyam's labours must be regarded as not less consonant with sound nosological views than those of the afflicted monarch's courtiers, until it can be shown that his treatment was worse than leaving Nature to herself. "They," says Froissart, "that were about the kynge sente the kynge's offrynge to a town called Aresneche, in the countie of Heynaulte, between Cambrey and Valancennes, in the whiche towne there was a churche parteyning to an Abbey of Saynt Waste in Arrasce wherein there lyeth a saynte, called Saynt Acquayre, of whom there is a shrine of sylver, which pylgrimage is sought farre and nere for the malady of the fransey; thyder was sent a man of waxe, representynge the Frenche Kynge, and was humbly offred to the Saynt, that he might be meane to God, to asswage the kynge's malady, and to sende him helthe. In lykewise the kynge's offrynge was sent to Saynt Hermyer in Romayes, which saynt had meryte to heal the fransey. And in lykewise offrynges were sent into other places for ye same entent."

The conclusion of Guyllyam's attendance is thus described:—"Trewe it is this sycknesse that the kyng took in the voyage towards Bretagne greatly abated the ioye of the realme of France, and good cause why, for when the heed is sicke the body canne have no ioye. No man durste openly speke thereof, but kepte it privy as moche as might be, and it was couertly kept fro the queene, for tyll she was delyuered and churched she knewe nothynge thereof, which tyme she had a doughter. The physician, myster Guyllyam, who had the chefe charge of healynge of the kynge, was styll aboute hym, and was ryght dyligent and well acquyted hymselfe, whereby he gate bothe honour and profyte; for lytell and lytell he brought the kynge in good estate, and toke away the feuer and the heate, and made hym to haue taste and appetyte to eate and drinke, slepe and rest, and knowledge of every thynge; howebeit, he was very feble, and lytell and lytell he made the kynge to ryde a huntynge and on hawkynge; and whanne tydynges was knowen through France howe the kynge was well mended, and had his memory again, every man was ioyfull and thanked God. The kynge thus beyng at Crayell, desyred to se the quene his wyfe and the dolphyn his sonne; so the quene came thyder to hym, and the chylde was brought thyder, the kynge made them good chere, and so lytell and lytell, through the helpe of God, the kynge recouered his helthe. And when mayster Guyllyam sawe the kynge in so good case he was ryght ioyfull, as reasone was, for he hade done a fayre cure, and so delyuered him to the dukes of Orlyance, Berrey, Burgoyne, and Burbone, and sayd: 'My lordes, thanked be God, the kynge is nowe in good state and helth, so I delyuer him, but beware lette no mane dysplease hym, for as yet his spyrytes be no fully ferme nor stable, but lytell and lytell he shall waxe stronge; reasonable dysporte, rest, and myrthe shall be moste profytable for hym; and trouble hym as lytell as may be with any counsayles, for he hath been sharpely handeled with a hote malady.' Than it was consydred to retaygne this mayster Guyllyam, and to gyve hym that he shulde be content with all, *whiche is the ende that all physicians requyre, to haue gyftes and rewardes*; he was desyred to abyde styll about the kynge, but he excused hymselfe, and sayd howe he was an olde impotent man, and coulde note endure the maner of courte, wherfore he desyred to returne into his owne countrey. Whan the counsayle sawe he wolde none otherwyse do, they gaue him leaue, and at his departing *gave him a thousand crownes, and retayned hym in wages with four horses whansover he wolde resorte to the courte*; howbeit, I beleve he never came there after, for whan he retournd to the cytie of Laon, there he contynued and dyed a ryche man: he left behynde him a xxx thousand frankes. All his dayes he was one of the greatest nygardes that ever was: all his pleasure was to get good and to spende nothynge, for in his howse he neuer spente past two souses of Parys in a day, but wolde eate and drinke in other mennes howses, where as he myght get it. *With this rodde lyghtly all physicyons are beaten.*"[19]

The humane advice given by Guyllym countenances the tradition that cards were invented for the amusement of his royal patient.

---

[19] Froissart's Chronicles, translated by John Bouchier, Lord Berners.

CHAPTER XII.

BLEEDING.

Fashion, capricious everywhere, is especially so in surgery and medicine. Smoking we are now taught to regard as a pernicious practice, to be abhorred as James the First abhorred it. Yet Dr. Archer, and Dr. Everard in his "Panacea, or a Universal Medicine, being a discovery of the wonderful virtues of Tobacco" (1659), warmly defended the habit, and for long it was held by the highest authorities to be an efficacious preservative against disease. What would schoolboys now say to being flogged for *not* smoking? Yet Thomas Hearne, in his diary (1720-21) writes—"Jan. 21, I have been told that in the last great plague in London none that kept tobacconists' shops had the plague. It is certain that smoking was looked upon as a most excellent preservative. In so much, that even children were obliged to smoak. And I remember that I heard formerly Tom Rogers, who was yeoman beadle, say, that when he was that year, when the plague raged, a school-boy at Eton, all the boys of that school were obliged to smoak in the school every morning, and that he was never whipped so much in his life as he was one morning for not smoaking."

Blood-letting, so long a popular remedy with physicians, has, like tobacco-smoking for medicinal purposes, fallen into disuse and contempt. From Hippocrates to Paracelsus, who, with characteristic daring, raised some objections to the practice of venesection, doctors were in the habit of drawing disease from the body as vintners extract claret from a cask, in a ruddy stream. In the feudal ages bleeding was in high favour. Most of the abbeys had a "flebotomaria" or "bleeding-house," in which the sacred inmates underwent bleedings (or "minutions" as they were termed) at stated periods of the year, to the strains of psalmody. The brethren of the order of St. Victor underwent five munitions annually—in September, before Advent, before Lent, after Easter, and at Pentecost.

There is a good general view of the superstitions and customs connected with venesection, in "The Salerne Schoole," a poem of which mention continually occurs in the writings of our old physicians. The poem commences with the following stanza:—

> "The 'Salerne Schoole' doth by these lines impart
> All health to England's king, and doth advise
> From care his head to keepe, from wrath his hart.
> Drink not much wine, sup light and soon arise,
> When meat is gone long sitting breedeth smart;

And afternoon still waking keep your eies.
*   *   *   *   *

Use three physicians still—first Doctor *Quiet*,
Next Doctor *Merriman* and Doctor *Dyet*.

"Of bleeding many profits grow and great
The spirits and sences are renew'd thereby,
Thogh these mend slowly by the strength of meate,
But these with wine restor'd are by-and-by;
By bleeding to the marrow commeth heate,
It maketh cleane your braine, releeves your eie,
It mends your appetite, restoreth sleepe,
Correcting humors that do waking keep:
All inward parts and sences also clearing,
It mends the voice, touch, smell, and taste, and hearing.

"*Three special months, September, Aprill, May,*
There are in which 'tis good to ope a vein—
In these three months the moon beares greatest sway,
Then old or young, that store of blood containe,
May bleed now, though some elder wizards say,
Some daies are ill in these, I hold it vaine;
September, Aprill, May have daies apeece,
That bleeding do forbid and eating geese,
And those are they, forsooth, of May the first,
Of t'other two, the last of each are worst.

"But yet those daies I graunt, and all the rest,
Haue in some cases just impediment,
As first, if nature be with cold opprest,
Or if the Region, Ile, or Continent,
Do scorch or freez, if stomach meat detest,
If Baths you lately did frequent,
Nor old, nor young, nor drinkers great are fit,
Nor in long sickness, nor in raging fit,
Or in this case, if you will venture bleeding,
The quantity must then be most exceeding.

"When you to bleed intend, you must prepare
Some needful things both after and before:
Warm water and sweet oyle both needfull are,
And wine the fainting spirits to restore;
Fine binding cloths of linnen, and beware
That all the morning you do sleepe no more;
Some gentle motion helpeth after bleeding,
And on light meals a spare and temperate feeding
To bleed doth cheare the pensive, and remove
The raging furies bred by burning love.

"Make your incision large and not too deep,
That blood have speedy yssue with the fume;
So that from sinnews you all hurt do keep.
Nor may you (as I toucht before) presume
In six ensuing houres at all to sleep,
Lest some slight bruise in sleepe cause an apostume;
Eat not of milke, or aught of milke compounded,
Nor let your brain with much drinke be confounded;
Eat no cold meats, for such the strength impayre,
And shun all misty and unwholesome ayre.

"Besides the former rules for such as pleases
Of letting bloud to take more observation;
*　　　*　　　*　　　*　　　*

To old, to young, both letting blood displeases.
By yeares and sickness make your computation.
First in the spring for quantity you shall
Of bloud take twice as much as in the fall;
In spring and summer let the right arme bloud,
The fall and winter for the left are good."

Wadd mentions an old surgical writer who divides his chapter on bleeding under such heads as the following:—1. What is to limit bleeding? 2. Qualities of an able phlebotomist; 3. Of the choice of instruments; 4. Of the band and bolster; 5. Of porringers; 6. *Circumstances to be considered at the bleeding of a Prince.*

Simon Harward's "Phlebotomy, or Treatise of Letting of Bloud; fitly serving, as well for an advertisement and remembrance to all well-minded chirurgians, as well also to give a caveat generally to all men to beware of the manifold dangers which may ensue upon rash and unadvised letting of bloud," published in the year 1601, contains much interesting matter on the subject of which it treats. But a yet more amusing work is one that Nicholas Gyer wrote and published in 1592, under the following title:—

"The English Phlebotomy; or, Method and Way of Healing by Letting of Bloud."

On the title-page is a motto taken from the book of Proverbs—"The horse-leach hath two daughters, which crye, 'give, give.'"

The work affords some valuable insight into the social status of the profession in the sixteenth century.

In his dedicatory letter to Master Reginald Scot, Esquire, the author says that phlebotomy "is greatly abused by vagabund horse-leaches and travailing tinkers, who find work almost in every village through whom it comes (having in truth neither knowledge, nor witte, nor honesty), the sober practitioner and cunning chirurgian liveth basely, is despised, and accounted a very abject amongst the vulgar sort." Of the medical skill of Sir Thomas Eliot, and Drs. Bulleyn, Turner, Penié, and Coldwel, the author speaks in terms of warm eulogy; but as for the tinkers aforementioned, he would regard them as murderers, and "truss them up at Ty-borne."

THE FOUNDERS OF THE MEDICAL SOCIETY OF LONDON
From the Original Painting.

Gyer, who indulges in continual reference to the "Schola Salerni," makes the following contribution to the printed metrical literature on Venesection:—

> *"Certaine very old English verses, concerning the veines and letting of bloud, taken out of a very auncient paper book of Phisicke notes:—*

"Ye maisters that usen bloud-letting,
And therewith getten your living;
Here may you learn wisdome good,
In what place ye shall let bloud.
For man, in woman, or in child,
For evils that he wood and wild.
There beene veynes thirty-and-two,
For wile is many, that must he undo.
Sixteene in the head full right,
And sixteene beneath I you plight.
In what place they shall be found,
I shall you tell in what stound.
Beside the eares there beene two,
That on a child mote beene undoe;
To keep his head from evil turning
And from the scale withouten letting.
And two at the temples must bleede,
For stopping and aking I reede;
And one is in the mid forehead,
For Lepry or for sawcefleme that mote bleede.
Above the nose forsooth is one,
That for the frensie mote be undone.
Also when the eien been sore,
For the red gowt evermore.
And two other be at the eien end.
If thy bleeden them to amend.
And the arch that comes thorow smoking,
I you tell withouten leasing.
And at the whole of the throat, there beene two,
That Lepry and straight breath will undoo.
In the lips foure there beene,
Able to bleede I tell it be deene,
Two beneath, and above also
I tell thee there beene two.
For soreness of the mouth to bleede,
When it is flawne as I thee reede.
And two in the tongue withouten lie,
Mote bleede for the quinancie.
And when the tongue is aught aking,
For all manner of swelling.
Now have I tolde of certaine,

That longer for the head I weene,
And of as many I will say,
That else where there beene in fay.
In every arme there beene fife,
Full good to blede for man and wife,
Cephalica is one I wis,
The head veyne he cleaped is,
The body above and the head;
He cleanseth for evil and qued.
In the bought of the arme also,
An order there must he undoo;
Basilica his name is,
Lowest he sitteth there y wis;
Forsooth he cleanseth the liver aright,
And all other members beneath I twight.
The middle is between the two,
Corall he is clipped also
That veine cleanseth withouten doubt;
Above and beneath, within and without.
For Basilica that I of told,
One braunched veine ety up full bold,
To the thomb goeth that one braunch;
The cardiacle he wil staunch,
That there braunch full right goeth,
To the little finger withouten oth;
Saluatell is his name,
He is a veine of noble fame;
There is no veine that cleanseth so clene,
The stopping of the liver and splene.
Above the knuckles of the feet,
With two veines may thou meet,
Within sitteth *Domestica,*
And without *Saluatica.*
*   *   *   *   *

All the veines thee have I told,
That cleanseth man both yong and old.
If thou use them at thy need,
These foresaid evils they dare not dread;
So that our Lord be them helping,
That all hath in his governing.
So mote it be, so say all wee,
Amen, amen, for charitee."

To bleed on May-day is still the custom with ignorant people in a few remote districts. The system of vernal minutions probably arose from that tendency in most men to repeat an act (simply because they have done it once) until it has become a habit, and then superstitiously to persevere in the habit, simply because it is a habit. How many aged people read certain antiquated journals, as they wear exploded garments, for no other reason than that they read the same sort of literature, and wore the same sort of habiliments, when young. To miss for once the performance of a periodically recurring duty, and so to break a series of achievements, would worry many persons, as the intermitted post caused Dr. Johnson discomfort till he had returned and touched it. As early as the sixteenth century, we have Gyer combating the folly of people having recourse to periodic venesections. "There cometh to my minde," he says, "a common opinion among the ignorant people, which do certainly beleeve that, if any person be let bloud one yere, he must be let bloud every yere, or else he is (I cannot tell, nor they neither) in how great danger. Which fonde opinion of theirs, whereof soever the same sprong first, it is no more like to be true, than if I should say: when a man hath received a great wound by chaunce in any part of his body, whereby he loseth much bloud; yet after it is healed, he must needs have the like wounde againe there the next yeare, to avoid as much bloud, or els he is in daunger of great sickness, yea, and also in hazard to lose his life."

The practitioners of phlebotomy, and the fees paid for the operation, have differed widely. In the middle of the last century a woman used the lancet with great benefit to her own pocket, if not to her patients, in Marshland, in the county of Norfolk. What her charge was is unknown, probably, however, only a few pence. A distinguished personage of the same period (Lord Radnor) had a great fondness for letting the blood (at the point of an amicable lancet—not a hostile sword) of his friends. But his Lordship, far from accepting a fee, was willing to remunerate those who had the courage to submit to his surgical care. Lord Chesterfield, wanting an additional vote for a coming division in the House of Peers, called on Lord Radnor, and, after a little introductory conversation, complained of a distressing headache.

"You ought to lose blood then," said Lord Radnor.

"Gad—do you indeed think so? Then, my dear lord, do add to the service of your advice by performing the operation. I know you are a most skilful surgeon."

Delighted at the compliment, Lord Radnor in a trice pulled out his lancet-case, and opened a vein in his friend's arm.

"By-the-by," asked the patient, as his arm was being adroitly bound up, "do you go down to the House to-day?"

"I had not intended going," answered the noble operator, "not being sufficiently informed on the question which is to be debated; but you, that have considered it, which side will you vote on?"

In reply, Lord Chesterfield unfolded his view of the case; and Lord Radnor was so delighted with the reasoning of the man (who held his surgical powers in such high estimation), that he forthwith promised to support the wily earl's side in the division.

"I have shed my blood for the good of my country," said Lord Chesterfield that evening to a party of friends, who, on hearing the story, were convulsed with laughter.

Steele tells of a phlebotomist who advertised, for the good of mankind, to bleed at "threepence per head." Trade competition has, however, induced practitioners to perform the operation even without "the threepence." In the *Stamford Mercury* for March 28, 1716, the following announcement was made:—"Whereas the majority of apothecaries in Boston have agreed to pull down the price of bleeding to sixpence, let these certifie that Mr Clarke, apothecary, will bleed anybody at his shop *gratis*."

The readers of Smollett may remember in one of his novels the story of a gentleman, who, falling down in his club in an apoplectic fit, was immediately made the subject of a bet between two friendly bystanders. The odds were given and accepted against the sick man's recovery, and the wager was duly registered, when a suggestion was made by a more humane spectator that a surgeon ought to be sent for. "Stay," exclaimed the good fellow interested in having a fatal result to the attack, "if he is let blood, or interfered with in any way, the bet doesn't hold good." This humorous anecdote may be found related as an actual occurrence in Horace Walpole's works. It was doubtless one of the "good stories" current in society, and was so completely public property, that the novelist deemed himself entitled to use it as he liked. In certain recent books of "ana" the incident is fixed on Sheridan and the Prince Regent, who are represented as the parties to the bet.

Elsewhere mention has been made of a thousand pounds *ordered* to be paid Sir Edmund King for promptly bleeding Charles the Second. A nobler fee was given by a French lady to a surgeon, who used his lancet so clumsily that he cut an artery instead of a vein, in consequence of which the lady died. On her death-bed she, with charming humanity and irony, made a will, bequeathing the operator a life annuity of eight hundred livres, on condition "that he never again bled anybody so long as he lived." In the *Journal Encylopédique* of Jan. 15, 1773, a somewhat similar story is told of a Polish princess, who lost her life in the same way. In her will, made *in extremis*, there was the following clause:—"Convinced of the injury that my unfortunate accident will occasion to the unhappy surgeon who is the cause of my death, I bequeath to him a life annuity of two hundred ducats, secured by my estate, and forgive his mistake from my heart: I wish this may indemnify him for the discredit which my sorrowful catastrophe will bring upon him."

A famous French Maréchal reproved the clumsiness of a phlebotomist in a less gratifying manner. Drawing himself away from the bungling operator, just as the incision was about to be made, he displayed an unwillingness to put himself further in the power of a practitioner, who, in affixing the fillet, had given him a blow with the elbow in the face.

"My Lord," said the surgeon, "it seems that you are afraid of the bleeding."

"No," returned the Maréchal, "not of the bleeding—but the bleeder."

Monsieur, brother of Louis XIV., had an insuperable aversion to the operation, however dexterous might be the operator. At Marly, while at table with the King, he was visited with such ominous symptoms, that Fochon, the first physician of the court, said—"You are threatened with apoplexy, and you cannot be too soon blooded."

But the advice was not acted on, though the King entreated that it might be complied with.

"You will find," said Louis, "what your obstinacy will cost you. We shall be awoke some of these nights to be told that you are dead."

The royal prediction, though not fulfilled to the letter, soon proved substantially true. After a gay supper at St. Cloud, Monsieur, just as he was about to retire to bed, quitted the world. He was asking M. de Ventadour for a glass of liqueur sent him by the Duke of Savoy, when he dropped down dead. Anyhow Monsieur went out of this life thinking of something nice. The Marquis of Hertford, with all his deliberation, could not do more.

The excess to which the practice of venesection was carried in the last century is almost beyond belief. The *Mercure de France* (April, 1728, and December, 1729) gives the particulars of the illness of a woman named Gignault. She was aged 24 years, was the wife of an hussar, and resided at St. Sauge, a town of the Nivernois. Under the direction of Monsieur Theveneau, Seigneur de Palmery, M.D., of St. Sauge, she was bled three thousand nine hundred and four times in nine months (*i. e.* from the 6th of September, 1726, to the 3rd of June, 1727). By the 15th of July, in the same year, the bleedings numbered four thousand five hundred and fifty-five. From the 6th of September, 1726, to the 1st of December, 1729, the blood-lettings amounted to twenty-six thousand two hundred and thirty. Did this really occur? Or was the editor of the *Mercure de France* the original Baron Munchausen?

Such an account as the above ranges us on the side of the German physician, who petitioned that the use of the lancet might be made penal. Garth's epigram runs:—

> "Like a pert skuller, one physician plies,
> And all his art and all his skill he tries;
> But two physicians, like a pair of oars,
> Conduct you faster to the Stygian shores."

It would, however, be difficult to imagine a quicker method to destroy human life than that pursued by Monsieur Theveneau. A second adviser could hardly have accelerated his movements, or increased his determination not to leave his reduced patient a chance of recovery.

"A rascal," exclaimed a stout, asthmatic old gentleman, to a well-dressed stranger on Holborn Hill—"a rascal has stolen my hat. I tried to overtake him— and I'm—so—out of breath—I can't stir another inch." The stranger eyed the old gentleman, who was panting and gasping for hard life, and then pleasantly observing, "Then I'm hanged, old boy, if I don't have your wig," scampered off, leaving his victim bald as a baby. M. Theveneau was the two thieves in one. He first brought his victim to a state of helplessness, and then "carried out his little system." It would be difficult to assign a proper punishment to such a stupid destroyer of human life. Formerly, in the duchy of Wurtemberg, the public executioner, after having sent out of the world a certain number of his fellow-creatures, was dignified with the degree of doctor of physic. It would not be otherwise than well to confer on such murderous physicians as M. Theveneau the honorary rank of hangman extraordinary.

The incomes that have been realized by blood-letting alone are not less than those which, in the present day, are realized by the administration of chloroform. An eminent phlebotomist, not very many years since, made a thousand per annum by the lancet.

About blood-letting—by the lancet, leeches, and cupping (or *boxing*, as it was called in Elizabeth's days, and much later)—the curious can obtain many interesting particulars in our old friend Bulleyn's works.

To open a vein has for several generations been looked on as beneath the dignity of the leading professors of medicine or surgery. In some cases phlebotomy was practised as a sort of specialty by surgeons of recognised character: but generally, at the close of the last century, it was left, as a branch of practice, in the hands of the apothecary. The occasions on which physicians have of late years used the lancet are so few, that it is almost a contribution to medical gossip to bring up a new instance. One of the more recent cases of a notability being let blood by a physician, was when Sir Lucas Pepys, on Oct. 2, 1806, bled the Princess of Wales. On that day, as her Royal Highness was proceeding to Norbury Park, to visit Mr. Locke, in a barouche drawn by four horses, the carriage was upset at Leatherhead. Of the two ladies who accompanied the Princess, one (Lady Sheffield) escaped without a bruise, but the other (Miss Cholmondley) was thrown to the ground and killed on the spot. The injuries sustained by the Princess were very slight, but Sir Lucas Pepys, who luckily happened to be in the neighbourhood at the time of the accident, bled her on his own responsibility, and with his own hand.

CHAPTER XIII.

RICHARD MEAD.

"Dr. Mead," observed Samuel Johnson, "lived more in the broad sunshine of life than almost any man."

Unquestionably the lot of Richard Mead was an enviable one. Without any high advantages of birth or fortune, or aristocratic connection, he achieved a European popularity; and in the capital of his own country had a social position that has been surpassed by no member of his profession. To the sunshine in which Mead basked, the lexicographer contributed a few rays; for when James published his Medicinal Dictionary, the prefatory letter to Mead, affixed to the work, was composed by Johnson in his most felicitous style.

"Sir, — That the Medicinal Dictionary is dedicated to you, is to be imputed only to your reputation for superior skill in those sciences which I have endeavoured to explain and to facilitate; and you are, therefore, to consider the address, if it be agreeable to you, as one of the rewards of merit; and, if otherwise, as one of the inconveniences of eminence.

"However you shall receive it, my design cannot be disappointed; because this public appeal to your judgment will show that I do not found my hopes of approbation upon the ignorance of my readers, and that I fear his censure least whose knowledge is the most extensive. I am, sir, your most obedient humble servant, — R. JAMES."

But the sunshine did not come to Mead. He attracted it. Polished, courtly, adroit, and of an equable temper, he seemed pleased with everybody, and so made everybody pleased with him. Throughout life he was a Whig—staunch and unswerving, notwithstanding the charges brought against him by obscure enemies of being a luke-warm supporter of the constitutional, and a subservient worshipper of the monarchical, party. And yet his intimate friends were of the adverse faction. The overbearing, insolent, prejudiced Radcliffe forgave him his scholarship and politics, and did his utmost to advance his interests.

Mead's family was a respectable one in Buckinghamshire. His father was a theological writer, and one of the two ministers of Stepney, but was ejected from his preferment for non-conformity on the 24th of August, 1662. Fortunately the dispossessed clerk had a private fortune on which to maintain his fifteen children, of whom Richard, the eleventh, was born on the eleventh of August, 1673. The first years of Richard's life were spent at Stepney, where the Rev. Matthew Mead continued to minister to a noncomformist congregation, keeping in house Mr. John

Nesbitt, afterwards a conspicuous nonconformist minister, as tutor to his children. In 1683 or 1684, it being suspected that Mr. Mead was concerned in certain designs against the government, the worthy man had to quit his flock and escape from the emissaries of power to Holland. During the father's residence abroad, Richard was sent to a classical school kept in Clerkenwell Close, by the nonconformist, Thomas Singleton, who had formerly been second master of Eton. It was under this gentleman's tuition that the boy acquired a sound and extensive knowledge of Latin and Greek. In 1690 he went to Utrecht; and after studying there for three years, proceeded to Leyden, where he studied botany and physic. His academical studies concluded, he travelled with David Polhill and Dr. Thomas Pellet, afterwards President of the College of Physicians, through Italy, stopping at Florence, Padua, Naples, and Rome. In the middle of 1696 he returned to London, with stores of information, refined manners, and a degree of Doctor of Philosophy and Physic, conferred on him at Padua, on the sixteenth of August, 1695. Settling at Stepney, and uniting himself closely with the nonconformists, he commenced the practice of his profession, in which he rapidly advanced to success. On the ninth of May, 1703, before he was thirty years of age, he was chosen physician of St. Thomas's Hospital, in Southwark. On obtaining this preferment he took a house in Crutched Friars, and year by year increased the sphere of his operations. In 1711 he moved to Austin Friars, to the house just vacated by the death of Dr. Howe. The consequences of this step taught him the value, to a rising doctor, of a house with a good reputation. Many of Howe's patients had got into a habit of coming to the house as much as to the physician, and Mead was only too glad to feel their pulses and flatter them into good humour, sound health, and the laudable custom of paying double fees. He was appointed Lecturer on Anatomy to the Company of Barbers and Surgeons.

He kept himself well before the public, as an author, with his "Mechanical Account of Poisons," published in 1702; and his treatise (1704), "De Imperio Solis et Lunæ in Corpora humana, et Morbis inde oriundis." He became a member of the Royal Society; and, in 1707, he received his M.D. diploma from Oxford, and his admission to the fellowship of the College of Physicians.

It has already been stated how Radcliffe engaged to introduce Mead to his patients. When Queen Anne was on her death-bed, the young physician was of importance enough to be summoned to the couch of dying royalty. The physicians who surrounded the expiring queen were afraid to say what they all knew. The Jacobites wanted to gain time, to push off the announcement of the queen's state to the last possible moment, so that the Hanoverians should not be able to take steps for quietly securing the succession which they desired. Mead, however, was too earnest a Whig to sacrifice what he believed to be the true interests of the country to any considerations of the private advantage that might be derived by currying favour with the Tory magnates, who, hovering about the Court, were debating how they could best make their game. Possibly his hopes emboldened him to speak the truth. Anyhow, he declared, on his first visit, that the queen would not live an hour. Charles Ford, writing to Swift, said, "This morning when I went there before nine, they told me she was just expiring. That account continued above three hours, and a report was carried to town that she was actually dead. She was not prayed for even in her own chapel at St. James's; and, *what is more infamous (!)* stocks arose three *per cent.* upon it in the city. Before I came away, she had recovered a warmth in her breast and one of her arms; and all the doctors agreed she would, in all probability, hold out till to-morrow—*except Mead, who pronounced, several hours before, she could not live two minutes, and seems uneasy it did not happen so.*" This was the tone universally adopted by the Jacobites. According to them, poor Queen Anne had hard measure dealt out to her by her physicians;—the Tory Radcliffe negatively murdered her by not saving her; the Whig Mead earnestly desired her death. Certainly the Jacobites had no reason to speak well of Mead, for the ready courage with which he stated the queen's demise to be at hand gave a disastrous blow to their case, and did much to seat George I. quietly on the throne. Miss Strickland observes, "It has always been considered that the prompt boldness of this political physician (*i. e.* Mead) occasioned the peaceable proclamation of George I. The queen's demise in one hour was confidently predicted by her Whig doctor. He was often taunted afterwards with the chagrin his countenance expressed when the royal patient, on being again blooded, recovered her speech and senses."

On the death of Radcliffe, the best part of his empire descended to Mead, who, having already reaped the benefit of occupying the nest which Howe vacated at the summons of death, wisely resolved to take possession of Radcliffe's vacated mansion in Bloomsbury Square. This removal from Austin Friars to the more fashionable quarter of town was effected without delay. Indeed, Radcliffe was not buried when Mead entered his house. As his practice lay now more in the West than the East end of town, the prosperous physician resigned his appointment at St. Thomas's, and, receiving the thanks of the grand committee for his services, was presented with the staff of a governor of the charity. Radcliffe's practice and house were not the only possessions of that sagacious practitioner which Mead contrived to acquire. Into his hands also passed the doctor's gold-headed cane of office. This wand became the property successively of Radcliffe, Askew, Pitcairn, and Baillie, the arms of all which celebrated physicians are engraved on its head. On the death of Dr. Baillie, Mrs. Baillie presented the cane, as an interesting professional relic, to the College of Physicians, in the library of which august and learned body it is now preserved. Some years since the late respected Dr. Macmichael made the adventures of this stick the subject of an agreeable little book, which was published under the title of "The Gold-Headed Cane."

The largest income Mead ever made in one year was £7000. For several years he received between £5000 and £6000 per annum. When the great depreciation of the currency is taken into account, one may affirm, with little fear of contradiction, that no living physician is at the present time earning as much. Mead, however, made his income without any avaricious or stingy practices. In every respect he displayed that generosity which has for generations been the glorious distinction of his profession. At home his fee was a guinea. When he visited a patient of good rank and condition, in consultation or otherwise, he expected to have two guineas, or even more. But to the apothecaries who waited on him at his coffee-houses, he charged (like Radcliffe) only half-a-guinea for prescriptions, written without seeing the patient. His evening coffee-house was Batson's, frequented by the profession even down to Sir William Blizard; and in the forenoons he received apothecaries at Tom's, near Covent Garden. In Mead's time the clergy, as a body, were unable to pay the demands which professional etiquette would have required the physician to make on them if he had any. It is still the humane custom of physicians and eminent surgeons not to accept fees from curates, half-pay officers in the army and navy, and men of letters; and no one has more reason than the writer of these pages to feel grateful for the delicacy with which they act on this rule, and the benevolent zeal with which they seem anxious to drown the sense of obligation (which a gratuitous patient necessarily experiences) in increased attention and kindness, as if their good deeds were a peculiar source of pleasure to themselves.

But in the last century the beneficed clergy were in a very different pecuniary condition from that which they at present enjoy. Till the Tithe Communication Act passed, the parson (unless he was a sharp man of business, shrewd and unscrupulous as a horse-jobber, and ready to have an unintermittent war with his parishioners) never received anything like what he was entitled to of the produce of the land. Often he did not get half his dues; and even when he did obtain a fair tithe, his receipts were small compared with what his successor in the present generation has from the same source. Agriculture was then in such a backward state, and land was so ill-cultivated, that the rector of a large parish of good land was justly entitled only to a sum that a modern rent-charge holder would regard with painful surprise if told that he might take nothing more for his share in the fruits of the earth. The beneficed clergy were a comparatively poor body. The curate perhaps was not in a worse state than he is in now, for the simple reason that a worse can hardly be. To add to the impoverished appearance of the clerical profession, there existed in every capital and country town the luckless nonconforming clergy, bereft of the emoluments of their vocation, and often reduced to a condition scarcely—if at all—removed from begging. The title of *Reverend* was still affixed to their names—their costume was still that of their order—and by large masses of the people they were regarded with more reverence and affection than the well-fed Vicars of Bray, who, with mealy mouths and elastic consciences, saw only the butter on one side of their bread, and not the dirt on the other. Archbishop Sancroft died on his little farm in Suffolk, having for years subsisted on about fifty pounds a-year. When such was the fate of an Archbishop of Canterbury, the straits to which the ejected vicars or disabled curates were brought can be imagined— but scarcely described. In the great towns these unfortunate gentlemen swarmed, gaining a wretched subsistence as ushers in schools, tutors, secretaries—not unfrequently as domestic servants.

In such a condition of the established church, the rule of never taking money from "the cloth" was almost invariably observed by the members of the medical profession.

Mead once—and only once—departed from this rule. Mr. Robert Leake, a fellow of St. John's College, Cambridge, called on the doctor and sought his advice. The patient's ill-health had been in a great degree effected by doctoring himself—

that is, exhibiting, according to his own notions of medical practice, some of Dr. Cheyne's prescriptions.

"Do as I tell you," said Mead, "and I'll set you up again."

For a time Leake cheerfully obeyed; but soon—although his case was progressing most favourably—he had the bad taste to suggest that a recurrence to some of Cheyne's prescriptions would be advisable. Mead, of course, was not pleased with such folly, but continued his attendance till his patient's health was restored. Leake then went through the form of asking to what amount he was in the physician's debt.

"Sir," answered Mead, "I have never yet, in the whole course of my practice, taken or demanded the least fee from any clergyman; but, since you have been pleased, contrary to what I have met with in any other gentleman of your profession, to prescribe to me rather than follow my prescriptions, when you had committed the care of your recovery to my skill and trust, you must not take it amiss, nor will, I hope, think it unfair, if I demand ten guineas of you."

With much reluctance, and a wry face, Leake paid the money, but the doctor subsequently returned him more than half of it.

Of course Mead did not gain the prize of his profession without a few rough contests with competitors in the race of honour. Woodward, the Professor of Physic at the Gresham College, attacked him with bitterness in his "State of Physic and Diseases," and made himself even more obnoxious in his personal demeanour to him in public. Some insult offered to him by Woodward so infuriated Mead, that the latter drew his sword and ordered his adversary to defend himself. The duel terminated in Mead's favour, as far as martial prowess was concerned, for he disarmed Woodward and ordered him to beg for his life.

"Never, till I am your patient," answered Woodward, happily.

The memory of this Æsculapian battle is preserved in an engraving in Ward's "Lives of the Gresham Professors." The picture is a view of Gresham Street College, with a gateway entering from Broad Street, marked 25, within which Woodward is represented as kneeling and submissively yielding his sword to Mead. Ward was one of Mead's warmest friends, and certainly on this occasion displayed his friendship in a very graceful and effective manner.

The doctor would gladly have never had to deal with a more dangerous antagonist than Woodward; but the time came when he had to run for safety, and that too from a woman. He was in attendance by the bed-side of the Duke of Marlborough, who was suffering from indisposition, when her Grace—the celebrated Sarah—flew into a violent rage at some remark which the physician had dared to make. She even threatened him with personal chastisement, and was proceeding to carry out her menaces, when Mead, recognizing the peril of his position, turned and fled from the room. The duchess ran after him, and, pursuing him down the grand staircase, vowed she would pull off his wig, and dash it in his face. The doctor luckily was a better runner than her Grace, and escaped.

Envy is the shadow of success, and detraction is the echo of its voice. A host of pamphleteers, with just courage enough to print lies, to which they had not the spirit to affix their obscure names, hissed their malignity at the fortunate doctor. The members of the Faculty, accustomed though they are to the jealousies and animosities which are important undercurrents in every fraternity, would in these days scarcely credit the accounts which could be given of the coarseness and baseness of the anonymous rascals who lampooned Mead. It is painful to know that some of the worst offenders were themselves physicians. In 1722, appeared "The Art of getting into Practice in Physick, here at present in London. In a letter to that very ingenious and most learned Physician (Lately come to Town), Dr Timothy Vanbustle, M.D.—A.B.C.," the writer of this satire attributes to the dead Radcliffe the practices to which Hannes was accused of having resorted. "Thus the famous R——fe, 'tis said, on his first arrival, had half the porters in town employed to call for him at all the coffee-houses and public places, so that his name might be known." The sting of the publication, the authorship of which by a strange error has been attributed *to* Mead, is throughout directed *at* him. It is more than suggested that he, to creep up into practice, had associated in early life with "women, midwives, nurses, and apothecaries," and that he had interested motives for being very gentle "in taking fees of the clergy, of whatsoever sect or opinion." Here is a stab that the reader of the foregoing pages can appreciate: "As to *Nostrums*, I cannot much encourage you to trade in these if you would propose to get universal business; for though they may serve to make you known at first, particularly in such a way, yet it will not promote general business, but on the contrary. *I rather therefore would advise you to court, flatter, and chime in with the chief in Play, and luckily a noted practitioner should drop, do you be as sure and ready to get into his house as he is into his coffin.*"

More scandal of this sort may be found in "An account of a Strange and Wonderful Dream. Dedicated to Doctor M——d," published 1719. It is insinuated in the dream that his Latin writings were not his own composition. The troubles of his domestic life are dragged before the public. "It unluckily happen'd that, just as Mulso discovered his wife's intrigues, his effects were seized on by his creditors, his chariot and horses were sold, and he himself reduced to the state of a foot-quack. In this condition he had continued to this day, had he not been retrieved from poverty and contempt by the recommendation of a physician of great note. Upon this he spruced up, looked gay, roll'd about in a chariot. At this time he fell ill of the *scribendi cacoethes*, and, by the help of two mathematicians and an usher, was delivered of a book in a learned language."

Mead did not long occupy Radcliffe's house in Bloomsbury Square. In 1719 he moved to the imposing residence in Ormond Street, to which in 1732 he added a gallery for the accommodation of his library and museum.

Of Mead's various contributions to medical literature it is of course not the province of this work to speak critically. The *Medica Sacra* is a literary curiosity, and so is the doctor's paper published in 1735, in which he recommends a compound of pepper and *lichen cinereus terrestris* as a specific against the bite of a mad dog. Dampier, the traveller, used this lichen for the same purpose. The reader need not be reminded of the popularity attained by this antidote, dividing the public favour, as it did, with Dr. James's *Turpeth Mineral*, and the *Musk* and *Cinnabar*.

Mead was married twice. His first wife was Ruth Marsh, the daughter of a pious London tradesman. She died in 1719, twenty years after her marriage, leaving behind her four children—three daughters, who all married well, and one son, William Mead. If any reliance is to be placed on the statements of the lampoon writers, the doctor was by no means fortunate in this union. He married, however, a second time—taking for his bride, when he was more than fifty years old, Anne, the daughter of Sir Rowland Alston, of Odell, a Bedfordshire baronet.

One of the pleasant episodes in Mead's life is his conduct towards his dear friend and political antagonist, Freind—the Jacobite physician, and Member of Parliament for Launceston. On suspicion of being concerned in the Atterbury plot, Freind was committed to the Tower. During his confinement, that lasted some months, he employed himself calmly on the composition of a Latin letter, "On certain kinds of Small-Pox," and the "History of Physic, from the time of Galen to the Commencement of the Sixteenth Century." Mead busied himself to obtain his friend's release; and, being called to attend Sir Robert Walpole, pleaded so forcibly for the prisoner, that the minister allowed him to be discharged on bail—his sureties being Dr. Mead, Dr. Hulse, Dr. Levet, and Dr. Hale. To celebrate the termination of Freind's captivity, Mead called together on a sudden a large party in Ormond Street, composed of men of all shades of opinion. Just as Freind was about to take his leave for his own residence in Albemarle Street, accompanied by Arbuthnot, who resided in Cork Street, Burlington Gardens, Mead took him aside into a private room, and presented him with a case containing the fees he had received from the Tory doctor's patients during his imprisonment. They amounted to no less than five thousand guineas.

Mead's style of living was very liberal. From the outset to the close of his career he was the companion of men whom it was an honour to treat hospitably. He was the friend of Pope, Newton, and Bentley. His doors were always open to every visitor who came from a foreign country to these shores, with any claim whatever on the goodwill of society. To be at the same time a patron of the arts, and a liberal entertainer of many guests, demands no ordinary expenditure. Mead died comparatively poor. The sale of his library, pictures, statues, and curiosities, realized about £16,000, and he had other property amounting to about £35,000; but, after the payment of his debts, not more than £20,000 remained to be divided amongst his four children. His only son, however, was amply provided for, having entered into the possession of £30,000 under will of Dr. Mead's unmarried brother Samuel, an eminent barrister, and a Commissioner of the Customs.

Fortunate beyond fortunate men, Mead had the great misfortune of living too long. His sight failed, and his powers underwent that gradual decay which is the saddest of all possible conclusions to a vigorous and dignified existence. Stories might be ferreted up of the indignities to which he submitted at the hands of a domineering valet. Long, however, before he sunk into second childhood, he excited the ridicule of the town by his vanity, and absurd pretensions to be a lady-killer. The extravagances of his amorous senility were whispered about; and, eventually, some hateful fellow seized hold of the unpleasant rumours, and published them in a scandalous novelette, called "The Cornutor of Seventy-five; being a genuine narrative of the Life, Adventures, and Amours of *Don Ricardo Honeywater*, Fellow of the Royal College of Physicians at Madrid, Salamanca, and Toledo, and President of the Academy of Sciences in Lapland; containing, amongst other most diverting particulars, his intrigue with Donna Maria W— —s, of Via Vinculosa—*anglice*, Fetter Lane—in the city of Madrid. Written, originally, in Spanish, by the Author of Don Quixot, and translated into English by a Graduate of the College of Mecca, in Arabia." The "Puella fabri," as Greenfield designates the damsel who warmed the doctor's aged heart, was the daughter of a blacksmith in Fetter Lane; and to please her, Mead—long past threescore years and ten—went to Paris, and learnt dancing, under Dupré, giving as an excuse that his health needed active muscular exercise.

Dr. Mead died on February 16, 1754, in his eighty-first year. He was buried in the Temple Church, by the side of his brother Samuel. His memory has been honoured with busts and inscriptions—in Westminster Abbey, and the College of Physicians.

Mead was not the first of his name to enter the medical profession. William George Meade was an eminent physician at Tunbridge Wells; and dying there on the 4th of November, 1652, was buried at Ware, in Hertfordshire. This gentleman left £5 a-year for ever to the poor; but he is more remarkable for longevity than generosity. He died at the extraordinary age of 148 years and nine months. This is one of the most astonishing instances of longevity on record. Old Parr, dying at 152 years of age, exceeded it only by 4 years. The celebrated Countess Desmond was some years more than 140 at the time of her death. Henry Read, minister of Hardwicke, Co. Northampton, numbered only 132 years; and the Lancashire woman (the *Cricket of the Hedge*) did not outlive the 141st year. But all these ages become insignificant when put by the side of the 169 years to which Henry Jenkins protracted his earthly sojourn.

CHAPTER XIV.

IMAGINATION AS A REMEDIAL POWER.

Astrology, alchemy, the once general belief in the healing effects of the royal touch, the use of charms and amulets, and mesmerism, are only various exhibitions of one superstition, having for their essence the same little grain of truth, and for their outward expression different forms of error. Disconnected as they appear at first sight, a brief examination discovers the common features which prove them to be of one family. By turns they have—each of them—given humiliating evidence of the irrational extravagances that reasoning creatures are capable of committing; and each of them, also, has conferred some benefits on mankind. The gibberish of Geber, and the alchemists who preceded and followed him, led to the study of chemistry, the utility and importance of which science we have only begun rightly to appreciate; and a curiosity about the foolishness of astrology led Sir Isaac Newton to his astronomical inquiries. Lord Bacon says—"The sons of chemistry, while they are busy seeking the hidden gold—whether real or not—have by turning over and trying, brought much profit and convenience to mankind." And if the delusions of talismans, amulets, and charms, and the impostures of Mesmer, have had no greater consequences, they have at least afforded, to the observant and reflective, much valuable instruction with regard to the constitution of the human mind.

In the history of these superstitions we have to consider the universal faith which men in all ages have entertained in planetary influence, and which, so long as day and night, and the moon and tides endure, few will be found so ignorant or so insensible as to question. The grand end of alchemy was to transmute the base metals into gold; and it proposed to achieve this by obtaining possession of the different fires transmitted by the heavenly bodies to our planet, and subjecting, according to a mysterious system, the comparatively worthless substances of the mineral world to the forces of these fires.

"Now," says Paracelsus, in his "Secrets of Alchemy," "we come to speake of a manifold spirit or fire, which is the cause of variety and diversity of creatures, so that there cannot one be found right like another, and the same in every part; as it may be seen in metals, of which there is none which hath another like itself; the *Sun* produceth his gold; the *Moon* produceth another metal far different, to wit, silver; *Mars* another, that is to say, iron; *Jupiter* produceth another kind of metal to wit, tin; *Venus* another, which is copper; and *Saturn* another kind, that is to say, lead: so that they are all unlike, and several one from another; the same appeareth to be as well amongst men as all other creatures, the cause whereof is the multiplicity of fire.... Where there is no great mixture of the elements, the Sun bringeth forth; where it is a little more thick, the Moon; where more gross, Venus; and thus, according to the diversity of mixtures, are produced divers metals; so that no metal appeared in the same mine like another."

This, which is an extract from Turner's translation of Paracelsus's "Secrets of Alchemy" (published in 1655), may be taken as a fair sample of the jargon of alchemy.

The same faith in planetary influence was the grand feature of astrology, which regarded all natural phenomena as the effects of the stars acting upon the earth. Diseases of all kinds were referable to the heavenly bodies; and so, also, were the properties of those herbs or other objects which were believed in as remedial agents. In ancient medicine, pharmacy was at one period only the application of the dreams of astrology to the vegetable world. The herb which put an ague or madness to flight, did so by reason of a mystic power imparted to it by a particular constellation, the outward signs of which quality were to be found in its colour or aspect. Indeed, it was not enough that "a simple," impregnated with curative power by heavenly beams, should be culled; but it had to be culled at a particular period of the year, at a particular day of the month, even at a particular hour, when the irradiating source of its efficacy was supposed to be affecting it with a peculiar force; and, moreover, it had to be removed from the ground or the stem on which it grew with a particular instrument or gesture of the body—a disregard of which forms would have obviated the kindly influence of the particular star, without whose benignant aid the physician and the drug were alike powerless.

Medical practitioners smile now at the mention of these absurdities. But many of them are ignorant that they, in their daily practice, help to perpetuate the observance of one of these ridiculed forms. The sign which every member of the Faculty puts before his prescriptions, and which is very generally interpreted as an abbreviation for *Recipe*, is but the astrological symbol of Jupiter.

It was on this principle that a belief became prevalent that certain objects, either of natural formation or constructed by the instruments of art, had the power of counteracting noxious agents. An intimate connection was supposed to exist between the form or colour of an external substance and the use to which it ought to be put. Red objects had a mysterious influence on inflammatory diseases; and yellow ones had a similar power on those who were discoloured with jaundice. Edward II.'s physician, John of Gaddesden, informs us, "When the son of the renowned King of England lay sick of the small-pox, I took care that everything round the bed should be of a red colour, which succeeded so completely that the Prince was restored to perfect health without a vestige of a pustule remaining." Even as late as 1765, this was put in practice to the Emperor Francis I. The earliest talismans were natural objects, with a more or less striking external character, imagined to have been impressed upon them by the planets of whose influence they were especially susceptible, and of whose virtues they were beyond all other substances the recipients. The amulet (which differs little from the talisman, save in that it must be worn suspended upon the person it is to protect, whereas the talisman might be kept by its fortunate possessor locked up in his treasure-house) had a like origin.

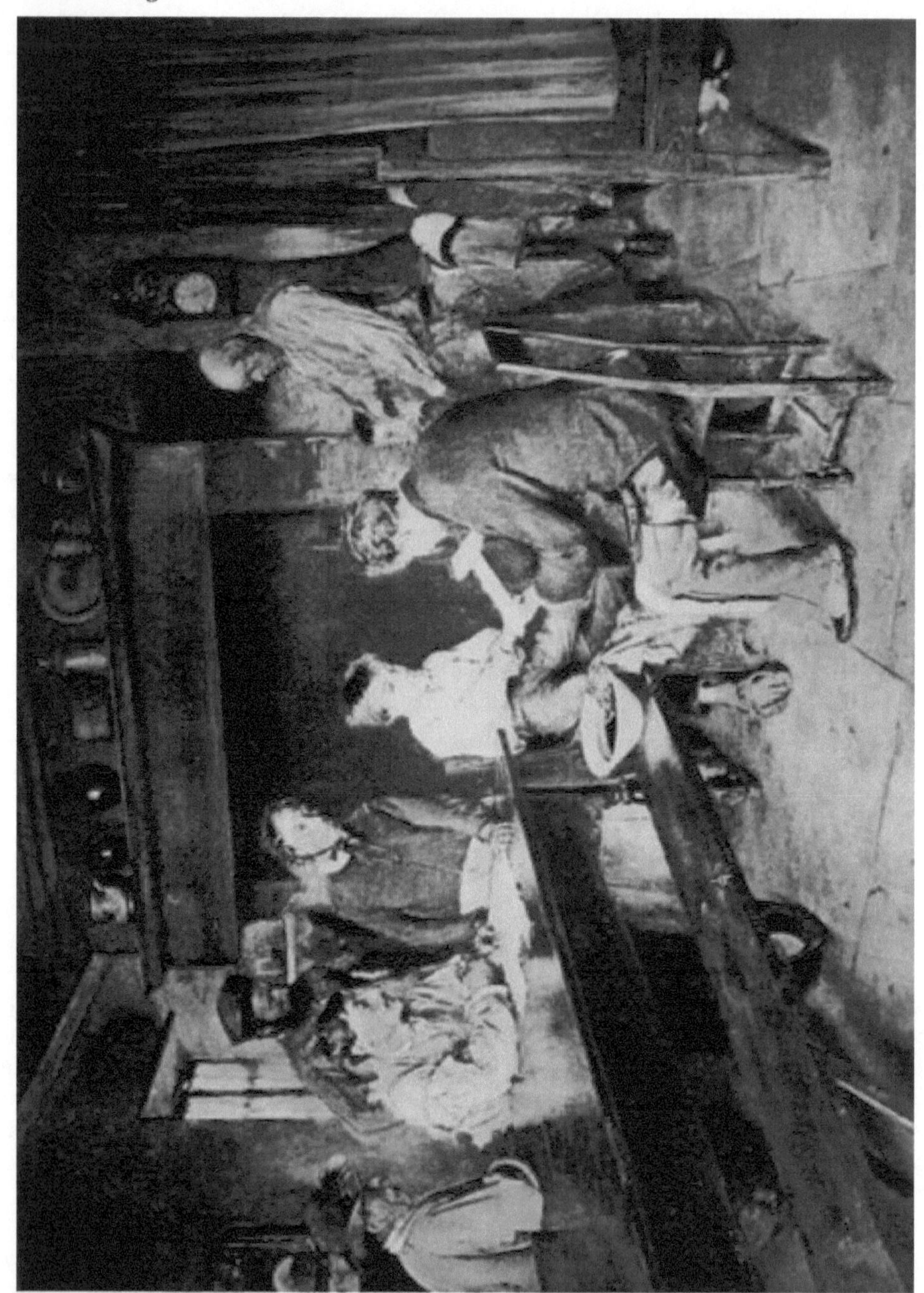

AN ACCIDENT[20]

From the Original Painting by Dagnan-Vouveret.

[20] Original by courtesy of William Wood & Co., New York.

But when once a superstitious regard was paid to the external marks of a natural object, it was a short and easy step to produce the semblances of the revered characters by an artificial process, and then bestow on them the reverential feelings which had previously been directed to their originals. The ordinary course taken by a superstition in its degradation is one where its first sentiment becomes lost to sight, and its form is dogmatically insisted on. It was so in that phase of feticism which consisted in the blind reliance put on artificial talismans and amulets. The original significance of the talisman—the truth which was embodied in it as the emblem of the unseen powers that had produced it, in accordance with natural operations—was forgotten. The rows of lines and scratches, and the variegations of its colour, were only thought of; and the cunning of man—ever ready to make a god for himself—was exerted to improve upon them. In the multitude of new devices came inscriptions of mystic numbers, strange signs, agglomerations of figures, and scraps from sacred rituals—Abraxas and Abracadabra, and the Fi-fo-fum nonsense of the later charms.

Creatures that were capable of detecting the influence of the planetary system on that portion of Nature which is unquestionably affected by it, and of imagining its presence in inanimate objects, which, to use cautious language, have never been proved by science to be sensible of such a power, of course magnified its consequences in all that related to the human intellect and character. The instant in which a man entered the world was regarded as the one when he was most susceptible. Indeed, a babe was looked upon as a piece of warm and pliant wax: and the particular planet which was in the ascendant when the nurse placed the new child of Adam amongst the people of earth stamped upon it a distinctive charactery. To be born under a particular star was then an expression that meant something. On the nature of the star it depended whether homunculus, squealing out its first agonies, was to be morose or gentle, patient or choleric, lively or saturnine, amorous or vindictive—a warrior or a poet—a dreamer or a man of action.

Laughing at the refinements of absurdity at which astrology had arrived in his day, the author of "Hudibras" says:—

> "There's but the twinkling of a star
> Between a man of peace and war;
> A thief and justice, fool and knave,
> A huffing officer and slave;
> A crafty lawyer and a pickpocket,
> A great philosopher and a blockhead;
> A formal preacher and a player,
> A learned physician and manslayer.
> As if men from stars did suck
> Old age, diseases, and ill-luck,
> Wit, folly, honour, virtue, vice,
> Travel and women, trade and dice;
> And draw, with the first air they breathe,
> Battle and murder, sudden death.
> Are not these fine commodities

> To be imported from the skies,
> And vended here amongst the rabble
> For staple goods and warrantable?"

Involved in this view of the universe was the doctrine that some exceptional individuals were born far superior to the mass of their fellow-creatures. Absurd as astrology was, still, its postulates having once been granted, the logic was unassailable which argued that those few on whose birth lucky stars had shone benignantly, had a destiny and an organization distinct from those of ordinary mortals. The dicta of modern liberalism, and the Transatlantic dogma that "all men are by nature born equal," would have appeared to an orthodox believer in this planetary religion nothing better than the ravings of madness or impiety. Monarchs of men, whatever lowly station they at first occupied in life, were exalted above others because they possessed a distinctive excellence imparted to them at the hour of birth by the silent rulers of the night. It was useless to strive against such authority. To contend with it would have been to wrestle with the Almighty—ever present in his peculiarly favoured creatures.

Rulers being such, it was but natural for their servile worshippers to believe them capable of imparting to others, by a glance of the eye or a touch of the hand, an infinitesimal portion of the virtue that dwelt within them. To be favoured with their smiles was to bask in sunshine amid perfumes. To be visited with their frowns was to be chilled to the marrow, and feel the hail come down like keen arrows from an angry sky. To be touched by their robes was to receive new vigour. Hence came credence in the miraculous power of the imposition of royal, or otherwise sacred hands. Pyrrhus and Vespasian cured maladies by the touch of their fingers; and, long before and after them, earthly potentates and spiritual directors had, both in the East and the West, to prove their title to authority by displaying the same faculty.

In our own country more than in any other region of Christendom this superstition found supporters. From Edward the Confessor down to Queen Anne, who laid her healing hands on Samuel Johnson, it flourished; and it was a rash man who, trusting to the blind guidance of human reason dared to question that manifestation of the divinity which encircles kingship. Doubtless the gift of money made to each person who was touched did not tend to bring the cure into dis-esteem. It can be easily credited that, out of the multitude who flocked to the presence of Elizabeth and the Stuart kings for the benefit of their miraculous manipulations, there were many shrewd vagabonds who had more faith in the coin than in the touch bestowed upon them. The majority, however, it cannot be doubted, were as sincere victims of delusion as those who, at the close of the last century, believed in the efficacy of metallic tractors, and those who now unconsciously expose their intellectual infirmity as advocates of electro-biology and spirit-rapping. The populace, as a body, unhesitatingly believed that their sovereigns possessed this faculty as the anointed of the Lord. A story is told of a Papist, who, much to his astonishment, was cured of the king's evil by Elizabeth, after her final rupture with the court of Rome.

"Now I perceive," cried the man, "by plain experience that the excommunication against the Queen is of no effect, since God hath blessed her with such a gift."

Nor would it be wise to suppose that none were benefited by the treatment. The eagerness with which the vulgar crowd to a sight, and the intense excitement with which London mobs witness a royal procession to the houses of Parliament, or a Lord Mayor's pageant on its way from the City to Westminster, may afford us some idea of the inspiriting sensations experienced by a troop of wretches taken from their kennels to Whitehall, and brought into personal contact with their sovereign—their ideal of grandeur! Such a trip was a stimulus to the nervous system, compared with which the shock of a galvanic battery would have been but the tickling of a feather. And, over and above this, was the influence of imagination, which in many ways may become an agent for restoring the tone of the nervous system, and so enabling Nature to overcome the obstacles of her healthy action.

Montaigne admirably treated this subject in his essay, "Of the Force of Imagination"; and his anecdote of the happy results derived by an unfortunate nobleman from the use of a flat gold plate, graven with celestial figures, must have occurred to many of his readers who have witnessed the beneficial effects which are frequently produced by the practices of quackery.

"These apes' tricks," says Montaigne, "are the main cause of the effect, our fancy being so far seduced as to believe that such strange and uncouth formalities must of necessity proceed from some abstruse science. Their very inanity gives them reverence and weight."

And old Burton, touching, in his "Anatomy of Melancholy," on the power of imagination, says, quaintly:—

"How can otherwise blear eyes in one man cause the like affection in another? Why doth one man's yawning make another man yawn? Why do witches and old women fascinate and bewitch children; but, as Wierus, Paracelsus, Cardan, Migaldus, Valleriola, Cæsar Vanninus, Campanella, and many philosophers think, the forcible imagination of one party moves and alters the spirits of the other. Nay more, they cause and cure, not only diseases, maladies, and several infirmities by this means, as 'Avicenna de Anim. 1. 4, sect. 4,' supposeth in parties remote, but move bodies from their places, cause thunder, lightning, tempests; which opinion Alkindus, Paracelsus, and some others approve of."

In this passage Burton touches not only on the effects of the imagination, but also on the impression which the nervous energy of one person may create upon the nervous sensibility of another. That such an impression can be produced, no one can question who observes the conduct of men in their ordinary relations to each other. By whatever term we christen it—endeavouring to define either the cause or its effect—we all concur in admitting that decision of character, earnestness of manner, enthusiasm, a commanding aspect, a piercing eye, or a strong will, exercise a manifest control over common natures, whether they be acting separately or in masses.

Of the men who, without learning, or an ennobling passion for truth, or a high purpose of any kind, have, unaided by physical force, commanded the attention and directed the actions of large numbers of their fellow creatures, Mesmer is perhaps the most remarkable in modern history. But we will not speak of him till we have paid a few minutes' attention to one of his predecessors.

The most notable forerunner of Mesmer in this country was Valentine Greatrakes, who, in Charles the Second's reign, performed "severall marvaillous cures by the stroaking of the hands." He was a gentleman of condition, and, at first, the dupe of his own imagination rather than a deliberate charlatan. He was born on the 14th of February, 1628, on his father's estate of Affane, in the County of Waterford, and was, on both sides, of more than merely respectable extraction, his father being a gentleman of good repute and property, and his mother being a daughter of Sir Edward Harris, Knt, a Justice of the King's Bench in Ireland. The first years of his school-life were passed in the once famous Academy of Lismore; but when he had arrived at thirteen years of age his mother (who had become a widow), on the outbreak of the rebellion, fled with him and his little brothers and sisters to England, where the fugitive family were hospitably entertained by Mr. Edmund Harris, a gentleman of considerable property, and one of the justice's sons. After concluding his education in the family of one John Daniel Getseus, a High-German minister of Stock Gabriel, in the County of Devon, Valentine returned to Ireland, then distracted with tumult and armed rebellion; and, by prudently joining the victorious side, re-entered on the possession of his father's estate of Affane. He served for six years in Cromwell's forces (from 1650 to 1656) as a lieutenant of the Munster Cavalry, under the command of the Earl of Orrery. Valentine's commission was in the earl's regiment; and, from the time of entering the army till the close of his career is lost sight of, he seems to have enjoyed the patronage and friendship of that nobleman's family.

When the Munster horse was disbanded in 1656, Valentine retired to Affane, and for a period occupied himself as an active and influential country gentleman. He was made Clerk of the Peace for the County of Cork, a Register for Transplantation, and a Justice of the Peace. In the performance of the onerous duties which, in the then disturbed state of Ireland, these offices brought upon him, he gained deserved popularity and universal esteem. He was a frank and commanding personage, of pleasant manners, gallant bearing, fine figure, and singularly handsome face. With a hearty and musical voice, and a national stock of high animal spirits, he was the delight of all festive assemblies, taking his pleasure freely, but never to excess. Indeed, Valentine was a devout man, not ashamed, in his own household, and in his bearing to the outer world, to avow that it was his intention to serve the Lord. But, though he had all the purity of Puritanism, there was in him no taint of sectarian rancour or uncharitableness. When an anonymous writer aspersed his reputation, he responded—and no one could gainsay his words—with regard to his public career:—"I studied so to acquit myself before God and man in singleness and integrity of heart, that, to the comfort of my soul, and praise of God that directed me, I can with confidence say I never took bribe nor reward from any man, though I had many and great ones before me (when I was Register for Transplantation); nor did I ever connive at or suffer a malefactor to go unpunished, if the person were guilty of any notorious crime (when I had power), nor did I ever take the fee belonging to my office, if I found the person were injured, or in want; nor did I ever commit any one for his judgment and conscience barely, so it led him not to do anything to the disturbance of the civil peace of the nation; nor did I take anything for my fee when he was discharged—for I bless God he has taken away a persecuting spirit from me, who would persuade all men to be Protestants, those principles being most consonant to Truth and the Word of God, in my judgment, and that profession which I have ever been of, and still am.... Yet (though there were orders from the power that then was, to all Justices of the Peace, for Transplanting all Papists that would not go to church), I never molested any one that was known or esteemed to be innocent, but suffered them to continue in the English quarters, and that without prejudice. So that I can truly say, I never injured any man for his conscience, conceiving that ought to be informed and not enforced."

On the Restoration, Valentine Greatrakes lost his offices, and was reduced to the position of a mere private gentleman. His estate at Affane was a small one; but he laboured on it with good results, introducing into his neighbourhood a more scientific system of agriculture than had previously been known there, and giving an unprecedented quantity of employment to the poor. Perhaps he missed the excitement of public business, and his energies, deprived of the vent they had for many years enjoyed, preyed upon his sensitive nature. Anyhow, he became the victim of his imagination, which, acting on a mind that had been educated in a school of spiritual earnestness and superstitious introspection, led him into a series of remarkable hallucinations. He first had fits of pensiveness and dejection, similar to those which tormented Cromwell ere his genius found for itself a more fit field of display than the management of a brewery and a few acres of marsh-land. Ere long he had an impulse, or a strange persuasion in his own mind (of which he was not able to give any rational account to another), which did very frequently suggest to him that there was bestowed on him the gift of curing the King's Evil, which for the extraordinariness of it, he thought fit to conceal for some time, but, at length communicated to his wife, and told her, "That he did verily believe that God had given him the blessing of curing the King's Evil; for, whether he were in private or publick, sleeping or waking, still he had the same impulse; but her reply was to him, that she conceived this was a strange imagination." Such is his statement.

Patients either afflicted with King's Evil, or presumed to be so, were in due course brought before him; and, on his touching them, they recovered. It may be here remarked that in the days when the Royal Touch was believed in as a cure for scrofula, the distinctions between strumous and other swellings were by no means ascertained even by physicians of repute; and numbers of those who underwent the manipulation of Anointed Rulers were suffering only from aggravated boils and common festering sores, from which, as a matter of course, nature would in the space of a few weeks have relieved them. Doubtless many of Valentine's patients were suffering, not under scrofulous affections, but comparatively innocent tumours; for his cures were rapid, complete, and numerous. A second impulse gave him the power of curing ague; and a third inspiration of celestial aura imparted to him command, under certain conditions, over all human diseases. His modes of operation were various. When an afflicted person was laid before him, he usually offered up a prayer to God to help him, to make him the humble instrument of divine mercy. And invariably when a patient derived benefit from his treatment, he exhorted him to offer up his thanks to his Heavenly Father. After the initiatory supplication the operator passed his hands over the affected part of the sick person's body, sometimes over the skin itself and sometimes over the clothes. The manipulations varied in muscular force from delicate tickling to violent rubbing, according to the nature of the evil spirits by which the diseased people were tormented. Greatrakes's theory of disease was the scriptural one: the morbific power was a devil, which had to be expelled from the frame in which it had taken shelter. Sometimes the demon was exorcised by a few gentle passes; occasionally it fled at the verbal command of the physician, or retreated on being gazed at through the eyes of the mortal it tormented; but frequently the victory was not gained till the healer rubbed himself—like the rubber who in our own day makes such a large income at Brighton—into a red face and a copious perspiration. Henry Stubbe, a famous physician in Stratford-upon-Avon, in his "Miraculous Conformist," published in 1666, gives the following testimony:—

"Proofs that he revives the Ferment of the Blood.—Mr Bromley's brother, of Upton upon Severne, after a long quartane Ague, had by a Metastasis of the Disease such a chilnesse in the habit of the body, that no clothes could possibly warme him; he wore upon his head many spiced caps, and tenne pounds weight of linen on his head. Mr Greatarick stripped him, and rubbed him all over, and immediately he sweat, and was hot all over, so that the bath never heated up as did the hand of Mr Greatarick's; this was his own expression. But Mr Greatarick causing him to cast off all that multitude of caps and cloaths, it was supposed that it frustrated the happy effect, for he felt the recourse of his disease in some parts rendered the cure suspicious. But as often as Mr Greatarick came and rubbed him he would be all in a flame againe for half-an-hour: the experiment whereof was frequently practised for five or six dayes at Ragly."

Greatrakes himself also speaks of his more violent curative exertions making him very hot. But it was only occasionally that he had to labour so vehemently. His eye, the glance of which had a fascinating effect on people of a nervous organization, and his fantastic ticklings, usually produced all the results required by his mode of treatment.

The fame of the healer spread far and wide. Not only from the most secluded parts of Ireland, but from civilized England, the lame and blind, the deaf, dumb, and diseased, made pilgrimages to the Squire of Affane. His stable, barn, and malthouse were crowded with wretches imploring his aid. The demands upon his time were so very many and great, that he set apart three days in the week for the reception of patients; and on those days, from six in the morning till six in the evening, he ministered to his wretched clients. He took no fee but gratitude on the part of those he benefited, and a cheering sense that he was fulfilling the commands of the founder of his religion. The Dean of Lismore cited him to appear before the ecclesiastical court, and render an account of his proceedings. He went, and on being asked if he had worked any cures, replied to the court that they might come to his house and see. The judge asked if he had a licence to practise from the ordinary of the diocese; and he replied that he knew of no law which prohibited any man from doing what good he could to others. He was, however, commanded by the court not to lay his hands again on the sick, until he had obtained the Ordinary's licence to do so. He obeyed for two days only, and went on again more earnestly than ever.

Let a charlatan or an enthusiast spread his sails, the breeze of fashion is always present, and ready to swell them. The Earl of Orrery took his quondam lieutenant by the hand, and persuaded him to go over to England to cure the Viscountess Conway of a violent headache, which, in spite of the ablest physicians of England and France, she had suffered from for many years. Lord Conway sent him an urgent invitation to do so. He complied, and made his way to Rugby, in Warwickshire, where he was unable to give relief to his hostess, but was hospitably entertained for a month. His inability to benefit Lady Conway did not injure his reputation, for he did not profess to be able to cure every one. An adverse influence—such as the sins of a patient, or his want of faith—was enough to counteract the healing power. In the jargon of modern mesmerism, which *practically* was only a revival of Greatrakes's extravagances, the physician could affect only those who were susceptible. But though Lady Conway was beyond the reach of his mysterious agency, the reverse was the case with others. The gentry and commonalty of Warwickshire crowded by thousands to him; and he touched, prayed over, and blessed them, and sent them away rejoicing. From Rugby he went to Worcester, at the request of the Lord Mayor and Aldermen of that city; and from Worcester he was carried up to London. Lord Arlington commanded him to appear at Whitehall, and mumble in his particular fashion for the amusement of Charles II. A man who could cure gout by a touch would have been an acquisition to such a court as then presided over English manners.

In London he immediately became a star. The fashion of the West, and the wary opulence of the East, laid their offerings at his feet. For a time he ruled from Soho to Wapping. Mr. Justice Godfrey gave him rooms for the reception of patients in his mansion in Lincoln's-inn-Fields; and thither flocked the mob of the indigent and the mob of the wealthy to pay him homage. Mr. Boyle (the brother of the Earl of Orrery), Sir William Smith, Dr. Denton, Dr. Fairclough, Dr. Faber, Sir Nathaniel Hobart, Sir John Godolphin, Dr. Wilkins, Dr. Whichcot, and Dr. Cudworth, were amongst his most vehement supporters of the sterner sex. But the majority of his admirers were ladies. The Countess of Devonshire entertained him in her palace; and Lady Ranelagh frequently amused the guests at her routs with Mr. Valentine Greatrakes, who, in the character of *the lion* of the season, performed with wondrous results on the prettiest or most hysterical of the ladies present. It was held as certain by his intimate friends that the curative property that came from him was a subtle aura, effulgent, and of an exquisitely sweet smell, that could only be termed the divine breath. "God," says Dr. Henry Stubbe, "had bestowed upon Mr. Greaterick a peculiar temperament, or composed his body of some particular ferments, the effluvia whereof, being introduced sometimes by a light, sometimes by a violent friction, should restore the temperament of the debilitated parts, re-invigorate the blood, and dissipate all heterogeneous ferments out of the bodies of the diseased by the eyes, nose, mouth, hands, and feet. I place the gift of healing in the temperament or composure of his body, because I see it is necessary that he touch them. Besides, the Right Honourable the Lord Conway observed one morning, as he came into his Lordship's chamber, a smell strangely pleasant, as if it had been of sundry flowers; and demanding of his man what sweet water he had brought into the room, he answered, *None*; whereupon his Lordship smelled upon the hand of Mr. Greaterick, and found the fragrancy to issue thence; and examining his bosom, he found the like scent there also." Dean Rust gave similar testimony; and "Sir Amos Meredith, who had been Mr. Greaterick's bed-fellow," did the like.

Amongst the certificates of cures performed, which Greatrakes published, are two to which the name of Andrew Marvell is affixed, as a spectator of the stroking. One of them is the following:—

"Mr Nicholson's Certificate.

"I, Anthony Nicholson, of Cambridge, Bookseller, have been affected sore with pains all over my body, for three-and-twenty years last past, have had advice and best directions of all the doctors there; have been at the bath in Somersetshire, and been at above one hundred pounds expense to procure ease, or a cure of these pains; and have found all the means I could be advised or directed to ineffectual for either, till, by the advice of Dr Benjamin Whichcot and Dean Rust, I applyed myself to Mr Greatrake's for help upon Saturday was sevenight, being the latter end of March, and who then stroked me; upon which I was very much worse, and enforced to keep my bed for five or six days; but then being stroked twice since, by the blessing of God upon Mr Greatrake's endeavours, I am perfectly eas'd of all pains, and very healthy and strong, insomuch as I intend (God willing) to return home towards Cambridge to-morrow morning, though I was so weak as to be necessitated to be brought up in men's arms, on Saturday last about 11 of the clock, to Mr Greatrake's. Attested by me this tenth day of April, 1666. I had also an hard swelling in my left arm, whereby I was disabled from using it; which being taken out by the said Mr Greatrake's, I am perfectly freed of all pain, and the use thereof greatly restored.

"ANTHONY NICHOLSON.

"In the presence of Andrew Marvell, Jas. Fairclough, Tho. Al- ured, Tho. Pooley, W. Popple."

There were worse features of life in Charles the Second's London than the popularity of Valentine Greatrakes; but his triumph was of short duration. His professions were made the butts of ridicule, to which his presence of mind and volubility were unable to respond with effect. It was asserted by his enemies that his system was only a cloak under which he offended the delicacy of virtuous women, and roused the passions of the unchaste. His tone of conversation was represented as compounded of the blasphemy of the religious enthusiast and the blasphemy of the profligate. His boast that he never received a fee for his remedial services was met by flat contradiction, and a statement that he received presents to the amount of £100 at a time from a single individual. This last accusation was never clearly disposed of; but it is probable that the reward he sought (if he looked for any) was restoration, through Court influence, to the commission of magistrates for his county, and the lost clerkship of the peace. The tide of slander was anyhow too strong for him, and he retired to his native country a less honoured though perhaps a not less honest man than he left it. Of his sincerity at the outset of his career as a healer there can be little doubt.

Valentine Greatrakes did unconsciously what many years after him Mesmer did by design. He in his remarkable career illustrated the power which a determined man may exercise over the will and nervous life of another.

As soon as the singular properties of the loadstone were discovered, they were presumed to have a strong medicinal effect; and in this belief physicians for centuries—and indeed almost down to present times—were in the habit of administering pulverized magnet in salves, plaisters, pills, and potions. It was not till the year 1660 that it was for the first time distinctly recorded in the archives of science, by Dr. Gilbert, of Colchester, that in a state of pulverization the loadstone no longer possessed any magnetic powers. But it was not till some generations after this that medical practitioners universally recognized the fact that powder of magnet, externally or internally administered, was capable of producing no other results than the presence of any ordinary ferruginous substance would account for. But long after this error had been driven from the domains of science, an unreasonable belief in the power of magnets applied externally to the body held its ground. In 1779-80, the Royal Society of Medicine in Paris made numerous experiments with a view to arrive at a just appreciation of the influence of magnets on the human system, and came to the conclusion that they were medicinal agents of no ordinary efficacy.

Such was the state of medical opinion at the close of the last century, when Perkins's tractors, which were supposed to act magnetically, became the fashion. Mr. Perkins was a citizen of Connecticut, and certainly his celebrated invention was worthy of the 'cutest people on the 'varsal earth. Barnum's swindles were modest ventures by comparison. The entire world, old and new, went tractor-mad. Every valetudinarian bought the painted nails, composed of an alloy of various metals (which none but Perkins could make, and none but Perkins sell), and tickled with their sharp ends those parts of his frame which were regarded as centres of disease.

The phenomena apparently produced by these instruments were astounding, and misled every observer of them; until Dr. Haygarth of Bath proved by a process to which objections was impossible, that they were referable not to metal points, but to the mental condition of those who used them. "Robert Thomas," says Dr. Haygarth in his interesting work, "aged forty-three, who had been for some time under the care of Dr. Lovell, in the Bristol Infirmary, with a rheumatic affection of the shoulder, which rendered his arm perfectly useless, was pointed out as a proper object of trial by Mr. J. W. Dyer, apothecary to the house. Tuesday, April 19th, having everything in readiness, I passed through the ward, and, in a way that he might suspect nothing, questioned him respecting his complaint. I then told him that I had an instrument in my pocket which had been very serviceable to many in his state; and when I had explained to him how simple it was, he consented to undergo the operation. In six minutes no other effect was produced than a warmth upon the skin, and I feared that this *coup d'essai* had failed. The next day, however, he told me that 'he had received so much benefit that it had enabled him to lift his hand from his knee, which he had in vain several times attempted on Monday evening, as the whole ward witnessed.' The tractors I used being made of lead, I thought it advisable to lay them aside, lest, being metallic points, the proof against the fraud might be less complete. Thus much, however, was proved, that the patent tractors possessed no specific power independent of simple metals. Two pieces of wood, properly shaped and painted, were next made use of; and in order to add solemnity to the farce, Mr. Barton held in his hand a stop-watch, whilst Mr. Lax minuted the effects produced. In four minutes the man raised his hand several inches; and he had lost also the pain in his shoulder, usually experienced when attempting to lift anything. He continued to undergo the operation daily, and with progressive good effect; for on the twenty-fifth he could touch the mantel-piece. On the twenty-seventh, in the presence of Dr. Lovell and Mr. J. P. Noble, two common iron nails, disguised with sealing-wax, were substituted for the pieces of mahogany before used. In three minutes he felt something moving from his arm to his hand, and soon after he touched the board of rules which hung a foot above the fire-place. This patient at length so far recovered that he could carry coals and use his arm sufficiently to help the nurse; yet, previous to the use of the spurious tractors, he could no more lift his hand from his knee than if a hundredweight were upon it, or a nail driven through it—as he declared in the presence of several gentlemen, whose names I shall have frequent occasion to mention. The fame of this case brought applications in abundance; indeed, it must be confessed that it was more than sufficient to act upon weak minds, and induce a belief that these pieces of wood and iron were endowed with some peculiar virtues."

The result of Dr. Haygarth's experiments was the overthrow of Perkins, and the enlightenment of the public as to the real worth of the celebrated metallic tractors. In achieving this the worthy physician added some interesting facts to the science of psychology. But of course his influence upon the ignorant and foolish persons he illuminated was only transient. Ere a few short years or even months were over, they had embraced another delusion—not less ridiculous, but more pernicious.

CHAPTER XV.

IMAGINATION AND NERVOUS EXCITEMENT. MESMER.

At a very early date the effects of magnetic influences, and the ordinary phenomena of nervous excitement, were the source of much confusion and perplexity to medical speculators, who, with an unsound logic that is perhaps more frequent than any other form of bad reasoning, accounted for what they could not understand by pointing to what they were only imperfectly acquainted with. The power of the loadstone was a mystery; the nervous phenomena produced by a strong will over a weak one were a mystery:—clearly the mysterious phenomena were to be attributed to the mysterious power. In its outset animal magnetism committed no other error than this. Its wilder extravagances were all subsequent to this assumption, that two sets of phenomena, which it has never yet been proved are nearly allied, were connected, the one with the other, in the relation of cause and effect, or as being the offspring of one immediate and common cause.

To support this theory, Mesmerism called into its service the old astrological views regarding planetary influence. But it held also that the subtle fluid, so transmitted to the animal life of our planet, was capable of being passed on in greater or less volumes of quantity and intensity. Nervous energy was only that subtle fluid which was continually passing and repassing in impalpable currents between the earth and the celestial bodies; and when, by reason of the nervous energy within him, any one exercised control over another, he was deemed only to have infused him with some of his own stock of spiritual aura. Here was a new statement of the old dream which had charmed the poets and philosophers of buried centuries; and as it was a view which did not admit of positive disproof, it was believed by its excited advocates to be proved.

One of the first British writers on animal magnetism was William Maxwell, a Scotch physician, who enunciated his opinions with a boldness and perspicacity which do him much credit. The first four of his twelve conclusions are a very good specimen of his work:—

"*Conclusio 1.*—Anima non solum in corpore proprio visibili, sed etiam extra corpus est, nec corpore organico circumscribitur.

"*Conclusio 2.*—Anima extra corpus proprium, communiter sic dictum, operatur.

"*Conclusio 3.*—Ab omni corpore radii corporales fluunt, in quibus anima sua præsentia, operatur; hisque energiam et potentiam operandi largitur. Sunt vero radii hi non solum corporales, sed et diversarum partium.

"*Conclusio 4.*—Radii hi, qui ex animalium corporibus emittuntur, spiritu vitali gaudent, per quem animæ mutationes dispensantur."

The sixty-fifth of the aphorisms with which Maxwell concludes his book is an amusing one, as giving the orthodox animal-magnetic view of that condition of the affections which we term love, and also as illustrating the connection between astrology and charms.

"*Aphorism 65.*—Imaginatione vero producitur amor, quando imaginatio exaltata unius imaginationi alterius dominatur, eamque fingit sigillatque; atque hoc propter miram imaginationis volubilitatem vicissim fieri potest. Hinc incantationes effectum nanciscuntur, licet aliqualem forsan in se virtutem possideant, sine imaginatione tamen hæc virtus propter universalitatem distribui nequit."

Long before animal magnetism was a stock subject of conversation at dinner-parties, there was a vague knowledge of its pretensions floating about society; and a curiosity to know how far its principles were reconcilable with facts, animated men of science and lovers of the marvellous. Had not this been the state of public feeling, the sensations created by Sir Kenelm Digby's sympathetic cures, Greatrake's administrations, Leverett's manual exercises, and Loutherbourg's manipulations, would not have been so great and universal.

But the person who turned the credulity of the public on this point to the best account was Frederick Anthony Mesmer. This man did not originate a single idea. He only traded on the old day-dreams and vagaries of departed ages; and yet he managed to fix his name upon a science (?), in the origination or development of which he had no part whatever; and, by daring charlatanry, he made it a means of grasping enormous wealth. Where this man was born is uncertain. Vienna, Werseburg in Swabia, and Switzerland, contend for the honour of having given him to the world. At Vienna he took his M.D. degree, having given an inaugural dissertation on "The Influence of the Planets upon the Human Body." His course of self-delusion began with using magnets as a means of cure, when applied externally; and he had resolutely advanced on the road of positive knavery, when, after his quarrel with his old instructor, Maximilian Hel, he threw aside the use of steel magnets, and produced, by the employment of his fingers and eyes, greater marvels than had ever followed the application of the loadstone or Perkins's tractors. As his prosperity and reputation increased, so did his audacity—which was always laughable, when it did not disgust by its impiety.

On one occasion, Dr. Egg Von Ellekon asked him why he ordered his patients to bathe in river, and not in spring water? "Because," was the answer, "river water is exposed to the sun's rays." "True," was the reply, "the water is sometimes warmed by the sun, but not so much so that you have not sometimes to warm it still more. Why then should not spring water be preferable?" Not at all posed, Mesmer answered, with charming candour, "Dear doctor, the cause why all the water which is exposed to the rays of the sun is superior to all other water is because it is magnetized. I myself magnetized the sun some twenty years ago."

But a better story of him is told by Madame Campan. That lady's husband was attacked with pulmonary inflammation. Mesmer was sent for, and found himself called upon to stem a violent malady, not to gull the frivolous Parisians, who were then raving about the marvels of the new system. He felt his patient's pulse, made certain inquiries, and then, turning to Madame Campan, gravely assured her that the only way to restore her husband to health was to lay in his bed, by his side one of three things—a young woman of brown complexion, a black hen, or an old bottle. "Sir," replied Madame Campan, "if the choice be a matter of indifference, pray try the empty bottle." The bottle was tried, but Mons. Campan grew worse. Madame Campan left the room, alarmed and anxious, and, during her absence, Mesmer bled and blistered his patient. This latter treatment was more efficacious. But imagine Madame Campan's astonishment, when on her husband's recovery, Mesmer asked for and obtained from him a written certificate that he had been cured by Mesmerism!

It is instructive to reflect that the Paris which made for a short day Mesmer its idol, was not far distant from the Paris of the Reign of Terror. In one year the man received 400,000 francs in fees; and positively the French government, at the instigation of Maurepas, offered him an annual stipend of 20,000 francs, together with an additional 10,000 to support an establishment for patients and pupils, if he would stay in France. One unpleasant condition was attached to this offer: he was required to allow three nominees of the Crown to watch his proceedings. So inordinately high did Mesmer rate his claims, that he stood out for better terms, and like the dog of the fable, by endeavoring to get too much, lost what he might have secured. Ere long the Parisians recovered something of common sense. The enthusiasm of the hour subsided: and the Royal Commission, composed of some of the best men of science to be found in the entire world, were enabled to explain to the public how they had been fooled by a trickster, and betrayed into practices scarcely less offensive to modesty than to reason. In addition to the public report, another private one was issued by the commissioners, urging the authorities, in the name of morality, to put a stop to the mesmeric mania.

Mesmer died in obscurity on the 5th of March, in the year 1815.

Animal magnetism, under the name of mesmerism, has been made familiar of late years to the ears of English people, if not to their understandings, by the zealous and indiscreet advocacy which its absurdities have met with in London and our other great cities. It is true that the disciples have outrun their master—that Mesmer has been out-mesmerized; but the same criticisms which have been here made on the system of the arch-charlatan may be applied to the vagaries of his successors, whether they be dupes or rogues. To electro-biologists, spirit-rappers, and table-turners the same arguments must be used as we employ to mesmerists. They must be instructed that phenomena are not to be referred to magnetic influence, simply because it is difficult to account for them; that it is especially foolish to set them down to such a cause, when they are manifestly the product of another power; and that all the wonders which form the stock of their conversation, and fill the pages of the *Zoist*, are to be attributed, not to a lately discovered agency, but to nervous susceptibility, imagination, and bodily temperament, aroused by certain well-known stimulants.

They will doubtless be disinclined to embrace this explanation of their marvels, and will argue that it is much more likely that a table is made by ten or twelve gentlemen and ladies to turn rapidly round, without the application of muscular force, than that these ladies and gentlemen should delude themselves into an erroneous belief that such a phenomenon has been produced. To disabuse them of such an opinion, they must be instructed in the wondrous and strangely delicate mechanism of the human intellect and affections. And after such enlightenment they must be hopelessly dull or perverse if they do not see that the metaphysical explanation of "their cases" is not only the true one, but that it opens up to view far more astonishing features in the constitution of man than any that are dreamt of in the vain philosophy of mesmerism. It is humiliating to think that these remarks should be an appropriate comment on the silliness of the so-called educated classes of the nineteenth century. That they are out of place, none can advance, when one of the most popular pulpit orators of London has not hesitated to commit to print, in a work of religious pretensions, the almost blasphemous suggestion that table-turning is a phenomenon consequent upon the first out-poured drops of "the seventh vial" having reached the earth.

CHAPTER XVI.

MAKE WAY FOR THE LADIES!

"For in all times, in the opinion of the multitude, witches and old women and impostors have had a competition with physicians. And what followeth? Even this, that physicians say to themselves, as Solomon expresseth it upon a higher occasion, 'If it befall to me as befalleth to the fools, why should I labour to be more wise?'"—Lord Bacon's *Advancement of Learning*.

It is time to say something about the ladies as physicians. Once they were the chief practitioners of medicine; and even to recent times had a monopoly of that branch of art over which Dr. Locock presides. The question has lately been agitated whether certain divisions of remedial industry ought not again to be set aside for them; and the patronage afforded to the lady who (in spite of the ridicule thrown on her, and the rejection of her advances by various medical schools to which she applied for admission as a student), managed to obtain a course of medical instruction at one of the London schools, and practised for a brief time in London previous to her departure for a locality more suited to her operations, would seem to indicate that public feeling is not averse to the thought of employing—under certain conditions and for certain purposes—female physicians.

Of the many doctresses who have flourished in England during the last 200 years, only a few have left any memorial of their actions behind them. Of *the wise women* (a class of practitioners, by-the-by, still to be found in many rural villages and in certain parts of London) in whom our ancestors had as much confidence as we of the present generation have in the members of the College of Physicians, we question if twoscore, including Margaret Kennix and Mrs. Woodhouse, of the Elizabethan era, could be rescued from oblivion. Some of them wrote books, and so, by putting their names "in print," have a slight hold on posthumous reputation. Two of them are immortalized by mention in the records of the "Philosophical Transactions for 1694." These ladies were Mrs. Sarah Hastings and Mrs. French. The curious may refer to the account there given of the ladies' skill; and also, for further particulars relative to Sarah Hastings, a glance may be given to M. de la Cross's "Memoirs for the Ingenious," published in the month of July, 1693. We do not care to transcribe the passages into our own pages; though, now that it is the fashion to treat all the unpleasant details of nursing as matters of romance, we presume there is nothing in the cases mentioned calculated to shock public delicacy.

A most successful "wise woman" was Joanna Stephens, an ignorant and vulgar creature, who, just before the middle of the last century, proclaimed that she had discovered a sovereign remedy for a painful malady, which, like the small-pox, has become in the hands of modern surgery so manageable that ere long it will rank as little more than "a temporary discomfort." Joanna was a courageous woman. She went straightway to temporal peers, bishops, duchesses, and told them she was the woman for their money. They believed her, testified to the marvellous cures which she had effected, and allowed her to make use of their titles to awe sceptics into respect for her powers. Availing herself of this permission, she published books containing lists of her cures, backed up by letters from influential members of the nobility and gentry.

In the April number of the *Gentleman's Magazine* for the year 1738, one reads—"Mrs. Stephens has proposed to make her medicine publick, on consideration of £5000 to be raised by contribution and lodged with Mr. Drummond, banker; he has received since the 11th of this month about £500 on that account." By the end of the month the banker had in his hands £720 8s. 6d.

This generous offer was not made until the inventor of the nostrums had enriched herself by enormous fees drawn from the credulity of the rich of every sect and rank. The subscription to pay her the amount she demanded for her secret was taken up enthusiastically. Letters appeared in the Journals and Magazines, arguing that no humane or patriotic man could do otherwise than contribute to it. The movement was well whipped up by the press. The Bishop of Oxford gave £10 10s.; Bishop of Gloucester, £10 10s.; The Earl of Pembroke, £50; Countess of Deloraine, £5 5s.; Lady Betty Jermaine, £21; Lady Vere Beauclerc, £10 10s.; Earl of Godolphin, £100; Duchess of Gordon, £5 5s.: Viscount Lonsdale, £52 10s.; Duke of Rutland, £50; the Bishop of Salisbury, £25; Sir James Lowther, Bart., £25; Lord Cadogan, £2 2s.; Lord Cornwallis, £20; Duchess of Portland, £21; Earl of Clarendon, £25; Lord Lymington, £5; Duke of Leeds, £21; Lord Galloway, £30; General Churchill (Spot Ward's friend), £10 10s.; Countess of Huntingdon, £10 10s.; Hon. Frances Woodhouse, £10 10s.; Sir Thomas Lowther, Bart., £5 5s.; Duke of Richmond, £30; Sir George Saville, Bart., £5 5s.

These were only a few of the noble and distinguished dupes of Joanna Stephens. Mrs. Crowe, in her profound and philosophic work, "Spiritualism, and the Age we live in," informs us that "the solicitude" about the subject of table-turning "displayed by many persons in high places, is the best possible sign of the times; and it is one from which she herself hopes that the period is arrived when we shall receive further help from God." Hadn't Joanna Stephens reason to think that the period had arrived when she and her remedial system would receive further help from God? What would not Read (we do not mean the empiric oculist knighted by Queen Anne, but the cancer quack of our own time) give to have such a list of aristocratic supporters? What would not Mrs. Doctor Goss (who in this year, 1861, boasts of the patronage of "ladies of the highest distinction") give for a similar roll of adherents?

The agitation, however, for a public subscription for Joanna Stephens was not so successful as her patrician supporters anticipated. They succeeded in collecting £1356 3s. But Joanna stood out: her secret should not go for less than £5000. "No pay, no cure!" was her cry. The next thing her friends did was to apply to Parliament for the required sum—and, positively, their request was granted. The nation, out of its taxes, paid what the individuals of its wealthy classes refused to subscribe. A commission was appointed by Parliament, that gravely inquired into the particulars of the cures alleged to be performed by Joanna Stephens; and, finding the evidence in favour of the lady unexceptionable, they awarded her the following certificate, which ought to be preserved to all ages as a valuable example of senatorial wisdom:—

"THE CERTIFICATE REQUIRED BY THE ACT OF PARLIAMENT.

March 5, 1739.

"We, whose names are underwritten, being the major part of the Justices appointed by an Act of Parliament, entitled, '*An Act for providing a Reward to Joanna Stephens, upon proper discovery to be made by her, for the use of the Publick, of the Medicines prepared by her— —*' —do certify, that the said Joanna Stephens did, with all convenient speed after the passing of the said Act, make a discovery to our satisfaction, for the use of the publick, of the said medicines, and of her method of preparing the same; and that we have examined the said medicines, and of her method of preparing of the same, and are convinced by experiment of the *Utility*, *Efficacy*, and *Dissolving Power* thereof.

"JO. CANT,	THO. OXFORD,
HARDWICKE, C.,	STE. POYNTZ,
WILMINGTON, P.,	STEPHEN HALES,
GODOLPHIN, C. P. S.,	JO. GARDINER,
DORSET,	SIM BURTON,
MONTAGUE,	PETER SHAW,
PEMBROKE,	D. HARTLEY,
BALTIMORE,	W. CHESELDEN,
CORNBURY,	C. HAWKINS,
M. GLOUCESTER,	SAM. SHARP."

When such men as Cheselden, Hawkins, and Sharp could sign such a certificate, we need feel no surprise at the conduct of Dr. Nesbit and Dr. Pellet (Mead's early friend, who rose to be president of the College of Physicians). These two gentlemen, who were on the commission, having some scruples about the words "dissolving power," gave separate testimonials in favour of the medicines. St. John Long's cause, it may be remembered, was advocated by Dr. Ramadge, a Fellow of the College.

The country paid its money, and obtained Joanna's prescriptions. Here is a portion of the lady's statement:—

"A full Discovery of the Medicines given by me, Joanna Stephens, and a particular account of my method of preparing and giving the same.

"My medicines are a Powder, a Decoction, and Pills.

"The Powder consists of egg-shells and snails—both calcined.

"The Decoction is made by boiling some herbs (together with a ball which consists of soap, swine's-cresses burnt to a blackness, and honey) in water.

"The Pills consist of snails calcined, wild carrot seeds, burdock seeds, ashen keys, hips and hawes—all burnt to a blackness—soap and honey.

"The powder is thus prepared:—Take hen's egg-shells, well drained from the whites, dry and clean; crush them small with the hands, and fill a crucible of the twelfth size (which contains nearly three pints) with them lightly, place it on the fire till the egg-shells be calcined to a greyish white, and acquire an acrid, salt taste: this will take up eight hours, at least. After they are thus calcined, put them in a dry, clean earthen pan, which must not be above three parts full, that there may be room for the swelling of the egg-shells in stacking. Let the pan stand uncovered in a dry room for two months, and no longer; in this time the egg-shells will become of a milder taste, and that part which is sufficiently calcined will fall into a powder of such a fineness, as to pass through a common hairsieve, which is to be done accordingly.

"In like manner, take garden snails, with their shells, cleaned from the dirt; fill a crucible of the same size with them whole, cover it, and place it on the fire as before, till the snails have done smoaking, which will be in about an hour—taking care that they do not continue in the fire after that. They are then to be taken out of the crucible, and immediately rubbed in a mortar to a fine powder, which ought to be of a very dark-grey colour.

> "*Note.*—If pit-coal be made use of, it will be proper—in order that the fire may the sooner burn clear on the top—that large cinders, and not fresh coals, be placed upon the tiles which cover the crucibles.

"These powders being thus prepared, take the egg-shell powder of six crucibles, and the snail-powder of one; mix them together, and rub them in a mortar, and pass them through a cypress sieve. This mixture is immediately to be put up into bottles, which must be close stopped, and kept in a dry place for use. I have generally added a small quantity of swine's-cresses, burnt to a blackness, and rubbed fine; but this was only with a view to disguise it.

"The egg-shells may be prepared at any time of the year, but it is best to do them in summer. The snails ought only to be prepared in May, June, July, and August; and I esteem those best which are done in the first of these months.

"The decoction is thus prepared:—Take four ounces and a half of the best Alicant soap, beat it in a mortar with a large spoonful of swine's-cresses burnt to a blackness, and as much honey as will make the whole of the consistence of paste. Let this be formed into a ball. Take this ball, and green camomile, or camomile flowers, sweet fennel, parsley, and burdock leaves, of each an ounce (when there are not greens, take the same quantity of roots); slice the ball, and boil them in two quarts of soft water half an hour, then strain it off, and sweeten it with honey.

"The pills are thus prepared:—Take equal quantities by measure of snails calcined as before, of wild carrot seeds, burdock seeds, ashen keys, hips and hawes, all burnt to a blackness, or, which is the same thing, till they have done smoaking; mix them together, rub them in a mortar, and pass them through a cypress sieve. Then take a large spoonful of this mixture, and four ounces of the best Alicant soap, and beat them in a mortar with as much honey as will make the whole of a proper consistence for pills; sixty of which are to be made out of every ounce of the composition."

Five thousand pounds for such stuff as this!—and the time was coming when the nation grudged an inadequate reward to Jenner, and haggled about the purchase of Hunter's Museum!

But a more remarkable case of feminine success in the doctoring line was that of Mrs. Mapp, who was a contemporary of Mrs. Stephens. Under the patronage of the Court, "Drop and Pill" Ward (or "Spot" Ward, as he was also called, from a mole on his cheek) was astonishing London with his cures, and his gorgeous equipage which he had the royal permission to drive through St. James Park, when the attention of the fashionable world was suddenly diverted to the proceeding of "Crazy Sally of Epsom." She was an enormous, fat, ugly, drunken woman, known as a haunter of fairs, about which she loved to reel, screaming and abusive, in a state of roaring intoxication. This attractive lady was a bone-setter; and so much esteemed was she for skill in her art, that the town of Epsom offered her £100 if she would reside there for a year. The following passage we take from the *Gentleman's Magazine* for 1736: "Saturday 31. In the *Daily Advertiser*, July 28, Joshua Ward, Esq., having the queen's leave, recites seven extraordinary cases of persons which were cured by him, and examined before her Majesty, June 7, objections to which had been made in the *Grub Street Journal*, June 24. But the attention of the public has been taken off from the wonder-working Mr. Ward to a strolling woman now at Epsom, who calls herself Crazy Sally; and had performed cures in bone-setting to admiration, and occasioned so great a resort, that the town offered her 100 guineas to continue there a year."

"Crazy Sally" awoke one morning and found herself famous. Patients of rank and wealth flocked in from every quarter. Attracted by her success, an Epsom swain made an offer of marriage to Sally, which she like a fool accepted. Her maiden name of Wallin (she was the daughter of a Wiltshire bone-setter of that name) she exchanged at the altar for that of Mapp. If her marriage was not in all respects fortunate, she was not burdened with much of her husband's society. He lived with her only for a fortnight, during which short space of time he thrashed her soundly twice or thrice, and then decamped with a hundred guineas of her earnings. She found consolation for her wounded affections in the homage of the world. She became a notoriety of the first water, and every day some interesting fact appeared about her in the prints and public journals. In one we are told "the cures of the woman bone-setter of Epsom are too many to be enumerated: her bandages are extraordinary neat, and her dexterity in reducing dislocations and setting fractured bones wonderful. She has cured persons who have been twenty years disabled, and has given incredible relief in the most difficult cases. The lame come daily to her, and she gets a great deal of money, persons of quality who attend her operations making her presents."

Poets sounded her praises. Vide *Gentleman's Magazine*, August, 1736:

"On Mrs Mapp, the Famous Bone-setter of Epsom.

> "Of late, without the least pretence to skill,
> Ward's grown a fam'd physician by a pill;
> Yet he can but a doubtful honour claim,
> While envious Death oft blasts his rising fame.
> Next travell'd Taylor fills us with surprise,
> Who pours new light upon the blindest eyes;
> Each journal tells his circuit through the land,
> Each journal tells the blessings of his hand;
> And lest some hireling scribbler of the town
> Injure his history, he writes his own.
> We read the long accounts with wonder o'er;
> Had he wrote less, we had believed him more.
> Let these, O Mapp, thou wonder of the age!
> With dubious arts endeavor to engage;
> While you, irregularly strict to rules,
> Teach dull collegiate pedants they are fools;
> By merit, the sure path to fame pursue—
> For all who see thy art must own it true."

Mrs. Mapp continued to reside in Epsom, but she visited London once a week. Her journeys to and from the metropolis she performed in a chariot drawn by four horses, with servants wearing splendid liveries. She used to put up at the Grecian Coffee-House, where Sir Hans Sloane witnessed her operations, and was so favourably impressed by them, that he put under her charge his niece, who was suffering from a spinal affection, or, to use the exact and scientific language of the newspapers, "whose back had been broke nine years, and stuck out two inches." The eminent lady went to the playhouse in Lincoln's-Inn-Fields to see the *Husband's Relief* acted. Her presence not only produced a crowded house, but the fact that she sate between Taylor the quack oculist on one side, and Ward the drysalter on the other, gave occasion for the production of the following epigram, the point of which is perhaps almost as remarkable as its polish:—

> "While Mapp to the actors showed a kind regard,
> On one side *Taylor* sat, on the other *Ward*;
> When their mock persons of the drama came,
> Both *Ward* and *Taylor* thought it hurt their fame;
> Wonder'd how Mapp could in good humour be,
> '*Zoons!*' crys the manly dame, 'it hurts not me;
> Quacks without art may either blind or kill,
> But demonstration proves that mine is skill.'"

On the stage, also, a song was sung in honour of Mrs. Mapp, and in derision of Taylor and Ward. It ran thus:—

"You surgeons of London, who puzzle your pates,
To ride in your coaches, and purchase estates,
Give over for shame, for pride has a fall,
And the doctress of Epsom has out-done you all.
Derry down, &c.

"What signifies learning, or going to school,
When a woman can do, without reason or rule,
What puts you to nonplus, and baffles your art;
For petticoat practice has now got the start.
Derry down, &c.

"In physic, as well as in fashions, we find
The newest has always its run with mankind;
Forgot is the bustle 'bout Taylor and Ward,
And Mapp's all the cry, and her fame's on record.
Derry down, &c.

"Dame Nature has given a doctor's degree—
She gets all the patients, and pockets the fee;
So if you don't instantly prove her a cheat,
She'll loll in her carriage, whilst you walk the street.
Derry down, &c."

On one occasion, as this lady was proceeding up the Old Kent Road to the Borough, in her carriage and four, dressed in a loosely-fitting robe-de-chambre, and manifesting by her manner that she had partaken somewhat too freely of Geneva water, she found herself in a very trying position. Her fat frame, indecorous dress, intoxication, and dazzling equipage, were in the eyes of the mob such sure signs of royalty, that she was immediately taken for a Court lady, of German origin and unpopular repute, whose word was omnipotent at St. James's.

Soon a crowd gathered round the carriage, and, with the proper amount of swearing and yelling, were about to break the windows with stones, when the spirited occupant of the vehicle, acting very much as Nell Gwyn did on a similar occasion, rose from her seat, and letting down the glasses, exclaimed, with an imprecation more emphatic than polite, "— —! Don't you know me? I am Mrs. Mapp, the bone-setter!"

This brief address so tickled the humour of the mob, that the lady proceeded on her way amidst deafening acclamations and laughter.

The Taylor mentioned as sitting on one side of Mrs. Mapp in the playhouse was a notable character. A cunning, plausible, shameless blackguard, he was eminently successful in his vocation of quack. Dr. King, in his "Anecdotes of his own Times," speaks of him with respect. "I was at Tunbridge," says the Doctor, "with Chevalier Taylor, the oculist. He seems to understand the anatomy of the eye perfectly well; he has a fine hand and good instruments, and performs all his operations with great dexterity; but he undertakes everything (even impossible cases), and promises everything. No charlatan ever appeared with fitter and more excellent talents, or to greater advantage; he has a good person, is a natural orator, and has a faculty of learning foreign languages. He has travelled over all Europe, and has always with him an equipage suitable to a man of the first quality; and has been introduced to most of the sovereign princes, from whom he has received many marks of their liberality and esteem."

Dr. King, in a Latin inscription to the mountebank, says:—

> "Hic est, hic vir est,
> Quem docti, indoctique omnes impense mirantur,
> Johannes Taylor;
> Cœcigenorum, cœcorum, cœcitantium,
> Quot quot sunt ubique,
> Spes unica—Solamen—Salus."

The Chevalier Taylor (as he always styled himself), in his travels about the country, used to give lectures on "The Eye," in whatever place he tarried. These addresses were never explanatory of the anatomy of the organ, but mere absurd rhapsodies on it as an ingenious and wonderful contrivance.

Chevalier's oration to the university of Oxford, which is still extant, began thus:—

"The eye, most illustrious sons of the muses, most learned Oxonians, whose fame I have heard celebrated in all parts of the globe—the eye, that most amazing, that stupendous, that comprehending, that incomprehensible, that miraculous organ, the eye, is the Proteus of the passions, the herald of the mind, the interpreter of the heart, and the window of the soul. The eye has dominion over all things. The world was made for the eye, and the eye for the world.

"My subject is Light, most illustrious sons of literature—intellectual light. Ah! my philosophical, metaphysical, my classical, mathematical, mechanical, my theological, my critical audience, my subject is the eye. You are the eye of England!

"England has two eyes—Oxford and Cambridge. They are the two eyes of England, and two intellectual eyes. You are the right eye of England, the elder sister in science, and the first fountain of learning in all Europe. What filial joy must exult in my bosom, in my vast circuit, as copious as that of the sun himself, to shine in my course, upon this my native soil, and give light even at Oxford!

"The eye is the husband of the soul!

"The eye is indefatigable. The eye is an angelic faculty. The eye in this respect is a female. The eye is never tired of seeing; that is, of taking in, assimilating, and enjoying all Nature's vigour."

When the Chevalier was ranting on in this fashion at Cambridge (of course there terming Oxford the *left* eye of England), he undertook to express every passion of the mind by the eye alone.

"Here you have surprise, gentlemen; here you have delight; here you have terror!"

"Ah!" cried an undergraduate, "there's no merit in that, for you tell us before-hand what the emotion is. Now next time say nothing—and let me guess what the feeling is you desire to express."

"Certainly," responded the Doctor, cordially; "nothing can be more reason-able in the way of a proposition. Now then, sir, what is this?"

"Oh, veneration, I suppose."

"Certainly—quite right—and this?"

"Pity."

"Of course, sir: you see it's impossible for an observant gentleman like your-self to misunderstand the language of the eye," answered the oculist, whose plan was only to assent to his young friend's decisions.

In the year 1736, when the Chevalier was at the height of his fame, he received the following humorous letter:—

> "DOMINE,—O tu, qui in oculis hominum versaris, et qua-mcunque tractas rem, *acu* tangis, salve! Tu, qui, instar Phœbi, lu-men orbi, et orbes luminibus reddis, iterum salve!
>
> "Cum per te Gallia, per te nostræ academiæ, duo regni lu-mina, clarius intuentur, cur non ad urbem Edinburgi, cum toties ubique erras, cursum tendis? nam quædam cœcitas cives illic invasit. Ipsos magistratus *Gutta Serena* occupavit, videntur enim videre, sed nihil vident. Idcirco tu istam *Scoticam Nebulam* ex oc-ulis remove, et quodcunque latet in tenebris, in lucem profer. Illi violenter carcerem, tu oculos leniter reclude; illi lucem Porteio ademerunt, tu illis lucem restitue, et quamvis fingant se duplic-iter videre, fac ut simpliciter tantum oculo irretorto conspiciant. Peractoque cursu, ad Angliam redi artis tuæ plenus, Toriosque (ut vulgo vocantur) qui adhuc cœcutiant et hallucinantur, illumi-nato. Ab ipsis clericis, si qui sint cœci ductores, nubem discute; immo ipso Sole lunaque, cum laborant eclipsi, quæ, instar tui ip-sius, transit per varias regiones obumbrans, istam molem caliginis amoveto. Sic eris Sol Mundi, sic eris non solum nomine Sartor, sed re Oculorum omnium resarcitor; sic omuis Charta Publica tuam Claritudinem celebrabit, et ubicunque frontem tuam ostendis, nemo non te, O vir spectatissime, admirabitur. Ipse lippus scrip-tor hujus epistolæ maxime gauderet te Medicum Illustrissimum, cum omnibus tuis oculatis testibus, Vindsoriæ videre.—VALE."

The Chevalier had a son and a biographer in the person of John Taylor, who, under the title of "John Taylor, Junior," succeeded to his father's trumpet, and blew it with good effect. The title-page of his biography of his father enumerates some half-hundred crowned or royal heads, to whose eyes the "Chevalier John Taylor, Opthalmiater Pontifical, Imperial, and Royal," administered.

But this work was feeble and contemptible compared with the Chevalier's autobiographic sketch of himself, in his proposal for publishing which he speaks of his loves and adventures, in the following modest style:—

"I had the happiness to be also personally known to two of the most amiable ladies this age has produced—namely, Lady Inverness and Lady Mackintosh; both powerful figures, of great abilities, and of the most pleasing address—both the sweetest prattlers, the prettiest reasoners, and the best judges of the charms of high life that I ever saw. When I first beheld these wonders I gazed on their beauties, and my attention was busied in admiring the order and delicacy of their discourse, &c. For were I commanded to seek the world for a lady adorned with every accomplishment that man thinks desirable in the sex, I could only be determined by finding their resemblance....

"I am perfectly acquainted with the history of Persia, as well before as since the death of Thamas Kouli Khan; well informed of the adventures of Prince Heraclius; was personally known to a minister he sent to Moscow in his first attempt to conquer that country; and am instructed in the cruel manner of putting out the eyes of conquered princes, and of cutting away the eyelids of soldiers taken in war, to make them unfit for service.

"I have lived in many convents of friars of different orders, been present at their creation to various degrees, and have assisted at numberless entertainments upon those occasions.

"I have been in almost every female nunnery in all Europe (*on account of my profession*), and could write many volumes on the adventures of these religious beauties.

"I have been present at the making of nuns of almost every order, and assisted at the religious feasts given on those occasions.

"I have met with a very great variety of singular religious people called Pilgrims.

"I have been present at many extraordinary diversions designed for the amusement of the sovereign, viz. hunting of different sorts of wild beasts, as in Poland; bull-fighting, as in Spain.

"I am well acquainted with all the various punishments for different crimes, as practised in every nation—been present at the putting of criminals to death by various ways, viz. striking off heads, breaking on the wheel, &c.

"I am also well instructed in the different ways of giving the torture to extract confession—and am no stranger to other singular punishments, such as impaling, burying alive with head above ground, &c.

"And lastly, I have assisted, have seen the manner of embalming dead bodies of great personages, and am well instructed in the manner practised in some nations for preserving them entire for ages, with little alteration of figure from what they were when first deprived of life....

"All must agree that no man ever had a greater variety of matter worthy to be conveyed to posterity. I shall, therefore, give my best care to, so to paint my thoughts, and give such a dress of the story of my life, that tho' I shall talk of the Great, the Least shall not find cause of offence."

The occasion of this great man issuing so modest a proposal to the public is involved in some mystery. It would seem that he determined to publish his own version of his adventures, in consequence of being dissatisfied with his son's sketch of them. John Taylor, Junior, was then resident in Hatton Garden, living as an eye-doctor, and entered into an arrangement with a publisher, without his father's consent, to write the Chevalier's biography. Affixed to the indecent pamphlet, which was the result of this agreement, are the following epistolary statements:—

"MY SON,—If you should unguardedly have suffered your name at the head of a work which must make us all contemptible, this must be printed in it as the best apology for yourself and father:—

"TO THE PRINTER.

"Oxford, Jan. 10, 1761.

"My dear and only son having respectfully represented to me that he has composed a work, intitled *My Life and Adventures*, and requires my consent for its publication, notwithstanding I am as yet a stranger to the composition, and consequently can be no judge of its merits, I am so well persuaded that my son is in every way incapable of saying aught of his father but what must redound to his honour and reputation, and so perfectly convinced of the goodness of his heart, that it does not seem possible I should err in my judgment, by giving my consent to a publication of the said work. And as I have long been employed in writing my own Life and Adventures, which will with all expedition be published, 'twill hereafter be left with all due attention to the candid reader, whether the Life of the Father written by the son, or the Life of the Father written by himself, best deserves approbation.

"THE CHEVALIER TAYLOR,
"Opthalmiater, Pontifical, Imperial, and Royal.

"* * * The above is a true copy of the letter my Father sent me. All the answer I can make to the bills he sends about the town and country is, that I have maintained my mother these eight years, and do this at the present time; and that, two years since, I was concerned for him, for which I have paid near £200.

"As witness my hand,
"JOHN TAYLOR, *Oculist*."

"Hatton Garden."

It is impossible to say whether these differences were genuine, or only feigned by the two quacks, in order to keep silly people gossiping about them. Certainly the accusations brought against the Chevalier, that he had sponged on his son, and declined to support his wife, are rather grave ones to introduce into a make-believe quarrel. But, on the other hand, when the Chevalier's autobiography appeared it was prefaced with the following dedicatory letter to his son:—

"My dear Son,—Can I do ill when I address to you the story of your father's life? Whose name can be so proper as your own to be prefixed to a work of this kind? You who was born to represent me living, when I shall cease to be—born to pursue that most excellent and important profession to which I have for so many years labored to be useful—born to defend my cause and support my fame—may I not *presume*, my son, that you will defend your father's cause? May I not *affirm* that you, my son, will support your father's fame? After having this said, need I add more than remind you—that, to a father, nothing can be so dear as a deserving son—nor state so desirable as that of the man who holds his successor, and knows him to be worthy. Be prosperous. Be happy.

> "I am, your affectionate Father,
> "The Chevalier John Taylor."

This unctuous address to "my lion-hearted boy" is equalled in drollery by many passages of the work itself, which (in the language of the title-page) "contains all most worthy the attention of a Traveller—also a dissertation on the Art of Pleasing, with the most interesting observations on the Force of Prejudice; numberless adventures, as well amongst nuns and friars as with persons in high life; with a description of a great variety of the most admirable relations, which, though told in his well-known peculiar manner, each one is strictly true, and within the Chevalier's own observations and knowledge."

Apart from the bombast of his style, the Chevalier's "well-known peculiar manner" was remarkable for little besides tautology and a fantastic arrangement of words. In his orations, when he aimed at sublimity, he indulged in short sentences each of which commenced with a genitive case followed by an accusative; after which came the verb succeeded by the nominative. Thus, at such crises of grandiloquence, instead of saying, "I will lecture on the wonders of the eye," he would invert the order to, "Of the eye on the wonders lecture will I." By doing this, he maintained that he surpassed the finest periods of Tully! There is a letter in Nichols's "Literary Anecdotes," in which a lecture given by this mountebank at Northampton is excellently described. "The doctor," says the writer, "appeared dressed in black, with a long light flowing ty'd wig; ascended a scaffold behind a large table raised about two feet from the ground, and covered with an old piece of tapestry, on which was laid a dark-coloured cafoy chariot-seat with four black bunches (used upon hearses) tyed to the corners for tassels, four large candles on each side of the cushion, and a quart decanter of drinking water, with a half-pint glass, to moisten his mouth."

The fellow boasted that he was the author of forty-five works in different languages. Once he had the audacity to challenge Johnson to talk Latin with him. The doctor responded with a quotation from Horace, which the charlatan took to be the doctor's own composition. "*He said a few words well enough*," Johnson said magnanimously when he repeated the story to Boswell. "Taylor," said the doctor, "is the most ignorant man I ever knew, but sprightly; Ward, the dullest."

John Taylor, Junr., survived his father more than fifteen years, and to the last had a lucrative business in Hatton Garden. His father had been oculist to George the Second; but this post, on the death of the Chevalier, he failed to obtain, it being given to a foreign *protégé* of the Duke of Bedford's. He made a great noise about the sufferings of the poor, and proposed to the different parishes of London to attend the paupers labouring under diseases of the eye at two guineas a-year for each parish. He was an illiterate, vulgar, and licentious scoundrel; and yet when he died, on the 17th September, 1787, he was honoured with a long memoir in the *Gentleman's Magazine,* as one "whose philanthropy was exerted so fully as to class him with a Hanway or a Howard."

If an apology is needed for giving so much space, in a chapter devoted to the ladies, to the John Taylors, it must be grounded on the fact that the Chevalier was the son of an honest widow woman who carried on a respectable business, as an apothecary and doctress, at Norwich. In this she resembled Mrs. Blood, the wife of the Colonel of that name, who for years supported herself and son at Romford, by keeping an apothecary's shop under the name of Weston. Colonel Blood was also himself a member of the Faculty. For some time, whilst meditating his *grand coup,* he practised as a doctor in an obscure part of the City, under the name of Ayliffe.

Two hundred years since the lady practitioners of medicine in the provinces not seldom had working for them pupils and assistants of the opposite sex, and this usage was maintained in secluded districts till a comparatively recent date. In Houghton's Collection, Nov. 15, 1695, is the following advertisement,—"If any Apothecary's Widow that keeps a shop in the country wants a journeyman that has lived 25 years for himself in London, and has had the conversation of the eminent physicians of the colledge, I can help to such an one."

CHAPTER XVII.

MESSENGER MONSEY.

Amongst the celebrities of the medical profession, who have left no memorial behind them more durable or better known than their wills in Doctors' Commons, was Messenger Monsey, the great-grandfather of our ex-Chancellor, Lord Cranworth.

We do not know whether his Lordship is aware of his descent from the eccentric physician. Possibly he is not, for the Monseys, though not altogether of a plebeian stock, were little calculated to throw éclat over the genealogy of a patrician house.

Messenger Monsey, who used with a good deal of unnecessary noise to declare his contempt of the ancestral honours which he in reality possessed, loved to tell of the humble origin of his family. The first Duke of Leeds delighted in boasting of his lucky progenitor, Jack Osborn, the shop lad, who rescued his master's daughter from a watery grave, in the Thames, and won her hand away from a host of noble suitors, who wanted—literally, the young lady's *pin*-money. She was the only child of a wealthy pinmaker carrying on his business on London Bridge, and the jolly old fellow, instead of disdaining to bestow his heiress on a 'prentice, exclaimed, "Jack won her, and he shall wear her!" Dr. Monsey, in the hey-day of his social fame, told his friends that the first of his ancestors of any note was a baker, and a retail dealer in hops. At a critical point of this worthy man's career, when hops were "down" and feathers were "up," to raise a small sum of money for immediate use he ripped open his beds, sold the feathers, and stuffed the tick with unsaleable hops. Soon a change in the market occurred, and once more operating on the couches used by himself and children, he sold the hops at a profit, and bought back the feathers. "That's the way, sir, by which my family hopped from obscurity!" the doctor would conclude.

We have reason for thinking that this ancestor was the physician's great-grandfather. As is usually found to be the case, where a man thinks lightly of the advantages of birth, Messenger was by no means of despicable extraction. His grandfather was a man of considerable property, and married Elizabeth Messenger, co-heir of Thomas Messenger, lord of Whitwell Manor, in the county of Norfolk, a gentleman by birth and position; and his father, the Rev. Robert Monsey, a Norfolk rector, married Mary, the daughter of Roger Clopton, rector of Downham. Of the antiquity and importance of the Cloptons amongst the gentle families of England this is no place to speak; but further particulars relative to the Monsey pedigree may be found by the curious in Bloomfield's "History of Norfolk." On such a descent a Celt would persuade himself that he represented kings and rulers. Monsey, like Sydney Smith after him, preferred to cover the whole question with jolly, manly ridicule, and put it out of sight.

Messenger Monsey was born in 1693, and received in early life an excellent education; for though his father at the Revolution threw his lot in with the non-jurors, and forfeited his living, the worthy clergyman had a sufficient paternal estate to enable him to rear his only child without any painful considerations of cost. After spending five years at St. Mary's Hall, Cambridge, Messenger studied physic for some time under Sir Benjamin Wrench, at Norwich. Starting on his own account, he practised for a while at Bury St. Edmunds, in Suffolk, but with little success. He worked hard, and yet never managed in that prosperous and beautiful country town to earn more than three hundred guineas in the same year. If we examined into the successes of medical celebrities, we should find in a great majority of cases fortune was won by the aspirant either annexing himself to, and gliding into the confidence of, a powerful clique, or else by his being through some lucky accident thrown in the way of a patron. Monsey's rise was of the latter sort. He was still at Bury, with nothing before him but the prospect of working all his days as a country doctor, when Lord Godolphin, son of Queen Anne's Lord Treasurer, and grandson of the great Duke of Marlborough, was seized, on the road to Newmarket, with an attack of apoplexy. Bury was the nearest point where medical assistance could be obtained. Monsey was summoned, and so fascinated his patient with his conversational powers that his Lordship invited him to London, and induced him to relinquish his country practice.

From that time Monsey's fortune was made. He became to the Whigs very much what, in the previous generation, Radcliffe had been to the Tories. Sir Robert Walpole genuinely loved him, seizing every opportunity to enjoy his society, and never doing anything for him; and Lord Chesterfield was amongst the most zealous trumpeters of his medical skill. Lively, sagacious, well-read, and brutally sarcastic, he had for a while a society reputation for wit scarcely inferior to Swift's; and he lived amongst men well able to judge of wit. Garrick and he were for many years intimate friends, until, in a contest of jokes, each of the two brilliant men lost his temper, and they parted like Roland and Sir Leoline—never to meet again. Garrick probably would have kept his temper under any other form of ridicule, but he never ceased to resent Monsey's reflection on his avarice to the Bishop of Sodor and Man.

"Garrick is going to quit the stage," observed the Bishop.

"That he'll never do," answered Monsey, making use of a Norfolk proverb, "so long as he knows a guinea is cross on one side and pile on the other."

This speech was never forgiven. Lord Bath endeavoured to effect a reconciliation between the divided friends, but his amiable intention was of no avail.

"I thank you," said Monsey; "but why will your Lordship trouble yourself with the squabbles of a Merry Andrew and quack doctor?"

When the tragedian was on his death-bed, Monsey composed a satire on the sick man, renewing the attack on his parsimony. Garrick's illness, however, terminating fatally, the doctor destroyed his verses, but some scraps of them still remain to show their spirit and power. A consultation of physicians was represented as being held over the actor:—

> "Seven wise physicians lately met,
> To save a wretched sinner;
> Come, Tom, said Jack, pray let's be quick,
> Or I shall lose my dinner.
> *   *   *   *   *
>
> "Some roared for rhubarb, jalap some,
> And some cried out for Dover;
> Lets give him something, each man said—
> Why e'en let's give him—over."

After much learned squabbling, one of the sages proposed to revive the sinking energies of the poor man by jingling guineas in his ears. The suggestion was acted upon, when—

> "Soon as the fav'rite sound he heard,
> One faint effort he try'd;
> He op'd his eyes, he stretched his hands,
> He made one grasp—and dy'd."

Though, on the grave closing over his antagonist, Monsey suppressed these lines, he continued to cherish an animosity to the object of them. The spirit in which, out of respect to death, he drew a period to their quarrel, was much like that of the Irish peasant in the song, who tells his ghostly adviser that he forgives Pat Malone with all his heart (supposing death should get the better of him)—but should he recover, he means to pay the rascal off roundly. Sir Walter Scott somewhere tells a story of a Highland chief, in his last moments declaring that he from the bottom of his heart forgave his old enemy, the head of a hostile clan—and concluding this Christian avowal with a final address to his son—"But may all evil light upon ye, Ronald, if ye e'er forgie the heathen."

Through Lord Godolphin's interest, Monsey was appointed physician to Chelsea College, on the death of Dr. Smart. For some time he continued to reside in St. James's: but on the death of his patron he moved to Chelsea, and spent the last years of his life in retirement—and to a certain extent banishment—from the great world. The hospital offices were then filled by a set of low-born scoundrels, or discharged servants, whom the ministers of various Cabinets had had some reason of their own for providing for. The surgeon was that Mr. Ranby who positively died of rage because Henry Fielding's brother (Sir John) would not punish a hackney coachman who had been guilty of the high treason of—being injured and abused by the plaintiff. With this man Monsey had a tremendous quarrel; but though in the right, he had to submit to Ranby's powerful connections.

This affair did not soften his temper to the other functionaries of the hospital with whom he had to associate at the hall table. His encounter with the venal elector who had been nominated to a Chelsea appointment is well known, though an account of it would hurt the delicacy of these somewhat prudish pages. Of the doctor's insolence the following is a good story:—

A clergyman, who used to bore him with pompous and pedantic talk, was arguing on some point with Monsey, when the latter exclaimed:—

"Sir, if you have faith in your opinion, will you venture a wager upon it?"

"I could—but I won't," was the reply.

"Then," rejoined Monsey, "you have very little wit, or very little money." The logic of this retort puts one in mind of the eccentric actor who, under somewhat similar circumstances, asked indignantly, "Then, sir, how *dare* you advance a statement in a public room which you are not prepared to substantiate with a bet!"

Monsey was a Unitarian, and not at all backward to avow his creed. As he was riding in Hyde Park with a Mr. Robinson, that gentleman, after deploring the corrupt morals of the age, said, with very bad taste, "But, Doctor, I talk with one who believes there is no God." "And I," retorted Monsey, "with one who believes there are three." Good Mr. Robinson was so horrified that he clapped spurs to his horse, galloped off, and never spoke to the doctor again.

Monsey's Whiggism introduced him to high society, but not to lucrative practice. Sir Robert Walpole always extoled the merits of his "Norfolk Doctor," but never advanced his interests. Instead of covering the great minister with adulation, Monsey treated him like an ordinary individual, telling him when his jokes were poor, and not hesitating to worst him in argument. "How happens it," asked Sir Robert, over his wine, "that nobody will beat me at billiards, or contradict me, but Dr. Monsey!" "Other people," put in the doctor, "get places—I get a dinner and praise." The Duke of Grafton treated him even worse. His Grace staved off paying the physician his bill for attending him and his family at Windsor, with promises of a place. When "the little place" fell vacant, Monsey called on the duke, and reminded him of his promise. "Ecod—ecod—ecod," was the answer, "but the Chamberlain has just been here to tell me he has promised it to Jack — —." When the disappointed applicant told the lord-chamberlain what had transpired, his Lordship replied, "Don't, for the world, tell his Grace; but before he knew I had promised it, here is a letter he sent me, soliciting for *a third person*."

Amongst the vagaries of this eccentric physician was the way in which he extracted his own teeth. Round the tooth sentenced to be drawn he fastened securely a strong piece of catgut, to the opposite end of which he affixed a bullet. With this bullet and a full measure of powder a pistol was charged. On the trigger being pulled, the operation was performed effectually and speedily. The doctor could only rarely prevail on his friends to permit him to remove their teeth by this original process. Once a gentleman who had agreed to try the novelty, and had even allowed the apparatus to be adjusted, at the last moment exclaimed, "Stop, stop, I've changed my mind!" "But I haven't, and you're a fool and a coward for your pains," answered the doctor, pulling the trigger. In another instant the tooth was extracted, much to the timid patient's delight and astonishment.

At Chelsea, to the last, the doctor saw on friendly terms all the distinguished medical men of his day. Cheselden, fonder of having his horses admired than his professional skill extolled, as Pope and Freind knew, was his frequent visitor. He had also his loves. To Mrs. Montague, for many years, he presented a copy of verses on the anniversary of her birth-day. But after his quarrel with Garrick, he saw but little of the lady, and was rarely, if ever, a visitor at her magnificent house in Portman Square. Another of his flames, too, was Miss Berry, of whom the loss still seems to be recent. In his old age, avarice—the very same failing he condemned so much in Garrick—developed itself in Monsey. In comparatively early life his mind was in a flighty state about money matters. For years he was a victim of that incredulity which makes the capitalist imagine a great and prosperous country to be the most insecure of all debtors. He preferred investing his money in any wild speculation to confiding it to the safe custody of the funds. Even his ready cash he for long could not bring himself to trust in the hands of a banker. When he left town for a trip, he had recourse to the most absurd schemes for the protection of his money. Before setting out, on one occasion, for a journey to Norfolk, incredulous with regard to cash-boxes and bureaus, he hid a considerable quantity of gold and notes in the fireplace of his study, covering them up artistically with cinders and shavings. A month afterwards, returning (luckily a few days before he was expected), he found his old house-maid preparing to entertain a few friends at tea in her master's room. The hospitable domestic was on the point of lighting the fire, and had just applied a candle to the doctor's notes, when he entered the room, seized on a pail of water that chanced to be standing near, and, throwing its contents over the fuel and the old woman, extinguished the fire and her presence of mind at the same time. Some of the notes, as it was, were injured, and the Bank of England made objections to cashing them.

To the last Monsey acted by his own rules instead of by those of other people. He lived to extreme old age, dying in his rooms in Chelsea College, on December 26th, 1788, in his ninety-fifth year; and his will was as remarkable as any other feature of his career. To a young lady mentioned in it, with the most lavish encomiums on her wit, taste, and elegance, was left an old battered snuff-box—not worth sixpence; and to another young lady, whom the testator says he intended to have enriched with a handsome legacy, he leaves the gratifying assurance that he changed his mind on finding her "a pert, conceited minx." After inveighing against bishops, deans, and chapters, he left an annuity to two clergymen who had resigned their preferment on account of the Athanasian doctrine. He directed that his body should not be insulted with any funeral ceremony, but should undergo dissection; after which, the "remainder of my carcase" (to use his own words) "may be put into a hole, or crammed into a box with holes, and thrown into the Thames." In obedience to this part of the will, Mr. Forster, surgeon, of Union Court, Broad Street, dissected the body, and delivered a lecture on it to the medical students in the theatre of Guy's Hospital. The bulk of the doctor's fortune, amounting to about £16,000, was left to his only daughter for life, and after her demise, by a complicated entail, to her *female* descendants. This only child, Charlotte Monsey, married William Alexander, a linen-draper in Cateaton Street, City, and had a numerous family. One of her daughters married the Rev. Edmund Rolfe, rector of Cockley Clay, Norfolk, of which union Robert Monsey Rolfe, Baron Cranworth of Cranworth, county of Norfolk, is the offspring.

Before making the above-named and final disposition of his body, the old man found vent for his ferocious cynicism and vulgar infidelity in the following epitaph, which is scarcely less characteristic of the society in which the writer had lived, than it is of the writer himself:—

"MOUNSEY'S EPITAPH, WRITTEN BY HIMSELF."

"Here lie my old bones; my vexation now ends;
I have lived much too long for myself and my friends.
As to churches and churchyards, which men may call holy,
'Tis a rank piece of priestcraft, and founded on folly.
What the next world may be never troubled my pate;
And be what it may, I beseech you, O fate,
When the bodies of millions rise up in a riot,
To let the old carcase of Mounsey be quiet."

Unpleasant old scamp though he in many respects was, Monsey retains even at this day so firm a hold of the affections of all students who like ferreting into the social history of the last century, that no chance letter of his writing is devoid of interest. The following specimen of his epistolary style, addressed to his fair patient, the accomplished and celebrated Mrs. Montague (his acquaintance with which lady has already been alluded to), is transcribed from the original manuscript in the possession of Dr. Diamond:—

"4th of March, a minute past 12.

"DEAR MADAME,

"Now dead men's ghosts are getting out of their graves, and there comes the ghost of a doctor in a white sheet to wait upon you. Your Tokay is got into my head and your love into my heart, and they both join to club their thanks for the pleasantest day I have spent these seven years; and to my comfort I find a man may be in love, and be happy, provided he does not go to book for it. I could have trusted till the morning to show my gratitude, but the Tokay wou'd have evaporated, and then I might have had nothing to talk of but an ache in my head and pain in my heart. Bacchus and Cupid should always be together, for the young gentleman is very apt to be silly when he's alone by himself; but when old toss-pot is with him, if he pretends to fall a whining, he hits him a cursed knock on the pate, and says: 'Drink about, you....' 'No, Bacchus, don't be in a passion. Upon my soul you have knocked out one of my eyes!' 'Eyes, ye scroundrel? Why, you have never had one since you were born.... Apollo would have couched you, but your mother said no; for then, says she, "he can never be blamed for his shot, any more than the people that are shot at." She knew 'twould bring grist to her mill; for what with those who pretended they were in love and were not so, and those who were really so and wouldn't own it, I shall find rantum scantum work at Cyprus,

Paphos, and Cythera. Some will come to acquire what they never had, and others to get rid of what they find very troublesome, and I shall mind none of 'em.' You see how the goddess foresaw and predicted my misfortunes. She knew I was a sincere votary, and that I was a martyr to her serene influence. Then how could you use me so like an Hyrcanian tygress, and be such an infidel to misery; that though I hate you mortally, I wish you may feel but one poor *half-quarter-of-an-hour* before you slip your breath—how shall I rejoice at your horrid agonies? *Nec enim lex justior ulla Quam necis artifices arte perire suâ*—Remember Me.

"My ills have disturbed my brain, and the revival of old ideas has set it a-boyling, that, till I have skim'd off the froth, I can't pretend to say a word for myself; and by the time I have cleared off the scum, the little grudge that is left may be burnt to the bottom of the pot.

"My mortal injuries have turned my mind,
And I could hate myself for being blind
But why should I thus rave of eyes and looks?
All I have felt is fancy—all from Books.
I stole my charmers from the cuts of Quarles,
And my dear Clarissa from the grand Sir Charles.
But if his mam or Cupid live above,
Who have revenge in store for injured love,
O Venus, send dire ruin on her head,
Strike the Destroyer, lay the Victress dead;
Kill the Triumphress, and avenge my wrong
In height of pomp, while she is warm and young.
Grant I may stand and dart her with my eyes
While in the fiercest pangs of life she lies,
Pursue her sportive soul and shoot it as it flies,
And cry with joy—There Montague lies flat,
Who wronged my passion with her barbarous Chat,
And was as cruel as a Cat to Rat,
As cat to rat—ay, ay, as cat to rat.
And when you got her up into your house,
Clinch yr, fair fist, and give her such a souse:
There, Hussy, take you that for all your Prate,
Your barbarous heart I do a-bo-mi-nate.
I'll take your part, my dearest faithful Doctor!
I've told my son, and see how he has mockt her!
He'll fire her soul and make her rant and rave;
See how she groans to be old Vulcan's slave.
The fatal bow is bent. Shoot, Cupid, shoot,
And there's your Montague all over soot.
Now say no more my little Boy is blind,
For sure this tyrant he has paid in kind.

She fondly thought to captivate a lord.
A lord, sweet queen? 'Tis true, upon my word.
And what's his name? His name? Why—
And thought her parts and wit the feat had done.
But he had parts and wit as well as she.
Why then, 'tis strange those folks did not agree.
Agree? Why, had she lived one moment longer,
His love was strong, but madam's grew much stronger.
Hiatus valde deflendus.
So for her long neglect of Venus' altar
I changed Cu's Bowstring to a silken Halter;
I made the noose, and Cupid drew the knot.
Dear mam! says he, don't let her lie and rot,
She is too pretty. Hold your tongue, you sot!
The pretty blockhead? None of yr. rogue's tricks.
Ask her, she'll own she's turned of thirty-six.
I was but twenty when I got the apple,
And let me tell you, 'twas a cursed grapple.
Had I but staid till I was twenty-five,
I'ad surely lost it, as you're now alive!
Paris had said to Juno and Minerva,
Ladies, I'm yours, and shall be glad to serve yer;
I must have bowed to wisdom and to power.
And Troy had stood it to this very hour,
Homer had never wrote, nor wits had read
Achilles' anger or Patroclus dead.
We gods and goddesses had lived in riot,
And the blind fool had let us all be quiet.
Mortals had never been stunn'd with!!!!!!!—
Nor Virgil's wooden horse play'd Hocus Pocus.
Hang the two Bards! But Montague is pretty.
Sirrah, you lie; but I'll allow she's witty.
Well! but I'm told she was so at fifteen,
Ay, and the veriest so that e'er was seen.
Why that I own; and I myself——

"But, hold! as in all probability I am going to tell a parcel of
cursed lies, I'll travel no further, lay down my presumptuous pen,
and go to bed; for it's half-past two, and two hours and an half is
full long enough to write nonsense at one time. You see what it is
to give a Goth Tokay: you manure your land with filth, and it pro-
duces Tokay; you enrich a man with Tokay, and he brings forth
the froth and filth of nonsense. You will learn how to bestow it
better another time. I hope what you took yourself had a better, or
at least no bad, effect. I wish you had wrote me a note after your
first sleep. There wou'd have been your sublime double-distilled,
treble-refined wit. I shouldn't have known it to be yours if it could

have been anybody's else.

"Pray don't show these humble rhimes to R——y. That puppy will write notes upon 'em or perhaps paint 'em upon signposts, and make 'em into an invitation to draw people to see the Camel and Dromedary—for I see he can make anything of anything; but, after all, why should I be afraid? Perhaps he might make something of nothing. I have wrote in heroics. Sure the wretch will have a reverence for heroics, especially for such as he never saw before, and never may again. Well, upon my life I will go to bed—'tis a burning shame to sit up so. I lie, for my fire is out, and so will my candle too if I write a word more.

"So I will only make my mark.　　**X**

"God eternally bless and preserve you from such writers."

"March 5th, 12 o'clock.

"Dear Mrs. Montague,

"My fever has been so great that I have not had any time to write to you in such a manner as to try and convince you that I had recovered my senses, and I could write a sober line. Pray, how do you do after your wine and its effects on you, as well as upon me? You are grown a right down rake, and I never expect you for a patient again as long as we live, the last relation I should like to stand to you in, and which nothing could make bearable but serving you, and that is a *J'ay pays* for all my misery in serving you ill.

"I am called out, so adieu."

"March 6th.

"How do you stand this flabby weather? I tremble to hear, but want to hear of all things. If you have done with my stupid West India Ly., pray send 'em, for they go to-morrow or next day at latest. 'Tis hardly worth while to trouble Ld L with so much chaff and so little wheat—then why you!

"Very true. 'Tis a sad thing to have to do with a fool, who can't keep his nonsense to himself. You know I am a rose, but I have terrible prickles. Dear madam, adieu. Pray God I may hear you are well, or that He will enable me to make you so, for you must not be sick or die. I'll find fools and rogues enough to be that for you, that are good for nothing else, and hardly, very hardly, good enough for that. Adieu, Adieu! I say Adieu, Adieu.

"M. M."

Truly did Dr. Messenger Monsey understand the art of writing a long letter about nothing.

CHAPTER XVIII.

AKENSIDE.

There were two Akensides—Akenside the poet, and Akenside the man; and of the *man* Akenside there were numerous subdivisions. Remarkable as a poet, he was even yet more noteworthy a private individual in his extreme inconsistency. No character is more commonplace than the one to which is ordinarily applied the word contradictory; but Akenside was a curiosity from the extravagance in which this form of "the commonplace" exhibited itself in his disposition and manners.

By turns he was placid, irritable, simple, affected, gracious, haughty, magnanimous, mean, benevolent, harsh, and sometimes even brutal. At times he was marked by a childlike docility, and at other times his vanity and arrogance displayed him almost as a madman. Of plebeian extraction, he was ashamed of his origin, and yet was throughout life the champion of popular interests. Of his real humanity there can be no doubt, and yet in his demeanour to the unfortunate creatures whom, in his capacity of a hospital-physician, he had to attend, he was always supercilious, and often cruel.

Like Byron, he was lame, one of his legs being shorter than the other; and of this personal disfigurement he was even more sensitive than was the author of "Childe Harold" of his deformity. When his eye fell on it he would blush, for it reminded him of the ignoble condition in which he was born. His father was a butcher at Newcastle-upon-Tyne; and one of his cleavers, falling from the shop-block, had irremediably injured the poet's foot, when he was still a little child.

Akenside was not only the son of a butcher—but, worse still, a Nonconformist butcher; and from an early period of his life he was destined to be a sectarian minister. In his nineteenth year he was sent to Edinburgh to prosecute his theological studies, the expenses of this educational course being in part defrayed by the Dissenters' Society. But he speedily discovered that he had made a wrong start, and persuaded his father to refund the money the Society had advanced, and to be himself at the cost of educating him as a physician. The honest tradesman was a liberal and affectionate parent. Mark remained three years at Edinburgh, a member of the Medical Society, and an industrious student. On leaving Edinburgh he practised for a short time as a surgeon at Newcastle; after which he went to Leyden, and having spent three months in that university took his degree of doctor of physic, May 16, 1744. At Leyden he became warmly attached to a fellow-student named Dyson; and wonderful to be related, the two friends, notwithstanding one was under heavy pecuniary obligations to the other, and they were very unlike each other in some of their principal characteristics, played the part of Pylades and Orestes, even into the Valley of Death. Akenside was poor, ardent, and of a nervous, poetic temperament. Dyson was rich, sober, and matter-of-fact, a prudent place-holder. He rose to be clerk of the House of Commons, and a Lord of the Treasury; but the atmosphere of political circles and the excitement of public life never caused his heart to forget its early attachment. Whilst the poet lived Dyson was his munificent patron, and when death had stepped in between them, his literary executor. Indeed, he allowed him for years no less a sum than £300 per annum.

Akenside was never very successful as a physician, although he thoroughly understood his profession, and in some important particulars advanced its science. Dyson introduced him into good society, and recommended him to all his friends; but the greatest income Akenside ever made was most probably less than what he obtained from his friend's generosity. Still, he must have earned something, for he managed to keep a carriage and pair of horses; and £300 per annum, although a hundred years ago that sum went nearly twice as far as it would now, could not have supported the equipage. His want of patients can easily be accounted for. He was a vain, tempestuous, crotchety little man, little qualified to override the prejudices which vulgar and ignorant people cherish against lawyers and physicians who have capacity and energy enough to distinguish themselves in any way out of the ordinary track of their professional duties.

He was admitted, by mandamus, to a doctor's degree at Cambridge; and became a fellow of the Royal Society, and a fellow of the Royal College of Physicians. He tried his luck at Northampton, and found he was not needed there; he became an inhabitant of Hampstead, but failed to ingratiate himself with the opulent gentry who in those days resided in that suburb; and lastly fixed himself in Bloomsbury Square (ætat. 27), where he resided till his death. After some delay, he became a physician of St. Thomas's Hospital, and an assistant physician of Christ's Hospital—read the Gulstonian Lectures before the College of Physicians, in 1755—and was also Krohnian Lecturer. In speeches and papers to learned societies, and to various medical treatises, amongst which may be mentioned his "De Dysentariâ Commentarius," he tried to wheedle himself into practice. But his efforts were of no avail. Sir John Hawkins, in his absurd Life of Dr. Johnson, tells a good story of Saxby's rudeness to the author of the "Pleasures of Imagination." Saxby was a custom-house clerk, and made himself liked in society by saying the rude things which other people had the benevolence to feel, but lacked the hardihood to utter. One evening, at a party, Akenside argued, with much warmth and more tediousness, that physicians were better and wiser men than the world ordinarily thought.

"Doctor," said Saxby, "after all you have said, my opinion of the profession is this: the ancients endeavoured to make it a science, and failed; and the moderns to make it a trade, and succeeded."

He was not liked at St. Thomas's Hospital. The gentle Lettsom, whose mild poetic nature had surrounded the author of "The Pleasures of Imagination" with a halo of romantic interest, when he entered himself a student of that school, was shocked at finding the idol of his admiration so irritable and unkindly a man. He was, according to Lettsom's reminiscences, thin and pale, and of a strumous countenance. His injured leg was lengthened by a false heel. In dress he was scrupulously neat and delicate, always having on his head a well-powdered white wig, and by his side a long sword. Any want of respect to him threw him into a fit of anger. One amongst the students who accompanied him on a certain occasion round the wards spat on the floor behind the physician. Akenside turned sharply on his heel, and demanded who it was that dared to spit in his face. To the poor women who applied to him for medical advice he exhibited his dislike in the most offensive and cruel manner. The students who watched him closely, and knew the severe disappointment his affections had suffered in early life, whispered to the novice that the poet-physician's moroseness to his female patients was a consequence of his having felt the goads of despised love. The fastidiousness of the little fellow at having to come so closely in contact with the vulgar rabble, induced him sometimes to make the stronger patients precede him with brooms and clear a way for him through the crowd of diseased wretches. Bravo, my butcher's boy! This story of Akenside and his lictors, pushing back the unsightly mob of lepers, ought to be read side by side with that of the proud Duke of Somerset, who, when on a journey, used to send outriders before him to clear the roads, and prevent vulgar eyes from looking at him.

On one occasion Akenside ordered an unfortunate male patient of St. Thomas's to take boluses of bark. The poor fellow complained that he could not swallow them. Akenside was so incensed at the man's presuming to have an opinion on the subject, that he ordered him to be turned out of the hospital, saying, "He shall not die under my care." A man who would treat his *poor* patients in this way did not deserve to have any *rich* ones. These excesses of folly and brutality, however, ere long reached the ears of honest Richard Chester, one of the governors, and that good fellow gave the doctor a good scolding, roundly telling him, "Know, thou art a servant of this charity."

Akenside's self-love received a more humorous stab than the poke administered by Richard Chester's blunt cudgel, from Mr. Baker, one of the surgeons at St. Thomas's. To appreciate the full force of the story, the reader must recollect that the jealousy, which still exists between the two branches of the medical profession, was a century since so violent that even considerations of interest failed in some cases to induce eminent surgeons and physicians to act together. One of Baker's sons was the victim of epilepsy, and frequent fits had impaired his faculties. Baker was naturally acutely sensitive of his child's misfortune, and when Akenside had the bad taste to ask to what study the afflicted lad intended to apply, the father answered, "I find he is not capable of making a surgeon, so I have sent him to Edinburgh to make a physician of him." Akenside felt this sarcasm so much, that he for a long time afterward refused to hold any intercourse with Baker.

But Akenside had many excuses for his irritability. He was very ambitious, and failed to achieve that success which the possession of great powers warranted him in regarding as his due. It was said of Garth that no physician understood his art more, or his trade less! and this, as Mr. Bucke, in his beautiful "Life of Arkenside," remarks, was equally true of the doctor of St. Thomas's. He had a thirst for human praise and worldly success, and a temperament that caused him, notwithstanding all his sarcasms against love, to estimate at their full worth the joys of married life; yet he lived all his days a poor man, and died a bachelor. Other griefs also contributed to sour his temper. His lot was cast in times that could not justly appreciate his literary excellences. His sincere admiration of classic literature and art and manners was regarded by the coarse herd of rich and stupid Londoners as so perfectly ridiculous, that when Smollett had the bad taste to introduce him into *Peregrine Pickle,* as the physician who gives a dinner after the manner of the ancients, the applause was general, and every city tradesman, with scholarship enough to read the novel, had a laugh at the expense of a man who has some claims to be regarded as the greatest literary genius of his time. The polished and refined circles of English life paid homage to his genius, but even in them he failed to meet with the cordial recognition he deserved. Johnson, though he placed him above Gray and Mason, did not do him justice. Boswell didn't see much in him. Horace Walpole differed from the friend who asked him to admire the "Pleasures of Imagination." The poets and wits of his own time had a high respect for his critical opinion, and admitted the excellence of his poetry—but almost invariably with some qualification. And Akenside was one who thirsted for the complete assent of the applauding world. He died after a brief illness in his forty-ninth year, on the 23rd of June, 1770; and we doubt not, when the Angel of Death touched him, the heart that ceased to beat was one that had known much sorrow.

Akenside's poetical career was one of unfulfilled promise. At the age of twenty-three he had written "The Pleasures of the Imagination." Pope was so struck with the merits of the poem, that when Dodsley consulted him about the price set on it by the author (£120), he told him to make no niggardly offer, for it was the work of no every-day writer. But he never produced another great work. Impressed with the imperfections of his achievement, he occupied himself with incessantly touching and re-touching it up, till he came to the unwise determination of re-writing it. He did not live to accomplish this suicidal task; but the portion of it which came to the public was inferior to the original poem, both in power and art.

CHAPTER XIX.

LETTSOM.

High amongst literary, and higher yet amongst benevolent, physicians must be ranked John Coakley Lettsom, formerly president of the Philosophical Society of London. A West Indian, and the son of a planter, he was born on one of his father's little islands, Van Dyke, near Tortola, in the year 1744. Though bred a Quaker, he kept his heart so free from sectarianism, and his life so entirely void of the formality and puritanic asceticism of the Friends, that his ordinary acquaintance marvelled at his continuing to wear the costume of the brotherhood. At six years of age he was sent to England for education, being for that purpose confided to the protection of Mr. Fothergill, of Warrington, a Quaker minister, and younger brother of Dr. John Fothergill. After receiving a poor preparatory education, he was apprenticed to a Yorkshire apothecary, named Sutcliffe, who, by industry and intelligence, had raised himself from the position of a weaver to that of the first medical practitioner of Settle. In the last century a West Indian was, to the inhabitants of a provincial district, a rare curiosity; and Sutcliffe's surgery, on the day that Lettsom entered it in his fifteenth year, was surrounded by a dense crowd of gaping rustics, anxious to see a young gentleman accustomed to walk on his head. This extraordinary demonstration of curiosity was owing to the merry humour of Sutcliffe's senior apprentice, who had informed the people that the new pupil, who would soon join him, came from a country where the feet of the inhabitants were placed in an exactly opposite direction to those of Englishmen.

Sutcliffe did not find his new apprentice a very handy one. "Thou mayest make a physician, but I think not a good apothecary," the old man was in the habit of saying; and the prediction in due course turned out a correct one. Having served an apprenticeship of five years, and walked for two the wards of St. Thomas's Hospital, where Akenside was a physician, conspicuous for supercilious manner and want of feeling, Lettsom returned to the West Indies, and settled as a medical practitioner in Tortola. He practised there only five months, earning in that time the astonishing sum of £2000; when, ambitious of achieving a high professional position, he returned to Europe, visited the medical schools of Paris and Edinburgh, took his degree of M.D. at Leyden on the 20th of June, 1769, was admitted a licentiate of the Royal College of Physicians of London in the same year, and in 1770 was elected a fellow of the Society of Antiquaries.

From this period till his death, in 1815 (Nov. 20), he was one of the most prominent figures in the scientific world of London. As a physician he was a most fortunate man; for without any high reputation for professional acquirements, and with the exact reverse of a good preliminary education, he made a larger income than any other physician of the same time. Dr. John Fothergill never made more than £5000 in one year; but Lettsom earned £3600 in 1783—£3900 in 1784—£4015 in 1785-and £4500 in 1786. After that period his practice rapidly increased, so that in some years his receipts were as much as £12,000. But although he pocketed such large sums, half his labours were entirely gratuitous. Necessitous clergymen and literary men he invariably attended with unusual solicitude and attention, but without ever taking a fee for his services. Indeed, generosity was the ruling feature of his life. Although he burdened himself with the public business of his profession, was so incessantly on the move from one patient to another that he habitually knocked up three pairs of horses a-day, and had always some literary work or other upon his desk, he nevertheless found time to do an amount of labour, in establishing charitable institutions and visiting the indigent sick, that would by itself have made a reputation for an ordinary person.

To give the mere list of his separate benevolent services would be to write a book about them. The General Dispensary, the Finsbury Dispensary, the Surrey Dispensary, and the Margate Sea-bathing Infirmary, originated in his exertions; and he was one of the first projectors of—the Philanthropic Society, St. Georges-in-the-Fields, for the Prevention of Crimes, and the Reform of the Criminal Poor; the Society for the Discharge and Relief of Persons Imprisoned for Small Debts; the Asylum for the Indigent Deaf and Dumb; the Institution for the Relief and Employment of the Indigent Blind; and the Royal Humane Society, for the recovery of the apparently drowned or dead. And year by year his pen sent forth some publication or other to promote the welfare of the poor, and succour the afflicted. Of course there were crowds of clever spectators of the world's work, who smiled as the doctor's carriage passed them in the streets, and said he was a deuced clever fellow to make ten thousand a-year so easily; and that, after all, philanthropy was not a bad trade. But Lettsom was no calculating humanitarian, with a tongue discoursing eloquently on the sufferings of mankind, and an eye on the sharp lookout for his own interest. What he was before the full stare of the world, that he was also in his own secret heart, and those private ways into which hypocrisy cannot enter. At the outset of his life, when only twenty-three years old, he liberated his slaves—although they constituted almost his entire worldly wealth, and he was anxious to achieve distinction in a profession that offers peculiar difficulties to needy aspirants. And when his career was drawing to a close, he had to part with his beloved countryseat because he had impoverished himself by lavish generosity to the unfortunate.

There was no sanctimonious affectation in the man. He wore a drab coat and gaiters, and made the Quaker's use of *Thou* and *Thee*; but he held himself altogether apart from the prejudices of his sect. A poet himself of some respectability, he delighted in every variety of literature, and was ready to shake any man by the hand—Jew or Gentile. He liked pictures and works of sculpture, and spent large sums upon them; into the various scientific movements of the time he threw himself with all the energy of his nature; and he disbursed a fortune in surrounding himself at Camberwell with plants from the tropics. He liked good wine, but never partook of it to excess, although his enemies were ready to suggest that he was always glad to avail himself of an excuse for getting intoxicated. And he was such a devoted admirer of the fair sex, that the jealous swarm of needy men who envied him his prosperity, had some countenance for their slander that he was a Quaker debauchee. He married young, and his wife outlived him; but as a husband he was as faithful as he proved in every other relation of life.

Saturday was the day he devoted to entertaining his friends at Grove Hill, Camberwell; and rare parties there gathered round him—celebrities from every region of the civilized world, and the best "good fellows" of London. Boswell was one of his most frequent guests, and, in an ode to Charles Dilly, celebrated the beauties of the physician's seat and his humane disposition:—

> "My cordial Friend, still prompt to lend
> Your cash when I have need on't;
> We both must bear our load of care—
> At least we talk and read on't."

> "Yet are we gay in ev'ry way,
> Not minding where the joke lie;
> On Saturday at bowls we play
> At Camberwell with Coakley."

> "Methinks you laugh to hear but half
> The name of Dr. Lettsom:
> From him of good—talk, liquors, food—
> His guests will always get some."

> "And guests has he, in ev'ry degree,
> Of decent estimation:
> His liberal mind holds all mankind
> As an extended Nation.

> "O'er Lettsom's cheer we've met a peer—
> A peer—no less than Lansdowne!
> Of whom each dull and envious skull
> Absurdly cries—'The man's down!'

> "Down do they say? How then, I pray,
> His king and country prize him!
> Through the whole world known, his peace alone
> Is sure t' immortalize him.

> "Lettsom we view a *Quaker* true,
> 'Tis clear he's so in one sense:
> His *spirit*, strong, and ever young,
> Refutes pert Priestley's nonsense.

> "In fossils he is deep, we see;
> Nor knows Beasts, Fishes, Birds ill;
> With plants not few, some from Pelew,
> And wondrous Mangel Wurzel!

> "West India bred, warm heart, cool head,
> The city's first physician;
> By schemes humane—want, sickness, pain,
> To aid in his ambition.
>
> "From terrace high he feasts his eye,
> When practice grants a furlough;
> And, while it roves o'er Dulwich groves,
> Looks down—even upon Thurlow."

The concluding line is an allusion to the Lord Chancellor's residence at Dulwich.

In person, Lettsom was tall and thin—indeed, almost attenuated: his face was deeply lined, indicating firmness quite as much as benevolence; and his complexion was of a dark yellow hue. His eccentricities were numerous. Like the founder of his sect, he would not allow even respect for royalty to make an alteration in his costume which his conscience did not approve; and George III., who entertained a warm regard for him, allowed him to appear at Court in the ordinary Quaker garb, and to kiss his hand, though he had neither powder on his head, nor a sword by his side. Lettsom responded to his sovereign's courtesy by presenting him with some rare and unpurchasable medals.

Though his writings show him to have been an enlightened physician for his time, his system of practice was not of course free from the violent measures which were universally believed in during the last century. He used to say of himself,

> "When patients sick to me apply,
> I physics, bleeds and sweats 'em;
> Then—if they choose to die,
> What's that to me—I lets 'em."—(I. Lettsom.)

But his prescriptions were not invariably of a kind calculated to depress the system of his patient. On one occasion an old American merchant, who had been ruined by the rupture between the colonies and the mother country, requested his attendance and professional advice. The unfortunate man was seventy-four years of age, and bowed down with the weight of his calamities.

"Those trees, doctor," said the sick man, looking out of his bed-room window over his lawn, "I planted, and have lived to see some of them too old to bear fruit; they are part of my family: and my children, still dearer to me, must quit this residence, which was the delight of my youth, and the hope of my old age."

The Quaker physician was deeply affected by these pathetic words, and the impressive tone with which they were uttered. He spoke a few words of comfort, and quitted the room, leaving on the table as his prescription—a cheque for a large sum of money. Nor did his goodness end there. He purchased the house of his patient's creditors, and presented it to him for life.

As Lettsom was travelling in the neighbourhood of London, a highwayman stopped his carriage, and, putting a pistol into the window, demanded him to surrender his money. The faltering voice and hesitation of the robber showed that he had only recently taken to his perilous vocation, and his appearance showed him to be a young man who had moved in the gentle ranks of life. Lettsom quickly responded that he was sorry to see such a well-looking young man pursuing a course which would inevitably bring him to ruin; that he would *give* him freely all the money he had about him, and would try to put him in a better way of life, if he liked to call on him in the course of a few days. As the doctor said this, he gave his card to the young man, who turned out to be another victim of the American war. He had only made one similar attempt on the road before, and had been driven to lawless action by unexpected pennilessness. Lettsom endeavoured in vain to procure aid for his *protégé* from the commissioners for relieving the American sufferers; but eventually the Queen, interested in the young man's case, presented him with a commission in the army; and in a brief military career, that was cut short by yellow fever in the West Indies, he distinguished himself so much that his name appeared twice in the *Gazette*.

On one of his benevolent excursions the doctor found his way into the squalid garret of a poor woman who had seen better days. With the language and deportment of a lady she begged the physician to give her a prescription. After inquiring carefully into her case, he wrote on a slip of paper to the overseers of the parish—

> "A shilling per diem for Mrs Moreton. Money, not physic, will cure her.   "LETTSOM."

Of all Lettsom's numerous works, including his contributions to the *Gentleman's Magazine*, under the signature of "Mottles," the anagram of his own name, the one most known to the general reader, is the "History of some of the Effects of Hard Drinking." It concludes with a scale of Temperance and Intemperance, in imitation of a thermometer. To each of the two conditions seventy degrees are allotted. Against the seventieth (or highest) degree of Temperance is marked "Water," under which, at distances of ten degrees, follow "Milk-and-Water," "Small Beer," "Cyder and Perry," "Wine," "Porter," "Strong Beer." The tenth degree of Intemperance is "Punch"; the twentieth, "Toddy and Crank"; the thirtieth, "Grog and Brandy and Water"; the fortieth, "Flip and Shrub"; the fiftieth, "Bitters infused in Spirits, Usquebaugh, Hysteric Water"; the sixtieth, "Gin, Aniseed, Brandy, Rum, and Whisky," in the morning; the seventieth, like the sixtieth, only taken day and night. Then follow, in tabular order, the vices, diseases, and punishments of the different stages of Intemperance. The mere enumeration of them ought to keep the most confirmed toper sober for the rest of his days:—

"*Vices.*—Idleness, Peevishness, Quarrelling, Fighting, Lying, Swearing, Obscenity, Swindling, Perjury, Burglary, Murder, Suicide.

"*Diseases.*—Sickness, Tremors of the Hands in the Morning, Bloatedness, Inflamed Eyes, Red Nose and Face, Sore and Swelled Legs, Jaundice, Pains in the Limbs, Dropsy, Epilepsy, Melancholy, Madness, Palsy, Apoplexy, Death.

"*Punishments.*—Debt, Black Eyes, Rags, Hunger, Hospital, Poor-house, Jail, Whipping, the Hulks, Botany Bay, Gallows!"

This reads like Hogarth's Gin Lane.

CHAPTER XX.

A FEW MORE QUACKS.

The term quack is applicable to all who, by pompous pretences, mean insinuations, and indirect promises, endeavour to obtain that confidence to which neither education, merit, nor experience entitles them.—Samuel Parr's Definition.

Of London's modern quacks, one of the most daring was James Graham, M. D., of Edinburgh, who introduced into England the juggleries of Mesmer, profiting by them in this country scarcely less than his master did on the Continent. His brother married Catherine Macaulay, the author of the immortal History of England, which no one now-a-days reads; the admired of Horace Walpole; the lady whose statue during her life-time, was erected in the chancel of the church of St. Stephen's, Walbrook. Graham's sister was married to Dr. Arnold, of Leicester, the author of a valuable book on Insanity.

With a little intellect and more knavery, Dr. Graham ran a course very similar to Mesmer. Emerging from obscurity in or about the year 1780, he established himself in a spacious mansion in the Royal Terrace, Adelphi, overlooking the Thames, and midway between the Blackfriars and Westminster Bridges. The river front of the house was ornamented with classic pillars; and inscribed over the principal entrance, in gilt letters on a white compartment, was "Templum Æsculapio Sacrum." The "Temple of Health," as it was usually spoken of in London, quickly became a place of fashionable resort. Its spacious rooms were supplied with furniture made to be stared at—sphynxes, dragons breathing flame, marble statues, paintings, medico-electric apparatus, rich curtains and draperies, stained glass windows, stands of armour, immense pillars and globes of glass, and remarkably arranged plates of burnished steel. Luxurious couches were arranged in the recesses of the apartments, whereon languid visitors were invited to rest; whilst the senses were fascinated with strains of gentle music, and the perfumes of spices burnt in swinging censers. The most sacred shrine of the edifice stood in the centre of "The Great Apollo Apartment," described by the magician in the following terms:—"This room is upwards of thirty feet long, by twenty wide, and full fifteen feet high in the ceiling; on entering which, words can convey no adequate idea of the astonishment and awful sublimity which seizes the mind of every spectator. The first object which strikes the eye, astonishes, expands, and ennobles the soul of the beholder, is a magnificent temple, sacred to health, and dedicated to Apollo. In this tremendous edifice are combined or singly dispensed the irresistible and salubrious influences of electricity, or the elementary fire, air, and magnetism; three of the greatest of those agents of universal principles, which, pervading all created being and substances that we are acquainted with, connect, animate, and keep together all nature;—or, in other words, principles which constitute, as it were, the various faculties of the material soul of the universe: *the Eternally Supreme Jehovah Himself* being the essential source—the Life of that Life—the Agent of those Agents—the Soul of that Soul—the All-creating, all-sustaining, all-blessing God!—not of this world alone—not of the other still greater worlds which we know compose our solar system! Not the creator, the soul, the preserver of this world alone—or of any of those which we have seen roll with uninterrupted harmony for so many thousands of years!—not the God of the millions of myriads of worlds, of systems, and of various ranks and orders of beings and intelligences which probably compose the aggregate of the grand, the vast, the incomprehensible system of the universe!—but the eternal, infinitely wise, and infinitely powerful, infinitely good God of the whole—the Great Sun of the Universe!"

This blasphemy was regarded in Bond Street and Mayfair as inspired wisdom. It was held to be wicked not to believe in Dr. Graham. The "Temple" was crowded with the noble and wealthy; and Graham, mingling the madness of a religious enthusiast with the craft of a charlatan, preached to his visitors and prayed over them with the zeal of Joanna Southcote. He composed a form of prayer to be used in the Temple, called "the Christian's Universal Prayer," a long rigmarole of spasmodic nonsense, to the printed edition of which the author affixed the following note: "The first idea of writing this prayer was suggested by hearing, one evening, the celebrated Mr Fischer play on the hautboy, with inimitable sweetness, *his long-winded* variations on some old tunes. I was desirous to know what effect that would have when extended to literary composition. I made the experiment as soon as I got home, on the Lord's Prayer, and wrote the following in bed, before morning:"

About the "Temple of Health" there are a few other interesting particulars extant. The woman who officiated in the "Sanctum Sanctorum" was the fair and frail Emma—in due course to be the wife of Sir William Hamilton, and the goddess of Nelson. The charges for consulting the oracle, or a mere admission in the Temple, were thus arranged. "The nobility, gentry, and others, who apply through the day, viz., from ten to six, must pay a guinea the first consultation, and half a guinea every time after. No person whomsoever, even personages of the first rank, need expect to be attended at their own houses, unless confined to bed by sickness, or to their room through extreme weakness; and from those whom he attends at their houses two guineas each visit is expected. Dr Graham, for reasons of the highest importance to the public as well as to himself, has a chymical laboratory and a great medicinal cabinet in his own house; and in the above fixed fees either at home or abroad, every expense attending his advice, medicines, applications, and operations, and *influences,* are included—a few tedious, complex, and expensive operations in the Great Apollo apartment only excepted."

But the humour of the man culminated when he bethought himself of displaying the crutches and spectacles of restored patients, as trophies of his victories over disease. "Over the doors of the principal rooms, under the vaulted compartments of the ceiling, and in each side of the centre arches of the hall, are placed walking-sticks, ear-trumpets, visual glasses, crutches, &c., left, and here placed as most honourable trophies, by deaf, weak, paralytic, and emaciated persons, cripples, &c., who, being cured, have happily no longer need of such assistances."

Amongst the furniture of the "Temple of Health" was a celestial bed, provided with costly draperies, and standing on glass legs. Married couples, who slept on this couch, were sure of being blessed with a beautiful progeny. For its use £100 per night was demanded, and numerous persons of rank were foolish enough to comply with the terms. Besides his celestial bed and magnetic tomfooleries, Graham vended an "Elixir of Life," and subsequently recommended and superintended earth-bathing. Any one who took the elixir might live as long as he wished. For a constant supply of so valuable a medicine, £1000, paid in advance, was the demand. More than one nobleman paid that sum. The Duchess of Devonshire patronized Graham, as she did every other quack who came in her way; and her folly was countenanced by Lady Spencer, Lady Clermont, the Comtesse de Polignac, and the Comtesse de Chalon.

Of all Dr. Graham's numerous writings one of the most ridiculous is "A clear, full, and faithful Portraiture, or Description, and ardent Recommendation of a certain most beautiful and spotless Virgin Princess, of Imperial descent! To a certain youthful Heir-Apparent, in the possession of whom alone his Royal Highness can be truly, permanently, and supremely happy. Most humbly dedicated to his Royal Highness, George, Prince of Wales, and earnestly recommended to the attention of the Members of both Houses of Parliament." When George the Third was attacked for the first time with mental aberration, Graham hastened down to Windsor, and obtaining an interview there with the Prince Regent, with thrilling earnestness of manner assured his Royal Highness that he would suffer in the same way as his father unless he married a particular princess that he (Dr. Graham) was ready to introduce to him. On the Prince inquiring the name of the lady, Graham answered, "Evangelical Wisdom." Possibly the royal patient would have profited, had he obeyed the zealot's exhortation. The work, of which we have just given the title, is a frantic rhapsody on the beauties and excellence of the Virgin Princess Wisdom, arranged in chapters and verses, and begins thus:—

"CHAP. 1."

"Hear! all ye people of the earth, and understand; give ear attentively, O ye kings and princes, and be admonished; yea, learn attentively, ye who are the rulers and the judges of the people."

"2. Let the inhabitants of the earth come before me with all the innocency and docility of little children; and the kings and governors, with all purity and simplicity of heart.

"3. For the Holy Spirit of Wisdom! or celestial discipline! flees from duplicity and deceit, and from haughtiness and hardness of heart; it removes far from the thoughts that are without understanding; and will not abide when unrighteousness cometh in."

The man who was fool enough to write such stuff as this had, however, some common sense. He detected the real cause of the maladies of half those who consulted him, and he did his utmost to remove it. Like the French quack Villars, he preached up "abstinence" and "cleanliness." Of the printed "general instructions" to his patients, No. 2 runs thus:—"It will be unreasonable for Dr Graham's patients to expect a complete and lasting cure, or even great alleviation of their peculiar maladies, unless they keep their body and limbs most perfectly clean with frequent washings, breathe fresh open air day and night, be simple in the quality and moderate in the quantity of their food and drink, and totally give up using deadly poisons and weakeners of both body and soul, and the canker-worms of estates, called foreign tea and coffee, red port wine, spirituous liquors, tobacco and snuff, gaming and late hours, and all sinful and unnatural and excessive indulgence of the animal appetites, and of the diabolical and degrading mental passions. On practising the above rules, and a widely-open window day and night, and on washing with cold water, and going to bed every night by eight or nine, and rising by four or five, depends the very perfection of bodily and mental health, strength, and happiness."

Many to whom this advice was given thought that ill-health, which made them unable to enjoy anything was no worse an evil than health brought on terms that left them nothing to enjoy. During his career Graham moved his "Temple of Health" from the Adelphi to Pall-Mall. But he did not prosper in the long-run. His religious extravagances for a while brought him adherents, but when they took the form of attacking the Established Church, they brought on him an army of adversaries. He came also into humiliating collision with the Edinburgh authorities.

Perhaps the curative means employed by Graham were as justifiable and beneficial as the remedies of the celebrated doctors of Whitworth in Yorkshire, the brothers Taylor. These gentlemen were farriers, by profession, but condescended to prescribe for their own race as well, always, however, regarding the vocation of brute-doctor as superior in dignity to that of a physician. Their system of practice was a vigorous one. They made no gradual and insidious advances on disease, but opened against it a bombardment of shot and shell from all directions. They bled their patients by the gallon, and drugged them by the stone. Their druggists, Ewbank and Wallis of York, used to supply them with a ton of Glauber's salts at a time. In their dispensary scales and weights were regarded as the bugbears of ignoble minds. Every Sunday morning they bled *gratis* any one who liked to demand a prick from their lancets. Often a hundred poor people were seated on the surgery benches at the same time, waiting for venesection. When each of the party had found a seat the two brothers passed rapidly along the lines of bared arms, the one doctor deftly applying the ligature above the elbow, and the other immediately opening the vein, the crimson stream from which was directed to a wooden trough that ran round the apartment in which the operations were performed. The same magnificence of proportion characterized their administration of kitchen physic. If they ordered a patient broth, they directed his nurse to buy a large leg of mutton, and boil it in a copper of water down to a strong decoction, of which a quart should be administered at stated intervals.

When the little Abbé de Voisenon was ordered by his physician to drink a quart of ptisan per hour he was horrified. On his next visit the doctor asked,

"What effect has the ptisan produced?"

"Not any," answered the little Abbé.

"Have you taken it all?"

"I could not take more than half of it."

The physician was annoyed, even angry that his directions had not been carried out, and frankly said so.

"Ah, my friend," pleaded the Abbé, *"how could you desire me to swallow a quart an hour? —I hold but a pint!"*

This reminds us of a story we have heard told of an irascible physician who died, after attaining a venerable age, at the close of the last century. The story is one of those which, told once, are told many times, and affixed to new personages, according to the whim or ignorance of the narrator.

"Your husband is very ill—very ill—high fever," observed the Doctor to the poor labourer's wife; "and he's old, worn, emaciated: his hand is as dry as a Suffolk cheese. You must keep giving him water—as much as he'll drink; and, as I am coming back to-night from Woodbridge, I'll see him again. There—don't come snivelling about me!—my heart is a deuced deal too hard to stand that sort of thing. But, since you want something to cry about, just listen—your husband *isn't going to die yet!* There, now you're disappointed. Well, you brought it on yourself. Mind lots of water—as much as he'll drink" ·

The doctor was ashamed of the feminine tenderness of his heart, and tried to hide it under an affectation of cynicism, and a manner at times verging on brutality. Heaven bless all his descendants, scattered over the whole world, but all of them brave and virtuous! A volume might be written on his good qualities; his only bad one being extreme irascibility. His furies were many, and sprung from divers visitations; but nothing was so sure to lash him into a tempest as to be pestered with idle questions.

"Water, sir?" whined Molly Meagrim. "To be sure, your honour—water he shall have, poor dear soul! But, your honour, how much water ought I to give him?"

"Zounds, woman! haven't I told you to give him as much as he'll take?—and you ask me how much! *How much?*—give him a couple of pails of water, if he'll take 'em. Now, do you hear me, you old fool? Give him a couple of pails."

"The Lord bless your honour—yes," whined Molly.

To get beyond the reach of her miserable voice the Doctor ran to his horse, and rode off to Woodbridge. At night as he returned, he stopped at the cottage to inquire after the sick man.

"He's bin took away, yer honour," said the woman, as the physician entered. "The water didn't fare to do him noan good—noan in the lessest, sir. Only then we couldn't get down the right quantity, though we did our best. We got down better nor a pail and a half, when he slipped out o' our hands. Ah, yer honour! if we could but ha' got him to swaller the rest, he might still be alive! But we did our best, Doctor!"

Clumsy empirics, however, as the Taylors were, they attended people of the first importance. The elder Taylor was called to London to attend Thurlow, Bishop of Durham, the brother of Lord Chancellor Thurlow. The representative men of the Faculty received him at the bishop's residence, but he would not commence the consultation till the arrival of John Hunter. "I won't say a word till Jack Hunter comes," roared the Whitworth doctor; "he's the only man of you who knows anything." When Hunter arrived, Taylor proceeded to his examination of the bishop's state, and, in the course of it, used some ointment which he took from a box.

"What's it made of?" Hunter asked.

"That's not a fair question," said Taylor, turning to the Lord Chancellor, who happened to be present. "No, no, Jack. I'll send you as much as you please, but I won't tell you what it's made of."

CHAPTER XXI.
ST. JOHN LONG.

In the entire history of charlatanism, however, it would be difficult to point to a career more extraordinary than the brilliant though brief one of St. John Long, in our own cultivated London, at a time scarcely more than a generation distant from the present. Though a pretender, and consummate quack, he was distinguished from the vulgar herd of cheats by the possession of enviable personal endowments, a good address, and a considerable quantity of intellect. The son of an Irish basket-maker, he was born in or near Doneraile, and in his boyhood assisted in his father's humble business. His artistic talents, which he cultivated for some time without the aid of a drawing-master, enabled him, while still quite a lad, to discontinue working as a rush-weaver. For a little while he stayed at Dublin, and had some intercourse with Daniel Richardson the painter; after which he moved to Limerick county, and started on his own account as a portrait-painter, and an instructor in the use of the brush. That his education was not superior to what might be expected in a clever youth of such lowly extraction, the following advertisement, copied from a Limerick paper of February 10, 1821, attests:—

"Mr John Saint John Long, Historical and Portrait Painter, the only pupil of Daniel Richardson, Esq., late of Dublin, proposes, during his stay in Limerick, to take portraits from Ittalian Head to whole length; and parson desirous of getting theirs done, in historical, hunting, shooting, fishing, or any other character; or their family, grouped in one or two paintings from life-size to miniature, so as to make an historical subject, choseing one from history."

"The costume of the period from whence it would be taken will be particularly attended to, and the character of each preserved."

"He would take views in the country, terms per agreement. Specimens to be seen at his Residence, No. 116, Georges Street, opposite the Club-house, and at Mr James Dodds, Paper-staining Warehouse, Georges Street.

"Mr Long is advised by his several friends to give instructions in the Art of Painting in Oils, Opeak, Chalk, and Water-colours, &c., to a limited number of Pupils of Respectability two days in each week at stated hours."

"Gentlemen are not to attend at the same hour the Ladies attend at. He will supply them in water-colours, &c."

How the young artist acquired the name of St. John is a mystery. When he blazed into notoriety, his admirers asserted that it came to him in company with noble blood that ran in his veins; but more unkind observers declared that it was assumed, as being likely to tickle the ears of his credulous adherents. His success as a provincial art-professor was considerable. The gentry of Limerick liked his manly bearing and lively conversation, and invited him to their houses to take likenesses of their wives, flirt with their daughters, and accompany their sons on hunting and shooting excursions. Emboldened by good luck in his own country, and possibly finding the patronage of the impoverished aristocracy of an Irish province did not yield him a sufficient income, he determined to try his fortune in England. Acting on this resolve, he hastened to London, and with ingratiating manners and that persuasive tongue which nine Irishmen out of ten possess, he managed to get introductions to a few respectable drawing-rooms. He even obtained some employment from Sir Thomas Lawrence, as colour-grinder and useful assistant in the studio; and was elected a member of the Royal Society of Literature, and also of the Royal Asiatic Society. But like many an Irish adventurer, before and after him, he found it hard work to live on his impudence, pleasant manners, and slender professional acquirements. He was glad to colour anatomical drawings for the professors and pupils of one of the minor surgical schools of London; and in doing so picked up a few pounds and a very slight knowledge of the structure of the human frame. The information so obtained stimulated him to further researches, and, ere a few more months of starvation had passed over, he deemed himself qualified to cure all the bodily ailments to which the children of Adam are subject.

He invented a lotion or liniment endowed with the remarkable faculty of distinguishing between sound and unsound tissues. To a healthy part it was as innocuous as water; but when applied to a surface under which any seeds of disease were lurking, it became a violent irritant, creating a sore over the seat of mischief, and stimulating nature to throw off the morbid virus. He also instructed his patients to inhale the vapour which rose from a certain mixture compounded by him in large quantities, and placed in the interior of a large mahogany case, which very much resembled an upright piano. In the sides of this piece of furniture were apertures, into which pipe-stalks were screwed for the benefit of afflicted mortals, who, sitting on easy lounges, smoked away like a party of Turkish elders.

With these two agents St. John Long engaged to combat every form of disease—gout, palsy, obstructions of the liver, cutaneous affections; but the malady which he professed to have the most complete command over was consumption. His success in surrounding himself with patients was equal to his audacity. He took a large house in Harley Street, and fitted it up for the reception of people anxious to consult him; and for some seasons every morning and afternoon (from 8 a.m. to 4 p.m.) the public way was blocked up with carriages pressing to his door. The old and the young alike flocked to him; but nine of his patients out of every ten were ladies. For awhile the foolish of every rank in London seemed to have but one form in which to display their folly. Needy matrons from obscure suburban villages came with their guineas to consult the new oracle; and ladies of the highest rank, fashion, and wealth, hastened to place themselves and their daughters at the mercy of a pretender's ignorance.

Unparalleled were the scenes which the reception-rooms of that notorious house in Harley Street witnessed. In one room were two enormous inhalers, with flexible tubes running outwards in all directions, and surrounded by dozens of excited women—ladies of advanced years, and young girls giddy with the excitement of their first London season—puffing from their lips the medicated vapour, or waiting till a mouth-piece should be at liberty for their pink lips. In another room the great magician received his patients. Some he ordered to persevere in inhalation, others he divested of their raiment, and rubbed his miraculous liniment into their backs, between their shoulders or over their bosoms. Strange to say, these lavations and frictions—which invariably took place in the presence of third persons, nurses or invalids—had very different results. The fluid, which, as far as the eye could discern, was taken out of the same vessel, and was the same for all, would instantaneously produce on one lady a burning excoriation, which had in due course to be dressed with cabbage-leaves; but on another would be so powerless that she could wash in it, or drink it copiously, like ordinary pump-water, with impunity. "Yes," said the wizard, "that was his system, and such were its effects. If a girl had tubercles in her lungs, the lotion applied to the outward surface of her chest would produce a sore, and extract the virus from the organs of respiration. If a gentleman had a gouty foot, and washed it in this new water of Jordan, at the cost of a little temporary irritation the vicious particles would leave the affected part. But on any sound person who bathed in it the fluid would have no power whatever."

The news of the wonderful remedy flew to every part of the kingdom; and from every quarter sick persons, wearied of a vain search after an alleviation of their sufferings, flocked to London with hope renewed once more. St. John Long had so many applicants for attention that he was literally unable to give heed to all of them; and he availed himself of this excess of business to select for treatment those cases only where there seemed every chance of a satisfactory result. In this he was perfectly candid, for time after time he declared that he would take no one under his care who seemed to have already gone beyond hope. On one occasion he was called into the country to see a gentleman who was in the last stage of consumption; and after a brief examination of the poor fellow's condition, he said frankly—

"Sir, you are so ill that I cannot take you under my charge at present. You want stamina. Take hearty meals of beefsteaks and strong beer; and if you are better in ten days, I'll do my best for you and cure you."

It was a safe offer to make, for the sick man lived little more than forty-eight hours longer.

But, notwithstanding the calls of his enormous practice, St. John Long found time to enjoy himself. He went a great deal into fashionable society, and was petted by the great and high-born, not only because he was a notoriety, but because of his easy manners, imposing carriage, musical though hesitating voice, and agreeable disposition. He was tall and slight, but strongly built; and his countenance, thin and firmly set, although frank in expression, caused beholders to think highly of his intellectual refinement, as well as of his decision and energy. Possibly his personal advantages had no slight influence with his feminine applauders. But he possessed other qualities yet more fitted to secure their esteem—an Irish impetuosity of temperament and a sincere sympathy with the unfortunate. He was an excellent horseman, hunting regularly, and riding superb horses. On one occasion, as he was cantering round the Park, he saw a man strike a woman, and without an instant's consideration he pulled up, leaped to the ground, seized the fellow bodily, and with one enormous effort flung him slap over the Park rails.

But horse-exercise was the only masculine pastime he was very fond of. He was very temperate in his habits; and although Irish gentlemen *used* to get tipsy, he never did. Painting, music, and the society of a few really superior women, were the principal sources of enjoyment to which this brilliant charlatan had recourse in his leisure hours. Many were the ladies of rank and girls of gentle houses who would have gladly linked their fortunes to him and his ten thousand a year.[21] But though numerous matrimonial overtures were made to him, he persevered in his bachelor style of life; and although he was received with peculiar intimacy into the privacy of female society, scandal never even charged him with a want of honour or delicacy towards women, apart from his quackery. Indeed, he broke off his professional connection with one notorious lady of rank, rather than gratify her eccentric wish to have her likeness taken by him in that remarkable costume—or no costume at all—in which she was wont to receive her visitors.

In the exercise of his art he treated women unscrupulously. Amidst the crowd of ladies who thronged his reception-rooms he moved, smiling, courteous, and watchful, listening to their mutual confidences about their maladies, the constitutions of their relations, and their family interests. Every stray sentence the wily man caught up and retained in his memory, for future use. To induce those to become his patients who had nothing the matter with them, and consequently would go to swell the list of his successful cases, he used the most atrocious artifices.

"Ah, Lady Emily, I saw your dear sister," he would say to a patient, "yesterday—driving in the Park—lovely creature she is! Ah, poor thing!"

"Poor thing, Mr. Long!—why, Catherine is the picture of health!"

"Ah," the adroit fellow would answer, sadly, "you think so—so does she—and so does every one besides myself who sees her; but—but—unless prompt remedial measures are taken that dear girl, ere two short years have flown, will be in her grave." This mournful prophecy would be speedily conveyed to Catherine's ears;

[21] A writer in the *Gentleman's Magazine* for 1843 observes:—"In England, after Sir Astley, whose superiority of mind or dexterity of hand stood uncontested, another practitioner in that category of the Faculty of which it has been said, 'Periculis nostris, et experimenta per mortes agunt medici,' the once famous St John Long was, I believe, the most largely requited. I had some previous knowledge of him, and in 1830 he showed me his pass-book with his bankers, Sir Claude Scott and Co., displaying a series of credits from July, 1829, to July, 1830, or a single year's operations, to the extent of £13,400, But the delusion soon vanished. One act of liberality on his part at that period, however, I think it fair to record. To a gentleman who had rendered him some literary aid, which his defective education made indispensable, he presented double, not only what he was assured would be an ample remuneration, but what exceeded fourfold the sum his friend would have been satisfied with, or had expected."

and, under the influence of that nervous dread of death which almost invariably torments the youthful and healthy, she would implore the great physician to save her from her doom. It was not difficult to quiet her anxious heart. Attendance at 41, Harley Street, for six weeks, during which time a sore was created on her breast by the corrosive liniment, and cured by the application of cabbage-leaves and nature's kindly processes, enabled her to go out once more into the world, sounding her saviour's praises, and convinced that she might all her life long expose herself to the most trying changes of atmosphere, without incurring any risk of chest-affection.

But Mr. Long had not calculated that, although nine hundred and ninety-nine constitutions out of every thousand would not be materially injured by his treatment, he would at rare intervals meet with a patient of delicate organization, on whom the application of his blistering fluid would be followed by the most serious consequences. In the summer of the year 1830, two young ladies, of a good Irish family, named Cashin, came to London, and were inveigled into the wizard's net. They were sisters; and the younger of them, being in delicate health, called on Mr. Long, accompanied by her elder sister. The ordinary course of inhalation and rubbing was prescribed for the invalid; and ere long, frightened by the quack's prediction that, unless she was subjected to immediate treatment, she would fall into a rapid consumption, the other young lady submitted to have the corrosive lotion rubbed over her back and shoulders. The operation was performed on the 3rd of August. Forthwith a violent inflammation was established: the wound, instead of healing, became daily and hourly of a darker and more unhealthy aspect; unable to bear the cabbage-leaves on the raw and suppurating surface, the sufferer induced her nurse to apply a comforting poultice to the part, but no relief was obtained from it. St. John Long was sent for, and the 14th (just eleven days after the exhibition of the corrosive liniment), he found his victim in a condition of extreme exhaustion and pain, and suffering from continued sickness. Taking these symptoms as a mere matter of course, he ordered her a tumbler of mulled wine, and took his departure. On the following day (Sunday, 15th) he called again, and offered to dress the wound. But the poor girl, suddenly waking up to the peril of her position, would not permit him to touch her, and, raising herself with an effort in her bed, exclaimed—

"Indeed, Mr. Long, you shall not touch my back again—you very well know that when I became your patient I was in perfect health, but now you are killing me!" Without losing his self-command at this pathetic appeal, he looked into her earnest eyes, and said, impressively—

"Whatever inconvenience you are now suffering, it will be of short duration, for in two or three days you will be in better health than you ever were in your life."

But his words did not restore her confidence. The next day (the 16th) Mr., now Sir Benjamin, Brodie was sent for, and found on the wretched girl's back an inflamed surface about the size of a plate, having in the centre a spot as large as the palm of his hand, which was in a state of mortification. The time for rescue was past. Sir Benjamin prescribed a saline draught to allay the sickness; and within twenty-four hours Catherine Cashin, who a fortnight before had been in perfect health and high spirits—an unusually lovely girl, in her 25th year—lay upon her bed in the quiet of death.

An uproar immediately ensued; and there was an almost universal cry from the intelligent people of the country, that the empiric should be punished. A coroner's inquest was held; and, in spite of the efforts made by the charlatan's fashionable adherents, a verdict was obtained from the jury of man-slaughter against St. John Long. Every attempt was made by a set of influential persons of high rank to prevent the law from taking its ordinary course. The issue of the warrant for the apprehension of the offender was most mysteriously and scandalously delayed: and had it not been for the energy of Mr. Wakley, who, in a long and useful career of public service, has earned for himself much undeserved obloquy, the affair would, even after the verdict of the coroner's jury, have been hushed up. Eventually, however, on Saturday, October 30, St. John Long was placed in the dock of old Bailey, charged with the manslaughter of Miss Cashin. Instead of deserting him in his hour of need, his admirers—male and female—presented themselves at the Central Criminal Court, to encourage him by their sympathy, and to give evidence in his favour. The carriages of distinguished members of the nobility brought fair freights of the first fashion of May-fair down to the gloomy court-house that adjoins Newgate; and belles of the first fashion sat all through the day in the stifling atmosphere of a crowded court, looking languishingly at their hero in the dock, who, from behind his barrier of rue and fennel, distributed to them smiles of grateful recognition. The Judge (Mr. Justice Park) manifested throughout the trial a strong partisanship with the prisoner; and the Marchioness of Ormond, who was accommodated with a seat on the bench by his Lordship's side, conversed with him in whispers during the proceedings. The summing up was strongly in favour of the accused; but, in spite of the partial judge, and an array of fashionable witnesses in favour of the prisoner, the jury returned a verdict of guilty.

As it was late on Saturday when the verdict was given, the judge deferred passing sentence till the following Monday. At the opening of the court on that day a yet greater crush of the *beau monde* was present; and the judge, instead of awarding a term of imprisonment to the guilty man, condemned him merely to pay a fine of £250, or to be imprisoned till such fine was paid. Mr. St. John Long immediately took a roll of notes from his pocket, paid the mulct, and leaving the court with his triumphant friends, accepted a seat in Lord Sligo's curricle, and drove to the west end of the town.

The scandalous sentence was a fit conclusion to the absurd scenes which took place in the court of the Old Bailey, and at the coroner's inquest. At one or the other of these inquiries the witnesses advanced thousands of outrageous statements, of which the following may be taken as a fair specimen:—

One young lady gave evidence that she had been cured of consumption by Mr. Long's liniment; she knew she had been so cured, because she had a very bad cough, and, after the rubbing in all the ointment, the cough went away. An old gentleman testified that he had for years suffered from attacks of the gout, at intervals of from one to three months; he was convinced Mr. Long had cured him, because he had been free from gout for five weeks. Another gentleman had been tortured with headache; Mr. Long applied his lotion to it—the humour which caused his headache came away in a clear limpid discharge. A third gentleman affirmed that Mr. Long's liniment had reduced a dislocation of his child's hip-joint. The Marchioness of Ormond, on oath, stated that she *knew* that Miss Cashin's back was rubbed with the same fluid as she and her daughters had used to wash their hands with; but she admitted that she neither *saw* the back rubbed, nor *saw* the fluid with which it was rubbed taken from the bottle. Sir Francis Burdett also bore testimony to the harmlessness of Mr. Long's system of practice. Mr. Wakley, in the *Lancet*, asserted that Sir Francis Burdett had called on Long to ask him if his liniment would give the Marquis of Anglesea a leg, in the place of the one he lost at Waterloo, if it were applied to the stump. Long gave an encouraging answer; and the lotion was applied, with the result of producing not an entire foot and leg—but a great toe!

Miss Cashin's death was quickly followed by another fatal case. A Mrs. Lloyd died from the effects of the corrosive lotion; and again a coroner's jury found St. John Long guilty of manslaughter, and again he was tried at the Old Bailey—but this second trial terminated in his acquital.

It seems scarcely creditable, and yet it is true, that these exposures did not have the effect of lessening his popularity. The respectable organs of the Press—the *Times*, the *Chronicle*, the *Herald*, the *John Bull*, the *Lancet*, the *Examiner*, the *Spectator*, the *Standard*, the *Globe, Blackwood*, and *Fraser*, combined in doing their best to render him contemptible in the eyes of his supporters. But all their efforts were in vain. His old dupes remained staunch adherents to him, and every day brought fresh converts to their body. With unabashed front he went everywhere, proclaiming himself a martyr in the cause of humanity, and comparing his evil treatment to the persecutions that Galileo, Harvey, Jenner, and Hunter underwent at the hands of the prejudiced and ignorant. Instead of uncomplainingly taking the lashes of satirical writers, he first endeavored to bully them into silence, and swaggering into newspaper and magazine offices asked astonished editors how they *dared* to call him a *quack*. Finding, however, that this line of procedure would not improve his position, he wrote his defence, and published it in an octavo volume, together with numerous testimonials of his worth from grateful patients, and also a letter of cordial support from Dr. Ramadge, M.D., Oxon., a fellow of the College of Physicians. In a ridiculous and ungrammatical epistle, defending this pernicious quack, who had been convicted of manslaughter, Dr. Ramadge displayed not less anxiety to blacken the reputation of his own profession, than he did to clear the fame of the charlatan whom he designated *"a guiltless and a cruelly persecuted individual!!!"* The book itself is one of the most interesting to be found in quack literature. On the title-page is a motto from Pope—"No man deserves a monument who could not be wrapped in a winding-sheet of papers written against him"; and amongst pages of jargon about humoral pathology, it contains confident predictions that if his victims had *continued* in his system, they would have lived. The author accuses the most eminent surgeons and physicians of his time of gross ignorance, and of having conspired together to crush him, because they were jealous of his success and envious of his income. He even suggests that the same saline draught, prescribed by Sir Benjamin Brodie, killed Miss Cashin. Amongst those whose testimonials appear in the body of the work are the *then* Lord Ingestre (his enthusiastic supporter), Dr. Macartney, the Marchioness of Ormond, Lady Harriet Kavanagh, the Countess of Buckinghamshire, and the Marquis of Sligo. The Marchioness of Ormond testifies how Mr. Long had miraculously cured her and her daughter of "headaches," and her youngest children of "smart attacks of feverish colds, one with inflammatory sore throat, the others with more serious bad symptoms." The Countess of Buckinghamshire says she is cured of "headache and lassitude"; and Lord Ingestre avows his belief that Mr. Long's system is "preventive of disease," because he himself is much less liable to catch cold than he was before trying it.

Numerous pamphlets also were written in defence of John St. John Long, Esq., M.R.S.L., and M.R.A.S. An anonymous author (calling himself a graduate of Trinity College, Cambridge, and Member of the Middle Temple), in a tract dated 1831, does not hesitate to compare the object of his eulogy with the author of Christianity. "But who can wonder at Mr Long's persecutions? The brightest character that ever stept was persecuted, even unto death! His cures were all perverted, but they were not the less complete; they were miraculous, but they were not the less certain!"

To the last St. John Long retained his practice; but death removed him from the scene of his triumphs while he was still a young man. The very malady, his control over which he had so loudly proclaimed, brought his career—in which knavery or self-delusion, doubtless both, played a part—to an end. He died of consumption, at the age of thirty-seven years. Even in the grave his patients honoured him, for they erected an elegant and costly monument to his memory, and adorned it with the following inscription.

"It is the fate of most men
To have many enemies, and few friends.
This monumental pile
Is not intended to mark the career,
But to shew
How much its inhabitant was respected
By those who knew his worth,
And the benefits
Derived from his remedial discovery.
He is now at rest,
And far beyond the praises or censures
Of this world.
Stranger, as you respect the receptacle of the dead
(As one of the many who will rest here),
Read the name of
John Saint John Long
without comment."

Notwithstanding the exquisite drollery of this inscription, in speaking of a plebeian quack-doctor (who, by the exercise of empiricism, raised himself to the possession of £5000 per annum, and the intimate friendship of numbers of the aristocracy) as the victim of "many enemies and few friends," it cannot be said to be open to much censure. Indeed, St. John Long's worshippers were for the most part of that social grade in which bad taste is rare, though weakness of understanding possibly may not be uncommon.

The sepulchre itself is a graceful structure, and occupies a prominent position in the Kensal Green cemetery, by the side of the principal carriage-way, leading from the entrance-gate to the chapel of the burial-ground. Immediately opposite to it, on the other side of the gravel drive, stands, not inappropriately, the flaunting sepulchre of Andrew Ducrow, the horse-rider, "whose death," the inscription informs us, "deprived the arts and sciences of an eminent professor and liberal patron." When any cockney bard shall feel himself inspired to write an elegy on the west-end grave-yard, he will not omit to compare John St. John Long's tomb with that of "the liberal patron of the arts and sciences," and also with the cumbrous heap of masonry which covers the ashes of Dr. Morrison, hygeist, which learned word, being interpreted, means "the inventor of Morrison's pills."

To give a finishing touch to the memoir of this celebrated charlatan, it may be added that after his death his property became the subject of tedious litigation; and amongst the claimants upon it was a woman advanced in years, and of an address and style that proved her to belong to a very humble state of life. This woman turned out to be St. John Long's wife. He had married her when quite a lad, had found it impossible to live with her, and consequently had induced her to consent to an amicable separation. This discovery was a source of great surprise, and also of enlightenment to the numerous high-born and richly-endowed ladies who had made overtures of marriage to the idolized quack, and, much to their surprise, had had their advances adroitly but firmly declined.

There are yet to be found in English society, ladies—not silly, frivolous women, but some of those on whom the world of intellect has put the stamp of its approval—who cherish such tender reminiscences of St. John Long, that they cannot mention his name without their eyes becoming bright with tears. Of course this proves nothing, save the credulity and fond infatuation of the fair ones who love. The hands of women decked Nero's tomb with flowers.

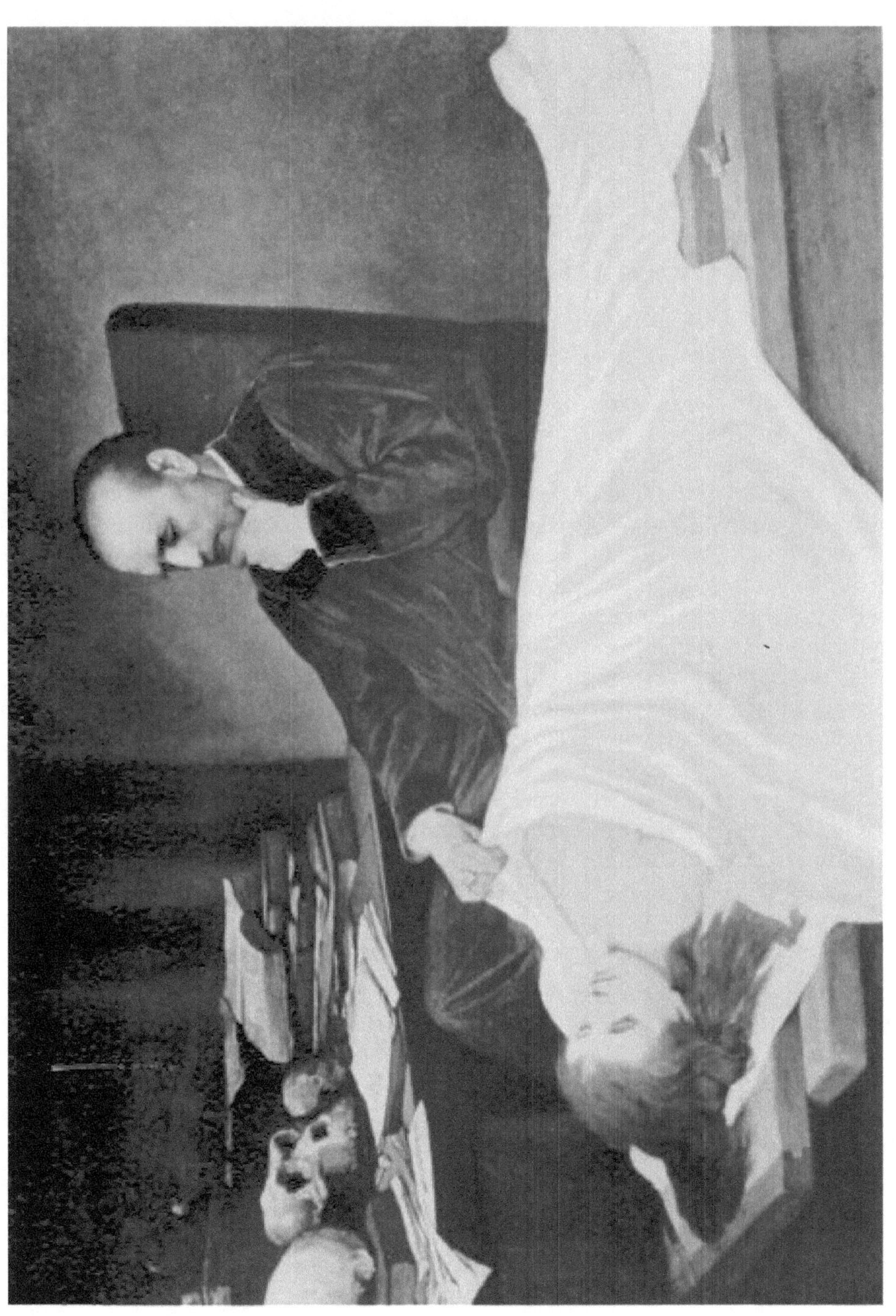

THE ANATOMIST

From the Original Painting by Max.

CHAPTER XXII.

THE QUARRELS OF PHYSICIANS.

For many a day authors have had the reputation of being more sensitive and quarrelsome than any other set of men. Truth to tell, they are not always so amiable and brilliant as their works. There is in them the national churlishness inducing them to nurse a contempt for every one they don't personally know, and a spirit of antagonism towards nearly every one they do. But to say this is only to say that they are made of British oak. Unfortunately, however, they carry on their contentions in a manner that gives them a wide publicity and a troublesome duration of fame. Soldiers, when they quarrelled in the last century, shot one another like gentlemen, at two paces' distance, and with the crack of their pistols the whole noise of the matter ceased. Authors, from time immemorial, have in their angry moments rushed into print, and lashed their adversaries with satire, rendered permanent by aid of the printer's devil,—thus letting posterity know all the secrets of their folly, whilst the merciful grave put an end to all memorial of the extravagances of their friends. There was less love between Radcliffe and Hannes, Freind and Blackmore, Gibbons and Garth, than between Pope and Dennis, Swift and Grub Street. But we know all about the squabbles of the writers from their poems; whereas only a vague tradition, in the form of questionable anecdotes, has come down to us of the animosities of the doctors—a tradition which would long ere this have died out, had not Garth—author as well as physician—written the "Dispensary," and a host of dirty little apothecaries contracted a habit of scribbling lampoons about their professional superiors.

Luckily for the members of it, the Faculty of Medicine is singularly barren of biographies. The career of a physician is so essentially one of confidence, that even were he to keep a memorial of its interesting occurrences, his son wouldn't dare to sell it to a publisher as the "Revelations of a Departed Physician." Long ere it would be decent or safe to print such a diary, the public would have ceased to take an interest in the writer. Pettigrew's "Life of Lettsom," and Macilwain's "Memoirs of Abernethy," are almost the only two passable biographies of eminent medical practitioners in the English language; and the last of these does not presume to enter fully on the social relations of the great surgeon. The lives of Hunter and Jenner are meagre and unworthily executed, and of Bransby Cooper's Life of his uncle little can be said that is not in the language of emphatic condemnation.

From this absence of biographical literature the medical profession at least derives this advantage—the world at large knows comparatively little of their petty feuds and internal differences than it would otherwise.

The few memorials, however, that we have of the quarrels of physicians are of a kind that makes us wish we had more. Of the great battle of the apothecaries with the physicians we have already spoken in the notice of Sir Samuel Garth. To those who are ignorant of human nature it may appear incredible that a body, so lovingly united against common foes, should have warred amongst themselves. Yet such was the case. A London druggist once put up at the chief inn of a provincial capital, whither he had come in the course of his annual summer ride. The good man thought it would hurt neither his health nor his interests to give "a little supper" to the apothecaries of the town with whom he was in the habit of doing business. Under the influence of this feeling he sallied out from "The White Horse," and spent a few hours in calling on his friends—asking for orders and delivering invitations. On returning to his inn, he ordered a supper for twelve—as eleven medical gentlemen had engaged to sup with him. When the hour appointed for the repast was at hand, a knock at the door was followed by the appearance of guest A, with a smile of intense benevolence and enjoyment. Another rap—and guest B entered. A looked blank—every trace of happiness suddenly vanishing from his face. B stared at A, as much as to say, "You be — —!" A shuffled with his feet, rose, made an apology to his host for leaving the room to attend to a little matter, and disappeared. Another rap—and C made his bow of greeting. "I'll try to be back in five minutes, but if I'm not, don't wait for me," cried B, hurriedly seizing his hat and rushing from the apartment. C, a cold-blooded, phlegmatic man, sat down unconcernedly, and was a picture of sleeping contentment till the entry of D, when his hair stood on end, and he fled into the inn-yard, as if he were pursued by a hyena. E knocked and said, "How d' you do?" D sprung from his chair, and shouted, "Good-bye!" And so it went on till, on guest No. 11 joining the party— that had received so many new comers, and yet never for an instant numbered more than three—No. 10 jumped through the window, and ran down the street to the bosom of his family. The hospitable druggist and No. 11 found, on a table provided for twelve, quite as much supper as they required.

Next morning the druggist called on A for an explanation of his conduct. "Sir," was the answer, "I could not stop in the same room with such a scoundrel as B." So it went straight down the line. B had vowed never to exchange words with C. C would be shot rather than sit at the same table with such a scoundrel as D.

"You gentlemen," observed the druggist, with a smile to each, "seem to be almost as well disposed amongst yourselves as your brethren in London; only they, when they meet, don't run from each other, but draw up, square their elbows, and fight like men."

The duel between Mead and Woodward, as it is more particularly mentioned in another part of these volumes, we need here only to allude to. The contest between Cheyne and Wynter was of a less bloody character. Cheyne was a Bath physician, of great practice and yet greater popularity—dying in 1743, at the age of seventy-two. At one time of his life he was so prodigiously fat that he weighed 32 stone, he and a gentleman named Tantley being the two stoutest men in Somersetshire. One day, after dinner, the former asked the latter what he was thinking about.

"I was thinking," answered Tantley, "how it will be possible to get either you or me into the grave after we die."

Cheyne was nettled, and retorted, "Six or eight stout fellows will do the business for me, but you must be taken at twice."

Cheyne was a sensible man, and had more than one rough passage of arms with Beau Nash, when the beau was dictator of the pump-room. Nash called the doctor in and asked him to prescribe for him. The next day, when the physician called and inquired if his prescription had been followed, the beau languidly replied:—

"No, i' faith, doctor, I haven't followed it. 'Pon honour, if I had I should have broken my neck, for I threw it out of my bed-room window."

But Cheyne had wit enough to reward the inventor of the white hat for this piece of insolence. One day he and some of his learned friends were enjoying themselves over the bottle, laughing with a heartiness unseemly in philosophers, when, seeing the beau draw near, the doctor said:—

"Hush, we must be grave now, here's a fool coming our way."

Cheyne became ashamed of his obesity, and earnestly set about overcoming it. He brought himself down by degrees to a moderate diet, and took daily a large amount of exercise. The result was that he reduced himself to under eleven stone, and, instead of injuring his constitution, found himself in the enjoyment of better health. Impressed with the value of the discovery he had made, he wrote a book urging all people afflicted with chronic maladies to imitate him and try the effects of temperance. Doctors, notwithstanding their precepts in favour of moderation, neither are, nor ever have been, averse to the pleasures of the table. Many of them warmly resented Cheyne's endeavours to bring good living into disrepute, possibly deeming that their interests were attacked not less than their habits. Dryden wrote,

> "The first physicians by debauch were made.
> Excess began, and sloth sustained the trade;
> By chase our long-liv'd fathers earned their food,
> Toil strung their nerves and purified their blood;
> But we, their sons, a pamper'd race of men,
> Are dwindled down to threescore years and ten.
> Better to hunt in fields for health unbought,
> Than fee the doctor for a nauseous draught;
> The wise for cure on exercise depend,
> God never made his work for man to mend."

Dr. Wynter arose to dispose of Cheyne in a summary fashion. Wynter had two good reasons for hating Cheyne: Wynter was an Englishman and loved wine, Cheyne was a Scotchman and loved milk.

Dr. Wynter to Dr. Cheyne.

> "Tell me from whom, fat-headed Scot,
> Thou didst thy system learn;

From Hippocrate thou hadst it not,
Nor Celsus, nor Pitcairn.

"Suppose we own that milk is good,
And say the same of grass;
The one for babes is only food,
The other for an ass.

"Doctor, one new prescription try
(A friend's advice forgive),
Eat grass, reduce thyself, and die,
Thy patients then may live."

Cheyne responded, with more wit and more good manners, in the following fashion:—

"DR. CHEYNE TO DR. WYNTER.

"My system, doctor, is my own,
No tutor I pretend;
My blunders hurt myself alone,
But yours your dearest friend.

"Were you to milk and straw confin'd,
Thrice happy might you be;
Perhaps you might regain your mind,
And from your wit be free."

"I can't your kind prescription try,
But heartily forgive;
'Tis natural you should wish me die,
That you yourself may live."

The concluding two lines of Cheyne's answer were doubtless little to the taste of his unsuccessful opponent.

In their contentions physicians have not often had recourse to the duel. With them an appeal to arms has rarely been resorted to, but when it has been deliberately made the combatants have usually fought with decision. The few duels fought between women have for the most part been characterized by American ferocity. Madame Dunoyer mentions a case of a duel with swords between two ladies of rank, who would have killed each other had they not been separated. In a feminine duel on the Boulevard St. Antoine, mentioned by De la Colombèire, both the principals received several wounds on the face and bosom—a most important fact illustrative of the pride the fair sex take in those parts.[22] Sometimes ladies have distinguished themselves by fighting duels with men. Mademoiselle Dureux fought her lover Antinotti in an open street. The actress Maupin challenged Dumény, but he declined to give her satisfaction; so the lady stripped him of watch and snuff-box, and bore them away as trophies of victory. The same lady, on another occasion, having insulted in a ball-room a distinguished personage of her own sex, was requested by several gentlemen to quit the entertainment. She

[22] *Vide* Millingen's "History of Duelling."

obeyed, but forthwith challenged and fought each of the meddlesome cavaliers—and killed them all! The slaughter accomplished, she returned to the ball-room, and danced in the presence of her rival. The Marquise de Nesle and the Countess Polignac, under the Regency, fought with pistols for the possession of the Duc de Richelieu. In or about the year 1827, a lady of Châteauroux, whose husband had received a slap in the face, called out the offender, and severely wounded him in a duel fought with swords. The most dramatic affair of honour, however, in the annals of female duelling occurred in the year 1828, when a young French girl challenged a *garde du corps* who had seduced her. At the meeting the seconds took the precaution of loading without ball, the fair principal of course being kept in ignorance of the arrangement. She fired first and saw her seducer remain unhurt. Without flinching, or changing colour, she stood watching her adversary, whilst he took a deliberate aim (in order to test her courage), and then, after a painful pause, fired into the air.

Physicians have been coupled with priests, as beings holding a position between the two sexes. In the Lancashire factories they allow women and clergymen the benefit of an entrée—because they don't understand business. Doctors and ladies could hardly be coupled together by the same consideration; but they might be put in one class out of respect to that gentleness of demeanour and suavity of voice which distinguish the members of the medical profession, in common with well-bred women.

Gentle though they be, physicians have, however, sometimes indulged in wordy wrangling, and then had recourse to more sanguinary arguments.

The duel between Dr. Williams and Dr. Bennet was one of the bloodiest in the eighteenth century. They first battered each other with pamphlets, and then exchanged blows. Matters having advanced so far, Dr. Bennet proposed that the fight should be continued in a gentlemanly style—with powder instead of fists. The challenge was declined; whereupon Dr. Bennet called on Dr. Williams, to taunt him with a charge of cowardice. No sooner had he rapped at the door, than it was opened by Williams himself, holding in his hand a pistol loaded with swanshot, which he, without a moment's parley, discharged into his adversary's breast. Severely wounded, Bennet retired across the street to a friend's house, followed by Williams, who fired another pistol at him. Such was the demoniacal fury of Williams, that, not contented with this outrage, he drew his sword, and ran Bennet through the body. But this last blow was repaid. Bennet managed to draw his rapier, and give his ferocious adversary a home-thrust—his sword entering the breast, coming out through the shoulder-blade, and snapping short. Williams crawled back in the direction of his house, but before he could reach it fell down dead. Bennet lived only four hours. A pleasant scene for the virtuous capital of a civilized and Christian people!

The example of Dr. Bennet and Dr. Williams was not lost upon the physicians of our American cousins. In the August of 1830, a meeting took place, near Philadelphia, between Dr. Smith and Dr. Jeffries. They exchanged shots at eight paces, without inflicting any injury, when their friends interposed, and tried to arrange the difficulty; but Dr. Jeffries swore that he would not leave the ground till some one had been killed. The principals were therefore put up again. At the second exchange of shots Dr. Smith's right arm was broken, when he gallantly declared that, as he was wounded, it would be gratifying to his feelings, to be killed. Third exchange of shots, and Dr. Smith, firing with his left arm, hits his man in the thigh, causing immense loss of blood. Five minutes were occupied in bandaging the wound; when Dr. Jeffries, properly primed with brandy, requested that no further obstacles might be raised between him and satisfaction. For a fourth time the mad men were put up—at the distance of six feet. The result was fatal to both. Dr. Smith dropped dead with a ball in his heart. Dr. Jeffries was shot through the breast, and survived only a few hours. The conduct of Dr. Jeffries during those last few hours was admirable, and most delightfully in keeping with the rest of the proceeding. On seeing his antagonist prostrate, the doctor asked if he was dead. On being assured that his enemy lived no longer, he observed, "Then I die contented." He then stated that he had been a school-mate with Dr. Smith, and that, during the fifteen years throughout which they had been on terms of great intimacy and friendship, he had valued him highly as a man of science and a gentleman.

One of the latest duels in which an English physician was concerned as a principal was that fought on the 10th of May, 1833, near Exeter, between Sir John Jeffcott and Dr. Hennis. Dr. Hennis received a wound, of which he died. The affair was brought into the Criminal Court, and was for a short time a *cause célèbre* on the western circuit; but the memory of it has now almost entirely disappeared.

As we have already stated, duels have been rare in the medical profession. Like the ladies, physicians have, in their periods of anger, been content with speaking ill of each other. That they have not lost their power of courteous criticism and judicious abuse, any one may learn, who, for a few hours, breathes the atmosphere of their cliques. It is good to hear an allopathic physician perform his duty to society by frankly stating his opinion of the character and conduct of an eminent homœopathic practitioner. Perhaps it is better still to listen to an apostle of homœopathy, when he takes up his parable and curses the hosts of allopathy. "Sir, I tell you in confidence," observed a distinguished man of science, tapping his auditor on the shoulder, and mysteriously whispering in his ear, "I know *things* about *that man* that would make him end his days in penal servitude." The next day the auditor was closeted in the consulting-room of *that man*, when that man said—quite in confidence, pointing as he spoke to a strong box, and jingling a bunch of keys in his pocket—"I have *papers* in that box, which, properly used, would tie a certain friend of ours up by the neck."

Lettsom, loose-living man though he was for a member of the Society of Friends, had enough of the Quaker element in him to be very fond of controversy. He dearly loved to expose quackery, and in some cases did good service in that way. In the *Medical Journal* he attacked, A. D. 1806, no less a man than Brodum, the proprietor of the Nervous Cordial, avowing that that precious compound had killed thousands; and also stating that Brodum had added to the crime of wholesale murder the atrocities of having been born a Jew, of having been a shoe-black in Copenhagen, and of having at some period of his chequered career carried on an ignoble trade in oranges. Of course Brodum saw his advantage. He immediately brought an action against Phillips, the proprietor of the *Medical Journal*, laying his damages at £5000. The lawyers anticipated a harvest from the case, and were proceeding not only against Phillips, but various newsvendors also, when a newspaper editor stept in between Phillips and Brodum, and contrived to settle the dispute. Brodum's terms were not modest ones. He consented to withdraw his actions, if the name of the author was given up, and if the author would whitewash him in the next number of the Journal, under the same signature. Lettsom consented, paid the two attorneys' bills, amounting to £390, and wrote the required puff of Brodum and his Nervous Cordial.

One of the singular characters of Dublin, a generation ago, was John Brenan, M.D., a physician who edited the *Milesian Magazine*, a scurrilous publication of the satirist class, that flung dirt on every one dignified enough for the mob to take pleasure in seeing him bespattered with filth. The man certainly was a great blackguard, but was not destitute of wit. How he carried on the war with the members of his own profession the following song will show:—

"THE DUBLIN DOCTORS.

"My gentle muse, do not refuse
To sing the Dublin Doctors, O;
For they're the boys
Who make the joys
Of grave-diggers and proctors, O.

We'll take 'em in procession, O,
We'll take 'em in succession, O;
But how shall we
Say who is he
Shall lead the grand procession, O?

Least wit and greatest malice, O,
Least wit and greatest malice, O,
Shall mark the man
Who leads the van,
As they march to the gallows, O.

First come then, Doctor Big Paw, O,
Come first then, Doctor Big Paw, O;
Mrs Kilfoyle
Says you would spoil
Its shape, did you her wig paw, O.

Come next, dull Dr Labat, O,
Come next, dull Dr Labat, O;
Why is it so,
You kill the doe,
Whene'er you catch the rabbit, O?

Come, Harvey, drunken dandy, O,
Come, Harvey, drunken dandy, O;

Thee I could paint
A walking saint,
If you lov'd God like brandy, O.

Come next, Doctor Drumsnuffle, O,
Come next, Doctor Drumsnuffle, O;
Well stuffed with lead,
Your leather head
Is thick as hide of Buffaloe.

Come next, Colossus Jackson, O,
Come next, Colossus Jackson, O;
As jack-ass mute,
A burthen brute,
Just fit to trot with packs on, O.

Come next, sweet Paddy Rooney, O,
Come next, sweet Paddy Rooney, O;
Tho' if you stay
Till judgment's day,
You'll come a month too soon-y, O.

Come next, sweet Breeny Creepmouse, O,
Come next, sweet Breeny Creepmouse, O;
Thee heaven gave
Just sense to shave
A corpse, or an asleep mouse, O.

For I say, creep-mouse Breeny, O,
For I say, creep-mouse Breeny, O;
Thee I can't sing
The fairy's king,
But I'll sing you their Queen-y O;

For I say, Dr Breeny, O,
For I say, Dr Breeny, O;
If I for once
Called you a dunce,
I'd shew a judgment weeny, O.

Come, Richards dull and brazen, O,
Come, Richards dull and brazen, O;
A prosperous drone,
You stand alone,
For wondering sense to gaze on, O.

Then come, you greasy blockhead, O,
Then come, you greasy blockhead, O;
Balked by your face,
We quickly trace,
Your genius to your pocket, O.

Come, Crampton, man of capers, O,
Come, Crampton, man of capers, O;

    *   *   *   *   *

And come, long Doctor Renney, O,
And come, long Doctor Renney, O;
If sick I'd fee
As soon as thee,
Old Arabella Denny, O.

Come, Tandragee Ferguson, O,
Come, Tandragee Ferguson, O;
Fool, don't recoil,
But as your foil
Bring Ireland or Puke Hewson, O.

Come, ugly Dr Alman, O,
Come, ugly Dr Alman, O;
But bring a mask,
Or do not ask,
When come, that we you call man, O.

    *   *   *   *   *

Come, Boyton, king of dunces, O,
Come, Boyton, king of dunces, O;
Who call you knave
No lies receive,
Nay, that your name each one says, O.

Come, Colles, do come, Aby, O,
Come, Colles, do come, Aby, O;
Tho' all you tell,
You'll make them well,
You always 'hould say may be, O.

Come, beastly Dr Toomy, O,
Come, beastly Dr Toomy, O;
If impudence
Was common sense
As you no sage ere knew me, O.

Come, smirking, smiling Beattie, O,
Come, smirking, smiling Beattie, O;
In thee I spy
An apple eye
Of cabbage and potaty, O.

Come, louse-bit Nasom Adams, O,
Come, louse-bit Nasom Adams, O;
In jail or dock
Your face would shock

It thee as base and bad damus, O.

Come next, Frank Smyth on cockney, O,
Come next, Frank Smyth on cockney, O;
Sweet London's pride,
I see you ride,
Despising all who flock nigh, O.

And bring your partner Bruen, O,
And bring your partner Bruen, O;
And with him ride
All by your side,
Like two fond turtles cooing, O.

Come next, Spilsberry Deegan, O,
Come next, Spilsberry Deegan, O;
With grace and air
Come kill the fair,
Your like we'll never, see 'gain, O.

Come, Harry Grattan Douglass, O,
Come, Harry Grattan Douglass, O;
A doctor's name
I think you claim,
With right than my dog pug less, O.

Come, Oronoko Harkan, O,
Come, Oronoko Harkan, O;
I think your face
Is just the place
God fix'd the blockhead's mark on, O.

Come, Christ-denying Taylor, O,
Come, Christ-denying Taylor, O;
Hell made your phiz
On man's a quiz,
But made it for a jailor, O.

Come, Packwood, come, Carmichael, O,
Come, Packwood, come, Carmichael, O;
Your cancer-paste,
The fools who taste,
Whom it kills not does nigh kill, O.

Come next, Adonis Harty, O,
Come next, Adonis Harty, O;
Your face and frame
Shew equal claim,
Tam Veneri quam Marti, O.

Here ends my song on Doctors, O,
Here ends my song on Doctors, O;

> Who, when all damn'd
> In hell are cramm'd,
> Will beggar all the Proctors, O."

Brenan (to do him justice) was as ready to fell a professional antagonist and brother with a bludgeon, hunting-whip, or pistol, as he was to scarify him with doggerel. He was as bold a fellow as Dr. Walsh, the Hibernian Æsculapius, who did his best to lay Dr. Andrew Marshall down amongst the daisies and the dead men. Andrew Marshall, when a divinity-student at Edinburgh, was insulted (whilst officiating for Stewart, the humanity professor) by a youngster named Macqueen. The insolence of the lad was punished by the professor (*pro tem.*) giving him a caning. Smarting with the indignity offered him, Macqueen ran home to his father, imploring vengeance; whereupon the irate sire promptly sallied forth, and entering Marshall's lodgings, exclaimed:—

"Are you the scoundrel that dared to attack my son?"

"Draw and defend yourself!" screamed the divinity student, springing from his chair, and presenting a sword-point at the intruder's breast. Old Macqueen, who had expected to have to deal only with a timid half-starved usher ready to crouch whiningly under personal castigation, was so astonished at this reception that he turned and fled precipitately. This little affair happened in 1775. As a physician Andrew Marshall was not less valiant than he had been when a student of theology. On Walsh challenging him, he went out and stood up at ten paces like a gentleman. Walsh, a little short fellow, invisible when looked at side-ways, put himself in the regular attitude, shoulder to the front. Marshall disdained such mean prudence, and faced his would-be murdered with his cheeks and chest inflated to the utmost. Shots were exchanged, Dr. Andrew Marshall receiving a ball in his right arm, and Dr. Walsh, losing a lock of hair—snipped off by his opponent's bullet, and scattered by the amorous breeze. Being thus the *gainer* in the affair, Dr. Andrew Marshall made it up with his adversary, and they lived on friendly terms ever afterwards. Why don't some of our living *medici* bury the hatchet with a like effective ceremony?

An affair that ended not less agreeably was that in which Dr. Brocklesby was concerned as principal, where the would-be belligerents left the ground without exchanging shots, because their seconds could not agree on the right number of paces at which to stick up their man. When Akenside was fool enough to challenge Ballow, a wicked story went about that the fight didn't come off because one had determined never to fight in the morning, and the other that he would never fight in the afternoon. But the fact was—Ballow was a paltry mean fellow, and shirked the peril into which his ill-manners had brought him. The lively and pleasant author of "Physic and Physicians," countenancing this unfair story, reminds us of the off-hand style of John Wilkes in such little affairs. When asked by Lord Talbot "How many times they were to fire?" the brilliant demagogue responded—

"Just as often as your Lordship pleases—I have brought *a bag of bullets and a flask of gunpowder* with me."

CHAPTER XXIII.
THE LOVES OF PHYSICIANS.

Honour has flowed to physicians by the regular channels of professional duty in but scant allowance. Their children have been frequently ennobled by marriage or for political services. Sir Hans Sloane's daughter Elizabeth, and manor of Chelsea, passed into the Cadogan family, the lady marrying the second Baron Cadogan. Like Sir Hans, Dr. Huck Sanders left behind him two daughters, co-heiresses of his wealth, of whom one (Jane) was ennobled through wedlock, the tenth Earl of Westmoreland raising her to be his second wife. Lord Combermere married the heiress of Dr. Gibbings, of Cork. In the same way Dr. Marwood's property came to the present Sir Marwood Elton by the marriage of his grandfather with Frances, the daughter and heiress of the Devonshire doctor. On the other hand, as instances of the offspring of physicians exalted to the ranks of the aristocracy for their political services, the Lords Sidmouth, Denman, and Kingsdown may be mentioned. Henry Addington, created Viscount Sidmouth, of the county of Devon, was the eldest son of Anthony Addington, M.D., of Reading—the physician who objected to fighting any brother physician who had not graduated at either Oxford or Cambridge. Dr. Anthony was the enthusiastic toady of the great Earl of Chatham. Devoted to his own interests and the Pitt family, he rose from the humble position of keeper of a provincial lunatic asylum to eminence in the medical profession. Coming up to town in 1754, under the patronage of Pitt, he succeeded in gaining the confidence of the Court, and was, with Dr. Richard Warren, Dr. Francis Willis, Dr. Thomas Gisborne, Sir Lucas Pepys, and Dr. Henry Revell Reynolds, examined, in 1782, by the committee appointed to examine "the physicians who attended his illness, touching the state of his Majesty's health." He took a very hopeful view of the king's case; and on being asked the foundation of his hopes, alluded to his experience in the treatment of the insane at Reading. The doctor had himself a passion for political intrigue, which descended to his son. The career of this son, who raised himself to the Speaker's chair in the House of Commons, to the dignity of First Minister of the Crown, and to the peerage of the realm, is matter of history.

Lord Denman was closely connected with the medical profession by family ties: his father being Dr. Denman, of Mount Street, Grosvenor Square, the author of a well-known work on a department of his profession; his uncle being Dr. Joseph Denman of Bakewell; and his two sisters having married two eminent physicians, Margaret being the wife of Sir Richard Croft, Bart., and Sophia the wife of Dr. Baillie. Lord Kingsdown's medical ancestor was his grandfather, Edward Pemberton, M.D., of Warrington.

But though the list of the ennobled descendants of medical practitioners might be extended to the limits of a volume, the writer of these pages is not aware of any case in which a doctor has, by the exercise of his calling, raised himself to the peerage. As yet, the dignity of a baronetcy is the highest honour conferred on the most illustrious of the medical faculty, Sir Hans Sloane being the first of the order to whom that rank was presented. More than once a physician has won admission into the *noblesse*, but the battle resulting in such success has been fought in the arena of politics or the bustle of the law courts. Sylvester Douglas deserted the counter, at which he commenced life an apothecary, and after a prolonged servitude to, or warfare with, the cliques of the House of Commons, had his exertions rewarded and his ambition gratified with an Irish peerage and a patrician wife. On his elevation he was of course taunted with the humility of his origin, and by none was the reproach flung at him with greater bitterness than it was by a brother *parvenu* and brother poet.

"What's his title to be?" asked Sheridan, as he was playing at cards; "what's Sylvester Douglas to be called?"

"Lord Glenbervie," was the answer.

"Good Lord!" replied Sheridan; and then he proceeded to fire off an *impromptu*, which he had that morning industriously prepared in bed, and which he subsequently introduced into one of his best satiric pieces.

> "Glenbervie, Glenbervie,
> What's good for the scurvy?
> For ne'er be your old trade forgot.
> In your arms rather quarter
> A pestle and mortar,
> And your crest be a spruce gallipot."

The brilliant partizan and orator displayed more wit, if not better taste, in his ridicule of Addington, who, in allusion to the rise of his father from a humble position in the medical profession, was ordinarily spoken of by political opponents as "The Doctor." On one occasion, when the Scotch members who usually supported Addington voted in a body with the opposition, Sheridan, with a laugh of triumph, fired off a happy mis-quotation from Macbeth, — "Doctor, the Thanes fly from thee."

Henry Bickersteth, Lord Langdale, was the luckiest of physicians and lawyers. He used the medical profession as a stepping-stone, and the legal profession as a ladder, and had the fortune to win two of the brightest prizes of life—wealth and a peerage—without the humiliation and toil of serving a political party in the House of Commons. The second son of a provincial surgeon, he was apprenticed to his father, and educated for the paternal calling. On being qualified to kill, he became medical attendant to the late Earl of Oxford, during that nobleman's travels on the Continent. Returning to his native town, Kirby Lonsdale, he for awhile assisted his father in the management of his practice; but resolved on a different career from that of a country doctor, he became a member of Caius College, Cambridge, and devoted himself to mathematical study with such success that, in

1808, when he was twenty-eight years old, he became Senior Wrangler and First Smith's prizeman. As late as the previous year he was consulted medically by his father. In 1811 he was called to the bar by the Inner Temple, and from that time till his elevation to the Mastership of the Rolls he was both the most hard-working and hard-worked of the lawyers in the Equity Courts, to which he confined his practice. In 1827 he became a bencher of his Inn; and, in 1835, although he was a staunch and zealous liberal, and a strenuous advocate of Jeremy Bentham's opinions, he was offered a seat on the judicial bench by Sir Robert Peel. This offer he declined, though he fully appreciated the compliment paid him by the Tory chieftain. He had not, however, to wait long for his promotion. In the following year (1836) he was, by his own friends, made Master of the Rolls, and created a peer of the realm, with the additional honour of being a Privy-Councillor. His Lordship died at Tunbridge Wells, in 1851, in his sixty-eighth year. It would be difficult to point to a more enviable career in legal annals than that of this medical lawyer, who won the most desirable honours of his profession without ever sitting in the House of Commons, or acting as a legal adviser of the Crown—and when he had not been called quite twenty-five years. To give another touch to this picture of a successful life, it may be added, that Lord Langdale, after rising to eminence, married Elizabeth, daughter of the Earl of Oxford, to whom he had formerly been travelling medical attendant.

Love has not unfrequently smiled on doctors, and elevated them to positions at which they would never have arrived by their professional labours. Sir Lucas Pepys, who married the Countess De Rothes, and Sir Henry Halford, whose wife was a daughter of the eleventh Lord St. John of Blestoe, are conspicuous amongst the more modern instances of medical practitioners advancing their social condition by aristocratic alliances. Not less fortunate was the farcical Sir John Hill, who gained for a bride the Honourable Miss Jones, a daughter of Lord Ranelagh—a nobleman whose eccentric opinion, that the welfare of the country required a continual intermixture of the upper and lower classes of society, was a frequent object of ridicule with the caricaturists and lampoon-writers of his time. But the greatest prize ever made by an Æsculapius in the marriage-market was that acquired by Sir Hugh Smithson, who won the hand of Percy's proud heiress, and was created Duke of Northumberland. The son of a Yorkshire baronet's younger son, Hugh Smithson was educated for an apothecary—a vocation about the same time followed for several years by Sir Thomas Geery Cullum, before he succeeded to the family estate and dignity. Hugh Smithson's place of business was Hatton Garden, but the length of time that he there presided over a pestle and mortar is uncertain. In 1736 he became a Fellow of the Society of Antiquaries, but he withdrew from that learned body, on the books of which his signature may be found, in the year 1740. A few months after this secession, Sir Hugh led to the altar the only child and heiress of Algernon Seymour, Duke of Somerset. There still lives a tradition that the lady made the offer to Sir Hugh immediately after his rejection by a famous belle of private rank and modest wealth. Another version of the story is that, when she heard of his disappointment, she observed publicly, "that the disdainful beauty was a fool, and that no other woman in England would be guilty of like folly." On hearing this, the baronet, a singularly handsome man, took courage to sue for that to which men of far higher rank would not have presumed to aspire. The success that followed his daring, of course, brought upon him the arrows of envy. He had won so much, however, that he could, without ill-humour, bear being laughed at. On being created Duke of Northumberland in 1766, he could afford to smile at a proposition that his coronet should be surrounded with senna, instead of strawberry-leaves; for, however much obscure jealousy might affect to contemn him, he was no fit object for disdain—but a gentleman of good intellect and a lordly presence, and (though he had mixed drugs behind a counter) descended from an old and honourable family. The reproach of being a Smithson, and no Percy, had more force when applied to the second duke in the Anti-Jacobin, than it had when hurled vindictively at the ex-doctor himself by the mediocrities of the *beau monde*, whom he had beaten on their own ground by superior attractions and accomplishments.

> "Nay," quoth the Duke, "in thy black scroll
> Deductions I espye—
> For those who, poor, and mean, and low,
> With children burthen'd lie.

> "And though full sixty thousand pounds
> My vassals pay to me,
> From Cornwall to Northumberland,
> Through many a fair countree;

> "Yet England's church, its king, its laws,
> Its cause I value not,
> Compared with this, my constant text,
> *A penny saved is got.*

> "No drop of princely Percy's blood
> Through these cold veins doth run;
> With Hotspur's castles, blazon, name,
> I still am *poor* Smithson."

Considering the opportunities that medical men have for pressing a suit in love, and the many temptations to gentle emotion that they experience in the aspect of feminine suffering, and the confiding gratitude of their fair patients, it is perhaps to be wondered at that only one medical duke is to be found in the annals of the peerage. When Swift's Stella was on her death-bed, her physician said, encouragingly—"Madam, you are certainly near the bottom of the hill, but we shall endeavour to get you up once more," the *naïve* reply of the poor lady was, "Doctor, I am afraid I shall be out *of breath* before I get to the top again." Not less touching was the fear expressed by Steele's merry daughter to her doctor, that she should "die *before the holidays.*" Both Stella and Sir Richard's child had left their personal charms behind them when they so addressed their physicians; but imagine, my brother, what the effect of such words would be on your susceptible heart, if they came from the lips of a beautiful girl. Would you not (think you) try to win other such speeches from her?—and if you tried, dear sir, surely *you* would succeed!

Prudence would order a physician, endowed with a heart, to treat it in the same way as Dr. Glynn thought a cucumber ought to be dressed—to slice it very thin, pepper it plentifully, pour upon it plenty of the best vinegar, and then—throw it away. A doctor has quite enough work on his hands to keep the affections of his patients in check, without having to mount guard over his own emotions. Thackeray says that girls make love in the nursery, and practise the arts of coquetry on the page-boy who brings the coals upstairs—a hard saying for simple young gentlemen triumphing in the possession of a *first* love. The writer of these pages could point to a fair dame, who enjoys rank amongst the highest and wealth equal to the station assigned her by the heralds, who not only aimed tender glances, and sighed amorously to a young waxen-faced, blue-eyed apothecary, but even went so far as to write him a letter proposing an elopement, and other merry arrangements, in which a carriage, everlastingly careering over the country at the heels of four horses, bore a conspicuous part. The silly maiden had, like Dinah, "a fortune in silvyer and gold," amounting to £50,000, and her blue-eyed Adonis was twice her age; but fortunately he was a gentleman of honour, and, without divulging the mad proposition of the young lady, he induced her father to take her away for twelve months' change of air and scene. Many years since the heroine of this little episode, after she had become the wife of a very great man, and the mother of children who bid fair to become ornaments to their illustrious race, expressed her gratitude cordially to this Joseph of the doctors, for his magnanimity in not profiting by the absurd fancies of a child, and the delicacy with which he had taken prompt measures for her happiness; and, more recently, she manifested her good will to the man who had offered her what is generally regarded as the greatest insult a woman can experience, by procuring a commission in the army for his eldest son.

The embarrassments Sir John Eliot suffered under from the emotional overtures of his fair patients are well known. St. John Long himself had not more admirers amongst the *élite* of high-born English ladies. The king had a strong personal dislike to Sir John,—a dislike possibly heightened by a feeling that it was sheer impudence in a doctor to capture without an effort the hearts of half the prettiest women amongst his subjects—and then shrug his shoulders with chagrin at his success. Lord George Germain had hard work to wring a baronetcy out of his Majesty for this victim of misplaced affection.

"Well," said the king, at last grudgingly promising to make Eliot a baronet—"my Lord, since you desire it, let it be; but remember he shall not be my physician."

"No, sir," answered Lord George—"he shall be your Majesty's baronet, and my physician."

Amongst other plans Sir John resorted to, to scare away his patients and patronesses, he had a death's-head painted on his carriage-panels; but the result of this eccentric measure on his practice and on his sufferings was the reverse of what he desired. One lady—the daughter of a noble member of a Cabinet—ignorant that he was otherwise occupied, made him an offer, and on learning to her astonishment that he was a married man, vowed that she would not rest till she had assassinated his wife.

Poor Radcliffe's loves were of a less flattering sort, though they resembled Sir John Eliot's in respect of being instances of reciprocity all on one side. But the amorous follies of Radcliffe, ludicrous though they became under the touches of Steele's pen, are dignified and manly when compared with the senile freaks of Dr. Mead, whose highest delight was to comb the hair of the lady on whom, for the time being, his affections were set.

Dr. Cadogan, of Charles the Second's time, was, like Sir John Eliot, a favourite with the ladies. His wont was to spend his days in shooting and his evenings in flirtation. To the former of these tastes the following lines refer:—

> "Doctor, all game you either ought to shun,
> Or sport no longer with the unsteady gun;
> But like physicians of undoubted skill,
> Gladly attempt what never fails to kill,
> Not lead's uncertain dross, but physic's deadly pill."

Whether he was a good shot we cannot say; but he was sufficiently adroit as a squire of dames, for he secured as his wife a wealthy lady, over whose property he had unfettered control. Against the money, however, there were two important points figuring under the head of "set-off"—the bride was old and querulous. Of course such a woman was unfitted to live happily with an eminent physician, on whom bevies of court ladies smiled whenever he went west of Charing Cross. After spending a few months in alternate fits of jealous hate and jealous fondness, the poor creature conceived the terrible fancy that her husband was bent on destroying her with poison, and so ridding his life of her execrable temper. One day, when surrounded by her friends, and in the presence of her lord and master, she fell on her back in a state of hysterical spasms, exclaiming:—

"Ah! he has killed me at last. I am poisoned!"

"Poisoned!" cried the lady-friends, turning up the whites of their eyes. "Oh! gracious goodness!—you have done it, doctor!"

"What do you accuse me of?" asked the doctor, with surprise.

"I accuse you—of—killing me—ee," responded the wife, doing her best to imitate a death-struggle.

"Ladies," answered the doctor, with admirable *nonchalance*, bowing to Mrs. Cadogan's bosom associates, "it is perfectly false. You are quite welcome to open her at once, and then you'll discover the calumny."

John Hunter administered a scarcely less startling reproof to his wife, who, though devoted in her attachment to him, and in every respect a lady worthy of esteem, caused her husband at times no little vexation by her fondness for society. She was in the habit of giving enormous routs, at which authors and artists, of all shades of merit and demerit, used to assemble to render homage to her literary powers, which were very far from common-place. A lasting popularity has attested the excellence of her song:—

> "My mother bids me bind my hair
> With bands of rosy hue;

Tie up my sleeves with ribbons rare,
And lace my boddice blue.

"'For why,' she cries, 'sit still and weep,
While others dance and play?'
Alas! I scarce can go or creep,
While Lubin is away.

"'Tis sad to think the days are gone,
When those we love are near;
I sit upon this mossy stone,
And sigh when none can hear.

"And while I spin my flaxen thread,
And sing my simple lay,
The village seems asleep or dead,
Now Lubin is away."

John Hunter had no sympathy with his wife's poetical aspirations, still less with the society which those aspirations led her to cultivate. Grudging the time which the labours of practice prevented him from devoting to the pursuits of his museum and laboratory he could not restrain his too irritable temper when Mrs. Hunter's frivolous amusements deprived him of the quiet requisite for study. Even the fee of a patient who called him from his dissecting instruments could not reconcile him to the interruption. "I must go," he would say reluctantly to his friend Lynn, when the living summoned him from his investigations among the dead, "and earn this d — —d guinea, or I shall be sure to want it to-morrow." Imagine the wrath of such a man, finding, on his return from a long day's work, his house full of musical professors, connoisseurs, and fashionable idlers—in fact, all the confusion and hubbub and heat of a grand party, which his lady had forgotten to inform him was that evening to come off! Walking straight into the middle of the principal reception-room, he faced round and surveyed his unwelcome guests, who were not a little surprised to see him—dusty, toilworn, and grim—so unlike what "the man of the house" ought to be on such an occasion.

"I knew nothing," was his brief address to the astounded crowd—"I knew nothing of this kick-up, and I ought to have been informed of it beforehand; but, as I have now returned home to study, I hope the present company will retire."

Mrs Hunter's drawing-rooms were speedily empty.

One of the drollest love stories in medical ana is that which relates to Dr. Thomas Dawson, a century since alike admired by the inhabitants of Hackney as a pulpit orator and a physician. Dawson was originally a Suffolk worthy, unconnected, however, with the eccentric John Dawson, who, in the reign of Charles the Second, was an apothecary in the pleasant old town of Framlingham, in that county. His father, a dissenting minister, had seven sons, and educated six of them for the Nonconformist pulpit. Of these six, certainly three joined the Established Church, and became rectors—two of the said three, Benjamin and Abraham, being controversial writers of considerable merit. Thomas Dawson adhered to the tenets of his father, and, combining the vocations of divine and physic-man, preached on

Sundays, and doctored during the rest of the week. He was Mead and Mead's father in one: though the conditions of human existence, which render it impossible for one person to be in two places at the same time, prevented him from leaving chapel to visit his patients, and the next minute urging the congregation to offer up a prayer for the welfare of the unfortunate sufferers. Amongst the doctor's circle of acquaintance Miss Corbett of Hackney was at the same time the richest, the most devout, and the most afflicted in bodily health. Ministering to her body and soul, Dr. Dawson had frequent occasions for visiting her. One day he found her alone, sitting with the large family Bible before her, meditating on perhaps the grandest chapter in all the Old Testament. The doctor read the words to which the forefinger of her right hand pointed—the words of Nathan to David: *"Thou art the man."* The doctor took the hint; and on the 29th of May, 1758, he found a wife—and the pious lady won a husband. The only offspring of this strange match was one son, a Mr. Dawson, who still resides at a very advanced age of life in the charming village of Botesdale, in Suffolk. When the writer of these pages was a happy little boy, making his first acquaintance with Latin and Greek, at the Botesdale Grammar School, then presided over by the pious, manly, and gentle — —, he was an especial pet with Mr. Dawson. The worthy gentleman's little house was in the centre of a large garden, densely stocked with apple and other fruit trees; and in it he led a very retired life, visited by only a very few friends, and tended by two or three servants—of whom one, an ancient serving man, acted as a valet, gardener, and groom to an antique horse which constituted Mr. Dawson's entire stud. The small urchin before-mentioned had free access at all times to the venerable gentleman, and used to bring him the gossip of the town and school, in exchange for apples and other substantial gifts. Thin and attenuated, diminutive, so as to be little more than a dwarf, with vagrant eager eye, hooked as to his nose, and with a long beard, snowy-white, streaming over his waistcoat, the octogenarian used to receive his fair-haired child-visitor. May he be happy—as may all old gentlemen be, who are kind to little schoolboys, and give them apples and "tips!"

The day that Abernethy was married he went down to the lecture-room to deliver his customary instruction to his pupils. His selection of a wife was as judicious as his marriage was happy; and the funny stories for long current about the mode in which he made his offer are known to be those most delusive of fabrications, fearless and extreme exaggerations of a little particle of the truth. The brutality of procedure attributed to the great surgeon by current rumour was altogether foreign to his nature. The Abernethy biscuit was not more audaciously pinned upon his reputation, than was the absurd falsehood that when he made his offer to his future wife he had only seen her once, and then wrote saying he should like to marry her, but as he was too busy to "make love," she must entertain his proposal without further preliminaries, and let him know her decision by the end of the week.

Of Sir John Eliot the fortunate, mention has already been made in this chapter. Let us now speak of John Eliot, the luckless hero of a biography published in 1787, under the title of "A Narrative of the Life and Death of John Eliot, M.D., containing an account of the Rise, Progress, and Catastrophe of his unhappy passion for Miss

Mary Boydell." A native of Somersetshire, John Elliot wrote a tragedy when only twelve years of age, and after serving an apprenticeship to a London apothecary, fell in love with one Miss Mary Boydell, a niece of a city alderman. The course of this gentleman's love ran smoothly till he chanced, by evil fortune, to read an announcement in a newspaper, that a Miss Boydell had, on the previous day, been led to the altar by some gentleman—not called Dr. John Elliot, certainly not himself. Never doubting that *the* Miss Boydell of the newspaper was *his* Miss Boydell, the doctor, without making any further inquiries after the perfidious fair one, sold his shop and fixtures, and ran off from the evil city of heartless women, to commune with beasts of the field and birds of the air in sylvan retirement. Not a little chagrined was Miss Boydell at the sudden disappearance of her ideal apothecary, whom her uncle, the alderman, stigmatized in round, honest, indignant language, as a big blackguard. After twelve years spent in wandering, "a forlorn wretch, over the kingdom," Dr. Elliott returned to London, set up once more in business, and began, for a second time, to drive a thriving trade, when Delilah again crossed his path. "One day," he says, telling his own story, "entering my shop (for I had commenced again the business of apothecary) I found two ladies sitting there, one of whom I thought I could recognize. As soon as she observed me, she cried out, 'Mr. Elliot! Mr. Elliot!' and fell back in a swoon. The well-known voice struck me like a shock of electricity—my affections instantly gushed forth—I fell senseless at her feet. When I came to myself, I found Miss Boydell sitting by my side." And *his* Miss Boydell was Miss Boydell still—innocent of wedlock.

Imogene being proved true, and Alonzo having come to life, the youthful couple renewed the engagement entered into more than twelve years before. The wedding-day was fixed, the wedding-clothes were provided, when uncle (the alderman), distrustful that his niece's scranny lover would make a good husband, induced her at the last moment to jilt him, and marry Mr. Nicols, an opulent bookseller. The farce was now to wear an aspect of tragedy. Infuriated at being, after all, *really* deceived, Dr. Elliot bought two brace of pistols, and bound them together in pairs. One pair he loaded only with powder; into the other he put the proper quantum of lead, as well as the pernicious dust. Armed with these weapons, he lay in wait for the destroyer of his peace. After some days of watching he saw her in Prince's Street, walking with the triumphant Nicols. Rushing up, he fired at her the two pistols (not loaded with ball), and then snatching the other brace from his pocket, was proceeding to commit suicide, when he was seized by the bystanders and disarmed.

The next scene in the drama was the principal court of the Old Bailey, with Dr. Elliot in the dock, charged with an attempt to murder Miss Boydell. The jury, being satisfied that the pistols were not loaded with ball, and that the prisoner only intended to create a startling impression on Miss Boydell's mind, acquitted him of that charge, and he was remanded to prison to take his trial for a common assault. Before this second inquiry, however, could come off, the poor man died in Newgate, July 22, 1787, of a broken heart—or jail fever. Ere his death, he took a cruel revenge of the lady, by writing an autobiographic account of his love experiences, in which appeared the following passage:—"Fascinated as I was by the charms of this faithless woman, I had long ceased to be sensible to these defects, or rather my impassioned imagination had converted them into perfections. But those who did not labour under the power of this magic were struck by her ungraceful exterior, and mine ears have not unfrequently been shocked to hear the tongue of indifference pronounce that the object of my passion was *ugly and deformed*. Add to this, that Miss Boydell has long since ceased to boast the bloom of youth, and then let any person, impartial and unprejudiced, decide whether a passion for her, so violent as that I have manifested, could be the produce of a slight and recent acquaintance, or whether it must not rather be the consequence of a long habit and inveterate intimacy." Such was the absurd sad story of John Elliot, author of "The Medical Almanack," "Elements of the Branches of Natural Philosophy," and "Experiments and Observations on Light and Colours."

The mournful love-story of Dr. John Elliot made a deep impression on the popular mind. It is found alluded to in ballads and chap-books, and more than one penny romance was framed upon it. Not improbably it suggested the composition of the following parody of Monk Lewis's "Alonzo the Brave and the Fair Imogene," which appeared at the close of the last century, during the first run of popularity which that familiar ballad obtained:—

"GILES BOLUS THE KNAVE AND BROWN SALLY GREEN.

"A ROMANCE BY M. G. LEWIS.

"A Doctor so grave and a virgin so bright,
Hob-a-nobbed in some right marasquin;
They swallowed the cordial with truest delight,
Giles Bolus the knave was just five feet in height,
And four feet the brown Sally Green.

"'And as,' said Giles Bolus, 'to-morrow I go
To physic a feverish land,
At some sixpenny hop, or perhaps the mayor's show,
You'll tumble in love with some smart city beau,
And with him share your shop in the Strand.'

"'Lord! how can you think so?' Brown Sally Green said,
'You must know mighty little of me;
For if you be living, or if you be dead,
I swear, 'pon my honour, that none in your stead,
Shall husband of Sally Green be.

"'And if e'er I by love or by wealth led aside
Am false to Giles Bolus the knave;
God grant that at dinner so amply suppli'd,
Over-eating may give me a pain in the side,
May your ghost then bring rhubarb to physic the bride,
And send her well-dosed to the grave.'

"To Jamaica the doctor now hastened for gold,
Sally wept till she blew her nose sore;

Yet scarce had a twelvemonth elaps'd, when behold!
A brewer quite stylish his gig that way roll'd,
And stopped it at Sally Green's door.

"His barrels, his bungs, and his brass-headed cane,
Soon made her untrue to his vows;
The stream of small beer now bewildered her brain;
He caught her while tipsy—denials were vain—
So he carried her home as his spouse.

"And now the roast-beef had been blest by the priest,
To cram now the guests had begun;
Tooth and nail, like a wolf, fell the bride on the feast
Nor yet had the clash of her knife and fork ceased,
When a bell (t'was the dustman's) toll'd one.

"Then first, with amazement, brown Sally Green found,
That a stranger was stuck by her side.
His cravat and his ruffles with snuff were embrown'd;
He ate not—he drank not—but, turning him round,
Sent some pudding away to be fried.

"His wig was turned forwards, and wort was his height,
His apron was dirty to view;
The women (oh! wondrous) were hushed at the sight,
The cats as they eyed him drew back (well they might),
For his body was pea-green and blue.

"Now, as all wish'd to speak, but none knew what to say,
They look'd mighty foolish and queer:
At length spoke the lady with trembling—'I pray,
Dear sir, that your peruke aside you would lay,
And partake of some strong or small beer.'

"The bride shuts her fly-trap—the stranger complies,
And his wig from his phiz deigns to pull.
Adzooks! what a squall Sally gave through surprise!
Like a pig that was stuck, how she opened her eyes,
When she recognized Giles's bare skull.

"Each miss then exclaimed, while she turn'd up her snout,
'Sir, your head isn't fit to be seen!'—
The pot-boys ran in, and the pot-boys ran out,
And couldn't conceive what the noise was about,
While the doctor addressed Sally Green.

"'Behold me, thou jilt-flirt! behold me!' he cri'd—
'I'm Bolus, whom some call the 'knave!'
God grant, that to punish your falsehood and pride,
You should feel at this moment a pain in your side.
Quick, swallow this rhubarb!—I'll physic the bride,

And send her well-dosed to the grave!'

"Thus saying, the physic her throat he forced down,
In spite of whate'er she could say:
Then bore to his chariot the maiden so brown,
Nor ever again was she seen in that town,
Or the doctor who whisked her away.

"Not long lived the brewer, and none since that time
To inhabit the brew-house presume;
For old women say that by order sublime
There Sally Green suffers the pain of her crime,
And bawls to get out of the room.

"At midnight four times in each year does her sprite
With shrieks make the chamber resound.
'I won't take the rhubarb!' she squalls in affright,
While a cup in his left hand, a draught in his right,
Giles Bolus pursues her around.

"With wigs so well powdered, twelve doctors so grave,
Dancing hornpipes around them are seen;
They drink chicken-broth, and this horrible stave
Is twanged through each nose, 'To Giles Bolus the knave,
And his patient the sick Sally Green.'"

In the court of love, Dr. Van Buchell, the empiric, may pass muster as a physician. When that droll charlatan lost his first wife, in 1775, he paid her the compliment of preserving her body with great care. Dr. Hunter, with the assistance of Mr. Cruikshank, injected the blood-vessels of the corpse with a carmine fluid, so that the cheeks and lips had the hue of healthy life; the cavities of the body were artistically packed with the antiseptics used by modern embalmers; and glass eyes were substituted in place of the filmy balls which Death had made his own. Decked in a dainty apparel of lace and finest linen, the body was then placed in a bed of thin paste of plaster of Paris, which, crystallizing, made a most ornamental couch. The case containing this fantastic horror had a glass lid, covered with a curtain; and as Van Buchell kept it in his ordinary sitting-room, he had the pleasure of introducing his visitors to the lifeless form of his "dear departed." For several years the doctor lived very happily with this slough of an immortal soul—never quarrelling with it, never being scolded by it—on the whole, enjoying an amount of domestic tranquility that rarely falls to one man's lot. Unwisely he made in advanced years a new alliance, and manifested a desire to be on with the new and the old love at the same time. To this Mrs. Van Buchell (No. 2) strongly objected, and insisted that the quaint coffin of Mrs. Van Buchell (No. 1) should be removed from the parlour in which she was expected to spend the greatest part of her days. The eccentric mode in which Buchell displayed his affection for his first wife was scarcely less repulsive than the devotion to the interests of anatomical science which induced Rondeletius to dissect the dead body of his own child in his theatre at Montpelier.

Are there no more loves to be mentioned? Yes; let these concluding pages tell an interesting story of the last generation.

Fifty years ago the picturesque, sunny town of Holmnook had for its physician one Dr. Kemp, a grave and reverend Æsculapius, punctilious in etiquette, with an imposing formality of manner, accurate in costume, in every respect a courtier of the old school. Holmnook is an antique market-town, square and compact, a capital in miniature, lying at the foot of an old feudal castle, in which the Bigods once held sway. That stronghold of moated towers was three centuries since the abode of a mighty Duke; Surrey, the poet earl, luckless and inspired, was born within its walls. The noble acres of the princely house fell into the hands of a *parvenu*—a rich, grasping lawyer;—that was bad. The lawyer died and went to his place, leaving the land to the poor;—that was better. And now the produce of the rich soil, which whilom sent forth a crop of mailed knights, supports a college of toil and time-worn peasants, saving their cold thin blood from the penury of the poor-house, and sheltering them from the contumelies of—Guardians of the Poor. Hard by the college, housing these ancient humble children of man, is a school, based on the same beneficent foundation, where the village lads are taught by as ripe a scholar and true a gentleman as ever came from the banks of Isis; and round which temple of learning they play their rough, noisy games, under the observation of the veterans of the bourg—the almsmen and almswomen who sit in the sun and on benches before their college, clad in the blue coats of the charity, and feeling no shame in them, though the armorial badge of that old lawyer is tacked upon them in red cloth.

Holmnook is unlike most other English towns of its size, abounding as it does in large antique mansions, formerly inhabited by the great officers and dependents on the ducal household, who in many cases were blood relations of the duke himself. Under the capacious windows of these old houses, in the streets, and round the market-square, run rows of limes, spreading their cool shade over the pinnacles of gabled roofs, and flinging back bars across the shining shingle which decorates the plaster walls of the older houses. In the centre of the town stands an enormous church, large enough to hold an entire army of Christians, and containing many imposing tombs of earls and leaders, long since gone to their account.

Think of this old town, its venerable dwellings—each by itself suggesting a romance. Hear the cooing and lazy flapping of pigeons, making continual holiday round the massive chimneys. Observe, without seeming to observe, the mayor's pretty daughter sitting at the open oriel window of the Guild-hall, merrily singing over her needle-work, and wondering if her bright ribbon has a good effect on passers below. Heed the jingle of a harpsichord in the rector's parlour. Be pleased to remember that the year is 1790—not 1860. Take a glass of stinging ale at "The Knight of Armour" hostelry—and own you enjoy it. Take another, creaming good-naturedly up under your lip, and confess you like it better than its predecessor. See the High Sheriff's carriage pass through the excited town, drawn by four enormous black horses, and having three Bacchic footmen hanging on behind. Do all this, and then you'll have a faint notion of Holmnook, its un-English picturesqueness, its placid joy, and experience of pomp.

Who is the gentleman emerging from the mansion on the causeway, in this year 1790—with white peruke and long pig-tail, snuff-coloured coat and velvet collar, tight dark nether garments, silk stockings, and shoes with buckles, volumes of white shirt-frill rising up under his chin? As he taps his shoes on his doorstep you can see he is proud of his leg, a pleasant pride, whether one has reason for it or not!

Seventy years of age, staid, decorous, and thoroughly versed in the social proprieties of the old world, now gone clean from us, like chivalry or chartism, Dr. Kemp was an important personage in Holmnook and its vicinity. An *éclat* was his that a country doctor does not usually possess. For he was of gentle blood, being a cadet of an old and wealthy family on the other side of the country, the representative of which hailed him "cousin," and treated him with the intimacy of kinship—the kinship of 1790.

Michael Kemp's youth had been spent away from Holmnook. Doubtless so polite and dignified a gentleman had once aimed at a brighter lot than a rural physician's. Doubtless he had a history, but he kept it to himself. He had never married! The rumour went that he had been disappointed—had undertaken the conquest of a high-born lady, who gave another ending to the game; and having conquered him, went off to conquer others. Ladies could do such things in the last century—when men had hearts.

Anyhow, Michael Kemp, M.D., was an old bachelor, of spotless honour, and a reputation that scandal never dared to trifle with.

A lady, much respected by the simple inhabitants of Holmsnook, kept his house.

Let us speak of her—fair and forty, comely, with matronly outlines, but graceful. Pleasant of voice, cheerful in manner, active in benevolence, Mistress Alice was a great favourite; no christening or wedding could go off without her for miles around. The doctor's grandest patients treated her as an equal; for apart from her personal claims to respect and good-will, she was, it was understood, of the doctor's blood—a poor relation, gentle by birth as she was by education. Mistress Alice was a great authority amongst the Holmnook ladies, on all matters pertaining to dress and taste. Her own ordinary costume was an artistic one. A large white kerchief, made so as to sit like a jacket, close and high round the throat, concealed her fair arms and shoulders, and reached down to the waist of her dress, which, in obedience to the fashion of the time, ran close beneath her arms. In 1790 a lady's waist at Holmnook occupied just about the same place where the drapery of a London belle's Mazeppa harness offers its first concealment to its wearer's charms. But it was on her foot-gear that Mistress Alice devoted especial care. The short skirts of that day encouraged a woman to set her feet off to the best advantage. Mistress Alice wore natty high-heeled shoes and clocked stockings—bright crimson stockings with yellow clocks.

Do you know what clocked stockings were, ladies? This writer is not deeply learned on such matters, but having seen a pair of Mistress Alice's stockings, he can tell you that they had on either side, extending from the heel upwards some six inches, flowers gracefully embroidered with a light yellow silk on the crimson ground. And these wreaths of broidery were by our ancestors called clocks. This writer could tell something else about Mistress Alice's apparel. She had for grand evenings of high festivity white kid gloves reaching up to the elbow, and having a slit at the tips of the forefinger and thumb of each hand. It was an ordinary fashion long syne. So, ladies could let out the tips of those digits to take a pinch of snuff!

One night Michael Kemp, M.D., Oxon., was called up to come with every possible haste to visit a sick lady, urgently in want of him. The night-bell was rung violently, and the messenger cried to the doctor over and over from the pavement below to make good speed. The doctor did his best to comply; but, as ill-luck would have it, after he had struck a light the candle illumined by it fell down, and left the doctor in darkness. This was very annoying to the good man, for he could not reconcile it to his conscience to consume time in lighting another, and yet it was hard for such a decorous man to make his hasty toilet in the dark.

He managed, however, better than he expected. His peruke came to hand all right; so did the tight inexpressibles; so did the snuff-coloured coat with high velvet collar; so did the buckled shoes. Bravo!

In another five minutes the active physician had groped his way down-stairs, emerged from his stately dwelling, and had run to his patient's house.

In a trice he was admitted; in a twinkle he was up the stairs; in another second he was by the sick lady's bedside, round which were seated a nurse and three eminent Holmnook gossips.

He was, however, little prepared for the reception he met with—the effect his appearance produced.

The sick lady, struggling though she was with severe pain, laughed outright.

The nurse said, "Oh my!—Doctor Kemp!"

Gossip No. 1 exclaimed, "Oh, you'll kill me!"

Gossip No. 2 cried, "I can't believe my eyes!"

Gossip No. 3 exploded with—"Oh, Doctor Kemp, do look at your stockings!"

And the doctor, obeying, did look at his stockings. One was of black silk—the other was a crimson one, with yellow clocks.

Was there not merry talk the next day at Holmnook! Didn't one hear blithe hearty laughter at every street corner—at every window under the limes?

What did they laugh about? What did they say?

Only this, fair reader—

"Honi soit qui mal y pense."

God bless thee, Holmnook! The bells of thy old church-tower are jangling in my ears though thou art a hundred miles away. I see the blue heavens kissing thy limes!

CHAPTER XXIV.

LITERATURE AND ART.

The old proverb says, "Every man is a physician or a fool by forty." Sir Henry Halford happening to quote the old saw to a circle of friends, Canning, with a pleasant humour smiling in his eyes, inquired, "Sir Henry, mayn't he be both?"

John Locke, according to academic registration, was not a physician till he was past forty. Born in 1632, he took his M.B. degree Feb. 6th, 1674. To what extent he exercised his profession is still a matter of dispute; but there is no doubt that he was for some period an active practitioner of it. Of his letters to Hans Sloane, that are still extant, the following is one:—

"Dear Sir,—

"I have a patient here sick of the fever at this season. It seems not violent; but I am told 'tis a sort that is not easily thrown off. I desire to know of you what your fevers in town are, and what methods you find most successful in them? I shall be obliged by your favour if you will give me a word or two by to-morrow's post, and direct it to me, to be left at Mr Harrison's, in the 'Crown,' at Harlow.

"I am, Sir,
"Your most humble servant,
"J Locke."

Popularly the name of Locke is as little associated with the profession of medicine as that of Sir James Mackintosh, who was a practising physician, till ambition and poverty made him select a more lucrative vocation, and turn his energies to the bar.

Distinguished amongst literary physicians was Andrew Borde, who studied Medicine at Oxford and Montpelier, and it is said acted as a physician in the service of Henry the Eighth. Borde's career has hitherto been a puzzle to antiquaries who, though interested in it, have been able to discover only little about it. It was his whim to sign himself Andrew Perforatus (his name really signifying "a cottage,"—"bordarius=a cottager"). In the same way after him Robert Fludd, the Rosicrucian doctor, adopted for his signature Robertus de Fluctibus. In his works he occasionally gives the reader a glimpse of his personal adventures; and from contemporary literature, as well as tradition, we learn enough to feel justified in believing that he created the cant term "Merry Andrew."

Of his freaks, about the most absurd was his conduct when acting as foreman of a jury in a small borough town. A prisoner was charged with stealing a pair of leather breeches, but though appearances were strongly against the accused (who was a notorious rogue), the evidence was so defective that to return a verdict of guilty on the charge was beyond the logic and conscience of the twelve good men and true. No course seemed open to them but to acquit the knave; when Andrew Borde prevailed on them, *as* the evidence of stealing the leather breeches was so defective, to bring him in guilty of manslaughter.

It is needless to say that the jurymen took Andrew's advice, and finding a verdict to the best of those abilities with which it had pleased God to bless them, astonished the judge and the public, not less than the prisoner, with the strange conclusion at which they had arrived.

Anthony à Wood and Hearne tell us the little that has hitherto been known of this eccentric physician. To that little an important addition may be made from the following letter, never before published, the original of which is in the State-Paper Office. The epistle is penned to Henry the Eighth's minister, Thomas Cromwell.

"Jesus.

"Offering humbly salutacyon with dew reverance. I certyffy yor mastershepp that I am now in Skotlonde in a lyttle universite or study namyd Glasko, where I study and practyce physyk as I have done in dyverse regyons and servyces for the sustentacyon off my lyvyng, assewring you that in ye parts that I am yn ye king's grace hath many hundred and in manner all men of presence (except some skolastycall men) that be hys adversarys. I resortt to ye Skotysh king's howse and to ye erle of Aryn, namyd Hamylton, and to ye Lord Evyndale, namyd Stuerd, and to many lords and lards as well spyrytuall as temporal, and truly I know their mynds, for they takyth me for a Skotysh man's sone, for I name my selff Karre, and so ye Karres kallyth me cosyn, thorow ye which I am in the more favor. Shortly to conclude; trust you no Skott for they wyll yowse flatterying wordes and all ys falshold. I suppose veryly that you have in Ynglond by hundred and thowsand Skotts and innumerable other alyons, which doth (specyally ye Skotts) much harme to the king's leege men throw their evyll wordes, for as I went thorow Ynglond I mett and was in company off many rurall felows, Englishmen that love nott our gracyose kyng. Wold to Jesu that some were ponyshed to geve others example. Wolde to Jesu also that you had never an alyen in yor realme, specyally Skotts, for I never knew alyen good for Ynglond except they knew proffytt and lucre should come to them so. In all parts of Chrystyndome that I have travylled in I know nott V Englishmen inhabytants except only scholers for learning. I pray to Jesu that alyens do in Ynglond no more harme to Ynglonde, and yff I myght do Ynglonde any servyce, specyally to my soveryn lord the kyng and to you, I would do ytt to spend and putt my lyfe in danger and jeberdy as far as any man. God be my judge. You have my hartt and shall be sure of me to the uttermost of my pore power. for I am never able to make you amends, for when I was in greatt thraldom, both bodyly and goastly, you of yor gentylnes sett me att liberte. Also I thank yor mastershepp for yor grett kyndnes that you have shewed me att Bysshopps Waltham, and that you gave me lycense to come to you ons in a qwarrtter. as sone as I come home I intende to come to you to submytt my selff to you to do with me what you wyll. for for lak of wytt paradventter I may in this wrettyng say that shall nott content you. but god be my judge I mene trewly both to my sovereyngne lord the kyng and to you. when I was kept in thrawldom in ye charterhouse and know neither ye kyngs noble acts nor you, then stultycyusly throw synstrall wordes I dyd as man of the others doth, butt after I was att lyberte manyfestly I aparsevyd ye ignorance and blyndnes that they and I wer yn. for I could never know no thynge of no maner of matter butt only by them, and they wolde cawse me wrett full incypyently to ye prior of London when he was in ye tower before he was putt to exicuyon. for ye which I trustt yor mastershepp hath pardonyd me, for god knoweth I was keppt in prison straytly, and glad I was to wrett att theyr request, but I wrott nothyng that I thought shold be agenst my prince nor you nor no other man. I pray god that you may provyde a good prior for that place of London, for truly there be many wylfull and obstynatt yowng men that stondeth to much in their owne consaytt and wyll nott be reformyd butt playth ye chyldryn, and a good prior wolde so serve them lyke chyldryn. News I have to wrett to you butt I yntende to be with ou shortly. for I am half wery off this baryn contry, as Jesu Chryst knowth, who ever keppe you in helthe and honor. a myle from Edynborough, the fyrst day off Apryll, by the hand of yor poer skoler and servantt, —Andrew Boorde Preest."

Literary physicians have, as a rule, not prospered as medical practitioners. The public harbour towards them the same suspicious and unfavourable prejudices as they do to literary barristers. A man, it is presumed, cannot be a master of two trades at the same time, and where he professes to carry on two it is usually concluded that he understands neither. To display the injustice of such views is no part of this writer's work, for the task is in better hands—time and experience, who are yearly adding to the cases that support the converse proposition that if a man is really a proficient in one subject, the fact is of itself a reason for believing him a master of a second.

Still, the number of brilliant writers who have enrolled themselves in the medical fraternity is remarkable. If they derived no benefit from their order, they have at least generously conferred lustre upon it. Goldsmith—though no one can say on what his claim to the title of doctor rested, and though in his luckless attempts to get medical employment he underwent even more humiliation and disgrace than fell to his lot as the drudge of Mrs. Griffiths—is one of the most pleasant associations that our countrymen have in connection with the history of "the Faculty." Smollett, like Goldsmith, tried ineffectually to escape from literary drudgery to the less irksome and more profitable duties that surround the pestle and mortar. Of Garth, Blackmore, Arbuthnot, and Akenside, notice has already been taken.

Anything like a complete enumeration of medical men who have made valuable contributions to *belles lettres* would fill a volume, by the writing of which very little good would be attained. By no means the least of them was Armstrong, whose portrait Thomson introduced into the "Castle of Indolence."

> "With him was sometimes joined in silken walk
> (Profoundly silent—for they never spoke),
> One shyer still, who quite detested talk;
> If stung by spleen, at once away he broke
> To grove of pine and broad o'ershadowing oak.
> There, inly thrilled, he wandered all alone,
> And on himself his pensive fury woke:
> He never uttered word, save when first shone
> The glittering star of eve—'Thank Heaven, the day is done.'"

His medical writings, and his best known poem, "The Art of Health," had he written nothing else, would in all probability have brought him patients, but the licentiousness of "The Economy of Love" effectually precluded him from ever succeeding as a family physician. Amongst Armstrong's poet friends was Grainger, the amiable and scholarly physician who enjoyed the esteem of Percy and Samuel Johnson, Shenstone and Sir Joshua. Soon after the publication of his translation of the "Elegies of Tibullus," (1758), Grainger went to the island of St. Christopher's, and established himself there as a physician. The scenery and industrial occupations of the island inspired him to write his most important poem, "The Sugar-Cane," which, in escaping such derision as was poured on Blackmore's effusions, owed its good fortune to the personal popularity of the author rather than its intrinsic merits. The following sample is a fair one:—

> "Destructive on the upland groves
> The monkey nation preys: from rocky heights,
> In silent parties they descend by night,
> And posting watchful sentinels, to warn
> When hostile steps approach, with gambols they
> Pour o'er the cane-grove. Luckless he to whom
> That land pertains! in evil hour, perhaps,
> And thoughtless of to-morrow, on a die
> He hazards millions; or, perhaps, reclines
> On luxury's soft lap, the pest of wealth;
> And, inconsiderate, deems his Indian crops
> Will amply her insatiate wants supply.

> "From these insidious droles (peculiar pest
> Of Liamigia's hills) would'st thou defen

Thy waving wealth, in traps put not thy trust,
However baited: treble every watch,
And well with arms provide them; faithful dogs,
Of nose sagacious, on their footsteps wait.
With these attack the predatory bands;
Quickly, th' unequal conflict they decline,
And chattering, fling their ill-got spoils away.
So when, of late, innumerous Gallic hosts,
Fierce, wanton, cruel, did by stealth invade
The peaceable American's domains,
While desolation mark'd their faithless rout;
No sooner Albion's martial sons advanc'd,
Than the gay dastards to their forests fled,
And left their spoils and tomahawks behind.
"Nor with less haste the whisker'd vermin race,
A countless clan, despoil the low-land cane.
"These to destroy, &c."

When the poem was read in MS. at Sir Joshua's house, the lines printed in italics were not part of the production, but in their place stood—

"Now, Muse, let's sing of *rats.*"

The immediate effect of such *bathos* was a burst of inextinguishable laughter from the auditors, whose sense of the ridiculous was by no means quieted by the fact that one of the company, slyly overlooking the reader, discovered that "the word had originally been *mice,* and had been altered to *rats,* as more dignified."

Above the crowd of minor medical *litterateurs* are conspicuous, Moore, the author of "Zeluco"; Dr. Aikin, one of whose many works has been already referred to; Erasmus Darwin, author of "The Botanic Garden"; Mason Good, the translator of "Lucretius," and author of the "Study of Medicine"; Dr. Ferriar, whose "Illustrations of Sterne" just doubled the value in the market of "Burton's Anatomy of Melancholy"; Cogan, the author of "Life and Opinions of John Buncle, jun."; Dr. Harrington, of Bath, editor of the "Nugæ Antiquæ"; Millingen, who wrote "The Curiosities of Medical Practice," and "The History of Duelling"; Dr. Paris, whose "Life of Sir Humphrey Davy," unsatisfactory as it is in many places, is still a useful book, and many of whose other writings will long remain of great value; Wadd, the humourous collector of "Medical Ana"; Dr. Merriman, the late contributor to the *Gentleman's Magazine* and *Notes and Queries;* and Pettigrew, the biographer of Lettsom. If the physicians and surgeons still living, who have openly or anonymously written with good effect on subjects not immediately connected with their profession, were placed before the reader, there would be found amongst them many of the most distinguished of their fraternity.

Apropos of the Dr. Harrington mentioned above, a writer says—"The Doctor for many years attended the Dowager Lady Trevor, relict of Lord Trevor, and last surviving daughter of Sir Richard Steele. He spoke of this lady as possessing all the wit, humour, and gaiety of her father, together with most of his faults. She was extravagant, and always in debt; but she was generous, charitable, and humane. She was particularly partial to young people, whom she frequently entertained most liberally, and delighted them with the pleasantry and volubility of her discourse. Her person was like that which her pleasant father described himself in the *Spectator*, with his short face, &c. A little before her death (which was in the month of December) she sent for her doctor, and, on his entering her chamber, he said, 'How fares your Ladyship!' She replied, 'Oh, my dear Doctor, ill fare! I am going to break up before the holidays!' This agreeable lady lived many years in Queen's Square, Bath, and, in the summer months, at St. Ann's Hill, Surrey, the late residence of Rt. Hon. Chas. James Fox."

Wolcot, better known as Peter Pindar, was a medical practitioner, his father and many of his ancestors having followed the same calling in Devonshire and Cornwall, under the names of Woolcot, Wolcott, Woolacot, Walcot, or Wolcot. After acquiring a knowledge of his profession in a somewhat irregular manner Wolcot found a patron in Sir William Trelawny, Bart., of Trelawny, co. Cornwall, who, on going out to assume the governorship of Jamaica, took the young surgeon with him to act as medical officer to his household. In Jamaica Wolcot figured in more characters than one. He was the governor's grand-master of the ceremonies, private secretary, and chaplain. When the King of the Mosquitoes waited on the new governor to express his loyal devotion to the King of England's representative, Wolcot had to entertain the royal guest—no difficult task as long as strong drink was in the way.

His Majesty—an enormously stout black brute—regarded intoxication as the condition of life most fit for kings.

> "Champagne the courtier drinks, the spleen to chase,
> The colonel Burgundy, and port his Grace."

The autocrat of the Mosquitoes, as the greatest only are, in his simplicity sublime, was contented with rum or its equivalent.

"Mo' drink for king! Mo' drink for king!" he would bellow, dancing round the grand-master of the governor's household.

"King," the grand-master would reply, "you are drunk already."

"No, no; king no drunk. Mo' drink for king! Broder George" (*i. e.* George III.) "love drink!"

Grand-Master.—"Broder George does not love drink: he is a sober man."

Autocrat.—"But King of Musquito love drink. Me will have mo' drink. Me love drink like devil. Me drink whole ocean!"

The different meagre memoirs of Peter Pindar are conflicting as to whether he ever received ordination from the hands of the Bishop of London. It seems most probable that he never did. But, consecrated or not, there is no doubt that he officiated as a colonial rector for some time. Droll stories of him as a parish priest used to circulate amongst his friends, as well as amongst his enemies. He read prayers and preached whenever a congregation appeared in his church, but three Sundays out of every four not a soul came to receive the benefit of his ministrations.

The rector was an admirable shot, and on his way from his house to church used to amuse himself with shooting pigeons, his clerk—also an excellent shot—walking behind with a fowling-piece in his hand, and taking part in the sport. Having reached the sacred edifice, his reverence and attendant opened the church door and waited in the porch ten minutes for the advent of worshippers. If none had presented themselves at the end of ten minutes, the pastor beat a retreat. If only a few black Christians straggled up, the rector bought them off with a few coins and then went home. One cunning old negro, who saw that the parson's heart was more with the wild-fowl of the neighboring bay than bent on the discharge of his priestly functions, after a while presented himself every Sunday, when the following interview and arrangement were regularly repeated:—

"What do you come here for, blackee?" the parson would exclaim.

"Why, massa, to hear your good sermon and all de prayer ob de church."

"Would not a *bit* or two do you more good?"

"Yes, massa doctor—me lub prayer much, but me lub money too."

The "bit or two" would then be paid, and the devotee would retire speedily from the scene. For an entire twelve-month was this *black*-mail exacted.

On his return to England, Wolcot, after a few unsuccessful attempts to establish himself in practice, relinquished the profession of physic as well as that of divinity, and, settling himself in London, made both fame and a good income by his writings. As a political satirist he was in his day almost without a rival, and the popularity of his numerous works would have placed a prudent man in lasting affluence. Improvidence, however, necessitated him to sell the copyright of his works to Messrs. Robinson, Golding, and Walker for an annuity of £250, payable half-yearly, during the remainder of his life. Loose agreements have always been the fashion between authors and publishers, and in the present case it was not clearly stated what "copyright of his works" meant. The publishers interpreted it as the copyright of both what the author had written at the time of making the agreement, and also of what he should subsequently write. Wolcot, however, declared that he had in the transaction only had regard to his prior productions. After some litigation and more squabbling, the publishers consented to take Wolcot's view of the case; but he never forgave them the discomfort they had caused him. His rancour against "the trade" increased with time, and inspired some of his most violent and unjust verses:—

> "Fired with the love of rhyme, and, let me say,
> Or virtue, too, I sound the moral lay;
> Much like St. Paul (who solemnly protests
> He battled hard at Ephesus with beasts),
> I've fought with lions, monkeys, bulls, and bears,
> And got half Noah's ark about my ears;
> Nay, more (which all the courts of justice know),
> Fought with the brutes of Paternoster Row."

For medicine Peter Pindar had even less respect than Garth had. He used to say "that he did not like the practice of it as an art. He was entirely ignorant, indeed, whether the patient was cured by the vis *medicatrix naturæ*, or the administration of a little pill, which was either directly or indirectly to reach the part affected." And for the practitioners of the art held in such low esteem, he cherished a contempt that he would at times display with true Pindaric warmth. In his two-act farce, "Physic and Delusion; or Jezebel and the Doctors," the dialogue is carried on in the following strain:—

> "*Blister.*— By God, old prig!
> Another word, and by my wig— —
>
> "*Bolus.*—Thy wig? Great accoucheur, well said,
> 'Tis of more value than thy head;
> And 'mongst thy customers—poor ninnies!
> Has helped thee much to bag thy guineas."

Amongst Peter Pindar's good services to the world was the protection he afforded to Opie (or Oppy, as it was at one time less euphoniously spelt and pronounced) the artist, when he was a poor country clown, rising at three o'clock in the summer mornings, to pursue his art with rude pieces of chalk and charcoal. Wolcot presented the boy with his first pencils, colours, and canvas, and put him in the way to paint portraits for the magnificent remuneration of half-a-guinea, and subsequently a guinea a-head. And it was to the same judicious friend that Opie, on leaving the provinces, owed his first success in London.

Wolcot used to tell some droll stories about his artist friend. Opie's indiscreet manner was a source of continual trouble to those who endeavoured to serve him; for, priding himself on being "a rough diamond," he took every pains that no one should fail to see the roughness. A lady sitter was anxious that her portrait should be "very handsome," and frankly told the painter so. "Then, madam," was the reply, "you wish to be painted otherwise than you are. I see you do not want your own face." Not less impudent was he at the close of his first year in London, in taking out writs against several sitters who were rather tardy in their payments.

Opie was not the only artist of celebrity deeply indebted to Peter Pindar. Bone, the painter in enamel, found an efficient friend in the same discerning lover of the arts. In this respect Wolcot was worthy of the profession which he deserted, and affected to despise; and his name will ever be honourably mentioned amongst those physicians who have fostered art, from the days of picture-loving Mead, down to those of the writer's very kind friend, Dr. Diamond, who gathered from remote quarters "The Diamond Collection of Portraits," which may be seen amongst the art treasures of Oxford.

One of the worthies of Dr. Diamond's family was Robertus Fludd, or De Fluctibus, the writer of Rosicrucian celebrity who gave Sterne more than one lesson in the arts of eccentricity. Sir Thomas Fludd of Milgate, Bearsted, co. Kent (grandson of David Fludd, *alias* Lloyd of Morton, in Shropshire), had five sons and a daughter. Of this offspring, one son, Thomas, purchased Gore Court, and fixed there a family, the vicissitudes of which may be learnt by a reference to Hasted's Kent. From this branch of the Fludds descended Dr. Diamond, who, amongst other curious family relics, possesses the diploma of Robertus de Fluctibus.

When Robertus de Fluctibus died, Sept. 8, 1637, in Coleman St., London, his body, under the protection of a herald of arms, was conveyed to the family seat in Kent, and was then buried in Bearsted Church, under a stone which he had before laid for himself. The monument over his ashes was ordered by him in his last will to be made after that of William Camden in the Abbey at Westminster. The inscription which marks his resting-place declares his, rather than our, estimate of his intellectual greatness;

> Magnificus non hæc sub odoribus urna vaporat,
> Crypta tegit cineres nec speciosa tuos.
> Quod mortale minus, tibi te committimus unum;
> Ingenii vivent hic monumenta tui
> Nam tibi qui similis scribit, moriturque, sepulchrum
> Pro totâ æternum posteritate facit.

More modest, and at the same time more humorous, is the epitaph, in Hendon Church, of poor Thomas Crossfield, whose name, alike as surgeon and politician, has passed from among men:—

> "Underneath Tom Crossfield lies,
> Who cares not now who laughs or cries.
> He always laughed, and when mellow
> Was a harum scarum sort of fellow.
> To none gave designed offence,
> So—*Honi soit qui mal y pense.*"

Amongst the medical poets there is one whom all scholarly physicians jealously claim as of their body—John Keats; he who, dying at Rome, at the age of twenty-six, wished his epitaph to be, "Here lies one whose name was writ in water." After serving his apprenticeship under an Edmonton surgeon, the author of "Endymion" became a medical student at St. Thomas's hospital.

Mention here, too, may be made of Dr. Macnish, the author of "The Anatomy of Drunkenness," and "The Modern Pythagorean"; and of Dr. Moir, the poet, whose death, a few years since, robbed the world of a simple and pathetic writer, and his personal acquaintance of a noble-hearted friend.

But of all modern English poets who have had an intimate personal connection with the medical profession, the greatest by far is Crabbe—

> "Nature's sternest painter, yet the best."

In 1754 George Crabbe was born in the old sea-faring town of Aldborough, in the county of Suffolk. His father, the collector of salt-duties, or salt-master of the town, was a churlish sullen fellow at the best of times; but, falling upon adversity in his old days, he became the *beau-ideal* of a domestic tyrant. He was not, however, without his respectable points. Though a poor man, he did his best to educate his children above the ranks of the very poor. One of them became a thriving glazier in his native town; another went to sea, and became captain of a Liverpool slave-ship; and a third, also a sailor, met with strange vicissitudes—at one time enjoying a very considerable amount of prosperity, and then suffering penury and persecution. A studious and a delicate lad, George, the eldest of the party, was designed for some pursuit more adapted to his disposition and physical powers than the avocations of working mechanics, or the hard duties of the marine service. When quite a child, he had, amongst the inhabitants of Aldborough, a reputation for mental superiority that often did him good service. On one occasion he chanced to offend a playmate—his senior and "master," as boys and savages term it—and was on the point of receiving a good thrashing nigh the roaring waves of old ocean, when a third boy, a common acquaintance, exclaimed in a voice of affright:—

"Yar marn't middle a' him; lit him aloone—he ha' got l'arning."

The plea was admitted as a good one, and the future bard, taking his benefit of clergy, escaped the profanation of a drubbing.

George was sent to two respectable schools, the one at Bungay, in Suffolk, and the other (the better of the two) at Stowmarket, in the same county. The expense of such an education, even if it amounted to no more than £20 per annum, was no small undertaking for the salt-master of a fishing-village; for Aldborough—now a handsome and much frequented provincial watering-place—was in 1750 nothing better than a collection of huts, whose humble inhabitants possessed little stake in the commonweal beyond the right of sending to parliament two members to represent their interests and opinions. On leaving school, in his fourteenth year, George was apprenticed to a country doctor of a very rough sort, who plied his trade at Wickham Brook, a small village near Bury St. Edmunds. It is a fact worthy of note, as throwing some light on the state of the profession in the provinces, that the apprentice shared the bed of his master's stable-boy. At Wickham Brook, however, the lad did not remain long to endure such indignity. He was removed from that scene of trial, and placed under the tutelage of Mr. Page, a surgeon of Woodbridge, a gentleman of good connections and polite tastes, and through the marriage of his daughter with the late famous Alderman Wood, an ancestor of a learned judge, who is not more eminent as a lawyer than beloved as a man.

It was during his apprenticeship to Mr. Page of Woodbridge that Crabbe made his first important efforts in poetry, publishing, in the year 1772, some fugitive pieces in *Wheble's Magazine*, and in 1775 "Inebriety, a poem, in three parts. Ipswich: printed and sold by C. Punchard, bookseller, in the Butter-market." While at Woodbridge, too, his friend Levett, a young surgeon of the neighborhood, took him over to Framlingham, introducing him to the families of that picturesque old town. William Springall Levett was at that time engaged to Alethea Brereton, a lady who, under the *nom de plume* of "Eugenia Acton," wrote certain novels that created a sensation in their brief day. Amongst them were "Vicissitudes of Genteel Life," "The Microcosm," and "A Tale without a Title." The love-making of Mr. Levett and Miss Eugenia de Acton was put a stop to by the death of the former, in 1774. The following epitaph, transcribed from the History of Framlingham, the work of the able antiquarian, Mr. Richard Green, is interesting as one of Crabbe's earlier compositions.

"What! though no trophies peer above his dust,

> Nor sculptured conquests deck his sober bust;
> What! though no earthly thunders sound his name,
> Death gives him conquest, and our sorrows fame!
> One sigh reflection heaves, but shuns excess,
> More should we mourn him, did we love him less."

Subsequently Miss Brereton married a gentleman named Lewis, engaged in extensive agricultural operations. However brief her literary reputation may have been, her pen did her good service; for, at a critical period of her husband's career, it brought her sums of much-needed money.

Mr. Levett's romance closed prematurely together with his life, but through him Crabbe first became acquainted with the lovely girl whom he loved through years of trial, and eventually made his wife. Sarah Elmy was the niece of John Tovell, *yeoman*, not *gentleman*—he would have scorned the title. Not that the worthy man was without pride of divers kinds, or that he did not hold himself to be a gentleman. He believed in the Tovells as being one of the most distinguished families of the country. A Tovell, by mere right of being a Tovell, could thrash more Frenchmen than any Englishman, not a Tovell, could. When the good man said, "I am nothing more than a plain yeoman," he never intended or expected any one to believe him, or to regard his words in any other light than as a playful protest against being deemed "a plain yeoman," or that modern hybrid, "a gentleman farmer."

He was a well-made, handsome, pleasant fellow—riding a good horse with the hounds—loving good cheer—enjoying laughter, without being very particular as to the cause of it—a little too much addicted to carousing, but withal an agreeable and useful citizen; and he lived at Parham Lodge, a house that a peer inhabited after him, without making any important alterations in the place.

On Crabbe's first introduction to Parham Lodge he was received with cordiality; but when it was seen that he had fallen in love with the squire's niece, it was only natural that "his presumption" should not at first meet the approval either of Mrs. Tovell or her husband. But the young people plighted troth to each other, and the engagement was recognized by the lady's family. It was years, however, before the wedding bells were set ringing. Crabbe's apprenticeship to Mr. Page finished, he tried ineffectually to raise the funds for a regular course of hospital instruction in London. Returning to Aldborough, he furnished a shop with a few bottles and a pound's worth of drugs, and set up as "an apothecary." Of course it was only amongst the poor of his native town that he obtained patients, the wealthier inhabitants of the borough distrusting the knowledge of a doctor who had not walked the hospitals. In the summer of 1778, however, he was appointed surgeon to the Warwickshire militia, then stationed at Aldborough, and in the following winter, on the Warwickshire militia being moved and replaced by the Norfolk militia, he was appointed surgeon to the latter regiment also. But these posts were only temporary, and conferred but little emolument on their holder. At length poverty drove the poet from his native town. The rest of his career is matter of notoriety. Every reader knows how the young man went to London and only escaped the death of Otway or Chatterton by the generous patronage of Burke, how through Burke's assistance he was ordained, became the Duke of Rutland's chaplain, obtained comfortable church preferment, and for a long span enjoyed an amount of domestic happiness that was as great and richly deserved as his literary reputation.

Crabbe's marriage with Sarah Elmy eventually conferred on him and his children the possession of Parham Lodge, which estate, a few years since, passed from them into the hands of wealthy purchasers. The poet also succeeded to other wealth through the same connection, an old-maid sister of John Tovell leaving him a considerable sum of money. "I can screw Crabbe up and down like an old fiddle," this amiable lady was fond of saying; and during her life she proved that her boast was no empty one. But her will was a handsome apology for all her little tiffs.

CHAPTER XXV.

NUMBER ELEVEN—A HOSPITAL STORY.

"Then, sir," said Mrs. Mallet, "if you'll only not look so frightened, I'll tell you how it was. It is now twenty years ago that I was very unfortunate. I was not more than thirty years of age, but I was old enough to have just lost a good husband and a dear little babe; and then, when I hadn't a sixpence in my pocket, I caught the fever, and had to go to a hospital. I wasn't used to trouble; for although I was nothing better than a poor man's child, I had known all my life nothing but kindness. I never had but one mistress,—my lady, who when she was the most beautiful young lady in all Devonshire, took me out of a village school, and raised me to be her maid; and her maid I was for twelve years—first down in Devonshire, and afterwards up in London, when she married (somewhat against the will of her family) a thorough good gentleman, but a poor one, who after a time took her out to India, where he became a judge, and she a grand lady. My dear mistress would have taken me out to India with her, only she was then too poor to pay for my passage out, and bear the expense of me there, where labour can be got so cheap, and native servants can live on a handful of rice a day. She, sir, is Lady Burridge—the same who gave me the money to start in this house with, and whose carriage you saw yesterday at my door.

"So my mistress went eastward, and I was left behind to marry a young man I had loved for some few years, and who had served during that time as clerk to my lady's husband. I was a young woman, and young women, to the end of the chapter, will think it a brave thing to fall in love. I thought my sweetheart was a handsomer and cleverer man than any other of his station in all London. I wonder how many girls have thought the same of their favourites! I went to church one morning with a fluttering heart and trembling knees, and came out under the porch thinking that all my life would ever afterwards be brighter, and lighter, and sunnier than it had been before. Well! in dancing into that pretty blunder, I wasn't a bigger fool than lots of others.

"And if a good husband is a great blessing (and she must be a paltry woman who can say nay to that), I was born to luck; for my husband was kind, good, and true—his temper was as sweet at home as his manners were abroad—he was hard-working and clever, sober and devout; and—though you may laugh at a woman of my age talking so like a romance—I tell you, sir, that if my life had to come all over again, I'd rather have the mischance of marrying my dear Richard, that the good fortune of wedding a luckier man.

"There's no doubt the game turned out ill for me. At first it seemed as if it would be just otherwise, for my husband had good health, plenty of work, and sufficient pay; so that, when my little girl came, her sweet face brought no shadow of anxiety with it, and we hoped she would be followed in due course by half-a-dozen more. But ere the dear babe had learned to prattle, a drear change came over the happy prospect. The fever crept over the gentle darling, and after she had suffered for a week or more, lying on my arms, God raised her from me into his happy home, where the beauty of summer reigns for ever, and the coldness of winter never enters. Richard and I took the body of our babe to the burial-ground, and saw it covered up in the earth which by turns gives all we get, and takes away from us all we have; and as we walked back to our deserted home, arm-in-arm, in the light of the summer's evening, we talked to each other more solemnly and tenderly than we had done for many a day. And the next morning he went back to his work in the office, from which he had absented himself since our child's death; and I encouraged him to cheer up, and not to give way to sorrow when I was not nigh to comfort him, but toil bravely and hopefully, as a man should; and in so advising him, I do not blush to say that I thought not only of what was best for his spirits, but also of what our necessity required—for we were only poor people, not at any time beforehand in the world, and now reduced by the cost of our little one's illness and funeral; and, sir, in this hard world we women, most times, have the best of it, for when the house is full of sorrow, we have little else to do but weep, but the men have to grieve and toil too.

"But poor Richard could not hold up his head. He came back from work that day pale and faint, and in the evening he had a chill and a heat-fit, that let me know the fever which had killed our little one had passed into him. The next day he could not leave his bed, and the doctor (a most kind man, who was always making rough jokes in a rough voice—just to hide his womanliness) said to me, 'If your husband goes down to his master's chambers in the Temple to-day, he had better stop at the coffin-maker's, in the corner of Chancery Lane, and leave his measure.' But Richard's case was not one for a jest, and he rapidly became worse than the doctor fancied he would be when he made that light speech. He was ill for six weeks, and then began slowly to mend; he got on so far as to sit up for two days for half-an-hour while he had his tea, and we were hoping that soon he would be able to be moved into the country—to my sister's, whose husband was an engineer at Stratford; but, suddenly, he had a relapse, and on the morning that finished the tenth week from his being seized, his arms let go their hold on my neck—and I was left alone!

"All during my babe's and Richard's long illness my sister Martha had behaved like a true sister to me. She was my only sister, and, to the best of my knowledge, the only relation I had in the world—and a good one she was; from girl to woman her heart always rung out clear like a bell. She had three young children, but even fear of contagion reaching them could not keep her from me in my trouble. She kept making the journey backwards and forwards, at least once a week, in the carrier's cart; and, though she had no money to spare, she brought me, with her husband's blessing, presents of wine, and jellies, and delicate meat, to buy which, I knew right well, she and her husband and her children must have pinched themselves down to scanty rations of bread and water. Her hands helped mine to put the flowers in poor Richard's coffin; she bore me up while I followed it, pale and trembling, to the grave; and when that horrible day was coming to an end, and she was about to return home, she took me into her arms, and covering me with kisses and caressings, and a thousand gentle sayings, as if I had been a child of her own, instead of her sister and a grown woman, she made me promise to come down to her at Stratford at the end of the week, and stay with her till God should give me strength and spirits and guidance, to work for myself again.

"But that promise was not kept. Next morning the rough-tender doctor came in, out of his mere goodness, to give me a friendly look, and a 'God speed you,' and found me, too, sickening for an illness. I knew, sir, he had made the discovery before his lips confessed a word; for when he had taken my wrist and felt my pulse, and looked up into my worn face, he turned pale, as if almost frightened, and such a look of grief came on his eyes and lips that he could not have said plainer, 'My poor woman! my poor woman! what I feared from the beginning, and prayed God not to permit, has come to pass at last.'

"Then I fairly broke down and cried bitterly; and I told the doctor how sore afflicted I was—how God had taken my husband and babe from me—how all my little means had been consumed in the expenses of nursing—how the little furniture in my rooms would not pay half what I owed to honest folk—and how, even in my unspeakable wretchedness, I could not ask the Almighty to take away my life, for I could not rest in death if I left the world without paying my just debts. Well, sir, the doctor sate down by me, and said, in his softest and simplest way:—

"'Come, come, neighbour, don't you frighten yourself. Be calm, and listen to me. Don't let the thought of debts worry you. What little I have done in the way of business for your poor child and husband I never wish to be paid for—so there's your greatest creditor disposed of. As for the others, they won't trouble you, for I'll undertake to see that none of them shall think that you have wronged 'em. I wish I could do more, neighbor; but I ain't a rich man, and I have got a wife and a regiment of little ones at home, who won't help, in the long run, to make me richer—although I am sure they'll make me happier. But now for yourself; you must go to the fever-hospital, to have your illness out; the physician who'll take care of you there is the cleverest in all London; and, as he is an old friend of mine, I can ask him to pay especial attention to you. You'll find it a pleasant, cheerful place, much more cool and comfortable than your rooms here; the nurses are all of them good people; and while lying on your bed there you won't have to fret yourself with thinking how you are to pay for the doctors, and medicine, and kitchen physic.'

"I was only too thankful to assent to all the doctor said; and forthwith he fetched a coach, put me into it, and took me off to the fever-hospital, to which his influence procured me instant admittance. Without delay I was conveyed to a large and comfortable bed, which, with another similar bed parallel to it, was placed against the wall at the end of a long gallery, containing twenty other beds. The first day of my hospital life I spent tranquilly enough; the languor of extreme exhaustion had soothed me, and my malady had not robbed me of my senses. So

I lay calmly on my couch and watched all the proceedings and arrangements of the great bed-room. I noticed how clean and white all the beds looked, and what kindly women the nurses were; I remarked what a wide space there was down the middle of the room between the two rows of beds, and again what large intervals there were between the beds on each side; I observed, too, that over every bed there was a ventilator set in the wall, and beneath the ventilator a board, on which was pinned a paper, bearing, in a filled-up printed form, the number of the bed to which it belonged, the date when the occupant was admitted to the ward, the names of the physician and nurse under whose charge she was, the medicine she was taking, and the diet on which she was put. It made me smile, moreover, to note how the nurses, when giving physic or nourishment, or otherwise attending to their charges, would frequently address them by the numbers on their boards, instead of their names.

"'Nurse, dear,' I asked, with a smile, when my attendant came near me, 'what's my name?'

"'Oh, dear!' said she, looking up at the board which had already been fixed over my head, 'your name is Number Eleven.'

"It would be hard for me to give you, sir, any notion of how these words, *Number Eleven*, took possession of my mind. This was the more strange, because the nurse did not usually call me by them; for she was a motherly creature, and almost always addressed me as 'poor dear,' or 'poor child'; and the doctors who had the charge of me spoke to me as 'friend,' or 'old friend,' or 'neighbor.' But all the same for that, I always thought of myself as Number Eleven; and ere many days, if any one had asked me what my name was, I could not for the life of me have remembered Abigail Mallet, but should have answered Number Eleven. The patient in the next bed to me was Number Twenty-two; she was, like myself, a poor woman who had just lost a husband and child by the fever, and both of us were much struck, and then drawn to each other, by discovering how we had suffered alike. We often interchanged a few words during the sorrowful hours of the long, hot nights, but our whisperings always turned on the same subject. 'Number Eleven,' I used to hear her poor thin lips murmur, 'are you thinking of your baby, dear?' 'To be sure, darling,' I would answer; 'I am awake, and when I am awake, I am always thinking of her.' Then most times she would inquire, 'Number Eleven, dear, which do you think of most—the little one or her father?' Whereto I would reply, 'I think of both alike, dear, for whenever I look at her, a fair young angel in heaven—she seems to be lying in her father's arms.' And after we had conversed so, No. 22 would be quiet for a few minutes; and often, in the silence of the night, I could at such times hear that which informed me the poor woman was weeping to herself—in such a way that she was happier for her tears.

"But my malady progressed unfavourably. Each succeeding night was worse to endure; and the morning light, instead of bringing refreshment and hope, only gave to me a dull, gloomy consciousness that I had passed hours in delirium, and that I was weaker and heavier in heart, and more unlikely than ever to hold my head up again. They cut all the hair off my head, and put blisters at the back of my neck; but the awful weight of sorrow and the gnawing heat kept on my brain all the same. I could no longer amuse myself with looking at what went on in the ward; I lost all care for the poor woman who lay in the next bed; and soon I tossed to and fro, and heeded nothing of the outer world except the burning, and aching, and thirst, and sleeplessness that encased me.

"One morning I opened my eyes and saw the doctor standing between me and No. 22, talking to the nurse. A fit of clearness passed over my understanding, such as people suffering under fever often experience for a few seconds, and I heard the physician say softly to the nurses, 'We must be careful and do our best, sister, and leave the rest to God. They are both very ill; this is now the fourth day since either of them recognized me. They must have more wine and brandy to help them through. Here, give me their boards.' On this, the nurse took down the boards, and handed them, one after the other, to the physician, and he, taking a pen from a clerk, who always attended him, wrote his directions on the papers, and handed them back to the nurse. Having heard and seen all this, I shifted in my bed, and after a few weak efforts to ponder on my terrible condition, and how awful a thing it is to die, I fell back into my former state of delirium and half-consciousness.

"The next distinct memory I have of my illness was when I opened my eyes and beheld a wooden screen standing between me and the next bed. My head felt as if it had been put into a closely fitting cap of ice; but apart from this strange sensation, I was free from pain. My body was easy, and my mind was tranquil. My nurse was standing at the foot of my bed, looking towards me with an expression of solemn tenderness; and by her side was another woman—as I afterwards found out, a new nurse, unaccustomed to the ways of the hospital.

"'What is that screen there for?' asked the novice.

"My nurse lowered her voice, and answered slowly, 'Number Eleven, poor soul, is dying; she'll be dead in half an hour; and the screen is there so that Number Twenty-Two mayn't see her.'

"'Poor soul!' said the novice, 'may God have mercy upon her!'

"They spoke scarcely above a whisper, but I heard them distinctly; and a solemn gladness, such as I used to feel, when I was a young girl, at the sound of church music, came over me at learning that I was to die. Only half an hour, and I should be with baby and Richard in heaven! Mixed with this thought, too, there was a pleasant memory of those I had loved and who had loved me—of sister Martha and her husband and children, of the doctor who had been so good to me and brought me to the hospital, of my lady in India, of many others; and I silently prayed the Almighty with my dying heart to protect and bless them. Then passed through me a fluttering of strange, soft fancies, and it was revealed to me that I was dead.

"By-and-by the physician came his round of the ward, stepping lightly, pausing at each bed, speaking softly to nurses and patients, and, without knowing it, making many a poor woman entertain kinder thoughts than she had ever meant to cherish of the wealthy and gentle. When he came to the end of the ward, his handsome face wore a pitiful air, and it was more by the movement of his lips than by the sound of his mouth that I knew what passed from him to the nurse.

"'Well, sister, well,' he said, 'she sleeps quietly at last. Poor thing! I hope and believe the next life will be a fairer one for her than this has been.'

"'Her sister has been written to,' observed the nurse.

"'Quite right; and how is the other?'

"'Oh, No. 22 is just the same—quite still, not moving at all, scarcely breathing, sir!'

"'Um!—you must persevere. Possibly she'll pull through. Good-bye, sister.'

"Late in the evening my sister Martha came. She was dressed in black, and led with her hand Rhoda, her eldest daughter. Poor Martha was very pale, and worn, and ill; when she approached the bed on which I lay, she seemed as if she would faint, and she trembled so painfully that my kind nurse led her behind the screen, so that she might recover herself out of my sight. After a few seconds—say two minutes—she stood again at the foot of my bed—calmer, but with tears in her eyes, and such a mournful loveliness in her sweet face as I had never seen before.

"'I shouldn't have known her, nurse,' she said, gazing at me for a short space and then withdrawing her eyes—'she is so much altered.'

"'Ah, dear!' answered the nurse, 'sickness alters people much—and death more.'

"'I know it, nurse—I know it. And she looks very calm and blissful—her face is so full of rest—so full of rest!'

"The nurse fetched some seats, and made Martha and Rhoda sit down side by side; and then the good woman stood by them, ready to afford them all comfort in her power.

"'How did she bear her illness?' inquired Martha.

"'Like an angel, dear,' answered the nurse. 'She had a sweet, grateful, loving temper. Whatever I did for her, even though my duty compelled me to give her pain, she was never fretful, but always concealed her anguish and said, "Thank you, dear, thank you, you are very good; God will reward you for all your goodness"; and as the end came nigher I often fancied that she had reasonable and happy moments, for she would fold her hands together, and say scraps of prayers which children are taught.'

"'Nurse,' replied my sister after a pause, 'she and I were the only children of our father, and we were left orphans very young. She was two years older than I, and she always thought for me and did for me as if she had been my mother. I could fill whole hours with telling you all the goodness and forbearance and love she displayed to me, from the time I was little or no bigger than my child here. I was often wayward and peevish, and gave her many hours of trouble, but though at times she could be hot to others she never spoke an unkind word to me. There was no sacrifice that she would not have made for me; but all the return I ever made was to worry her with my evil jealous temper. I was continually imagining unchristian things against her: that she slighted me; that, because she had a mistress who made much of her, she didn't care for me; that she didn't think my children fit to be proud of. And I couldn't keep all these foolish thoughts in my head to myself, but I must needs go and speak them out to her, and irritate her to quarrel with me. But she always returned smooth words to my angry ones, and I had never a fit of my unjust temper but she charmed me out of it, and showed me my error in such a way that I was reproved, without too much humiliation, and loved her more than ever. Oh! dear friend, dear good nurse, if you have a sister, don't treat her, as I did Abigail, with suspicion and wicked passion; for should you, all the light speeches of your frowardness will return to you, and lie heavy on your heart when hers shall beat no more.'

"When Martha had said this she cried very bitterly; and as I lay dead on my bed, and listened to her unfair self-reproaches, I longed to break the icy bonds that held me, and yearned to clasp her to my breast. Still, though I could neither move nor utter a sound, it thrilled me with gladness to see how she loved me.

"'Mother,' said little Rhoda, softly, 'don't cry. We shan't be long away from Aunt and her baby, for when this life is done we shall go to them. You know, mother, you told me so last night.'

"It was not permitted to me to hear any more. A colder chill came over my brain—and, wrapt in unconsciousness and deep stillness, I lay upon my bed.

"My next recollection is of beholding the gray dawn stream in through the half-opened windows, and of wondering, amid vague reminiscences of my previous sensations, how it was that a dead person could take notice of the world it moved in when alive. It is not enough to say that my experience of the last repose was pleasant to me; I was rejoiced and greatly delighted by it. Death, it seemed then, was no state of cold decay for men to shudder at with affright—but a condition of tranquility and mental comfort. I continued to muse on this remarkable discovery for an hour and more, when my favourite nurse reappeared to relieve the woman who had taken the night-watch, and approached me.

"'Ah!' she surprised me by saying, as a smile of congratulation lighted her face, 'then you are alive this morning, dear, and have your handsome eyes wide open.'

"This in my opinion was a singularly strange and inappropriate address; but I made no attempt to respond to it, for I knew that I was dead. and that the dead do not speak.

"'Why, dear heart,' resumed the nurse, kneeling by my side and kissing me, 'can't you find your tongue? I know by your eyes that you know me; the glassy stare has left them. Come, do say a word, and say you are better.'

"Then a suspicion flashed across my brain, and raising my right hand slightly, I pointed to the bed of No. 22, and asked, 'How is she?—how is she?'

"'Don't frighten yourself, dear,' answered the nurse, 'she isn't there. She has been moved. She doesn't have that bed my longer!'

"'Then it is *she* who is dead, nurse; and all the rest was a dream? It is she who is dead?'

"'Hush, hush, dear! she has gone to rest—'

"Yes! it was all clear to me. Not I but my unfortunate companion had died; and in my delirious fancy I had regarded the friends who came to see her, and convey her to the grave, as my sister Martha and her little daughter Rhoda. I did not impart to the nurse the delusion of which I had been the victim; for, as is often the case with the sick, I was sensitive with regard to the extreme mental sickness into which I had fallen, and the vagaries of my reason. So I kept my secret to the best of my power; and having recognised how much better I was, how the fever had quitted my veins and the weight had left my head, I thanked God in my heart for all his mercies, and once more cherished a hope that he might see fit to restore me to health.

"My recovery was rapid. At the end of a fortnight I was moved into the convalescents' ward, and was fed up with wine and meat in abundance. I had every reason to be thankful for all the kindness bestowed on me in the hospital, and all the good effect God permitted that kindness to have. But one thing troubled me very much and cut me to the quick. Ever since I had been in the hospital my sister had neither been to see me, nor sent to inquire after me. It was no very difficult business to account for her neglect of me. She had her good qualities (even in the height of my anger I could not deny that), but she was of a very proud high temper. She could sacrifice anything but her pride for love of me. I had gone into an hospital, had received public charity, and she hadn't courage to acknowledge a sister who had sunk so low as that! But if she was proud so was I; I could be as high and haughty as she; and, what was more, I would show her that I could be so! What, to leave her own sister—her only sister—who had worked for her when she was little, and who had loved her as her own heart! I would resent it! Perhaps fortune might yet have a turn to make in my favour; and if so I would in my prosperity remember how I had been treated in my adversity. I am filled with shame now, when I think on the revengeful imaginations which followed each other through my breast. I am thankful that when my animosity was at its height my sister did not present herself before me; for had she done so, I fear that, without waiting for an explanation from her, I should have spoken hasty words that (however much I might have afterwards repented them, and she forgiven them) would have rendered it impossible for us to be again the same as we were before. I never mentioned to any one—nurse or patient—in the convalescent ward, the secret of my clouded brows, or let out that I had a friend in the world to think of me or to neglect me. Hour after hour I listened to women and girls and young children, talking of home pleasures and longing to be quite well, and dismissed from the confinement of the hospital, and anticipating the pleasure which their husbands, or mothers, or sisters, or children, would express at welcoming them again; but I never gave a word of such gossip; I only hearkened, and compared their hopes with my desolation, morosely and vindictively. Before I was declared perfectly restored I got very tired of my imprisonment; indeed the whole time I was in the convalescent ward my life was wearisome, and without any of the pleasures which the first days of my sickness had had. There was only one inmate of the ward to which I was at first admitted, as yet, amongst the convalescents; none of them knew me, unless it was by my number—a new one now, for on changing my ward I had changed my number also. The nurses I didn't like so well as my first kind attendant; and I couldn't feel charitably, or in any way as a Christian ought to feel, to the poor people by whom I was surrounded.

"At length the day came for my discharge. The matron inquired of me where I was going; but I would not tell her; I would not acknowledge that I had a sister—partly out of mere perverseness, and partly out of an angry sense of honour; for I was a country-bred woman, and attached to the thought of 'going into a hospital' a certain idea of shame and degradation, such as country people attach to 'going on the parish', and I was too proud to let folk know that my sister had a sister in an hospital, when she clearly flinched from having as much said of her.

"Well, finding I was not in a communicative humour, the matron asked no more questions; but, giving me a bundle containing a few articles of wearing apparel, and a small donation of money, bade me farewell; and without saying half as much in the way of gratitude as I ought to have said, I walked out from the hospital garden into the wide streets of London. I did not go straight to my old lodgings, or to the house of the doctor who had been so kind to me; but I directed my steps to an inn in Holborn, and took a place in the stage-cart for Stratford. As I rode slowly to my sister's town I thought within myself how I should treat her. Somehow my heart had softened a great deal towards her during the few last days; a good spirit within me had set me thinking of how she had helped me to nurse my husband and baby—how she had accompanied me when I followed them to their graves—how she and her husband had sacrificed themselves so much to assist me in my trial; and the recollection of these kindnesses and proofs of sisterly love, I am thankful to know, made me judge Martha much less harshly. Yes! yes! I would forgive her! She had never offended me before! She had not wronged me seven times, or seventy times seven, but only *once*! After all, how much she had done for me! Who was I, that I should forget all that she had done, and judge her only by what she had left undone?

"The stage-cart reached Stratford as the afternoon began to close into evening; and when I alighted from it, I started off at a brisk pace, and walked to my sister's cottage that stood on the outskirts of the town. Strange to say, as I got nearer and nearer to her door my angry feelings became fainter and fainter, and all my loving memories of her strong affection for me worked so in me that my knees trembled beneath me, and my eyes were blinded with tears—though, if I had trusted my deceitful, wicked, malicious tongue to speak, I should still have declared she was a bad, heartless, worthless, sister.

"I reached the threshold, and paused on the step before it, just to get my breath and to collect as much courage and presence of mind as would let Martha know that, though I forgave her, I still was fully aware she might have acted more nobly. When I knocked, after a few seconds, little Rhoda's steps pattered down the passage, and opened the door. Why, the child was in black! What did that mean? Had anything happened to Martha or her husband, or little Tommy? But before I could put the question Rhoda turned deadly white, and ran back into the living-room. In another instant I heard Tommy screaming at the top of his voice; and in a trice

I was in the room, with Martha's arms flung round my neck, and her dear blessed eyes covering me with tears.

"She was very ill in appearance; white and haggard, and, like Rhoda and Tommy, she too was dressed in black. For some minutes she could not speak a word for sobbing hysterically; but when at last I had quieted her and kissed Rhoda, and cossetted Tommy till he had left off screaming, I learnt that the mourning Martha and her children wore was in my honour. Sure enough Martha had received a notice from the hospital of my death; and she and Rhoda had not only presented themselves at the hospital, and seen there a dead body which they believed to be mine, but they had also, with considerable expense, and much more loving care, had it interred in the Stratford churchyard, under the impression that in so doing they were offering me the last respect which it would be in their power to render me. The worst of it was that poor Martha had pined and sorrowed so for me that she seemed likely to fall into some severe illness.

"On inquiry it appeared that the morning when I and No. 22 were so much worse, and the doctor altered the directions of our boards, the nurse by mistake put the No. 22 board over my bed, and my board (No. 11) over the bed of the poor woman who had died. The consequence was that, when the hospital clerk was informed that No. 11 had died, he wrote to the doctor who placed me in the hospital, informing him of my death, and the doctor communicated the sad intelligence to my sister.

"The rest of the story you can fill up, sir, for yourself, and without my assistance you can imagine how it was that, while in a state of extreme exhaustion, and deeming myself dead, I heard my sister, in a strong agony of sorrow and self-reproach, say to my nurse, 'Oh, dear friend—dear good nurse—if you have a sister, don't treat her, as I did Abigail, with suspicion and wicked passion; for should you, all the light speeches of your frowardness will return to you, and lie heavy on your heart when hers shall beat no more.'"

CHAPTER XXVI.
MEDICAL BUILDINGS.

The medical buildings of London are seldom or never visited by the sight-seers of the metropolis. Though the science and art of nursing have recently been made sources of amusement to the patrons of circulating libraries, the good sense and delicacy of the age are against converting the wards of an hospital into galleries for public amusement. In the last century the reverse was the case. Fashionable idlers were not indeed anxious to pry into the mysteries of Bartholomew's, Guy's, and St. Thomas's hospitals; for a visit to those magnificent institutions was associated in their minds with a risk of catching fevers or the disfiguring small-pox. But Bethlehem, devoted to the entertainment and cure of the insane, was a favourite haunt with all classes. "Pepys," "The London Spy," "The Tatler," and "The Rake's Progress," give us vivid pictures of a noisy rout of Pall Mall beaus and belles, country fly-catchers, and London scamps, passing up and down the corridors of the great asylum, mocking its unhappy inmates with brutal jests, or investigating and gossiping about their delusions and extravagances with unfeeling curiosity. Samuel Johnson enlivened himself with an occasional stroll amongst the lunatics, just as he periodically indulged himself with witnessing a hanging, a judicial flogging, or any other of the pleasant spectacles with which Hogarth's London abounded. Boswell and he once strolled through the mansions of the insane; and on another occasion, when he visited the same abode with Murphy, Foote, and Wedderburne (afterwards Lord Loughborough), the philosopher's "attention was arrested by a man who was very furious, and who, while beating his straw, supposed it was William, Duke of Cumberland, whom he was punishing for his cruelties in Scotland in 1746." Steele, when he took three schoolboys (imagine the glee of Sir Richard's schoolboy friends out with him for a frolic) in a hackney coach to show them the town, paid his respects to "the lions, the tombs, Bedlam, and the other places, which are entertainments to raw minds because they strike forcibly on the fancy." In the same way Pepys "stept into Bedlam, and saw several poor miserable creatures in chains, one of whom was *mad with making verses*," a form of mental aberration not uncommon in these days, though we do not deem it necessary to consign the victims of it to medical guardianship.

The original Bethlehem hospital was established by Henry VIII., in a religious house that had been founded in 1246, by Simon Fitz-Mary, Sheriff of London, as an ecclesiastical body. The house was situated at Charing-cross, and very soon the king began to find it (when used for the reception of lunatics) disagreeably near his own residence. The asylum was therefore removed, at a "cost nigh £17,000," to

Bishopgate Without, where it remained till 1814, and the inmates were removed to the present noble hospital in St. George's Fields, the first stone of which was laid April 18th, 1812.

One of the regulations of old Bedlam has long since been disused. The harmless lunatics were allowed to roam about the country with a tin badge—the star of St. Bethlehem—on the right arm. Tenderness towards those to whom the Almighty has denied reason is a sentiment not confined to the East. Wherever these poor creatures went they received alms and kindly entreatment. The ensign on the right arm announced to the world their lamentable condition and their need of help, and the appeal was always mercifully responded to. Aubrey thus describes their appearance and condition:—

"Till the breaking out of the Civil Wars Tom o' Bedlams did travel about the country. They had been poor distracted men, but had been put into Bedlam, where recovering some soberness, they were licentiated to go a-begging, *i. e.* they had on their left arm an armilla of tin, about four inches long; they could not get it off. They wore about their necks a great horn of an ox in a string of baudry, which, when they came to an house for alms, they did wind, and they did put the drink given them into this horn, whereto they did put the stopple. Since the wars I do not remember to have seen any one of them."

The custom, however, continued long after the termination of the Civil War. It is not now the humane practice to label our fools, so that society may at once recognise them and entertain them with kindness. They still go at large in our public ways. Facilities are even given them for effecting an entrance into the learned professions. Frequently they are docketed with titles of respect, and decked with the robes of office. But however gratifying this plan may be to their personal vanity it is not unattended with cruelty. Having about them no external mark of their sad condition, they are often, through carelessness and misapprehension—not through hardness of heart—chastised with undue severity. "Poor Tom, thy horn is dry," says Edgar, in "Lear." Never may the horn of mercy be dry to such poor wretches!

It is needless to say that Easter holiday-makers are no longer permitted in swarms, on the payment of two-pence each, to race through the St. Bethlehem galleries, insulting with their ribaldry the most pitiable of God's afflicted creatures. A useful lesson, however, is taught to the few strangers who still, as merely curious observers, obtain admission for a few minutes within the walls of the asylum—a lesson conveyed, not by the sufferings of the patients, so much as by the gentle discipline, the numerous means of innocent amusement, and the air of quiet contentment, which are the characteristics of a well-managed hospital for the insane.

Not less instructive would it be for many who now know of them only through begging circulars and charity dinners, to inspect the well-ventilated, cleanly—and it may be added, *cheerful*—dwellings of the impoverished sick of London. The principal hospitals of the capital, those, namely, to which medical schools are attached, are eleven in number—St. George's, the London (at Mile End), University College, King's, St. Mary's, Westminster, Middlesex, and Charing-cross, are for the most part dependent on voluntary contributions for support, the Westminster Hospital (instituted 1719) being the first hospital established in this kingdom on the voluntary system. The three other hospitals of the eleven have large endowments, Bartholomew's and Guy's being amongst the wealthiest benevolent foundations of the country.

Like Bethlehem, St. Thomas's Hospital was originally a religious house. At the dissolution of the monasteries it was purchased by the citizens of London, and, in the year 1552, was opened as an hospital for the sick. At the commencement of the last century it was rebuilt by public subscription, three wards being erected at the cost of Thomas Frederick, and three by Guy, the founder of Guy's Hospital.

The first place of precedency amongst the London Hospitals is contended for by St. Bartholomew's and Guy's. They are both alike important by their wealth, the number of patients entertained within their walls, and the celebrity of the surgeons and physicians with whom their schools have enriched the medical profession; but the former, in respect of antiquity, has superior claims to respect. Readers require no introduction to the founder of Bartholomew's, for only lately Dr. Doran, in his "Court Fools," gave a sketch of Rahere—the minstrel and jester, who spent his prime in the follies and vices of courts, and his riper years in the sacred offices of the religious vocation. He began life a buffoon, and ended it a prior—presiding over the establishment to the creation of which he devoted the wealth earned by his abused wit. The monk chronicler says of him: "When he attained the flower of youth he began to haunt the households of noblemen and the palaces of princes; where, under every elbow of them, he spread their cushions with apeings and flatterings, delectably anointing their eyes—by this manner to draw to him their friendships. And yet he was not content with this, but often haunted the king's palace; and, among the press of that tumultuous court, enforced himself with jollity and carnal suavity, by the which he might draw to him the hearts of many one." But the gay adventurer found that the ways of mirth were far from those of true gladness; and, forsaking quips, and jeers, and wanton ditties for deeds of mercy, and prayer, and songs of praise, he long was an ensample unto men of holy living; and "after the years of his prelacy (twenty-two years and six months), the 20th day of September (A. D. 1143), the clay-house of this world forsook, and the house everlasting entered."

In the church of St. Bartholomew may still be seen the tomb of Dr. Francis Anthony, who, in spite of the prosecutions of the College of Physicians, enjoyed a large practice, and lived in pomp in Bartholomew Close, where he died in 1623. The merits of his celebrated nostrum, the *aurum potabile*, to which Boyle gave a reluctant and qualified approval, are alluded to in the inscription commemorating his services:—

> "There needs no verse to beautify thy praise,
> Or keep in memory thy spotless name.
> Religion, virtue, and thy skill did raise
> A three-fold pillar to thy lasting fame.
>
> Though poisonous envy ever sought to blame

Or hide the fruits of thy intention,
Yet shall all they commend that high design
Of purest gold to make a medicine,
That feel thy help by that thy rare invention."

Boyle's testimony to the good results of the *aurum potabile* is interesting, as his philosophic mind formed a decided opinion on the efficacy of the preparation by observing its operation in *two* cases—persons of great note. "Though," he says, "I have long been prejudiced against the *aurum potabile*, and other boasted preparations of gold, for most of which I have no great esteem, yet I saw such extraordinary and surprising effects from the tincture of gold I spake of (prepared by two foreign physicians) upon persons of great note, with whom I was particularly acquainted, both before they fell sick and after their dangerous recovery, that I could not but change my opinion for a very favourable one as to some preparations of gold."

Attached to his priory of St. Bartholomew's, Rahere founded an hospital for the relief of poor and sick persons, out of which has grown the present institution, over the principal gateway of which stands, burly and with legs apart—like a big butcher watching his meat-stall—an effigy of Henry VIII. Another of the art treasures of the hospital is the staircase painted by Hogarth.

If an hospital could speak it could tell strange tales—of misery slowly wrought, ambition foiled, and fair promise ending in shame. Many a toilworn veteran has entered the wards of St. Bartholomew's to die in the very couch by the side of which in his youth he daily passed—a careless student, joyous with the spring of life, and little thinking of the storm and unkind winds rising up behind the smiles of the nearer future. Scholars of gentle birth, brave soldiers of proud lineage, patient women whose girlhood, spent in luxury and refinement, has been followed by penury, evil entreatment, and destitution, find their way to our hospitals—to pass from a world of grief to one where sorrow is not. It is not once in awhile, but daily, that a physician of any large charitable institution of London reads a pathetic tale of struggle and defeat, of honest effort and bitter failure, of slow descent from grade to grade of misfortune—in the tranquil dignity, the mild enduring quiet, and noiseless gratitude of poor sufferers—gentle once in fortune, gentle still in nature. One hears unpleasant stories of medical students, their gross dissipations and coarse manners. Possibly these stories have their foundation in fact, but at best they are broad and unjust caricatures. This writer in his youth lived much amongst the students of our hospitals, as he did also amongst those of our old universities, and he found them simple and manly in their lives, zealous in the pursuit of knowledge, animated by *a professional esprit* of the best sort, earnestly believing in the dignity of their calling, and characterised by a singular ever-lively compassion for all classes of the desolate and distressed. And this quality of mercy, which unquestionably adorns in an eminent degree the youth of our medical schools, he has always regarded as a happy consequence of their education, making them acquainted, in the most practical and affecting manner, with the sad vicissitudes of human existence.

Guy's hospital was the benevolent work of a London bookseller, who, by perseverance, economy, and lucky speculation, amassed a very large fortune. Thomas Guy began life with a stock of about £200, as a stationery and bookseller in a little corner house between Cornhill and Lombard-st., taking out his freedom of the Stationers' Company in 1668. He was a thrifty tradesman, but he won his wealth rather by stock-jobbing than by the sale of books, although he made important sums by his contract with the University of Oxford for their privilege of printing bibles. Maitland informs us, "England being engaged in an expensive war against France, the poor seamen on board the royal navy, for many years, instead of money received tickets for their pay, which those necessitous but very useful men were obliged to dispose of at thirty, forty, and sometimes fifty in the hundred discount. Mr. Guy, discovering the sweets of this traffick, became an early dealer therein, as well as in other government securities, by which, and his trade, he acquired a very great estate." In the South-sea stock he was not less lucky. He bought largely at the outset, held on till the bubble reached its full size, and ere the final burst sold out. It may be questioned whether Guy's or Rahere's money was earned the more honourably,—whether to fawn, flatter, and jest at the table of princes was a meaner course of exertion than to drive a usurious trade with poor sailors, and fatten on a stupendous national calamity. But however basely it may have been gathered together, Guy's wealth was well expended, in alleviating the miseries of the same classes from whose sufferings it had been principally extracted. In his old age Guy set about building his hospital, and ere his death, in 1724, saw it completed. On its erection and endowment he expended £238,292 16s. 5d. To his honour it must be stated that, notwithstanding this expenditure and his munificent contributions to other charities, he had a considerable residue of property, which he distributed amongst his poor relations.

Of the collegiate medical buildings of London, the one that belongs to the humblest department of the profession is the oldest, and for that reason—apart from its contents, which are comparatively of little value—the most interesting. Apothecaries' Hall, in Water Lane, Blackfriars, was built in 1670. Possibly the size and imposing aspect of their college stimulated the drug-vendors to new encroachments on the prescriptive and enacted rights of the physicians. The rancour of "The Dispensary" passes over the merits (graces it has none) of the structure, and designates it by mentioning its locality—

> "Nigh where Fleet Ditch descends in sable streams,
> To wash his sooty Naiads in the Thames,
> There stands a structure on a rising hill,
> Where tyros take their freedom out to kill."

Amongst the art-treasures of the hall are a portrait of James I. (who first established the apothecaries as a company distinct from the grocers), and a bust of Delaune, the lucky apothecary of that monarch's queen, who has already been mentioned in these pages.

The elegant college of the physicians, in Pall Mall east, was not taken into use till the 25th of June, 1825, the doctors migrating to it from Warwick Hall, which is now in the occupation of the butchers of Newgate Market. Had the predecessors of the present tenants been "the surgeons," instead of "the physicians," the change of masters would have given occasion for a joke. As it is, not even the consolation of a jest can be extracted from the desecration of an abode of learning that has many claims on our affection.

In "The Dispensary," the proximity of the college dome to the Old Bailey is playfully pointed at:—

> "Not far from that most celebrated place,
> Where angry justice shows her awful face,
> Where little villains must submit to fate,
> That great ones may enjoy the world in state,
> There stands a dome, majestic to the sight,
> And sumptuous arches bear its oval height;
> A golden globe, placed high with artful skill,
> Seems, to the distant sight, a gilded pill:
> This pile was, by the pious patron's aim,
> Raised for a use as noble as its frame.
> Nor did the learn'd society decline
> The propagation of that great design;
> In all her mazes, Nature's face they view'd,
> And, as she disappear'd, their search pursued.
> Wrapt in the shade of night, the goddess lies,
> Yet to the learn'd unveils her dark disguise,
> But shuns the gross access of vulgar eyes."

The Warwick Lane college was erected on the college at Amen Corner (to which the physicians removed on quitting their original abode in Knight-Rider Street), being burnt to the ground in the great fire of 1666. Charles II. and Sir John Cutler were ambitious of having their names associated with the new edifice, the chief fault of which was that, like all the other restorations following the memorable conflagration, it was raised near the old site. Charles became its pious patron, and Sir John Cutler its munificent benefactor. The physicians duly thanked them, and honoured them with statues, Cutler's effigy having inscribed beneath it, "Omnis Cutleri cedat labor Amphitheatro."

So far, so good. The fun of the affair remains to be told. On Sir John's death, his executors, Lord Radnor and Mr. Boulter, demanded of the college £7000, which covered in amount a sum the college had borrowed of their deceased benefactor, and also the sum he pretended to have given. Eventually the executors lowered their claim to £2000 (which, it is reasonable to presume, had been *lent* by Sir John), and discontinued their demand for the £5000 given. Such being the stuff of which Sir John was made, well might Pope exclaim:—

> "His Grace's fate sage Cutler could foresee,
> And well (he thought) advised him, 'Live like me.'
> As well his Grace replied, 'Like you, Sir John?
> That I can do when all I have is gone.'"

In consideration of the £5000 retained of the niggard's money, the physicians allowed his statue to remain, but they erased the inscription from beneath it.

The Royal College of Surgeons in London was not incorporated till the year 1800—more than half a century after the final disruption of the surgeons from the barbers—and the college in Lincoln's Inn Fields was not erected till 1835. Its noble museum, based on the Hunterian Collection, which the nation purchased for £15,000, contains, amongst its treasures, a few preparations that are valuable for their historical associations or sheer eccentricity, rather than for any worth from a strictly scientific point of view. Amongst them are Martin Van Buchell's first wife, whose embalmment by William Hunter has already been mentioned; the intestines of Napoleon, showing the progress of the disease which was eventually fatal to him; and the fore-arms (preserved in spirits) of Thomas Beaufort, third son of John of Gaunt, Duke of Lancaster.

The writer had recently submitted to his notice, by Dr. Diamond of Twickenham, a very interesting and beautifully penned manuscript, relating to these remains, of which the following is a copy:—

"Bury St Edmunds.

"Joseph Pater scripsit, when thirteen years of age.

"On the 20th of February, 1772, some labourers, employed in breaking up part of the old abbey church, discovered a leaden coffin, which contained an embalmed body, as perfect and entire as at the time of its death; the features and lineaments of the face were perfect, which were covered with a mask of embalming materials. The very colour of the eyes distinguishable; the hairs of the head a brown, intermixed with some few gray ones; the nails fast upon the fingers and toes as when living; stature of the body about six feet tall, and genteelly formed. The labourers, for the sake of the lead (which they sold to Mr Faye, a plummer, in this town, for about 15s), stript the body of its coffin, and threw it promiscuously amongst the rubbish. From the place of its interment it was soon found to be the remains of Thomas Beaufort, third son of John de Gaunt, Duke of Lancaster, by his third duchess, Lady Catherine Swineford, relict of Sir Otho de Swineford, of Lincolnshire. He took the name of Beaufort from the place of his birth, a castle of the duke's, in France. He was half-brother to King Henry IV., created Duke of Exeter and Knight of the Garter; in 1410, Lord Chancellor of England; in 1412, High Admiral of England, and Captain of Calais; he commanded the Rear-Guard of his nephew King Henry the Fifth's army at the battle of Agincourt, on the 25th of October, 1415; and in 1422, upon the death of King Henry the Fifth, was jointly with his brother, Henry, Cardinal Bishop of Winchester, appointed by the Parliament to the government, care, and education of the royal infant, Henry the Sixth. He married Margaret, daughter of Sir Thomas Nevil, by whom he had issue only one son, who died young. He was a great benefactor to this church, died at East Greenwich, 1427, in the 5th year of King Henry ye Sixth, and was interred in this Abbey, near his duchess (as he had by his will directed), at the entrance of the Chapel of our Lady, close to the wall. On the 24th of February following, the mangled remains were enclosed in an oak coffin, and buried about eight feet deep, close to the north side of the north-east pillar, which formerly assisted to support the Abbey belfry. Before its re-interment, the body was mangled and cut with the most savage barbarity by Thomas Gery Cullum, a young surgeon in this town, lately appointed

Bath King-at-Arms. The skull sawed in pieces, where the brain appeared it seemed somewhat wasted, but perfectly contained in its proper membranes; the body ript open from the neck to the bottom, the cheek cut through by a saw entering at the mouth; his arms chopped off below the elbows and taken away. One of the arms the said Cullum confesses to have in spirits. The crucifix, supposed to be a very valuable one, is missing. It is believed the body of the duchess was found (within about a foot of the Duke's) on the 24th of February. If she was buried in lead she was most likely conveyed away clandestinely the same night. In this church several more of the antient royal blood were interred, whose remains are daily expected to share the same fate. Every sensible and humane mind reflects with horror at the shocking and wanton inhumanity with which the princely remains of the grandson of the victorious King Edward the Third have been treated—worse than the body of a common malefactor, and 345 years after his death. The truth of this paragraph having been artfully suppressed, or very falsely represented in the county newspapers, and the conveyance of public intelligence rendered doubtful, no method could be taken to convey a true account to the public but by this mode of offering it."

The young surgeon whose conduct is here so warmly censured was the younger son of a Suffolk baronet. On the death of his brother he succeeded to the family estate and honours, and having no longer any necessity to exert himself to earn money, relinquished medical practice. He was born in 1741 and died in 1831. It is from him that the present baronet, of Hawstead Place and Hardwicke House, in the county of Suffolk, is descended.

The fore-arms, now in the custody of the College of Surgeons, were for a time separated. One of them was retained by Mr. Cullum, and the other, becoming the property of some mute inglorious Barnum, was taken about to all the fairs and wakes of the county, and exhibited as a raree-show at a penny a peep. The vagrant member, however, came back after a while to Mr. Cullum, and he presented both of the mutilated pertions to their present possessors.

CHAPTER XXVII.

THE COUNTRY MEDICAL MAN.

The country doctor, such as we know him—a well-read and observant man, skilful in his art, with a liberal love of science, and in every respect a gentleman—is so recent a creation, that he may almost be spoken of as a production of the present century. There still linger in the provinces veteran representatives of the ignorance which, in the middle of the last century, was the prevailing characteristic of the rural apothecary. Even as late as 1816, the law required no medical education in a practitioner of the healing art in country districts, beyond an apprenticeship to an empiric, who frequently had not information of any kind, beyond the rudest elements of a druggist's learning, to impart to his pupils. Men who commenced business under this system are still to be found in every English county, though in most cases they endeavour to conceal their lack of scientific culture under German or Scotch diplomas—bought for a few pounds.

Scattered over these pages are many anecdotes of provincial doctors in the sixteenth and seventeenth centuries, from which a truthful but not complimentary picture of their order may be obtained. Indeed, they were for the most part vulgar drunken knaves, with just learning enough to impose on the foolish crowds who resorted to them. The most brilliant of the fraternity in Henry the Eighth's reign was Andrew Borde, a Winchester practitioner. This gentleman was author and buffoon, as well as physician. He travelled about the country from market to fair, and from fair to market, making comic orations to the crowds who purchased his nostrums, singing songs, and enlivening the proceedings when they were becoming dull with grimaces of inexpressible drollery. It was said of Sir John Hill,

> "For physic and farces
> His equal there scarce is;
> His farces are physic,
> His physic a farce is."

Borde's physic doubtless was a farce; but if his wit resembled physic, it did so, not (like Hill's) by making men sick, but by rousing their spirits and bracing their nerves with good hearty laughter. Everywhere he was known as "Merry Andrew," and his followers, when they mounted the bank, were proud to receive the same title.

Mr. H. Fleetwood Sheppard communicated in the year 1855, some amusing anecdotes to "Notes and Queries" about the popular Dorsetshire doctor—little Dr. Grey. Small but warlike, this gentleman, in the reign of James the First, had a following of well-born roisterers that enabled him to beard the High Sheriff at the assizes. He was always in debt, but as he always carried a brandy-flask and a brace of loaded pistols in his pocket or about his neck, he neither experienced the mental harass of impecuniosity nor feared bailiffs. In the hour of peril he blew a horn, which he wore suspended to his person, and the gentlemen of his body-guard rallied round him, vowing they were his "sons," and would die for him. Says the MS.—"This Doctor Grey was once arreste by a pedler, who coming to his house knocked at ye dore as yey (he being desirous of Hobedyes) useth to doe, and ye pedler having gartars upon his armes, and points, &c., asked him whether he did wante any points or gartars, &c., pedler like. Grey hereat began to storme, and ye other tooke him by ye arme, and told him that he had no neede be so angry, and holdinge him fast, told him y he had ye kinge's proces for him, and showed him his warrant. 'Hast thou?' quoth Grey, and stoode stil awhile; but at length, catchinge ye fellowe by both ends of his collar before, held him fast, and *drawinge out a great rundagger, brake his head in two or three places.*"

Again, Dr. Grey "came one day at ye assizes, wheare ye sheriffe had some sixty men, and he wth his twenty sonnes, ye trustyest young gentlemen and of ye best sort and rancke, came and drancke in Dorchester before ye sheriffe, and bad who dare to touch him; *and so after awhile blew his horn and came away.*" On the same terms who would not like to be a Dorsetshire physician?

In 1569 (*vide* "Roberts' History of the Southern Counties") Lyme had no medical practitioner. And at the beginning of the seventeenth century Sir Symonds D'Ewes was brought into the world at Coxden Hall, near Axminster, by a female practitioner, who deformed him for life by her clumsiness. Yet more, Mrs. D'Ewes set out with her infant for London, when the babe, unable to bear the jolting of the carriage, screamed itself into a violent illness, and had to be left behind at Dorchester under the care of another doctress—Mrs. Margaret Waltham. And two generations later, in 1665, the Rev. Giles Moore, of Essex, had to send twenty-five miles for an ordinary medical man, who was paid 12s. per visit, and the same distance for a physician, whose fee was £1—a second physician, who came and stayed two days, being paid £1 10s.

Of the country doctors of the middle and close of the last century, Dr. Slop is a fair specimen. They were a rude, vulgar, keen-witted set of men, possessing much the same sort of intelligence, and disfigured by the same kind of ignorance, as a country gentleman expects now to find in his farrier. They had to do battle with the village nurses at the best on equal terms, often at a disadvantage; masculine dignity and superior medical erudition being in many districts of less account than the force of old usage, and the sense of decorum that supported the lady practitioners. Mrs. Shandy had an express provision in her marriage settlement, securing her from the ignorance of country doctors. Of course, in respect to learning and personal acquirements, the rural practitioners, as a class, varied very much, in accordance with the intelligence and culture of the district in which their days were spent, with the class and character of their patients, and with their own connections and original social condition. On his Yorkshire living Sterne came in contact with a rought lot. The Whitworth Taylors were captains and leaders of the army in which Dr. Slop was a private. The original of the last-mentioned worthy was so ill-read that he mistook Lithopædii Senonensis Icon for the name of a distinguished surgical authority, and, under this erroneous impression, quoted Lithopædus Senonensis with the extreme of gravity.

This Lithopædus Senonensis story is not without its companions. A prescription, in which a physician ordered *extract, rad valer.*, and immediately under it, as an ingredient in the same mixture, a certain quantity of *tinctura ejusdem*, sorely perplexed the poor apothecary to who it was sent to be dispensed. *Tinctura ejusdem!* What could it be! *Ejusdem!* In the whole pharmacopoeia such a drug was not named. Nothing like it was to be found on any label in his shop. At his wits' end, the poor fellow went out to a professional neighbour, and asked, in an off-hand way, "How are you off for *Tinctura Ejusdem*? I am out of it. So can you let me have a little of yours." The neighbour, who was a sufficiently good classical scholar to have *idem, eadem, idem* at his tongue's end, lamented that he too was "out of the article." and sympathizingly advised his *confrère*, without loss of time, to apply for some at Apothecaries' Hall. What a delightful blunder to make to a *friend*, of all the people in the world! The apothecary must have been a dull as well as an unlettered fellow, or he would have known the first great rule of his art—"When in doubt—*Use water!*" A more awkward mistake still was that made by the young dispenser, who, for the first time in his life, saw at the end of a prescription the words *pro re natâ*. What could they mean? *pro re natâ!* What could *pro re natâ* have to do with a mixture sent to a lady who had just presented her husband with an heir. With the aid of a Latin Dictionary, the novice rendered *pro re natâ* "for the thing born." Of course. Clearly the mixture was for the baby. And in a trice the compound to be taken by an adult, as circumstances should indicate a necessity for a dose, was sent off for the "little stranger."

May not mention here be made of thee, ancient friend of childhood, Roland Trevor? The whole country round, for a circle of which the diameter measured thirty fair miles, thou wert one of the most popular doctors of East Anglia. Who rode better horses? Who was the bolder in the hunt, or more joyous over the bottle? Cheery of voice, with hearty laughter rolling from purple lips, what company thou wert to festive squires! The grave some score years since closed over thee, when ninety-six years had passed over thy head—covering it with silver tresses, and robbing the eye of its pristine fire, and the lip of its mirthful curl. The shop of a country apothecary had been thy only *Alma Mater*; so, surely, it was no fault of thine if thy learning was scanty. Still, in the pleasant vales of Loes and Wilford is told the story of how, on being asked if thou wert a believer in *phrenology*, thou didst answer with becoming gravity, "I never keep it, and I never use it. But I think it highly probable that, given frequently and in liberal doses, it would be very useful in certain cases of irregular gout."

Another memory arises of a country doctor of the old school. A huge, burly, surly, churlish old fellow was Dr. Standish. He died in extremely advanced age, having lived twenty-five years in the present century. A ferocious radical, he was an object of considerable public interest during the period of political excitement consequent on the French Revolution. Tom Paine, the Thetford breeches-maker of whom the world has heard a little, was his familiar friend and correspondent. It was rumoured throughout the land that "government" had marked the doctor out for destruction.

"Thar sai," the humbler Suffolk farmers used to gossip amongst themselves, "thar sai a picter-taikin chap hav guv his poortright to the King. And Billy Pitt ha'sin it. And oold King Georgie ha' swaren as how that sooner nor later he'll hav his hid" (*i. e.* head).

The "upper ten" of Holmnook, and the upper ten-times-ten of the distance round about Holmnook, held themselves aloof from such a dangerous character. But the common folk believed in and admired him. There was something of romance about a man whom George III. and Billy Pitt were banded together to destroy.

Standish was a man of few words. "Down with the bishops!" "Up with the people!" were his stock sentiments. He never approached nearer poetry than when (yellow being then the colour of the extreme liberal party in his district) he swore "there worn't a flower in the who' o' crashun warth lookin' at but a sunflower, for that was yallow, and a big un."

The man had no friends in Holmnook or the neighbourhood; but every evening for fifty years he sate, in the parlour of the chief inn, drinking brandy-and-water, and smoking a "churchwarden." His wife—(his wooing must have been of a queer sort)—a quiet, inoffensive little body, sometimes forgot she was but a woman, and presumed to have an opinion of her own. On such occasions Standish thrashed her soundly with a dog-whip. In consequence of one of these castigations she ran away from her tyrant. Instead of pursuing her, Dr. Standish merely inserted the following advertisement in the county paper:—

"*Dr Standish to all whom it may concern.*—Dr Standish's wife having run away, he wants a housekeeper. Dr Standish doesn't want good looks in a woman: but she must know how to hold her tongue and cook a plain joint. He gives ten pounds. Mrs Standish needn't apply—she's too much of a lady."

But poor Mrs. Standish did apply, and, what is more, obtained the situation. She and her lord never again had any quarrel that obtained publicity; and so the affair ended more happily than in all probability it would have done had Sir Creswell Creswell's court been then in existence. Standish's practice lay principally amongst the mechanics and little farmers of the neighborhood. Much of his time was therefore spent in riding his two huge lumbering horses about the country. In his old age he indulged himself in a gig (which, out of respect to radical politics, he painted with a flaring yellow paint); but, at the commencement of the present century, the by-roads of Suffolk—now so good that a London brougham drawn by one horse can with ease whisk over the worst of them at the rate of ten miles an hour—were so bad that a doctor could not make an ordinary round on them in a wheeled carriage. Even in the saddle he ran frequent risk of being mired, unless his horse had an abundance of bone and pluck.

Standish's mode of riding was characteristic of the man. Straight on he went, at a lumbering six miles an hour trot—dash, dosh, dush!—through the muddy roads, sitting loosely in his seat, heavy and shapeless as a sack of potatoes, looking down at his brown corduroy breeches and his mahogany top-boots (the toes of which pointed in directly opposite directions), wearing a perpetual scowl on his brows, and never either rising in his stirrups or fixing himself to the saddle with his knees. Not a word would he speak to a living creature in the way of civil greeting.

"Doctor, good morning to you," an acquaintance would cry out; "'tis a nice day!"

"Ugh!" Standish would half grunt, half roar, trotting straight on—dish, dosh, dush!

"Stop, doctor, I am out of sorts, and want some physic," would be the second form of address.

"Then why the — — — — didn't you say so, instead of jawing about the weather?" the urbane physician would say, checking his horse.

Standish never turned out an inch for any wayfarer. Sullen and overbearing, he rode straight on upon one side of the road; and, however narrow the way might be, he never swerved a barley-corn from his line for horse or rider, cart or carriage. Our dear friend Charley Halifax gave him a smart lesson in good manners on this point. Charley had brought a well-bred hackney, and a large fund of animal spirits, down from Cambridge to a title for orders in mid-Suffolk. He had met Standish in the cottages of some of his flock, and afterwards meeting elsewhere, had greeted him, and had no greeting in return. It was not long ere Charley learnt all about the clownish apothecary, and speedily did he devise a scheme for humbling him. The next time he saw Standish in the distance, trotting on towards him, Charley put his heels to his horse, and charged the man of drugs at full gallop. Standish came lumbering on, disdaining to look before him and ascertain who was clattering along at such a pace. On arriving within six feet of Standish's horse, Halifax fell back on his curb-rein, and pulled up sharp. Astonished, but more sensible than his master, Standish's horse (as Charley knew would be the case) suddenly came to a dead stop, on which Standish rolled over its head into the muddy highway. As he rolled over, he threw out a volley of oaths. "Ah, doctor," cried Charley, good-humoredly, "I said I would make you speak to me." Standish was six feet high, and a powerful man. For a few moments, on recovering his legs, he looked as if he contemplated an assault on the young parson. But he thought better of it; and, climbing into his seat once more, trotted on, without another word—dish, dosh, dush! The incident didn't tend to soften his feelings toward the Established Church.

The country doctor of the last century always went his rounds on horseback booted and spurred. The state of the roads rendered any other mode of travelling impracticable to men who had not only to use the highways and coach-roads, but to make their way up bridle-paths, and drifts, and lanes, to secluded farmsteads and outlying villages. Even as late as the last generation, in Suffolk, where now people drive to and fro at the rate of twelve miles an hour, a doctor (whom the writer of these pages has reason to think of with affection) was more than once mired, on a slightly-built blood horse, so effectually, that he had to dismount ere the animal could be extricated; and this happened in roads that at the present time are, in all seasons, firm as a garden walk.

Describing the appearance of a country doctor of this period, a writer observes—"When first I saw him, it was on Frampton Green. I was somewhat his junior in years, and had heard so much of him that I had no small curiosity to see him. He was dressed in a blue coat and yellow buttons, buckskins, well-polished jockey-boots, with handsome silver spurs, and he carried a smart whip with a silver handle. His hair, after the fashion, was done up in a club, and he wore a broad-brimmed hat." Such was the appearance of Jenner, as he galloped across the vale of Gloucester, visiting his patients. There is little to remind us of such a personage as this in the statue in Trafalgar Square, which is the slowly-offered tribute of our gratitude to Edward Jenner for his imperishable services to mankind. The opposition that Jenner met with in his labours to free our species from a hideous malady that, destroying life and obliterating beauty, spared neither the cottage nor the palace, is a subject on which it is painful to reflect. The learned of his own profession and the vulgar of all ranks combined to persecute and insult him; and when the merit of his inestimable discovery was acknowledged by all intelligent persons, he received from his country a remuneration that was little better than total neglect.

While acting as an apprentice to a country surgeon he first conceived the possibility of checking the ravages of small-pox. A young servant woman, who accidentally said that she was guarded from that disease by having "had cow-pox," first apprized him that amongst the servants of a rural population a belief existed that the virus from the diseased cow, on being absorbed by the human system, was a preventive against small-pox. From that time, till the ultimate success of his inquiries, he never lost sight of the subject.

The ridicule and misrepresentation to which he was subjected are at this date more pleasant for us to laugh at than, at the time, they were for him to bear. The ignorant populace of London was instructed that people, on being vaccinated, ran great risks of being converted into members of the bovine family. The appearance of hair covering the whole body, of horns and a tail, followed in many cases the operation. The condition of an unhappy child was pathetically described, who, brutified by vaccine ichor, persisted in running on all-fours and roaring like a bull. Dr. Woodville and Dr. Moseley opposed Jenner, the latter with a violence that little became a scientific inquirer. Numerous were the squibs and caricatures the controversy called forth. Jenner was represented as riding on a cow—an animal certainly not adapted to show the doctor ("booted and spurred" as we have just seen him) off to the best advantage. Of Moseley the comic muse sung:

> "Oh, Moseley! thy book, nightly phantasies rousing,
> Full oft makes me quake for my heart's dearest treasure;
> For fancy, in dreams, oft presents them all browsing
> On commons, just like little Nebuchadnezzar.
> *There*, nibbling at thistle, stand Jem, Joe, and Mary,
> On their foreheads, O horrible! crumpled horns bud:
> There Tom with his tail, and poor William all hairy,
> Reclined in a corner, are chewing the cud."

If London was unjust to him, the wiseacres of Gloucestershire thought that burning was his fit punishment. One dear old lady, whenever she saw him leaving his house, used to run out and attack him with indescribable vivacity. "So your book," cried this charming matron, in genuine Gloucestershire dialect, "is out at last. Well! I can tell you that there bean't a copy sold in our town, nor shan't neither, if I can help it." On hearing, subsequent to the publication of the book (a great offence to the old lady!), some rumours of vaccination failures, the same goodie bustled up to the doctor and cried, with galling irony, "Shan't us have a general inoculation now?"

But Jenner was compensated for this worthy woman's opposition in the enthusiastic support of Rowland Hill, who not only advocated vaccination in his ordinary conversation, but from the pulpit used to say, after his sermon to his congregation, wherever he preached, "I am ready to vaccinate to-morrow morning as many children as you choose; and if you wish them to escape that horrid disease, the small-pox, you will bring them." A Vaccine Board was also established at the Surrey Chapel—*i. e.* the Octagon Chapel, in Blackfriars Road.

"My Lord," said Rowland Hill once to a nobleman, "allow me to present to your Lordship my friend, Dr. Jenner, who has been the means of saving more lives than any other man."

"Ah!" observed Jenner, "would that I, like you, could say—souls."

There was no cant in this. Jenner was a simple, unaffected, and devout man. His last words were, "I do not marvel that men are grateful to me, but I am surprised that they do not feel gratitude to God for making me a medium of good."

Of Jenner's more sprightly humour, the following epigrams from his pen (communicated to the writer of these pages by Dr. E. D. Moore of Salop), are good specimens.

"TO MY SPANISH CIGAR.

"Soother of an anxious hour!
Parent of a thousand pleasures!
With gratitude I owe thy power
And place thee 'mongst my choicest treasures.
Thou canst the keenest pangs disarm
Which care obtrudes upon the heart;
At thy command, my little charm,
Quick from the bosom they depart."

"ON THE DEATH OF JOHN AND BETTY COLE.

"Why, neighbours, thus mournfully sorrow and fret?
Here lie snug and cosy old John and his Bet;
Your sighing and sobbing ungodly and rash is,
For two knobs of coal that have now gone to ashes."

"ON MISS JENNER AND MISS EMILY WORTHINGTON TEARING THE
"GLOBE" NEWSPAPER.

"The greatest curse that hath a name
Most certainly from woman came.
Two of the sex the other night—
Well arm'd with talons, venom, spite,—
Pull'd caps, you say?—a great wonder!
By Jove, they pull'd the globe asunder!"

Dr. Jenner was very fond of scribbling *currente calamo* such verses as these. The following specimens of his literary prowess have, we believe, never before been published.

HANNAH BALL.—A SONG.

"Farewell, ye dear lasses of town and of city,
Sweet ladies, adieu to you all!
Don't show a frown, though I tune up a ditty
In praise of fair Hannah Ball.

"T'other eve, as I rambled her snug cottage by,
Sly Cupid determined my fall,
The rogue, 'stead of darts, shot the beams of her eye,
The eye of my fair Hannah Ball.

"So sweetly she look'd, when attired so fine,
In her Dunstable hat and her shawl,
Enraptured I cried—''Tis a Goddess divine.'
'No indeed'—she replied—'Hannah Ball.'

"The bosom of Delia, tho' whiter than snow,
Is no more than black velvet pall—
Compared with my Hannah's—I'd have you to know—
The bosom of fair Hannah Ball.

"The honey the bee from her jessamine sips
You'd swear was as bitter as gall,
Could you taste but the sweets that exhale from the lips,
From the lips of the fair Hannah Ball.

"What's rouge, or carmine, or the blush of the rose?
Why, dead as the lime on the wall,
Compared with the delicate colour that glows
On the cheek of my fair Hannah Ball.

"When David melodiously play'd to appease
The troubled emotions of Saul,
Were his sounds more enchanting—ah, tell me, than these?
'Hannah Ball, oh! the fair Hannah Ball.'

"Near yonder fair copse as I pensively rove
In an eve, when the dews 'gin to fall;

To my sighs how kind echo responds from the grove—
'Hannah Ball, oh! the fair Hannah Ball.'

"With graces so winning see Rossi advance
But what's all his grace?—Why a sprawl—
With my Hannah compared, as she skims through the dance—
The lovely, the fair Hannah Ball.

"The song of the Mara—tho' great is her skill,
Believe me's no more than a squall,
Compared with the rapturous magical trill
Of my charming, my fair Hannah Ball.

"For oft in the meads at the close of the day,
Near yon murmuring rivulet's fall,
Have I heard the soft nightingale's soul-piercing lay,
And thought 'twas my fair Hannah Ball.

"To her eyes in Love's language I've told a soft tale,
But, alas! they replied not at all;
Yet bashfulness oft will our passions conceal;
Oh! the modest, the fair Hannah Ball.

"Ye Gods! would you make the dear creature my wife,
With thanks would I bow to you all;
How smoothly would then run the wheels of my life,
With my charming, my fair Hannah Ball.

"But should my petition be flung from the skies,
I'll take the bare bodkin or awl;
Yes! the cold seal of Death shall be fix'd on my eyes,—
What's Life without fair Hannah Ball."

This is a happy little satire on a vilage scandal. The Methodist parson and Roger were amongst the doctor's rustic neighbours.

On a quarrel between Butler, the Methodist parson of Frampton, and Roger his clerk. Butler accused the clerk of stealing his liquors, and the clerk accused Butler of stealing his bacon.

"Quoth good parson Butler to Rogers his clerk,
'How things come to light that are done in the dark!
My wine is all pilfer'd,—a sad piece of work,—
But a word with thee, Richard—I see thou'rt no Turk.'

"'What evil befall us!'—quoth Dick in reply,
Whilst contempt methodistical glanced from his eye,—
'My bacon's slipt off too—alas, sir! 'tis true,
And the fact seems to whisper that—you are no Jew.'"

The most daring of Jenner's epigrams, out of the scores that we have perused, is the following—

ON READING ADAM SMITH.

"The priests may exclaim against cursing and swearing,
And tell us such things are quite beyond bearing;
But 'tis clear as the day their denouncing's a sham;
For a thousand good things may be learnt from *Adam*."

Babbage, in his "Decline of Science in England," has remarked that "some of the most valuable names which adorn the history of English science have been connected with this (the medical) profession." Of those names many have belonged to country doctors; amongst which Jenner has a conspicuous place.[23]

Jenner was a bright representative of that class of medical practitioners—sagacious, well-instructed, courageous, and self-dependent in intellect—who, at the close of the last century, began to spring up in all parts of the country, and have rapidly increased in number; so that now the prejudiced, vulgar, pedantic doctors of Sterne's and Smollett's pages are extinct—no more to be found on the face of the earth than are the drunken squires who patronized and insulted them.

Of such a sort was Samuel Parr, the father of the famous classic scholar and Whig politician of the same name. The elder Parr was a general practitioner at Harrow, "a man" (as his son described him) "of a very robust and vigorous intellect." Educated in his early years at Harrow School, Samuel Parr (the son) was taken from that splendid seminary at the age of fourteen years and apprenticed to his father. For three or four years he applied himself to the mastery of the elements of surgical and medical knowledge—dispensing medicines, assisting at operations, and performing all the duties which a country doctor's pupil was expected to perform. But he had not nerve enough for the surgical department of the profession. "For a physician," he used to say, "I might have done well, but for a surgeon nev-

[23] Medical readers will be amused with the following letter, written by Dr. Jenner, showing as it does the excess of caution with which he prepared his patients for the trifling operation of vaccination.

"Sir,

"I was absent from home when your obliging letter of the 24th November arrived; but I do not think this is likely to occur again for some time, and I shall therefore be very happy to take your little family under my care at the time you mention—the latter end of January. Our arrangements must be carefully made, as the children must be met here by proper subjects for transferring the Vaccine Lymph; for on the accuracy of this part of the process much depends. It may be necessary to observe also, that among the greatest impediments to vaccination (indeed the greatest) is an eruptive state of the skin on the child intended to receive the infection. On this subject I wrote a paper so long ago as the year 1804, and took much pains to circulate it; but I am sorry to say the attention that has been paid to it by the Faculty in general has been by no means equal to its importance. This is a rock on which vaccination has been often wreck'd; but there is no excuse, as it was so clearly laid down in the chart.

"I am, Sir, your obedient
"and very humble servant,
"EDWARD JENNER."

er." His father consequently sent him to Cambridge, and allowed him to turn his intellects to those pursuits in which Nature had best fitted him to excel. Dr. Parr's reminiscences of this period of medical instruction were nearly all pleasant—and some of them were exquisitely droll. At that early age his critical taste and faculty caused him to subject the prescriptions that came under his notice to a more exact scrutiny than the dog-Latin of physicians usually undergoes.

"Father," cried the boy, glancing his eye over a prescription, "here's another mistake in the grammar!"

"Sam," answered the irritable sire, "d—— the prescription, make up the medicine."

Laudanum was a preparation of opium just then coming into use. Mr. Parr used it at first sparingly and cautiously. On one occasion he administered a small quantity to a patient, and the next day, pleased with the effects of the dose, expressed his intention (but hesitatingly) to repeat it.

"You may do that safely, sir," said the son.

"Don't be rash, boy. Beginners are always too bold. How should you know what is safe?" asked the father.

"Because, sir," was the answer, "when I made up the prescription yesterday, I doubled the dose."

"Doubled the dose! How dared you do that?" exclaimed the angry senior.

"Because, sir," answered little Sam, coolly, "*I saw you hesitate.*"

The father who would not feel pride in such a son would not deserve to have him.

Though Parr made choice of another profession he always retained a deep respect for his father's calling and the practitioners of it; medical men forming a numerous and important portion of his acquaintance. In his years of ripest judgment he often declared that "he considered the medical professors as the most learned, enlightened, moral, and liberal class of the community."

How many pleasant reminiscences this writer has of country surgeons—a class of men interesting to an observer of manners, as they comprise more distinct types of character than any other professional body. Hail to thee, Dr. Agricola! more yeoman than *savant*, bluff, hearty, and benevolent, hastening away from fanciful patients to thy farm, about which it is thy pleasure, early and late, to trudge, vigilant and canny, clad in velveteen jacket and leathern gaiters, armed with spud-stick or double-barrel gun, and looking as unlike Andrew Borde or Dr. Slop as it is possible to conceive mortal! What an eccentric, pious, tyrannical, most humane giant thou art! When thou wast mayor of thy borough, what lawless law didst thou maintain! With thine own arm and oaken stick didst thou fustigate the drunken poacher who beat his wife; and the little children, who made a noise in the market-square on a Sunday, thou didst incarcerate (for the sake of public morality) in "the goose-house" for two hours; but (for the sake of mercy) thou didst cause to be served out to each prisoner one large gingerbread bun—to soften the hardships of captivity. When the ague raged, and provisions were scarce in what the poor still refer to as "the bad year," what prescriptions didst thou, as parish doctor, shower down on the fever-ridden?—Mutton and gin, beef and wine—such were thy orders! The parsons said bravo! and clapt thee on the back; but the guardians of the poor and the relieving officers were up in arms, and summoned thee before a solemn tribunal at the union-house—"the board!" in fact. What an indignant oath and scream of ridicule didst thou give, when an attorney (Sir Oracle of "the board") endeavoured to instil into thy mind the first principles of supply and demand, and that grandest law of political economy—to wit, if there are too many poor people in a neighbourhood, they must be starved out of it into one where they will not be in the way; and if there are too many poor people in the entire world, they must be starved out of that also into another, where there'll be more room for them! And what was thy answer to the chairman's remark, "Doctor, if mutton and gin are the only medicines that will cure the sick poor, you must supply them yourself, in accordance with your contract"? What was thy answer? Why, a shower of butchers' and vintners' bills, pulled from the pockets of thy ancient gray coat—bills all receipted, and showing that, before asking the ratepayers for a doit, thou hadst expended every penny of thy salary of £150 on mutton and gin, beef and wine—for the sick poor! What a noble answer to a petty taunt! The chairman blushed. The attorney hurried away, saying he had to be present at an auction. The great majority of "the board" came to a resolution, engaging to support you in your schemes for helping the poor through the bad year. But the play was not yet at an end. Some rumours of what had occurred at the board reaching the ears of a few poor peasants, they made bold to thank thee for thy exertions in their behalf. How didst thou receive them?—With a violent harrangue against their incorrigible laziness and dishonesty—an assurance that half their sufferings sprung from their own vices—and a vehement declaration that, far from speaking a good word for them to the guardians, thou didst counsel the sternest and cruellest of measures.

A man of another mould and temper was the writer's dear friend, Felix. Gentle and ardent, tranquil as a summer evening, and unyielding as a rock, modest but brave, unobtrusive but fearless, he had a mind that poets only could rightly read. Delicate in frame, as he was refined in intellect, he could not endure rude exertion or vulgar pleasure. Active in mind, he still possessed a vein of indolence, thoroughly appreciating the pleasure of dreaming the whole day long on a sunny chair in a garden, surrounded with bright flowers and breathing a perfumed air. In the hot season the country people used to watch their doctor traversing the country in his capacious phaeton. Alone, without a servant by his side, he held the reins in his hands, but in his reveries altogether forgot to use them. Sometimes he would fall asleep, and travel for miles in a state of unconsciousness, his great phlegmatic horse pounding the dust at the rate of five miles an hour. The somni-driverous doctor never came to harm. His steed knew how to keep on the left-hand side of the road, under ordinary circumstances passing all vehicles securely, but never thinking of overtaking any; and the country people, amongst whom the doctor spent his days, made his preservation from bodily harm an object of their especial care. Often did a rustic wayfarer extricate the doctor's equipage from a perilous position, and then send it onwards without disturbing the gentleman by waking him. The same placid, equable man was Felix in society, that he was on these professional excursions—nothing alarming or exciting him. It was in his study that the livelier elements of his nature came into play. Those who, for the first time, conversed with him in private on his microscopic and chemical pursuits, his researches in history, or his labours in speculative or natural philosophy, caught fire from his fire and were inspired with his enthusiasm.

Felix belonged to a class daily becoming more numerous; Miles was of a species that has already become rare—the army surgeon. The necessities of the long war caused the enrolment of numbers of young men in the ranks of the medical profession, whose learning was not their highest recommendation to respect. An old navy surgeon, of no small wit, and an infinite capacity for the consumption of strong liquors—wine, brandy, whisky, usquebaugh (anything, so long as it was strong)—gave a graphic description to this writer of his examination on things pertaining to surgery by the Navy Board.

"Well," said the narrator, putting down his empty glass and filling it again with Madeira—"I was shown into the examination-room. Large table, and half-a-dozen old gentlemen at it. 'Big-wigs, no doubt,' thought I; 'and sure as my name is Symonds, they'll pluck me like a pigeon.'

"'Well, sir, what do you know about the science of your profession?' asked the stout man in the chair.

"'More than he does of the practice, I'll be bound,' tittered a little wasp of a dandy—a West End ladies' doctor.

"I trembled in my shoes.

"'Well, sir,' continued the stout man, 'what would you do if a man was brought to you during action with his arms and legs shot off? Now, sir, don't keep the Board waiting! What would you do? Make haste!'

"'By Jove, sir!' I answered—a thought just striking me—'I should pitch him overboard, and go on to some one else I could be of more service to.'

"By — —! every one present burst out laughing; and they passed me directly, sir—passed me directly!"

The examiners doubtless felt that a young man who could manifest such presence of mind on such an occasion, and so well reply to a terrorizing question, might be trusted to act wisely on other emergencies.

Many stories of a similar kind are very old acquaintances of most of our readers.

"What"—an examiner of the same Board is reported to have said to a candidate—"would you have recourse to if, after having ineffectually tried all the ordinary diaphoretics, you wanted to throw your patient, in as short a time as possible, into a profuse perspiration?"

"I should send him here, sir, to be examined," was the reply.

Not less happy was the audacity of the medical student to Abernethy.

"What would you do," bluntly inquired the surgeon, "if a man was brought to you with a broken leg?"

"Set it, sir," was the reply.

"Good—very good—you're a very pleasant, witty young man; and doubtless you can tell me what muscles of my body I should set in motion if I kicked you, as you deserve to be kicked, for your impertinence."

"You would set in motion," responded the youth, with perfect coolness, "the flexors and extensors of my right arm; for I should immediately knock you down."

If the gentlemen so sent forth to kill and cure were not overstocked with professional learning, they soon acquired a knowledge of their art in that best of all schools—experience. At the conclusion of the great war they were turned loose upon the country, and from their body came many of the best and most successful practitioners of every county of the kingdom. The race is fast dying out. A Waterloo banquet of medical officers, serving in our army at that memorable battle, would at the present time gather together only a small number of veterans. This writer can remember when they were plentiful; and, in company with two or three of the best of their class, he spent many of the happiest days of his boyhood. An aroma of old camp life hung about them. They rode better horses, and more boldly, than the other doctors round about. However respectable they might have become with increased years and prosperity, they retained the military knack of making themselves especially comfortable under any untoward combination of external circumstances. To gallop over a bleak heath, through the cold fog of a moonless December night; to sit for hours in a stifling garret by a pauper's pallet; to go for ten days without sleeping on a bed, without undressing, and with the wear of sixteen hours out of every twenty-four spent on horseback—were only features of "duty," and therefore to be borne manfully, and with generous endurance, at the time—and, in the retrospect, to be talked of with positive contentment and hilarity. They loved the bottle, too—as it ought to be loved: on fit occasions drinking any given quantity, and, in return, giving any quantity to drink; treating claret and the thinner wines with a levity at times savouring of disdain; but having a deep and unvarying affection for good sound port, and, at the later hours, very hot and very strong whisky and water, *with* a slice of lemon in each tumbler. How they would talk during their potations! What stories and songs! George the Fourth (even according to his own showing) had scarce more to do in bringing about the victory at Waterloo than they. Lord Anglesey's leg must have been amputated thrice; for this writer knew three surgeons who each—separately and by himself—performed the operation. But this sort of boasting was never indulged in before the —th tumbler.

May a word not be here said on the toping country doctor? Shame on these times! ten years hence one will not be able to find a bibulous apothecary, though search be made throughout the land from Dan to Beersheba! Sailors, amongst the many superstitions to which they cling with tenacity, retain a decided preference for an inebrious to a sober surgeon. Not many years since, in a fishing village on the eastern coast, there flourished a doctor in great repute amongst the poor; and his influence over his humble patients literally depended on the fact that he was sure, once in the four-and-twenty hours, to be handsomely intoxicated. Charles Dickens has told the public how, when he bought the raven immortalised in "Barnaby Rudge," the vendor of that sagacious bird, after enumerating his various accomplishments and excellences, concluded, "But, sir, if you want him to come out very strong, you must show him a drunk man." The simple villagers of Flintbeach had a firm faith in the strengthening effects of looking at a tipsy doctor. They always postponed their visits to Dr. Mutchkin till evening, because then they had the benefit of the learned man in his highest intellectual condition. "Dorn't goo to he i' the mornin', er can't doctor noways to speak on tills er's had a glass," was the advice invariably given to a stranger not aware of the doctor's little peculiarities.

Mutchkin was unquestionably a shrewd fellow, although he did his best to darken the light with which nature had endowned him. One day, accompanied by his apprentice, he visited a small tenant farmer who had been thrown on his bed with a smart attack of bilious fever. After looking at his patient's tongue and feeling his pulse, he said somewhat sharply:—

"Ah! 'tis no use doing what's right for you, if you will be so imprudent."

"Goodness, doctor, what do you mean?" responded the sick man; "I have done nothing imprudent."

"What!—nothing imprudent? Why, bless me, man, you have had green peas for dinner."

"So I have, sir. But how did you find that out?"

"In your pulse—in your pulse. It was very foolish. Mind, you mayn't commit such an indiscretion again. It might cost you your life."

The patient, of course, was impressed with Mutchkin's acuteness, and so was the apprentice. When the lad and his master had retired, the former asked:—

"How did you know he had taken peas for dinner, sir? Of course it wasn't his pulse that told you."

"Why, boy," the instructor replied, "I saw the pea-shells that had been thrown into the yard, and I drew my inference."

The hint was not thrown away on the youngster. A few days afterwards, being sent to call on the same case, he approached the sick man, and, looking very observant, felt the pulse.

"Ah!—um—by Jove!" exclaimed the lad, mimicking his master's manner, "this is very imprudent. It may cost you your life. Why, man, you've eaten a horse for your dinner."

The fever patient was so infuriated with what he naturally regarded as impertinence, that he sent a pathetic statement of the insult offered him to Mutchkin. On questioning his pupil as to what he meant by accusing a man, reduced with sickness, of having consumed so large and tough an animal, the doctor was answered—

"Why, sir, as I passed through from the yard I saw the saddle hanging up in the kitchen."

This story is a very ancient one. It may possibly be found in one of the numerous editions of Joe Miller's facetiæ. The writer has, however, never met with it in print, and the first time he heard it, Dr. Mutchkin, of Flintbeach, was made to figure in it in the matter above described.

The shrewdness of Mutchkin's apprentice puts us in mind of the sagacity of the hydropathic doctor, mentioned in the "Life of Mr Assheton Smith." A gentleman devoted to fox-hunting and deep potations was induced, by the master of the Tedworth Hunt, to have recourse to the water cure, and see if it would not relieve him of chronic gout, and restore something of the freshness of youth. The invalid acted on the advice, and in obedience to the directions of a hydropathic physician, proceeded to swathe his body, upon going to his nightly rest, with wet bandages. The air was chill, and the water looked—very—cold. The patient shivered as his valet puddled the bandages about in the cold element. He paused, as a schoolboy does, before taking his first "header" for the year on a keen May morning; and during the pause much of his noble resolve oozed away.

"John," at last he said to his valet, "put into that d — — water half a dozen bottles of port wine, to warm it."

John having carried out the direction, the bandages, saturated with port wine and water, were placed round the corpulent trunk of the invalid. The next morning the doctor, on paying his visit and inspecting the linen swathes, instead of expressing astonishment at their discoloration with the juice of the grape, observed, with the utmost gravity:—

"Ah, the system is acting beautifully. See, the port wine is already beginning to leave you!"

A different man from Dr. Mutchkin was jovial Ambrose Harvey. Twenty years ago no doctor throughout his county was more successful—no man more beloved. By natural strength of character he gained leave from society to follow his own humours without let, hindrance, or censure. Ladies did not think the less highly of his professional skill because he visited them in pink, and left their bedsides to ride across the country with Lord Cheveley's hounds. Six feet high, handsome, hearty, well-bred, Ambrose had a welcome wherever there was joy or sickness. To his little wife he was devotedly attached and very considerate; and she in return was very fond, and—what with woman is the same thing—very jealous of him. He was liked, she well knew, by the country ladies, many of whom were so far her superiors in rank and beauty and accomplishments, that it was only natural in the good little soul to entertain now and then a suspicious curiosity about the movements of her husband. Was it nothing but the delicate health of Lady Ellin that took him so frequently to Hove Hall? How it came about, from what charitable whisperings on the part of kind friends, from what workings of original sin in her own gentle breast, it would be hard to say; but 'tis a fact that, when Hove Hall was mentioned, a quick pain seized the little wife's heart and colour left her cheek, to return again quickly, and in increased quantity. The time came when she discovered the groundlessness of her fears, and was deeply thankful that she had never, in any unguarded moment, by clouded brow, or foolish tears, or sharp reply, revealed the folly of her heart. Just at the time that Mrs. Ambrose was in the midst of this trial of her affection, Ambrose obtained her permission to drive over to a town twelve miles distant, to attend the hunt dinner. The night of that dinner was a memorable one with the doctor's wife. Ambrose had promised to be home at eleven o'clock. But twelve had struck, and here he had not returned. One o'clock—two o'clock! No husband! The servants had been sent to bed four hours ago; and Mrs. Ambrose sate alone in her old wainscotted parlour, with a lamp by her side, sad, and pale, and feverish—as wakeful as the house-dog out of doors, that roamed round the house, barking out his dissatisfaction at the prolonged absence of his master.

At length, at half-past two, a sound of wheels was at the door, and in another minute Ambrose entered the hall, and greeted his little wife. Ah, Mrs. Ellis, this writer will not pain you by entering into details in this part of his story. In defence of Ambrose, let it be said that it was the only time in all his married life that he paid too enthusiastic homage to the god of wine. Something he mumbled about being tired, and having a headache, and then he walked, not over-steadily, upstairs. Poor Mrs. Ambrose! It was not any good asking *him*, what had kept him out so late. Incensed, frightened, and jealous, the poor little lady could not rest. She must have one doubt resolved. Where had her husband been all this time? Had he been round by Hove Hall? Had she reflected, she would have seen his Bacchic drowsiness was the best possible evidence that he had not come from a lady's drawing-room. But jealousy is love's blindness. A thought seized the little woman's head; she heard the step of Ambrose's man in the kitchen, about to retire to rest. Ah, he could tell her. A word from him would put all things right. Quick as thought, without considering her own or her husband's dignity, the angry little wife hastened down-stairs, and entered the kitchen where John was paying his respects to some supper and mild ale that had been left out for him. As evil fortune would have it, the step she had taken to mend matters made them worse.

"Oh, John," said the lady, telling a harmless fib, "I have just come to see if cook left you out a good supper."

John—most civil and trustworthy of grooms—rose, and posing himself on his heels, made a respectful obeisance to his mistress, not a little surprised at her anxiety for his comfort. But, alas! the potations at the hunt-dinner had not been confined to the gentlemen of the hunt. John had, in strong ale, taken as deep draughts of gladness as Ambrose had in wine. At a glance his mistress saw the state of the case, and in her fright, losing all caution, put her question point-blank, and with imperious displeasure—"John, where have you and your master been?—tell me instantly."

An admirable servant—honest and well-intentioned at all times—just then confused and loquacious—John remembered him how often his master had impressed upon him that it was his duty not to gossip about the places he stopped at in his rounds, as professional secrecy was a virtue scarcely less necessary in a doctor's man-servant than in a doctor. Acting on a muddle-headed reminiscence of his instructions, John reeled towards his mistress, endeavouring to pacify her with a profusion of duteous bobbings of the head, and in a tone of piteous sympathy, and with much incoherence, made this memorable answer to her question: "I'm very sorry, mum, and I do hope, mum, you won't be angry. I allus wish to do you my best duty—that I do, mum—and you're a most good, affable missus, and I, and cook, and all on us are very grateful to you."

"Never mind that. Where have you and your master been? That's my question."

"Indeed, mum—I darnatellye, it would bes goodasmeplace wi' master. I dare not say where we ha' been. For master rekwested me patikler not to dewulge."

But thou hadst not wronged thy wife. It was not thine to hurt any living thing, dear friend. All who knew thee will bear witness that to thee, and such as thee, Crabbe pointed not his bitter lines:—

> "But soon a loud and hasty summons calls,
> Shakes the thin roof, and echoes round the walls;
> Anon a figure enters, quaintly neat,
> All pride and business, bustle and conceit,
> With looks unalter'd by these scenes of woe,
> With speed that entering speaks his haste to go;
> He bids the gazing throng around him fly,
> And carries Fate and Physic in his eye;
> A potent quack, long versed in human ills,
> Who first insults the victim whom he kills,
> Whose murd'rous hand a drowsy bench protect,
> And whose most tender mercy is neglect.
> Paid by the Parish for attendance here,
> He wears contempt upon his sapient sneer.
> In haste he seeks the bed where misery lies,
> Impatience mark'd in his averted eyes;
> And, some habitual queries hurried o'er,
> Without reply, he rushes to the door;
> His drooping patient, long inured to pain,
> And long unheeded, knows remonstrance vain;
> He ceases now the feeble help to crave
> Of man, and mutely hastens to the grave."

THE END.

INDEX.

M

P

Q

R

Roger Clopton *166*

S

Samuel Johnson *18, 26, 128, 140, 229, 248*
Sim Burton *155*
Sir Amos Meredith *146*
Sir Astley Cooper *4, 36, 91*
Sir Benjamin Brodie *55, 85, 197*
Sir Benjamin Wrench *167*
Sir Creswell Creswell *259*
Sir Edmund King *37, 59, 61, 125*
Sir Everard Digby *20*
Sir F. Baring *91*
Sir Godfrey Kneller *58, 61*
Sir Humphrey Davy *29, 230*
Sir James Clarke *7*
Sir John Ayliffe *85*
Sir John Cheke *71*
Sir John Cutler *253*
Sir John Hill *29, 213, 256*
Sir John Jeffcott *205*
Sir Kenelm Digby *18, 19, 20, 21, 23, 28, 150*
Sir Nathaniel Hobart *145*
Sir Richard Blackmore *25, 37, 59, 60, 101, 105*
Sir Richard Croft *211*
Sir Richard Jebb *81, 108, 109*
Sir Richard Knightley *107*
Sir Rowland Alston *134*
Sir Symonds D'ewes *257*
Sir Theodore Mayerne *10, 13, 75, 89*
Sir Thomas Browne *18, 19*
Sir Thomas Hilton *17*
Sir Thomas Lawrence *191*
Sir Thomas Millington *37*
Sir William Blizard *59, 131*
Sir William Butts *84, 85*
St. John Long *155, 190, 191, 192, 193, 194, 195, 196, 197, 198, 215*
Sylvester Douglas *212*

T

Thomas Calfe *13*
Thomas Campanella *3*
Thomas Crossfield *234*
Thomas Messenger *166*